Modern Political Thought

Raymond Plant

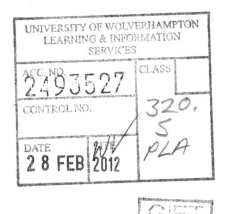

BLACKWELL
Oxford UK & Cambridge USA

Copyright © Raymond Plant 1991

First published 1991
Reprinted 1992, 1993

Blackwell Publishers
108 Cowley Road, Oxford, OX4 1JF, UK

238 Main Street, Suite 501
Cambridge, Massachusetts 02142, USA

British Library Cataloguing in Publication Data

A CIP catalogue record for this book is available from the British Library.

Library of Congress Cataloging in Publication Data

Plant, Raymond.
  Modern Political Thought/Raymond Plant.
    p. cm.
  Includes bibliographical references.
  ISBN 0–631–14223–1 (hardback) ISBN 0–631–14224–X (pbk.)
  1. Political science – Methodology. 2. Political science – Philosophy. I. Title.
JA73.P56   1991
320.5—dc20

                                                            90–40348
                                                                 CIP

Typeset in 11 on 13 pt Sabon
by Butler and Tanner Ltd, Frome and London
Printed in Great Britain by T. J. Press (Padstow) Ltd, Padstow, Cornwall.

This book is printed on acid-free paper.

Legitimacy means that there are good arguments for a political order's claim to be recognised as right and just; a legitimate order deserves recognition. Legitimacy means a political order's worthwhileness to be recognised.

J. Habermas, *Legitimation Problems in the Modern State*

If the foundations be destroyed, what can the righteous do?

Psalm 11

Contents

Preface

This book has two interrelated aims. The first is to introduce students to debates in modern political philosophy. Of course, this cannot be done in a comprehensive way in one volume. I hope, however, that I have surveyed sufficient of the field and have discussed a wide enough range of arguments and styles of thinking for students to go on to work for themselves on these and other topics within the discipline. The second aim of the book is to introduce students to some of the differences in methodology within political philosophy as it is currently practised. In most cases, however, these are not just methodological disputes, important though such disputes are; rather in many cases they represent different conceptions of the aims and nature of the discipline. It goes without saying that it is important for students to realize that there are these different approaches, yielding in some cases different accounts of the project of political philosophy. As an introduction, the book makes no claims to originality. All that I have done is to attempt to explain the salient issues as I see them and invite others to participate in the debates which the book seeks both to record and interpret. I have used rather a lot of quotation in the book, in an attempt to let writers speak for themselves when possible.

This book has taken an inordinate amount of time to write. Just how long can be gauged by the fact that the tent which I bought with the advance from Blackwells has now worn out. It has been Blackwell's loyalty which has kept me going when it looked as though the project would be abandoned and I am extremely grateful to many people there for encouraging me over the years: to Rene Oliveri, who first suggested that I should write the book; to Sue Corbett, my first editor; to Stephan

Chambers, her successor; and to Simon Prosser, who has encouraged me during the final stages.

I have incurred many other debts during the writing of the book. Many of the ideas in it were tried out in seminars at Hillel Steiner's home when I taught philosophy in the University of Manchester. The standards of discussion which Hillel insisted on made these seminars a highlight of my academic career. Other members of the seminar to whom I owe a great deal are Harry Lesser, Keekok Lee, John Harris, Alastair Edwards, Ursula Vogel, Norman Geras and Ian Steedman. My other Manchester mentor, Geraint Parry, also taught me a great deal about political philosophy and the history of political thought. Some of the chapters were written during a year in Oxford when I was supposed to be doing something else. I had the good fortune to be attached to Nuffield and thanks are due to the Warden and Fellows of the College for their hospitality and friendship. Among Nuffield colleagues, David Miller and Nevil Johnson were a great help to me. While in Oxford I was a member of All Souls Legal and Social Thought Group and I learned a great deal from attending the weekly seminars there. Listening to debates between Amartya Sen, Derek Parfit, Ronald Dworkin, John Gray, Alan Ryan, Steven Lukes, James Griffin, Charles Taylor, Joseph Raz and John Rawls taught me much about contemporary political thought.

I have lived for twelve years in a very supportive department in Southampton, and among the theorists I have to thank Peter Johnson, Liam O'Sullivan, Ronnie Beiner and Ian Forbes for all the help they have given me. Michael Bourn, a Faculty colleague, has also been a great support to me. Although our interests are very different he helped me as a guide and supporter when I was Dean and looked likely to be completely submerged by paper and committees.

The book is dedicated to my father, who died while I was writing it. When I was an adolescent he gave me his copy of John Stuart Mill's *Essay on Liberty*, which he had studied as a member of the Fire Brigade Union; he thus unintentionally introduced me to the discipline which has now preoccupied me for twenty-five years. I also owe a debt to the shades of Bach, Mozart and Beethoven during some long hours in my study, in fact I used up two tapes of *Bist du bei mir*. My secretary, Sandra Wilkins, has been of enormous help to me, coping uncomplainingly with my gross inefficiency. Katherine, my wife, Nicholas, Matthew and

Richard, our sons, have supported me over the years in ways which I cannot begin to repay and I hope they are pleased that the book has now seen the light of day.

I am naturally responsible for any errors and mistaken judgements which the book contains.

Raymond Plant

1

Shaking the Foundations of Political Theory

I doubt that, but from self evident propositions by necessary consequences, as incontestable as those in mathematics, the measures of right and wrong can be made out.
John Locke, *An Essay Concerning Human Understanding*

... in saying that a certain type of action is right or wrong, I am not making any factual statement, not even a statement about my own state of mind. I am merely expressing certain moral sentiments. And the man who is ostensibly contradicting me is really expressing his moral sentiments. So there is plainly no sense in asking which of us is in the right. For neither of us is asserting a genuine proposition.
A. J. Ayer, *Language, Truth and Logic*

In this opening chapter we shall be concerned with the question of whether issues in political theory are capable of being resolved on a rational basis. The issues which I have in mind, and which have been characteristic of the subject since the time of Plato, are concerned with questions such as: What is justice? Are there human rights and if so what are they? What is the role of the state? Do individuals have definable needs and if so who has an obligation to satisfy them? Should a government seek the greatest happiness of the greatest number and, if it should, what is the place for minorities within this rubric? Are there morally just grounds for interfering in the affairs of another state? What gives a government legitimacy and a state sovereignty? What sorts of claims on resources does the recognition of merit or desert embody? How far is the majority justified in imposing its moral outlook on the rest of society? Can we give an adequate account of the moral basis of social and political institutions? What is the best form of government? In dealing with these sorts of questions it can be seen that political philosophy is a branch of moral philosophy in that it is concerned with the question of justifying the right way or ways and identifying the wrong ways in which political power is to be exercised and the nature of the claims which citizens can make on the state and on each other.

In the West we are heirs to an intellectual tradition which includes all the great philosophers who wrote about politics – Plato, Aristotle, Augustine, Aquinas, Hobbes, Locke, Rousseau, Hegel, Marx and Mill – which assumes that questions of the sort mentioned above, that is questions about political morality, can be answered in rational and objective ways. By making this assumption these thinkers rejected the view that issues of political morality are a matter of individual preference, feeling, attitude or desire. There is, on their view, a rationally based answer which can be given to the questions of political morality and, it might be claimed, it is this assumption, which we might call foundationalism, in the sense of providing a rational basis for political action, which gives political theory its right to be seen as an academic discipline. After all, if political morality is just a matter of individual preferences and commitment it would seem on the face of it to lack the cognitive or epistemological basis for it to be regarded as a genuine academic discipline. Feelings and preferences about political morality might be regarded as a suitable subject for the psychology of politics, but if preferences and feelings cannot be rationally grounded then as such there can be no academic discipline dealing with them. While it would be true to say that there have been examples of this attitude in the history of philosophy, Protagoras for example comes to mind,[1] it is nevertheless only in this century that the idea that issues of political morality are simply a matter of preference has become pervasive, and the development of this attitude, which has been connected with a wide-ranging and subtle theory of knowledge, has led to a major question mark being placed at the side of the viability of political philosophy as an academic discipline.

The death of political theory

In 1956 Peter Laslett published an influential essay[2] on the death of political philosophy in which he argued that the growth of logical positivism was responsible for the death of the subject in the sense that positivism dismissed the cognitive claims of the subject and thus its status as an academic study. However, since the publication of Laslett's essay there has been a major revival of the subject, so in order for us to get to grips with the nature of our discipline, it is necessary to explain the reasons for its death and subsequent resurrection. Only in this way can we understand whether the subject can be put on a secure cognitive footing.

First of all we need to see what sorts of claims were made by the 'classical' political theorists so that we can appreciate why, by the 1950s, the foundations on which these claims had been made seemed to have been fatally undermined.

Traditional[3] or classical political theory had been concerned with the nature of the good life, with the institutional arrangements which would be necessary for human beings to flourish, for their needs to be met or their rational capacities realized. At the same time there was also a preoccupation with political right – with the nature of law, justice, the best form of government, the rights and duties of individuals and with the distributive organization of society. Political theories were therefore of the right and the good. As such these theories implied claims about the cognitive principles on which they were based. These theories purported to convey some truths about the fundamental nature of politics, to make claims which could be regarded as objective and inter-subjectively valid. This truth and objectivity was, in different theories, based upon different assumptions: sometimes about reason, sometimes about empirical experience, sometimes about intuition, and occasionally revelation. In all of these cases though, the claims the political philosopher made were supposed to be vindicated by some epistemological authority such as reason or experience so that ultimately claims about fundamental human needs, goals, purposes, relationships and the forms of rule appropriate to these which entered into a particular political philosophy were supposed to be *true*. Usually political philosophies have been part of a wider philosophical system in which the cognitive basis of the political claims is established. Very good examples of this could be the work of Plato, Hobbes, Hegel and Mill. These thinkers were concerned, at least in part, with working out the cognitive basis on which claims in political philosophy were to be advanced. Despite their big differences, they did not see political theory as embodying subjectivist claims based merely on preference or feeling. They took the view that there were truths to be stated about fundamental political issues and they themselves provided some account of the cognitive capacities and the epistemological grounds on which these claims to truth were advanced.

Of course, the very fact that there were major differences in the conclusions reached by political philosophers cast some doubt upon the epistemological assumptions on which the theories were built. After all there is very little use in developing rival theories of politics, each of which claims to embody the truth about political morality, without any criterion for enabling us to decide the adequacy of the cognitive basis of these moral theories. Indeed, this lack of an epistemological criterion is not just an accidental or contingent matter for the theories, because claims about the nature of human knowledge were, for example in the writings of Plato and Hobbes just to take two instances, bound up with the conclusions of the theories. It seemed that there could be no *independent* epistemological criterion in terms of which the cognitive claims of rival theories could be adjudicated. The theories themselves set up standards of cognitive truth which then became internal to the theories, such that an appeal to some theory independent principle or independent criterion is not possible.

However, in terms of its impact on polical theory the major critical development was undoubtedly logical positivism. This philosophical doctrine went right to the heart of the cognitive status of political philosophy and provided what seemed to be very cogent grounds for regarding political philosophy as irredeemably subjective and as a pseudo subject.

Logical positivism and the death of political philosophy

Although the critique was developed in a period of very sharp political conflict in the 1930s, logical positivist philosophers such as Shlick, Carnap, Von Neurath and A. J. Ayer were not directly interested in political questions. Their radical critique of the cognitive claims of political theory were an indirect consequence of espistemological theories they had developed in more or less total indifference to the claims of political theorists. In order to see the importance of the positivist critique of political theory and to see whether the subject has a genuine cognitive basis, we must look in some detail at the nature and significance of the positivist case, and because this was developed in relation to a discussion of truth in logic, mathematics and science rather than politics, its adequate discussion must take us away from the field of politics in the first instance.

Logical positivist theories, of which A. J. Ayer's *Language, Truth and Logic*[4] is the best example in English, were profoundly influenced by the writings of the great Austrian philosopher Ludwig Wittgenstein, and in particular his *Tractatus Logico-Philosophicus*[5] which was first published in 1922. In this book Wittgenstein asserted three theses which are of interest in our context. The first was that logic and mathematics consists of tautologies, the second is that language has a truth-functional structure and that its basic elements are names, the third, which is most important for our purposes and which was a consequence of the first two, is that no ethical or moral statements can convey definite cognitive information. These three theses are closely related and we need to indicate in more detail their precise significance. Wittgenstein followed Russell and Whitehead in the view, which they developed in *Principia Mathematica*[6], that the basic structure of mathematics could be derived from logic and that in a sense the truths of mathematics are conventional rather than revealing 'facts' about numbers and their relationships. That is to say, given certain definitions of basic terms, and a particular understanding of the rules of inference, the whole structure of mathematical truth could be generated. But these forms of truth depend upon the definitions of the terms and the rules of reference. In a sense, they are true by definition. It may *appear* that we make new discoveries in mathematics, but this is only because the remote consequences of definition are difficult to foresee and have to be teased out with great complication and elaboration. On this view Plato, for example, was therefore mistaken in thinking that mathematical structures depicted a set of real relationships between Forms or Ideas of numbers. Mathematical truths are rather tautological, recording the remote (and sometimes surprising) consequences of definition and rules of inference rather than real relationships in a world of non-sensible objects. The conventional character of mathematics does not mean that it is any less useful, it is rather an analysis of the kinds of truths which mathematics and logic convey. Mathematics and logic, or the laws of reason, do not give us access to some non-empirical non-tangible world of ideas as opposed to a set of tautologies.

The second thesis of interest to us set out in *Tractatus Logico-Philosophicus* is that language has a structure and that this can be laid bare by logical analysis. In Wittgenstein's view this analysis will reveal language as being truth-functional. That is to say (crudely) that complex propositions in the language which we use to convey information can be shown to be analysable into component propositions. Obviously at some point this process of analysis has to stop and we are left with the basic building blocks of language, what he calls 'elementary propositions'.[7] In Wittgenstein's view, these elementary propositions, and this is a point of crucial importance, consist of names.[8] Why should this be so and why should this very abstract point be so vital? If our language does have to yield basic building blocks or units of meaning-elementary propositions, then we have to explain how these elementary propositions get their meaning. This is crucial because they convey meaning to all other parts of the truth-functional structure. There seem to be two alternative ways in which elementary propositions could acquire meaning. One way (which is incoherent) would be to say that the meaning of an elementary proposition could be given in another proposition, that is to say a proposition which would explicate its meaning. This is incoherent, however, because if an elementary proposition depended for its meaning upon another proposition, it could no longer be considered as basic, rather the proposition which gave sense to the proposition in question would itself be more fundamental, but then the question could again be asked how does this proposition derive its sense? It is clear that this strategy will not lead to a conclusion and, in addition, will make meaning wholly internal to langauge rather than dependent upon some representation of the world. As Wittgenstein puts the point:

> If the world had no substance then whether one proposition has meaning would depend upon whether another proposition was true.[9]

To solve the problem of meaning in a language and thus to explain how it can communicate truth we have to try to determine basic linguistic units which have to satisfy two requirements: (a) their meaning has to be given directly rather than being mediated by other propositions; (b) they have to relate in some direct way to the world. In Wittgenstein's view, only names satisfy this requirement, so elementary propositions consist of names. Names solve the problem because a name can be given meaning without this meaning being mediated by further propositions. This is done by producing the object which it names. Names refer directly to the world because names refer to objects and objects are their meaning.[10] Consequently, if meaningful uses of langauge have, in the end, to turn upon the fact that names, the basic units of meaning, refer directly to objects, then this has clear consequences for moral and political thinking. If the propositions contained in normative political writing are not susceptible of this analysis then they are not meaningful. Wittgenstein does not say what the objects are which names ultimately refer to, but if, as the positivists argued, they should be taken to be either material objects or direct sense experiences, then clearly political language is in deep trouble. In what sense do terms like good, right, need, interest, justice refer to objects, or could be analysed in such a way that they could be held to refer to objects?

The final thesis in the *Tractatus* is the one which draws this conclusion. Moral and evaluative language generally does not admit of this truth-functional analysis and moral 'objects' cannot be spoken about in a cognitively meaningful manner. As he says in the famous paragraph 6.42 of the *Tractatus*:

It is impossible for there to be propositions of ethics.

Propositions can express nothing of what is higher.

It is clear that ethics cannot be put into words. Ethics is transcendental.

and in 6.53:

The correct method in philosophy would really be the following: to say nothing except what can be said, i.e. the propositions of natural science . . . and then when anyone wanted to say something metaphysical, to demonstrate to him that he had failed to give a meaning to certain signs in his propositions.

There can be no cognitive theory of value whether the value be moral, aesthetic or political. This does not mean that values are unimportant, indeed they may be of overriding importance, but they have to be exhibited in our commitments, in the ways in which we live our lives, and *not* reflected in some sort of theoretical structure which seeks to state truths about the nature of these values.

The *Tractatus* was a powerful although somewhat enigmatic work written in an aphoristic and unelaborated manner and it was the positivists who turned its ideas into a theory with a radical epistemological cutting edge. It is perhaps difficult for students of politics to understand why this theory was so important because its central tenets seem to be very abstruse, but we might say rather informally that its appeal lies mainly in the fact that the logical tools which it utilized had played a role in elucidating the structure of mathematics, itself a key tool in understanding the nature of the world, and the use of the tools of logical analysis in the field of ordinary language held out the possibility of accounting for its structural properties and the way in which its meaning could be accounted for. In addition, when elementary, basic or protocol propositions were interpreted in a radically empiricist way as the positivists did, it seemed that the theory was able to explain the meaningful and objective nature of scientific language and the subjectivism and unresolvability of a good deal of moral and metaphysical writing. In the positivists' hands the theory became the view that only those complex uses of language which could be shown to be built up out of elementary propositions describing basic experiences of material objects, were meaningful. That is to say, science, natural and factual uses of language are meaningful, whereas metaphysical theories of value which sought to give a foundation to moral and political conceptions of the good life are nonsense. The principle at stake here became known as the *verification principle*, that is, that a proposition is meaningful if and only if it can be empirically verified.[11] To give a meaning to the basic signs of a language is the fundamental problem and this meaning is given by the reference of these signs to empirical experiences. Consequently, if a proposition is meaningful it must be possible to show that either it directly refers to experience or, if it is a complex proposition, it can be shown, after analysis, to refer to direct sense experience. One caveat was entered subsequently, namely that a meaningful proposition does not have to refer to *directly available* sense experience, but rather experiences the nature of which could *in principle* be specified.[12] By this more permissive criterion the proposition 'There are mountains on the other side of the moon' could be regarded as meaningful because it was possible to specify the kinds of experience which would verify it, even though in the 1930s when the positivists wrote, they were currently unavailable; whereas the proposition 'The state is the actuality of the ethical will' is always in principle unverifiable because we cannot even in principle specify those experiences which would verify it.

The consequences of these views for moral and political philosophy were very radical. In so far as moral and political philosophy characteristically were normative exercises, recommending values, perspectives and arrangements whether in the sphere of personal morality or in the public domain of morality they are unverifiable – it is not possible to assign an empirical meaning to the signs employed. What account could the positivists therefore offer for normative and ethical language about 'good', 'right', justice, virtue, the best form of government etc.?

They took the view that such forms of language do not state facts. While for example the statements:

> The cat is on the mat
> This is a good book
> National Socialism is inhuman

are ostensibly similar in having a subject–predicate form in which a quality is assigned to a subject, it would be a mistake to assimilate these sentences to the same mode of meaning. While the first has a cognitive content because empirical meaning can be assigned to the words in it, this is not true in the second and third case. We could agree on all the empirical characteristics of the book and disagree about its aesthetic or other evaluative qualities and there would be no further empirical evidence which could settle the matter between us. On this view, the same would be true of the third example. At the same time, to regard the meaning of the word 'good' as relying for its reference and meaning on some non-empirical quality such as a Platonic Form or Idea or a non-natural property[13] of any sort would be to confirm its metaphysical and non-sensible status. Evaluative and normative propositions about the human good are not empirically based and do not convey a cognitive content.

They still have an important function in human life, however, and this is an expressive one. Moral language serves to express or evince emotional attitudes. It is irreducibly subjective and attitudinal.[14] To advance a case for a set of political arrangements is to do no more than to express our favourable attitude towards them. It is important to see that moral language *expresses* emotional attitudes, but does not describe them. Of course, emotional reactions can be described but they are of no interest in morality except to the psychologist or the sociologist of morals. Typically normative language has emotive rather than cognitive meaning, it has a subjective and not an objective status.

It follows from this that normative moral and political philosophy in which conceptions of the human good are advanced is a *pseudo* subject. It purports to seek the truth, to be intersubjective and to convey information of a sort. But, in fact, political and moral philosophy is merely the expression of attitude on the part of the philosopher. Positivists naturally drew the conclusion that moral and political philosophy as an objective account of political principles is nonsense in the literal sense. The philosophers' own personal preferences as expressed in a deceptive form in works of moral and political philosophy are no more valid or worthy of respect than any one else's,[15] a point made quite graphically by Margaret Macdonald when she argues:

> To assert that 'Freedom is better than slavery' or 'All men are of equal worth' is not to state a fact but to choose a side. It announces this is where I stand.

It might be thought, however, that this argument proceeds far too quickly, and for two reasons. In the first place it might be argued that some political theories claim to be based upon factual premises; in the second place, so the critic might argue, emotional attitudes are not just taken up in an empirical vacuum: our attitudes and preferences are somehow related to our beliefs about the world and are thus empirically verifiable. The strategy of the positivist when faced with these two points is to accept what is said in both cases but to deny that these points make any difference to the cognitive status of the conclusions.

He may well argue, for example, that some political theories, such as those of Hobbes, Aristotle or John Stuart Mill, seek to base themselves on facts about human nature, and in the case of Mill this connection is seen particularly strongly. In the *Essay on Utilitarianism* he argues that the ends of life, the things we take to be desirable in and for themselves, must be grounded in the *actual facts* about human desire.[16] It is Mill's view that human beings desire happiness as an intrinsic end, that is, for its own sake, and this is a factual observation which supports the conclusion that happiness is what human beings find desirable in itself. Similarly, as we shall see later, Hobbes's account of the nature of the sovereign is concerned to draw conclusions about the necessity of the sort of power the sovereign wields from facts about human desire, particularly the desire for power, and the relationships between individuals which follow from a proper understanding of their nature.

The positivist critic might be prepared to accept that the propositions about human nature in these cases are empirical, they could in principle be verified and then be meaningful. What he will concentrate upon, however, is the nature of the support which these empirical propositions are supposed to give to normative and evaluative conclusions and here reference is made to a crucial critical weapon in the positivist arsenal, namely 'Hume's Fork', that is to say the principle of reasoning first set out with clarity by David Hume in the eighteenth century, namely that factual premises in an argument cannot yield normative, moral or evaluative conclusions.[17] This argument is usually known as the principle that 'ought' cannot be derived from an 'is'. That is to say it articulates the principle that there can be nothing in the conclusion of a valid argument which is not already present in the premises. If we draw an evaluative conclusion then either the premises contain evaluative elements, in which case they are not verifiable, or the inference cannot go through if the premises do not contain normative elements. An example will make this clear. The syllogism:

> All men need food in order to live
>
> This man needs food
> Therefore he ought to get it

is not a valid argument. Either the first two premises are wholly empirical

and therefore contain no reference to 'ought' and therefore the conclusion does not follow, or there is a suppressed premise which we are
assuming namely that all men ought to have their needs met, which is
certainly a normative proposition which would add support to the
evaluative conclusion, but equally is not an empirical proposition and
would not therefore be acceptable as part of a valid piece of cognitive
reasoning.

Similarly, if the strategy is adopted of giving moral values an empirical
definition, as for example Bentham did in his identification of 'good'
with 'pleasure', a similar argument can be deployed, first developed by
G. E. Moore in *Principia Ethica*. The argument is called the 'open
question' argument and is held by Moore to expose what he calls the
naturalistic fallacy.[18] If we take seriously Bentham's definition of 'good'
as 'pleasure', then it must follow that the question:

> This is pleasant but is it good?

could make no more sense than:

> This is a bachelor but is he unmarried?

If the terms in the first question did in fact have the same meaning
the question would be as meaningless as the second to someone who
understands English. But we do recognize the question as meaningful;
in fact it poses a frequent moral problem. This shows that Bentham's
theory cannot be taken as an account of an *actual* definition or moral
usage. It is rather a recommendation[19] that we begin to use the word in
this way, a recommendation based upon a supposedly factual account
of the nature of desire and motivation. However, if this is so we are
back with the earlier point that factual theories of human nature do not,
without being conjoined with moral principles or evaluative statements,
allow us to deduce moral conclusions.

As we saw, however, there was the possibility that the defensive
political and moral philosopher could argue that even if moral and
political language is an expression of emotional attitudes, nevertheless
such attitudes depend upon our beliefs about facts. For example, if I
envy someone it is because that person has a particular quality(ies) or
possession(s) or both and this is a factual matter which can be tested in

a wholly empirical manner. The positivists, of course, recognized this and C. L. Stevenson distinguished very clearly in *Ethics and Language*[20] between the attitudinal and the belief elements in moral principles. However, the argument about deriving 'an ought from an is' becomes relevant again here. Beliefs are capable of being empirically assessed but in so far as they have a factual content it is not possible to derive moral conclusions from them. Beliefs do not *entail* attitudes, whatever support they may give to attitudes falls short of logical entailment. It is thus possible to draw different moral conclusions from exactly the same set of factual beliefs. Of course, it may be that in many moral and political arguments what is at stake is a disagreement about belief and these disagreements can be resolved in principle by empirical research – for example, into whether capital punishment deters murder. But even if factual evidence could settle this disagreement it would not *entail* any particular moral attitude towards the moral rightness or wrongness of capital punishment.

In all of these cases, therefore, the positivist wants to deny that moral and political principles can be derived from factual enquiries into this or that aspect of human nature and human society. Facts and values are separate and there can be no logical entailment between them. If all of this is so then it deals a death blow to the classical tradition of political thought because typically it does seek to speak about what is right and good in politics and to do this in a way which is linked to what are taken to be facts about the human condition. The positivist rejects the entailment postulated in this link and wishes to regard political philosophy as a pseudo form of enquiry, one that cannot, at the end of the day, give a cognitive content to the signs that it uses in its specifically normative aspect. Issues of moral and political principle are important, but they are irreducibly subjective, expressing attitudes and preferences, recording decisions and commitments. But this cannot be an academic study. The philosopher's commitment and attitude would only be worth further attention if they were entailed by the factual enquiries they make, but they are not and for logical reasons cannot be.

It is clear, therefore, how these strictures would apply to the classical tradition in political thought. Factual accounts of human nature and human relationships cannot logically support normative conclusions about how the political community ought to be organized or what basic political goods are. If such accounts already contain normative or evaluative statements they are to be construed as the expression of private preference. Finally, these normative terms cannot be translated into empirical ones because either the definition will be an analytic truth and G. E. Moore's 'open question' will not make sense, whereas it does in fact; or the assimilation of the moral term to the evaluative one has to be seen as a recommendation and has only subjective force. There is no way through this critique in the positivist view by claiming that moral values are *sui generis* and known to reason, intuition, moral sense or whatever, because meaningful propositions have to be translatable into empirical terms to be meaningful, in accordance with the canons laid down in the *Tractatus*, and the deliverances of moral sense or intuition are not so translatable.

Political theory and the positivist critique

If we agree with this critique, what approaches to political studies are acceptable? Positivism sanctions two approaches which are complementary. In the first place there is space for a wholly empirical study of political behaviour; second, there is a role for the logical analysis of political concepts. A behaviourist approach is clearly sanctioned by the positivist account of the relationship between theory and experience. Any meaningful theory has to be composed of propositions which can be defined in terms of empirical sense contents. In the case of politics this seems to require two things: an individualistic reductionist approach to social and political phenomena, and a behaviourist approach to the study of political attitudes. Some kind of methodological individualism is required for political science because no empirical sense can be attached to concepts relating to social 'wholes' such as 'state', 'community', 'nation', 'polity' unless these concepts can be used in sets of statements which refer only to the empirically detectable behaviour of individuals. A reductive analysis of these concepts has to be undertaken as they can be meaningful only if they are translatable without remainder into conjunctions of sentences which describe the behaviour of individuals. This has both this scientific methodological aspect and a substantive political point. Positivists argued that many holistic political theories appear to regard certain kinds of institutions – the state, the political community, the race – as having an existence over and above the individuals who compose it, demanding loyalty, duties and obligations from citizens. However, if social wholes are indeed wholly resolvable into actions of individuals (in the material mode of speech), or if sentences about social wholes are translatable without remainder into sentences about the actions of individuals (in the formal mode of speech), then political concepts are empirical and we can see their apparently mysterious and substantive references for what they are – not institutions which transcend individuals but 'shorthand' ways of referring to the complex actions of individuals.

The actions in question here are to be understood as patterns of physical behaviour, rather than their physical features being understood as in some sense caused by private and empirically inaccessible mental states. This thesis in its most uncompromising form was the thesis of physicalism developed by Rudolph Carnap, which receives its most relevant expression for our purposes in his paper 'Psychology in Physical Language'.[21] The language of mental states is itself to be translated into terms denoting physical, palpable behavioural goings-on.

A behavioural and reductive science of politics was therefore legitimate on positivist grounds. Political theory would be on a par with normal theory in the sciences, it would be the body of generalizations which it might be hoped would one day issue from sufficiently committed and large-scale empirical study. Political theory would be empirical and not normative, explanatory and not recommendatory, morally neutral rather than undergirding some particular conception of the good.

There was, however, an opening for another approach to the theoretical study of politics sanctioned within the positivist framework. In the same way as positivists such as A. J. Ayer had argued that an important task of philosophers of science lay in the logical analysis of scientific concepts,[22] that is those concepts used in scientific theories, to clarify their meaning and help to give them a wholly empirical, non-metaphysical and operational meaning, so too this role was open to political philosophy with respect to political concepts. In this sense political philosophy was an adjunct of political science, clarifying the concepts used in science and argument to attempt to evacuate them of anything other than a descriptive and empirical meaning so that the terms of political discourse could be used in ways which were neutral between ideological and moral perspectives. The hope would be that in the same way as scientific theories could be advanced and scientific phenomena described and identified irrespective of the moral and other commitments of scientists, so too political science could go forward in a value-free manner once the basic concepts of that science had been clarified and given a reductive empirical definition, and that political argument could proceed with clear concepts and agreed definitions. Positivism therefore sanctioned two approaches to the study of politics which could live alongside one another: a behavioural science of politics adopting a reductionistic methodological individualist perspective and the logical analysis of political concepts. Only this second activity was theoretical, the former is observational and empirical. Political theory and philosophy, if it is to be a viable discipline, has to abandon its concern with the right and the good based on these ideas are on non-cognitive preferences and attitudes and concern itself with the analysis of political concepts with the purpose of producing concepts which can be morally neutral and will fill the same kind of descriptive operational role in political science as scientific concepts play in natural science. This attitude has bitten very deeply into political science and can be illustrated with two quotations from distinguished practitioners of the subject. The first passage is from David Easton, a senior political scientist, who endorses the categorical division of beliefs between the empirical and the evaluative and non-cognitive, central to positivism:

> [An] assumption, generally adopted today in the social sciences, holds that values can ultimately be reduced to emotional responses conditioned by the individuals' total life experiences. In this interpretation . . . facts and values are logically heterogeneous. The factual aspect of a proposition refers to part of reality; hence it can be tested with reference to the facts. In this way we check its truth. The moral aspect of a proposition, however, expresses only the emotional response of an individual to a state of real or supposed facts . . . Although we can say that the aspect of a proposition referring to a fact can be true or false, it is meaningless to characterise the value aspect of a proposition in this way.[23]

The second quotation comes from Felix Oppenheim, who adopts the positivist view of the restricted and non-normative role of political theory when he argues as follows:

For the purposes of a scientific study of politics, we must attempt to provide basic political concepts with explications acceptable to anyone regardless of his normative or ideological commitments so that the truth or falsity of statements in which these concepts thus defined occur will depend exclusively on inter-subjectively ascertainable evidence.[24]

Both these passages envisage a role for political theory which is fundamentally different from the foundational and prescriptive role which was central to the Western tradition of political thought. This is not of course to say that classical political theory did not shed light upon political concepts – one only needs to think of Rousseau's writing on equality or Hegel's theory of Civil Society to see this, but the whole range of assumptions compared with those in Oppenheim's work were really quite different.

The past fifteen years or so, however, have seen the growth of work in political theory which gives it a place and a role in political study more like that found in the classical tradition. Having been pronounced dead in 1956 what accounts for its resurrection? And in the hands of Rawls,[25] Nozick,[26] Walzer,[27] Dworkin,[28] Gewirth[29] and others, is it of the same form as found in the classical tradition?

The decline of positivism

Perhaps one of the most basic reasons for the change of fortune has been the decline of positivism as a potent force in philosophy, a fact which itself needs considerable explanation.

In the first place positivism seemed to have the advantage of providing a principle – the verification principle – which would allow a very clear distinction to be drawn between sentences which have a clear cognitive content from those which do not, and as we have seen, this had an enormous critical impact upon political theory. However, the very clarity of the distinction soon seemed to be dubious. It was, for example, very difficult to give a coherent account of the verification principle itself. Clearly it is not a tautology or true by definition (and it could hardly have done the work required of it by logical positivism if it had been an analytical truth), but at the same time it was not itself a generalization from experience (and in fact if this is what it purported to be, most of the empirical evidence would have been against it). If all meaningful statements are, on the principle of verifiability, either tautologies or empirically verifiable, what of the formulation of the verification principle itself? It would be awkward to be put in the position of having to argue that the statement in terms of which we could distinguish between sense and nonsense, namely the statement articulating the criterion of verifiability, is itself non-sensical. One way out of this suggested itself – that of arguing that the principle is a *rule*, rather than a statement. The basic question to be asked about a statement is whether it is true or false; rules, however, are not true or false, but correct or incorrect, sensible or unfounded, good or bad rules.[30] So the principle of verifiability becomes a recommendation that we should adopt it as a policy and treat statements in the ways articulated in the rule. This is hardly satisfactory, however, because while a statement is either true or false and this is why it is accepted, we have to be able to give a *reason* for adopting the rule. What kind of reason could we have for adopting the verification principle? Two rather general answers suggest themselves. The first would be that to adopt it as our basic epistemological rule would somehow bring us into line with reality.[31] This is, however, extremely dubious because it assumes that we are able to describe the nature of reality on the one hand and then recommend an epistemological rule which will allow us to make only those state-ments which are consistent with that reality. It does not take much philosophical sophistication to see that there is a circularity at work here. If our conception of reality (prior to adopting the verifiability criterion) is the correct one, then we arrive at it in advance of formulating the criterion which is supposed to distinguish between sense and non-sense in our conceptions. The whole idea of comparing an epis-temological policy with reality is a very peculiar one because the policy is supposed to be the criterion of what is real and unreal, and in language what is sense or what is nonsense. This strategy for saving the verification principle from the threat posed to it by its own adoption is therefore a very weak one.

The alternative account of why the principle of verifiability should be adopted as a rule is that in some sense the principle articulates the basic assumption of natural science and that because science has so large, so effective and so crucial a part in our culture we ought to adopt as a basic epistemological rule that which comes closest to encapsulating a scientific orientation.[32] There are, however, two clear difficulties with this. In the first place it is not at all clear that the principle of verification does encapsulate a basic scientific assumption. Indeed, Karl Popper has argued the opposite case that verifiability would lead to a very large gap in the rationality of science. We can usually only verify statements when we are able to enumerate completely all the things covered by the statement – for example that I have three green pens in my pocket. This can be completely verified, but scientific laws are *not* like this because they are usually of unrestricted generality, for example:

All gases expand when heated

Because this covers an indefinite number of cases it cannot be fully verified and because of the indefinite number we cannot work out a probability calculation of how far particular verifiable examples make the general rule more probable. Verifiability cannot be the criterion of science otherwise science cannot account for a rational acceptance of some of its most fundamental laws. Popper in fact proposed a different criterion, that of falsification so that while we do not know on an inductive verification basis that 'all swans are white', we can falsify this statement by finding one black swan. This account led Popper to accept an important role for creative imagination in science in the framing of hypotheses which could be falsified by experiment. The main point for our purposes, however, is that verifiability was soon regarded as being a very weak candidate for the basic epistemological assumption of natural science. In its turn this had the more general effect of loosening the hold that the verification principle had in epistemology.

In addition though, there was something very odd about the whole argument that the verification principle should be adopted as being the basic rule of a scientific attitude. What possible explanation could be given as to why we should adopt such an attitude? We have already seen that the positivist could not argue without circularity that the rule would bring our statements into line with scientific reality because what was real/unreal, sense/nonsense was supposed to depend upon the principle. It would seem that the supposed verificationist basis for a scientific approach was a matter of recommendation but, as we saw earlier, such a recommendation would have, on the positivist's own criterion, no cognitive power – it would merely be an expression of preference and as such could be accepted or rejected – any empirical evidence, assuming this to be at all relevant, would not *entail* the acceptance or rejection of the recommendation.

At this basic epistemological level therefore, positivism lost a very great deal of its power and led to a much more permissive approach to questions of meaning and sense. The critique of positivism was also given a major boost by the later work of Wittgenstein, particularly *The Blue and Brown Books*,[33] *Philosophical Investigations*,[34] *Zettel*,[35] and *On Certainty*,[36] in which he subjected the arguments of the *Tractatus Logico-Philosphicus* to intense criticism. Given the way the *Tractatus* inspired positivism, this subsequent work by Wittgenstein is of very great significance for the nature of political philosophy in a post-positivist world. However, we shall discuss this further in the final chapter in the context of a consideration of the current debate between foundationalists and communitarians: those who believe that political philosophy is concerned with providing a basic universal foundation for political judgement and those who think that political philosophy is concerned with a coherent and self-conscious understanding of the political and moral values which suffuse a particular society.

It is, however, important to recognize that while the overall positivist programme has collapsed, nevertheless certain aspects of it are still very much alive, in particular the fact/value distinction and anti-naturalism in ethics. Both of these slightly different positions are of the utmost importance in political philosophy, particularly in relation to arguments about human nature. On a naturalistic view a philosophical account of politics has to be rooted in a conception of human nature which, in turn, is supposed not merely to record some moral decision or commitment in regard to human nature but somehow to reveal the truth about human nature and human flourishing and thus the type of social order which will best allow human beings with this nature to realize their capacities and powers. The next chapter will focus more closely on these issues.

Notes

1   For an account of Protagoras see E. Barker, *The Political Thought of Plato and Aristotle*, Dower, New York, 1959, pp. 30 ff, and G. G. Kerferd, *The*

Sophistic Movement, Cambridge University Press, Cambridge, 1987.

2 P. Laslett, 'Introduction' to *Philosophy, Politics and Society*, series 1, Blackwell, Oxford, 1956.

3 For a sceptical view about the possibility of characterizing a tradition of thought in this way, see Q. Skinner. 'Meaning and Understanding in the History of Ideas', *History and Theory*, 8, 1969.

4 A. J. Ayer's *Language, Truth and Logic*, first published in 1936, provides the most accessible introduction to logical postivism. References here are to the Penguin edition of 1971.

5 L. Wittgenstein, *Tractatus Logico-Philosophicus*, Routledge and Kegan Paul, London, 1961. For a range of interpretations of this complex work see E. Anscombe, *An Introduction to Wittgenstein's Tractatus*, Hutchinson, London, 1959. J. Griffin, *Wittgenstein's Logical Atonism*, The Clarendon Press, Oxford, 1964; D. Favrholdt, *An Interpretation and Critique of Wittgenstein's Tractatus*, Monksgaard, Copenhagan, 1964.

6 B. Russell and A. N. Whitehead, *Principia Mathematica*, The University Press, Cambridge, 1925.

7 See *Tractatus*, proposition 4.221.

8 See ibid., propositions 3.202; 3.203; 3.22; 4.22.

9 Ibid. proposition 2.0211; see also Wittgenstein, *The Blue and Brown Books*, 2nd edn, Blackwell, Oxford, 1969, p. 1.

10 See *Tractatus*, proposition 3.203; 3.23.

11 For a discussion of various formulations of the verification principle see Ayer, *Language, Truth and Logic*.

12 Ibid., p. 12.

13 As G. E. Moore argued in *Principia Ethica*, Cambridge University Press, Cambridge, 1959.

14 See Ayer, *Language, Truth and Logic*, ch. 6 'Critique of Ethics and Theology', pp. 145–8.

15 M. Macdonald, 'Natural Rights', in *Philosophy, Politics and Society*, ed. Laslett, p. 49.

16 See J. S. Mill, 'Utilitarianism', in *John Stuart Mill and Jeremy Bentham: Utilitarianism and Other Essays*, ed. A. Ryan, Penguin, Harmondsworth, 1987.

17 D. Hume, *Treatise on Human Nature*, ed. L. A. Selby-Bigge, The Clarendon Press, Oxford, 1888.

18 Moore, *Principia Ethica*, pp. 15ff.

19 This is Ayer's interpretation, see 'The Principle of Utility', in *Philosophical Essays*, Macmillan, London, 1963, p. 263.

20 C. L. Stevenson, *Ethics and Language*, Yale University Press, New Haven, 1948.

21 Reprinted in A. J. Ayer (ed.), *Logical Positivism*, Free Press, New York, 1959.

22 See Ayer, *Language, Truth and Logic*, chs 2 and 3.

23 D. Easton, *The Political System*, Knopf, New York, 1953, p. 221.

24 F. Oppenheim 'Facts and Values in Politics', *Political Theory*, 1, no. 1, 1973, p. 56.

25 J. Rawls, *A Theory of Justice*, The Clarendon Press, Oxford, 1972.

26 R. Nozick, *Anarchy, State and Utopia*, Blackwell, Oxford, 1974.

27 M. Walzer, *Spheres of Justice*, Martin Robertson, Oxford, 1983.

28 R. Dworkin, *Taking Rights Seriously*, Duckworth, London, 1977; *Laws Empire*, Fontana, London, 1986.

29 A. Gewirth, *Reason and Morality*, Chicago University Press, Chicago, 1980.

30 See A. J. Ayer, 'On What There Must Be', in *Metaphysics and Common Sense*, Macmillan, London, 1967.

31 This seems to have been Carnap's view in *The Logical Structure of the World*, Routledge, London, 1967, pp. xv-xviii.

32 Carnap, *Logical Structure*.

33 Wittgenstein, *The Blue and Brown Books*.

34 L. Wittgenstein, *Philosophical Investigations*, Blackwell, Oxford, 1958.

35 L. Wittgenstein, *Zettel*, Blackwell, Oxford, 1967.

36 L. Wittgenstein, *On Certainty*, Blackwell, Oxford, 1969.

2

Human Nature and Political Theory

... all political and social theorists, I venture to claim, depend on some model of man in explaining what moves people and accounts for institutions. Such models are sometimes hidden but never absent, and the rise of behavioural political science has only enriched the stock. There is no more central or pervasive topic in the study of politics.

Martin Hollis, *Models of Man*

In the previous chapter we discussed the problems involved in providing a metaphysical grounding for political theories and how such attempts at metaphysical grounding had been thrown on the defensive by logical positivism. One area in which this issue is particularly acute is in relation to ideas about human nature and in relation to ideas about natural law – a set of laws discoverable by reason which were supposed to set out the institutional embodiment of the requirements which would provide for the fulfilment of human nature. The idea here is that human nature is not something just empirically discovered, but rather that our nature has to be considered against a more general metaphysical background which relates to the place of human life and agency in the natural order and to an account of the fundamental purposes and drives of human beings. The sweep and metaphysical background of this idea is well brought out by Jurgen Habermas in his essay 'Legitimation Problems in the Modern State':

Classical natural law is a theory dependent on world views. It was still quite clear to Christian Wolff at the end of the eighteenth century that political philosophy 'presupposes in all its doctrines ontology, natural psychology, cosmology, theology and the whole of metaphysics.'[1]

Even with the decline of the full blown positivist programme such views are still not open to us. We find it difficult to imagine how a full-scale metaphysic could be constructed as a foundation for political principle and thus for political legitimacy. However, before assuming this view in its entirety, in this chapter I want to discuss some of the ways in which the idea of human nature, against a metaphysical background in many cases, has been used by philosophers to provide a basis for the legitimacy of some forms of government compared to others. In this sense the reader will become aware in more detail of some of the salient issues at stake.

In the chapter we shall look at the work of Aristotle just because his arguments present in a particularly clear way some of the issues at stake here. We shall then move on to look at Hobbes, who adopts what he sees as a rational, scientific attitude towards his understanding of human nature. Finally we shall look at Hume, who is an interesting case for us since as a radical empiricist he is one of the inspirational figures of the positivist movement, yet, even within his own empiricist approach, he does have a central place for a general political theory of the sort which the positivists denied and one which, furthermore, trades upon an extended account of human nature. Towards the end of the chapter we shall go on to consider some modern theorists, such as Eric Fromm and Herbert Marcuse, who have drawn extensively from Freud to enable us to examine both what the political implications of a psychological theory would be and the extent to which the moral language typical of earlier attempts to understand human nature can in fact be displaced by a theory which seeks some scientific and non-moral basis for its political arguments.   The issue at stake in this debate is whether a theory of human nature can provide us with a neutral basis for determining the nature of political morality and the appropriate shape of institutions for this morality or whether, in the words of Alasdair MacIntyre:

I cannot look to human nature as a neutral standard, asking which forms of social and moral life would give to it the most adequate expression. For each form of life carries with it its own picture of human nature. The choice of a form of life and the choice of a view of human nature go together.[2]

At the end of the chapter I shall then go on to discuss MacIntyre's claim and to see what follows from it, to assess whether or not theories of human nature can in any sense be the bedrock of political theory.

Aristotle: human nature and human function

Aristotle is the political philosopher who links an account of politics most closely to an account of human nature and the conception of the human good derived from that account, and the theory he derives from this produces a highly unified conception of politics and citizenship oriented to the idea of the political community realizing a particular conception of the human good. The question on which I want to focus is the extent to which in Aristotle it is true, as Habermas argues in his essay on 'Legitimation in the Modern State', that 'The ethics and politics of Aristotle are unthinkable without the connection to physics and metaphysics.'[3] If it turns out to be the case that Aristotle's arguments are in fact inseparable from a metaphysical position which we can no longer possibly share, then neo-Aristotelians such as Hannah Arendt, Leo Strauss, J. Ritter, William Galston, Ronald Beiner and others have to explain how a revised form of Aristotelian politics can be formulated independently of metaphysical assumptions on which it originally rested. If it turns out that, in MacIntyre's words, Aristotle's ethics presupposes his 'metaphysical biology',[4] then how far is the Aristotelian enterprise of linking politics to an account of human nature and the human good drawn from that biology vitiated by the failure of that biology? As we saw in the last chapter there has been in this century a strong move against ethical naturalism, led by G. E. Moore, who claimed to have diagnosed the naturalistic fallacy in the sense of linking an understanding of moral terms with an account of human nature. However, as MacIntyre argues in *After Virtue*, Aristotle's theory presupposes that there is no such naturalistic fallacy and that the human good can be defined in terms of some general features of human nature.[5]

The connection between an account of politics and an account of the human good is insisted upon right at the beginning of the Politics:

> Observation shows us, first, that every polis (or state) is a species of association, and, secondly, that all associations are instituted for the purpose of attaining some good – for all men do all acts with a view to achieving something which is, in their view, good. We may hold therefore (on the basis of what we actually observe) that all associations aim at some good; and we may also hold that the association which is the most sovereign of all, and includes all the rest, will pursue this aim most, and will thus be directed to the most sovereign of all goods. This most sovereign and inclusive association is the polis, as it is called or the political association.[6]

The political community is therefore concerned with advancing and securing the most general form of human good; other types of enterprise are devoted to more specific goods:

> Since, therefore, politics makes use of the other practical sciences, and lays it down besides what we must do and what we must not do, its end must include theirs. And that end, in politics as well as in ethics, can only be the good for man.[7]

How is this good to be determined and thus the ends or purposes of political life and the criterion of political judgement arrived at? Aristotle's answer to this question is in two parts. In the first part he tries to demonstrate that happiness is the ultimate end or goal of human action; the second part of the argument, and the one most salient for the purposes of this discussion, is designed to appeal to a conception of human functioning or basic human nature, which will then give an overall content to the idea of happiness. The metaphysical difficulties tend to relate to this second part of his enterprise.

In the *Nicomachean Ethics* Aristotle argues that a knowledge of the good for man is vital in politics and that this good is related to the characterization of human action. In his view every deliberate action or pursuit has for 'its object the attainment of some good' and granted that this is so, we must go on to ask 'What do we take to be the end of politics?' or what is the same question in another form: What is the supreme good attainable in our actions? Aristotle argues that by the supreme good, or the supreme end, he has in mind the idea of a goal of action which is desired for itself and not as a means to secure further ends:

Assuming that there is one such theory which alone is an end beyond which there are no further ends, we may call *that* the good of which we are in search ... An object pursued for its own sake possesses a higher degree of finality than one pursued with an eye to something else.[8]

In Aristotle's view happiness (eudaemonia – which includes ideas of flourishing and well-being) is such an end. Other good things in life such as honour, pleasure and intelligence, while they are clearly desirable for themselves, are nevertheless chosen because of the belief that they will be instrumental in promoting happiness or well-being. In parenthesis it might be noted here that the fact that he includes pleasure, which is a feeling or sensation, as one of the things which is instrumental to happiness shows that he does not, as we are liable to do, equate happiness with pleasure, nor does he equate happiness with any subjective sensation. As we shall see, given his view of human nature, he believes that happiness has an objective content and one that can give us criteria for political judgement of the form of the state in which human beings can fulfil their real nature and flourish.

Given then that eudaemonia is a final goal or purpose of human action and that it is not just a subjective sensation but an objective standard of flourishing and well-being, what is it and how is its objectivity to be demonstrated? This is a crucial question for Aristotle because what is at stake here is the supreme good on which the purpose of political life is founded. His answer to this question is in terms of the idea of human function or characteristic work, both of which are used as translations of the Greek word, εργον (ergon). However, before we go into this idea in detail we need to see that Aristotle bases his approach to an understanding of human life on more general views of teleology which he developed in general terms in his philosophy of nature in his *Physics*, and with reference to biological life of which man is a part in his book *The Parts of Animals*. In the *Physics* he argues as follows:

Further, when a series has a completion, all the preceeding steps are for the sake of this. Now surely, as in intelligent action, so in nature; and as in nature, so it is in each action if nothing interferes. Now intelligent action is for the sake of an end; therefore the nature of things also is so ... Each step then in a series is for the

sake of the next. . . . If therefore artificial products are for the sake
of an end, so are natural products.[9]

Given this teleological account of nature, and given that human beings
are part of nature, this teleological explanation applies in human life as
well. This is explained in detail in *The Parts of Animals*:

> As every instrument and every bodily member subsumes some
> partial end, that is to say, some special action, so the whole body
> must be destined to minister to some plenary sphere of action.
> Thus the saw is made for sawing, for sawing is a function, and
> not sawing for the saw. Similarly the body too must somehow or
> another be made for the soul, and each part of it for some sub-
> ordinate function to which it is adapted.[10]

This means that we can only explain something in terms of its end
(telos, τελος), which in turn means that we have to have a conception
of the telos before we can explain what is in fact done whether in terms
of the organs of the body, or in terms of ethics and politics:

> Now the order of development is the reverse of the real order.
> What is later in the formative process is earlier by its nature, and
> what comes at the end of the process is first by its nature. Thus a
> house, though it comes after the bricks and stones, is not there for
> the sake of them, they are there for the sake of the house. . . . And
> the same applies to materials of every kind.[11]

So, although as we shall see, observation and detailed knowledge of
a particular society and its practices is crucial for ethics in Aristotle's
view, there is an unavoidable a priori element arising from his teleological account of the natural order of which man is a part. As we
cannot explain a saw purely by observation without an understanding
of the purpose or function of a saw, so we cannot understand human
life and in particular ethics and political institutions without some
conception of the nature of the human good and the human ergon.
There are two parts to a teleological explanation, as Aristotle makes
clear in *The Parts of Animals*. The first is the account of the good which
explains the action or process in question; the second is the necessity of

the particular materials, actions and movements which explain how that good is achieved. These ideas are central to the explanation of ethics and politics.

The idea of function, Aristotle argues, gives us a foundation for an objective characterization of human well-being or the human good in the following way. In our lives we are aware that people undertake a wide variety of professions and callings – he mentions a flautist or a sculptor or craftsman – and when we reflect upon these professions we become aware that there is a special talent or excellence which is required by the exercise of that particular calling and which is embodied in the job and this talent is the ergon in this particular case. That is to say, we have objective criteria for determining the excellence of a craftsman and these are given by the particular talents required by the role. We know the good which the flautist seeks which then explains the necessity of his doing what he does in the way that he does it. Aristotle then goes on to generalize from these cases. While we all have particular functions as sculptors, fathers, husbands, soldiers etc., in Aristotle's view, we also have a function which goes beyond or transcends these particular functions:

> Is it likely that joiners and shoemakers have certain functions or specialised activities, while man as such has none but has been left by Nature as a functionless being . . .[12]

To try to determine the function or characteristic work of man, we would have to try to determine what is distinctive about human life. In the same way we can account for the movement of the lips and eyelids[13] in the body by seeing what overall purpose they serve. If this could be identified then the fulfilment of this distinctive function will constitute that form of happiness or well-being which it is the purpose of the political community to foster. In Aristotle's view this distinctive functioning is not to be found merely in the act of living or physical survival[14] because we find the same drives are at work in the animal and vegetable kingdom – hence physical nurture and growth cannot be the characteristic ergon of human beings, although these are of course features of their lives. Nor can this characteristic be found in the bodily sensations which human beings experience[15] because again these are to be found in the animal kingdom. The distinctive characteristic of human life is to be found in reason, in the exercise of our rational capacities which are not possessed by other creatures and from these considerations Aristotle arrives at the conclusion that the function of man is the exercise of these rational capacities:

> The function of a man is the exercise of his non-corporeal faculties or soul in accordance with or at least not divorced from, a rational principle. The function of an individual and of a good individual in the same class – a harp player, for example, and a good harp player, and so through the classes – is generically the same, except that we must add superiority in accomplishment to the function, the function of the harp player is merely to play on the harp, while the function of the good harp player is to play it well. The function of man is a certain form of life, namely an activity of the soul exercised in combination with a rational principle or reasonable ground of action. The function of a good man is to exert such activity well.... If these assumptions are granted, we conclude that the good for man is an activity of soul in accordance with goodness.[16]

As he himself recognizes, however, this merely provides us with an outline of the human good; there is a need to fill this in and to show the relationship between the exercise of these rational capacities and human virtue and then to the goal of the political community. This is where the a priori theory connects back with observation. A good deal of the remainder of *Nicomachean Ethics* is concerned both with a detailed account of how people in his sort of society in fact think about the human good, and he sees this as confirming his a priori reasoning, and also using this material to fill out in detail the general account of the human good which he has presented. Thus he is concerned not just with philosophical reasoning but with ενδοξα (endoxa), with what people actually think.[17] Thus he links up reason, a conception of human flourishing and thus an account of human virtue and how these are seen, articulated and embodied in a particular form of life. This connection between reason and practical social virtue is vital for Aristotle because, of course, an evil man can act on rational grounds, that is to say he acts on what he takes to be rational grounds. In Aristotle's view there has to be a connection between the exercise of reason and virtue – as he says: The human function and its associated good will be one and the same for all persons and its realization in collective form will constitute the good life. This connection is forged by Aristotle in his doctrine of the *mean* relating as it does, acting for reasons and virtue. By 'the mean' Aristotle should not be taken as counselling a doctrine of moderation in all things, rather it requires the balanced, proper, appropriate or rational response to a situation. So, for example, if we are faced with an evil or wrong-doing then the mean will be the appropriate response to *that* degree of evil – to do in response no more and no less than one should. The point is made very clearly in *Nicomachean Ethics*:

> It is possible, for example, to feel fear, boldness, desire, anger, pity, and pleasures and pains generally, too much or too little, or to the right amount. If we feel them too much or too little, we are wrong. But to have these feelings at the right times and on the right occasions towards the right people and for the right motive and in the right way is to have them in the right measure, that is somewhere between the two extremes; and this is what characterises goodness.[18]

To act virtuously is to act according to the mean and this entails that the virtuous persons will have 'a rational element in their souls – which we commend because it encourages them to perform the best actions in the right way'. As Aristotle understands this, however, this process is not one of applying some clearly objective criterion which could be reduced to a set of scientific maxims. He rejects Plato's view of an absolute answer to moral dilemmas which could be given once we know the nature and the Form of the good, in favour of a more specific account of practical judgement. As Taylor puts the point:

> The practically wise man (phronimos) has a knowledge of how to behave in each particular circumstance which can never be equated with or reduced to general truths. Practical wisdom (phronesis) is a not fully articulable sense rather than a kind of science.[19]

This is the main theme of Book VI of the *Nicomachean Ethics*. The phronimos will have his judgement informed by general considerations about the nature of the good as Aristotle has identified it, but he will be concerned with the specificity of each case. In this sense phronesis judges particular cases in the context of general principles but it is not a matter of applying a set of codified general rules in a mechanical way, a theme to which we shall return.

So given that moral goodness is central to political science, and that moral goodness is this condition of the psyche in which people act for the right reasons in the right circumstances, it follows that:

> the statesman ought to have some inkling of psychology, just as the doctor who is a specialist in the diseases of the life must have a general knowledge of physiology. Indeed, such a general background is even more necessary for the statesman in view of the fact that his science is of a higher order than the doctor's ... therefore the stateman should also be a psychologist.[20]

Given that it is the duty of the statesman to foster virtuous action and given that these virtues are linked to a correct account of the role of reason in human life, it follows that an account of human nature and human psychology is fundamental to our understanding of how the political community can develop what is truly good for man. Political science is therefore a practical activity, setting the goals in terms of human goodness and flourishing which the good state aims to foster – but these goals are not just a matter of subjective preference, they can be grounded by considering the characteristic ergon of human beings and this will provide us with a set of criteria of judgement in terms both of the goals themselves and the appropriate means of attaining them, that is to say, the institutional standards which are likely to develop human excellence as Aristotle understands it and this is the subject matter of his *Politics*. This point is also reinforced by his argument in the *Politics* that the human good as he understands it requires social cooperation – the exercise of the virtues which is described in detail in *Nicomachean Ethics* and only barely outlined above, requires a political community not merely to provide the means of subsistence, but also the sphere of participation and deliberation which are essential for the development of the rational nature of man as he sees it.

So, for example, if the human good consisted in mere survival there could be a state of slaves of animals, or equally if the encouragement of a particular form of goodness were not the aim of the state, a state could be understood as it was by the sophist Lycophron and, as we shall see, by modern liberals, as a guarantor of men's rights against one another.[21] The polis has a richer role than merely preventing one person doing harm to another; it is rather a rule of life 'such as will make the members of a polis good and just'.[22] Because we can arrive at an objective conception of the good life, understood as the exercise of the virtues described in the *Ethics*, the polis cannot be understood as:

> an association for residence on a common site, or for the sake of preventing mutual injustice and easing exchange. These are indeed conditions which must be present before a polis can exist; but the presence of all these conditions is not enough, in itself, to constitute a Polis. What constitutes a polis is an association of households and clans in a good life, for the sake of attaining a perfect and self-sufficing existence.[23]

The exercise of the human ergon of reason requires that in the sphere of politics citizens should be able to participate in politics, to rule and be ruled, to engage in political deliberation and in judicial functions, and to be involved in the election of magistrates and other officers of the state. Aristotle also draws other conclusions about the nature of citizenship from his argument about the distinctive capacities of human beings in the sense that he regards some groups as not possessing the appropriate capacities to a full extent. In Book I, Chapter V of the *Politics* he argues that both women, whose functions are different, and slaves do not possess these capacities. Indeed, in the case of a slave he argues that they possess reason only in so far as they can recognize its exercise in others. Citizenship in a polis directed towards realizing distinctively human capacities, has therefore to exclude both women and slaves.

Aristotle's argument raises deep questions about the nature of theories of human nature in relation to politics in that theories of human nature of the sort likely to be relevant to politics embody an illicit functional view of human nature – that theories of this sort presuppose that there is some overriding purpose or function to human life which appropriate political institutions will foster.

However, it can be argued as a matter of history and sociology that while we may still retain some idea of the ergon or definitive nature of certain particular human activities – for example, being a teacher or philosopher, we have been losing agreement about the ergon of other specific human roles, for instance being a mother. Feminists, for example, challenge the conventional account of what the ergon in relation to mothering is, but if this is true of specific human roles it is even more true of the nature of the human ergon as such – the characteristic work of human beings apart from their specific roles. On this view, in a liberal and pluralistic culture which is devoid of either a theological or metaphysical view about the definitive nature and work of human beings the attempt to ground political theory in a doctrine about human nature is bound to fail and the common good relating to this definitive work of man to be secured by the state is an illusion.

However, this historico-sociological argument can also be given more definitive philosophical backing drawn from existentialist writers, particularly Sartre, who have been very concerned to reject the view that human beings have a definitive nature and purpose to fulfil. The argument here is that while there may in fact be a function or ergon for the parts of the body and which can be determined by identifying the relation of the specific parts or organs to the structure of the body as a whole, to assume that human beings have a definite nature and a function is to treat human nature instrumentally. A thing can only have a function if it serves and is created to serve some external end or purpose. However, the existentialist argues, if we are devoid of some kind of theological or metaphysical background which constitutes the external reference for determining the ergon of human nature, then we cannot say that man has an essence.[24] Theories of human nature presuppose that essence precedes existence, that human beings instantiate a predetermined nature and function, whereas for the existentialist the reverse is the case: existence precedes essence. Human beings find themselves in a world without theological and metaphysical certainties and they create their own nature by their subjective choices. These choices of principle and practice cannot be based upon external authority such as the alleged nature of man, because there are no inescapable forms of such authority and if I choose as an authority a religious or a metaphysical conception of man's nature these authorities are only authorities because I have *chosen* to regard them as such. Thus Sartre argues:

man first of all exists, encounters himself, surges up in the world – and defines himself afterwards. If man as the existentialist sees him is not definable, it is because to begin with he is nothing. He will not be anything until later, and then he will be what he makes of himself. . . . Man simply is.[25]

As a free person my nature is indeterminate and is built up as a consequence of my choice. I am not a thing with some kind of pre-determined essence to fulfil. Man is *l'être pour soi*, a being who, if he is true to his humanity and not living a life of bad faith, of obedience to authorities which he has not self-consciously chosen, cannot be labelled because he does not have a function or telos. To treat human beings as if they fulfilled a pre-existing essence is to treat them as instruments for some external end. But shorn of the theological and metaphysical theory which would provide such an end, man is a self-creating being – creating his own nature and purposes through his/her free choices – as Sartre says, following Dostoevsky:

Si Dieu n'existent pas, tout serait possible.[26]

As we have seen, therefore, attempts to ground conceptions of political morality in theories of human nature meet very great difficulties in our culture. Modernity has undermined both the practical moral agreements about the purposes of individuals which may have characterized some earlier societies and made the claim for a shared human essence appear plausible, and equally philosophical speculation and the growth of scientific secularism have undermined the intellectual assumptions on which such theories of the human essence are based. In this sense, therefore, the general thrust of this argument is very much in the direction that human nature is not some kind of external standard which could be used to justify a particular morality or conception of the purposes of politics in defining a common good for persons. Rather our morality and our views on human nature interpenetrate one another and one cannot be foundational. This therefore looks as if political philosophy will have to be interpretive, bringing out the assumptions about human purposes and values which may be lodged deep in a particular moral or political tradition, looking at its coherence and the claims which might, within that tradition, be based upon it, but giving up any idea that an essence of man could be identified which would be an external foundation of political morality and of universal salience.

There is, however, a further aspect of Aristotle's work which is of great salience for the political theorist. I have stressed in the above account that there are two central strands to his argument. One is the a priori dimension which looks to some general, universal account of human purposes, resting upon his metaphysical biology; the other is his concern with endoxa, with the articulated values of a particular society, in his case the Athenian polis, and part of the philosophical project is to bring these together in a comprehensive theory. A complete political theory will be one which in Aristotle's view links an account of some universal principles and values with some account of how these are realized in particular historical circumstances. However, there are clear possibilities for tension between these two strands of thought. It could be argued that a good deal of modern thought has moved in the universalist direction of trying to generate a general theory of a priori reasons for action and for political judgement without paying sufficient attention to the values of particular societies and how such a priori principles bear on the values and institutions of particular societies. It is clear enough why political philosophy has in fact gone in this universalist direction and this is to do partly with the function of reason and partly growing moral diversity. Reason is a universal idea. The criteria of reason are supposed to be indifferent to circumstances and location, an idea which in the ancient world is found in Plato and in Cicero; in Aristotle too it comes out in relation to his metaphysical theory about the nature of human life and how this is linked with his general physical theory and his biology. These are universal features of the human condition. These claims of reason have become more and more reinforced in the modern world, particularly since the Enlightenment.

With the collapse of religious or even mythological bases of political legitimacy, it has been part of the quest of political philosophy to provide universal reasons for political legitimacy and this perhaps comes out most clearly in doctrines about human rights which are thought to apply to all persons everywhere. In this perspective political order has to be founded on the demands of reason and not the local and specific values of particular states. However, in the past ten years or so, there has been a revival of interest in political theory attempting to theorize not in a universal and general way but in trying to comprehend the values of political communities. This communitarian thought stands in explicit contrast to the universalizing tendencies which I have mentioned. In Aristotle, however, both dimensions are held together, but there is a clear tension between them, a tension which has been noted by modern political theorists. C. Taylor notes it in his book *Sources of the Self*;[27] MacIntyre does in *After Virtue*;[28] John McDowell notes some of the same issues in his Aristotelian essay 'Virtue and Reason', in which he contrasts the idea of phronesis, which in his view means approaching morality from the 'inside out' on the basis of an assumed understanding of what it is to act virtuously, with the Platonic approach which is from the 'outside in', that is to say, involving the idea of applying a set of codified rules to the resolution of moral disputes;[29] and the German philosopher Gadamer gives a particularly good account of how Aristotle sees the link between the two in his essay 'Über die Möglichkeit einer philosophischen Ethic' (On The Possibility of Philosophical Ethics).

> Philosophical ethics is in the same situation in which everyone finds himself. What counts as right, what we consent or object to in judging ourselves or others follows our general ideas of what is good and just; but it aquires genuine determinateness only in the concrete reality of the case, which is not a case of applying a general rule ... Above all it is not different from it insofar as it includes the same task of application to given circumstances that belongs to all moral knowledge.[30]

Aristotle's attempt to link the universal claims of moral knowledge, of what can be identified by reason and particular circumstances, is still a problem which haunts contemporary political philosophy and in the final chapter we shall take it up again when we come to consider modern debates on similar topics. For the moment, however, we will resume our task of looking at the way in which philosophers have sought to ground an account of politics on an account of human nature. In doing this we turn next to Thomas Hobbes, who rejected Aristotle in a particularly withering way and sought to present an account of the relationship between human nature and politics which was consistent with his understanding of empirical science, one which was miles away from Aristotle's teleological and metaphysical view.

Thomas Hobbes: science and human nature

Anxiety for the future time, disposeth men to inquire into the causes
of things: because the knowledge of them, maketh men the better
able to order the present to their best advantage.[31]

Thomas Hobbes of Malmesbury, probably the greatest and most systematic of British political philosophers, was preoccupied with working
out the conditions of social and political security. This is not at all
surprising. He was born prematurely, his birth occasioned by the news
of the approach of the Spanish Armada in 1588; he reached maturity
during the turbulent reign of Charles I and experienced exile and the
period of the Commonwealth with all its turmoil and religious and
political fanaticism. It is sometimes argued that political philosophy is
at its most lively and salient during periods of political upheaval, and
Hobbes exemplifies this case as well as anyone, although it is equally
true of Plato, St. Augustine, Machiavelli, Marx and Rawls. Hobbes,
deeply marked by the political breakdown of the civil war, argued that
the nature of politics and political power had to be understood in
scientific terms. If we could arrive at a correct scientific account of
human nature and basic human drives, we could derive an account of
how human beings basically relate to one another and under what sort
of political authority they would need to live in order to remedy the
defects of the social relations as these were likely to be in the light of
the scientific account of human nature.

Hobbes derived his account of science from the science of his own
day and in particular from Galileo and Harvey, a contemporary who
wrote on the circulation of the blood. He took from these thinkers a
scientific method and a principle of explanation of natural phenomena
in terms of the laws of motion. Hobbes's genius lay in the fact that he
extended these theories from natural objects to the world of human
motives and purposes. A scientific account of these purposes would
provide us with an account of cause and effect in human affairs, or from
causes to possible effects, and this knowledge could then be used in the
context of human motivation to determine the political preconditions
for an ordered, stable and peaceful society. Thus, although Hobbes
disagreed with Aristotle over most things they were alike in at least one
respect, namely in wanting to find an understanding of the nature and

the aims of politics upon a conception of human nature, however different these conceptions in fact turned out to be.

In Hobbes's view, human nature is to be understood and explained in the same way as any other natural phenomena, there is, as it were, no gap in the laws of physics, they apply equally well to the explanation of the circumstances of human life. The laws of physics in Hobbes's view are concerned with the laws of motion and the fundamental constituents of reality are items of matter in motion. In order to transpose this explanation to the sphere of human life, it is necessary to provide definitions of the basic elements in human nature in terms of matter in motion. These definitions, in Hobbes's rather peculiar use of the term, provide us with basic causes; effects are to be understood as the deductive consequences of such definitional causes.[32] Hence, in his view, scientific explanation is both causal and demonstrative, like geometry:

> Seeing then that truth consisteth in the right ordering of names in our affirmations, a man that seeketh precise truth has need to remember what every name he uses stands for, and to place it accordingly, or else he will find himself entangled in words ... And therefore in geometry ... men begin at settling the signification of their words; which settling of significations they call definitions, and place them at the beginning of this reckoning.[33]

Hence in *Leviathan*, Hobbes's masterpiece in political philosophy, he begins with materialist, matter-in-motion, definitions of basic human experiences, drives and motivations. There is not the space to discuss these definitions in any detail but it is necessary to pay attention to some to understand the place they have in Hobbes's political theory and the role of the conception of human nature in the elaboration of this theory.

It is central to his view, however, that a proper understanding of causes is essential both to an adequate political philosophy and to civil peace, which in turn depends upon there being an agreed civil philosophy. We can only determine the proper role, function and legitimacy of government if we have a proper understanding of the causes which have led to the setting up of civil power. He argues this point strongly in *Leviathan*:

Ignorance of the causes, the original constitution of Right, Equity, Law and Justice, disposeth a man to make custom and Example the rule of his actions ... like little children they have no other rule of good and evil manners (p. 165).

A sense of the legitimacy of government cannot rest upon custom, tradition or for that matter on myth or any other kind of narrative about the history and culture of the society; it has rather to be founded on a proper, that is to say scientific, account of causes.

Given Hobbes's mechanistic view of all physical things as matter in motion, he understands thoughts, feelings and states of consciousness generally[34] as a by-product of the physiological movements of the body. These internal physiological processes Hobbes calls the vital motions of the body, that is to say, they are what sustain the life of the organism, and in Hobbes's view desire, aversion, pleasure and pain, as conscious experiences, are closely linked to sustaining this vital motion. What we desire and what we find pleasant are those things which we calculate will secure the vital motions of the body, for example pleasure:

This motion which is called appetite, and for the appearance of it delight, and pleasure, seemeth to be a corroboration of vital motion and a help thereunto.[35]

Pain equally is what the mind perceives as impeding vital motion and is a signal that vital motion or life is in danger. These ideas are linked by Hobbes to the idea that all the fundamental drive of all living things is to go on living and hence a desire for life and an aversion to death are the two fundamental motives for Hobbes. From this it follows, given his understanding of pleasure and pain, that our basic motives are a desire for pleasure and an absence of pain. Given Hobbes's understanding of what, on a scientific basis, he believes human nature to be like, he can go on to give an account of moral ideas such as good and evil. These cannot in Hobbes's view be absolutes, they are always relative to the individual and his calculation of pleasure and pain:

whatsoever is the object of any man's appetite or desire, that is it which he for his part calleth good: and the object of his hate and aversion, evil; and of his contempt, vile and inconsiderable. For these words of good, evil and contemptible, are ever used with relation to the person that useth them: there being nothing simply and absolutely so; nor any common rule of good and evil to be taken from the nature of objects themselves, but from the person of the many.[36]

Whereas on Aristotle's view we are able to work out a definite account of the good for human beings from his account of man's distinctive ergon or function, Hobbes' reasoning takes us in the opposite direction, namely that because we are all physiologically determined beings it follows that good and evil are correlated with individual subjective sensations and these vary from individual to individual. Hence, there cannot be any *natural* agreement on what is good for man, each individual will differ in his asssessment of good and evil just because their sensations differ. This is a matter of prime political importance for Hobbes. If we are to have moral agreement, as part of a settled and secure life, the agreement has to be artifically contrived by the power of government or as Hobbes puts it, 'an arbitrator or judge, whom men disagreeing shall by consent set up, and make his gestures the rule thereof'. The exercise of governmental power is a necessary remedy for the lack of any natural moral agreement, the consequences of which, seen in the light of other aspects of Hobbes's theory of human nature, are disastrous. Hobbes's account of power is particularly important here. In Chapter X of *Leviathan* he defines power as 'a present means to attain some future good'. That is to say, my power is my ability to get what will satisfy my desires, secure me pleasure and, what is the same thing, to promote my good. In the absence of political authority and with it moral agreement, Hobbes argues that there is in mankind 'a perpetual and restless desire of power after power that closeth only in death'. As he puts it:

Life itself is but motion and can never be without desire.[37]

Unless one can acquire more and more power, one cannot be sure of the 'means to live well'. Yet this desire for an assured level of satisfaction of desire is itself a fundamental psychological and physiological feature of human life.

These fundamental drives in human nature both for power after power and the security to achieve this are also combined with Hobbes's assumption that people are roughly equal to one another, so that in a natural state no single individual is able, for very long, to dominate all others. In the absence of government, with no moral agreement and no rule-governed framework to regulate their lives, human life will be marked by a propensity to quarrel and disagree. In a world of scarce resources to satisfy desires and in the absence of agreement each individual will be in competition with all others for power and for satisfaction, and in this situation, of what life would be like without government, human beings will be in a state of war. Such a state of war, however, while a consequence of basic human drives in the absence of a government, also has the effect of undermining the possibility of the satisfaction of such drives both in the sense of satisfying desires and having some sense of security in that satisfaction. Many objects of satisfaction would be absent in such a society – industry, agriculture, navigation, trade, cooperative building; 'no arts; no letters; no society; and which is worst of all continual fear, and danger of violent death; and the life of man, solitary, poor, nasty, brutish and short'.[38] In addition, there would be no security of property 'no *mine* and *thine* distinct; but only that to be everyman's, that he can get; and for so long as he can keep it'.[39] This Hobbes concludes is the ill condition into which man is placed by 'mere nature'. To those who, in a political society, which does have government, security and a rule-governed structure, believe that Hobbes has painted an unrealistically bleak picture of what man's inclinations are in the absence of government, Hobbes says this. He asks us to consider our normal everyday reactions to other people, which he believes embody deep distrust:

> Let him consider with himself, when taking a journey, he arms himself, and seeks to go well accompanied; when going to sleep he locks his doors; when even in his house he locks his chests; and this when he knows there be laws, and public officers, armed to revenge all injuries shall be done him . . . Does he not there as much accuse mankind by his actions, as I do my words.[40]

So understood naturalistically or scientifically, man is in a dilemma, his physiological drives push each individual into a position in which the very possibility of the satisfaction of desire is a very fragile one, and each individual is haunted by the fear of violent death, which as the cessation of desire and vital movement is the worst evil that can happen to anyone.

In this situation we seek a means of remedying the position we are placed in in 'mere nature' or the state of nature, and this remedy is Hobbes's explanation of the necessity of an absolute form of government. In Hobbes's view both our passion and our reason can lead to a position in which a solution to the dilemma can be achieved.[41] Our passions lead us to desire social peace as a necessary condition of satisfying our desires in as secure and predictable a way as possible and reason points us in the direction of the means to securing this end. These means are embodied in what Hobbes calls the Laws of Nature, each of which is 'a precept or general rule, found out by reason, by which a man is forbidden to do that which is destructive of his life, or taketh away the mean of preserving the same; and to omit that by which he thinketh it best preserved'.[42] There are three fundamental laws of nature, or prudential maxims which can provide the means of escape from the state of competitive war in the state of nature: these are:

1 To seek peace and follow it and by all means that we can, defend ourselves.
2 That as far as he believes it to be necessary for peace and self-defence to lay down this right to all things and be contented with as much liberty against other men, as he would allow against himself.
3 Men perform their covenants made.

Given the nature of human nature and the consequences which follow from the unrestrained attempt to realize basic human drives and desires, a resolution of the human predicament requires the establishment of a sovereign by the act of choosing to renounce the rights which each individual has in the state of nature, the right in question here being understood as the liberty which each person has to use his own power as he thinks fit to satisfy his desires. Without a limitation on this right, there can be no social peace and its restraint is a precondition of government. Such laying down of a right is rational for each person because he sees it as a necessary condition for peace and security, or 'commodious living' as Hobbes calls it, but because the right is renounced to secure these goods we can never in Hobbes's view renounce that fundamental right, power or liberty to resist those who 'assume by force or take away life'. The authority of government over an individual is therefore set up by a covenant embodying a mutual renunciation of rights, but this renunciation must of necessity stop short at removing the power to protect one's own life, even against government. Hence government, or commonwealth, is to be understood in Hobbes' view as a contractual remedy for that 'miserable condition of war, which is necessarily consequence, ... to the natural passions of men, where there is no power to keep them in awe'. Without such a government, every man will 'lawfully rely upon his own strength and for caution against all other men'. Because of the extremity of the human condition without a sovereign government to keep men 'in awe', it is necessary for the sovereignty of government to be absolute subject to the caveat already entered, namely that a man has a liberty to disobey when the government threatens him with death.

> A covenant not to defend myself from force by force is always void.[43]

All the other liberties of the citizen depend upon the silence of the laws: 'where the sovereign has prescribed no rule, there the subject hath the liberty to do or to forebear, according to his own discretion.'[44] Given that the whole rationale for government is the exercise of the power to protect citizens from the consequences of 'mere nature', it follows that if the government somehow loses this power then citizens have no duty to continue to obey the sovereign. The obligation to obey the sovereign is 'understood to last as long, and no longer, than the power lasteth, by which he is able to protect them'.[45] We can never have a duty to relinquish our right to protect ourselves if the sovereign cannot do it.

Hobbes, therefore, like Aristotle, derives a conception of the nature and purposes of government from an account of human nature. However, there the similarity ends. Hobbes rejects Aristotle's view that there is a way of providing an account of the human virtues from an account of man's distinctive nature. Taken individually each person does not have a function, a distinctive work in which his self-realization is to be found; rather human happiness is 'a continual progress of ... desire from one object to another, the attaining of the former, being still the way to the latter'. Given his account of human nature, the political realm for Aristotle was the arena in which human beings came to realize their nature, whereas for Hobbes, politics is purely instrumental, a remedy for the inconveniences and horrors of human life, given human nature as he understands it. Indeed, as a consequence, citizens are kept out of politics; it is not an area within which citizens participate, rather it is an absolute power to keep men 'in awe' and to which they are subject. These radically different conceptions of the nature and purposes of politics turn upon quite different views about human nature and the consequent necessities and opportunities of human life. In these accounts, these views of human nature are foundational and in each case the author invites us to accept their accounts of politics by agreeing to the truth of their theories of human nature. In this sense, therefore, human nature is taken to be the objective basis upon which a correct conception of politics is to be based. So, to use the ideas developed in the first chapter, each of these theories can be taken as foundational and they both embody the same assumption about the crucially foundational nature of conceptions of human capacities and powers.

Hume: interests, sympathy and politics

Mankind are so much the same, in all times and places, that history informs us of nothing new or strange in this particular. Its chief use is only to discover the constant and universal principles of human nature, by showing them in all varieties of circumstances and situations and furnishing us with materials from which we may form our observations and become acquainted with the regular springs of human action and behaviour. These records of wars, intrigues, factions and revolutions, are so many collections of experiments by which the politician or moral philosopher fixes the principles of his science . . .[46]

This is a forthright statement of the claim that a theory of human nature underpins the attempt to gain a scientific perspective on politics. Although, as we shall see, Hume's theory of human nature and history is more complex than this bald statement would lead us to believe,[47] nevertheless human history shows a close similarity of basic moral sentiments and human motivations and it is out of his understanding of these that Hume develops his conception of politics. A proper conception of politics cannot be built upon an account of the 'casual humours and characters of particular men' only in this way will 'politics admit of general truths'.

In order to become clear about Hume's account of human nature and its place in generating general truths in politics we have to turn to his *Treatise on Human Nature*, which has the subtitle 'An Attempt to Introduce the Experimental Method of Reasoning into Moral Subjects' – so again the close connection between an account of the human mind and political philosophy, understood as a branch of moral philosophy, is insisted upon. The *Treatise* is divided into three books: 'Of the Understanding', 'Of the Passions', 'Of Morals', and in the first of these books Hume gives an account of the capacities and powers of the human mind which severely restricts the role of reason in the forming of moral and political judgement and which leaves space for the role of sentiment and interest in the development of judgement in these fields. For our purposes it will be important to concentrate upon these aspects of Hume's arguments which lead him to claim *contra* Aristotle, for example, that moral judgements can be given a rational foundation. On the face of it this seems a paradoxical claim for Hume to make because he has already claimed that there are general truths to be attained in politics and that politics can be reduced to a science. He therefore has to show that the falsity of the view that there are rational foundations for political principles is still consistent with the view that there are general truths to be arrived at.

In Book I of the *Treatise* Hume had developed a radically empiricist position in which he argues that reason has only two functions, to judge matters of fact or relations between ideas. Reason essentially is the discovery of truth or falsehood and these qualities refer to 'agreement or disagreement either to real relations of ideas or to real existence and matters of fact',[48] anything else is not capable of being true or false and hence not susceptible to the judgement of reason. By matters of fact here, Hume means those disagreements which can be resolved by reference to direct sense, impression or experience; by ideas Hume means logical relations between concepts, concepts which are themselves derived in various ways from sense impressions. Truth and falsity and therefore the claims of reason are restricted to matters of sense impression, or what can be derived from it. The ends and goals of human life are not like this and cannot therefore prescribe for us the goals of life in general or social and political life in particular. Hume drew this conclusion with the aid of several different arguments. The first argument is that judgements of moral and political value are action-guiding: that is to say they produce acts of volition and will whereas in Hume's view reason is inert in this regard:

> Since morals, therefore, have an influence upon the actions and upon the affections, it follows that they cannot be deriv'd from reason; and that because reason alone, as we have already prov'd, can never have any such influence. Morals excite passions, and procure or prevent actions. Reason of itself is utterly impotent in this particular. The rules of morality, therefore, are not conclusions of our reason ... As long as it allowed, that reason has no influence on our passions and actions, 'tis in vain to pretend, that morality is discovered only by a deduction of reason.[49]

Reasoning can only be about means and not about ends, given the empiricist framework from which Hume begins, and by itself, therefore, cannot produce action. Given that reason can only adjudicate matters of fact, or relations of ideas, Hume challenges the ethical rationalist or realist who believes that moral judgements are based upon reason, to show what are either the matters of fact or the conceptual relations which underpin moral and political judgements. In the case of matters of fact Hume brings forward two arguments to show that moral judgements cannot be derived in this way. If morality was a purely factual matter, then moral qualities such as good, bad, right or wrong, should be revealed to perception. However, Hume argues that this is not so:

> But can there be any difficulty in proving that vice and virtue are not matters of fact, whose existence we can infer by reason? Take any action allowed to be vicious: Wilful murder, for instance. Examine it in all lights, and see if you can find the matter of fact, or real existence which you call vice. In whichever way you take it, you will find only certain passions, motives, volitions and thoughts. There is no other matter of fact in the case. The vice entirely escapes you, as long as you consider the object. You can never find it, till you turn your reflexion into your own breast, and

find a sentiment of disapprobation, which arises in you towards this action. Here is the matter of the fact; but 'tis the object of feeling, not of reason. It lies in yourself, not in the object.[50]

Moral values are not a part of the objective world, they are ways of talking about our own sentiments which arise, in a way which we see is important for Hume, from the 'constitution of your nature'. This point, as we shall see, becomes central to Hume's account of the nature of morality and politics.

The second argument which Hume employs to reject the claim that morality can be understood as a factual matter and thus amenable to reason, has been central to subsequent arguments in moral philosophy, and as we saw in the first chapter, is important to logical positivism. The argument, sometimes known as 'Hume's Fork', claims that there is a logical gap in any argument which seeks to derive moral conclusions from purely factual, descriptive premises:

> In every system of morality, which I have hitherto met with, I have always remark'd, that the author proceeds for some time in the ordinary way of reasoning, and establishes the being of a God, or makes observations concerning human affairs; when of a sudden I am surprized to find, that instead of the usual copulations of propositions, *is*, and *is not*, I meet with no proposition that is not connected with an ought or ought not. The change is imperceptible, but is however of the last consequence. For as this *ought* or *ought not* expresses some new relation or affirmation, 'tis necessary that should be observed and explained; and at the same time that a reason should be given, for what seems altogether inconceivable, how this new relation can be a deduction from others, which are entirely different from it.[51]

This principle turns upon the idea that there cannot be anything in the conclusion of a valid argument which is not present in the conjoined premises in the argument. There is therefore a gap between facts and values and in this sense, reasoning based upon factual considerations cannot lead us to moral conclusions.

The other alternative role for reason would be to take the view that moral goals can be determined by reasoning about moral concepts or moral ideas, what Hume calls 'the comparing of ideas, and the discovery of their relations'. Hume's strategy in rejecting this form of formal ethical rationalism is to argue that if the 'same relations have different characters, it must evidently follow, that these characters are not discovered merely by reason.' This is a difficult idea but Hume puts the point in terms of an example. Why is it that we regard incest in humans as morally wrong, but not in the case of animals?[52] It would appear here that we have the same relations: father and daughter for example, but we condemn sexual relations in one case but not in the other. It might be argued that human beings are, unlike animals, endowed with reason, the faculty which *ought* to restrain them. However, Hume counters this argument by claiming that this reasoning is circular, 'For before reason can perceive this turpitude, the turpitude must exist; and consequently is independent of the decision of our reason, and is their object more properly than their effect.'[53] That is to say, the lack of reason may hinder animals from perceiving the moral relations in which they stand but 'can never hinder these duties from existing: since they must antecedently exist in order for them to be perceived'.

Hence, morality is not prescribed by reason but by our sentiments and we must now turn to Hume's positive account of sentiments in human nature and their importance for his view of politics. The sentiment which Hume regards as most basic to social life is that of *sympathy* which he regards as both a distinctive and common feature of human nature.

This idea of sympathy or fellow feeling, or a sentiment of humanity is central to Hume's account of social and political life and morality. He takes the view that while, as he has shown, morality is not a matter based upon reason, but rather on sentiment, it is not for that reason arbitrary or subjective.[54] When we engage in moral discourse we address our language to all and expect others to agree with our moral assessments which would not be the case if morality were merely a matter of taste.

> 'Tis only when a character is considered in general, without reference to our particular interest, that it causes such a feeling or sentiment, as denominates it morally good or evil.[55]

Sympathy or humanity is a common human attribute, which Hume takes to be *sui generis* and not to be reducible to a long-term form of self-love, as for example it was for Hobbes, a view which he took to be more like a satire rather than a true delineation or description of human nature. How then does sympathy work, given Hume's empiricist assumptions? In a moral context, in which I appraise the conduct of another person under a moral category such as 'hypocritical', I am led to consider the typical consequences of hypocritical actions and the kinds of deceptions which this involves. With all these deceptions I am moved to experience a sensation of pain myself and this is a primary impression from which arises the moral disapprobation. We feel moral disapproval of those forms of behaviour which I believe cause painful consequences in human life. While this mechanism of sympathy is a constant in human life, and accounts for our moral judgements, Hume believes that the way it operates is influenced by all sorts of local circumstances and conditions and is stronger for relatives, friends and people united by nationality and ties of blood, but nevertheless in Hume's view the principle does in fact operate at a general level even towards those who are removed from us in space and time:

> Sympathy, we shall allow, is much further than our concern for
> ourselves, and sympathy with persons remote from us, much
> further than that with persons near and contiguous: but for this
> very reason it is necessary for us, in our calm judgments and
> discourse concerning the characters of men, to neglect all these
> differences and render our sentiments more public and social ...
> The intercourse of sentiments, therefore in society and conver-
> sation, makes us form some general unalterable standard by which
> we may approve or disapprove of characters and manners.[56]

Moral judgements, although not based upon reason, are equally not just the evincing of emotion and feeling, they do make a claim to general acceptance and this claim is based upon the criterion of humanity or sympathy. However, for the moment this is all rather general and we need to consider the social and political implications of Hume's view that there are common standards of moral and political judgement based upon sympathy and the sentiment of humanity and this issue takes us to Hume's arguments about the nature of justice to be found in Book 3 Part II of the *Treatise*. As we have seen, Hume claims that the rational sentiment of sympathy leads us to take into account the pleasures and pains of others as well as our own experiences and this leads us to a common standard of judgement so that we come to attach the same sort of moral importance to the pleasures and pains of anyone whether they are relatives, friends, a member of the same society or another. These points relate to justice in the following way. Assume for the moment the factual claim which, as we shall see, Hume notes, namely that justice is concerned with upholding of existing rules of property and that if these rules are not upheld then society will become destructive and anarchical; then we have to go on to ask, as Hume's own philosophy itself requires us to do, why should these factual claims lead us to regard justice as a virtue? The only answer possible in Hume's theory is that the sentiment of sympathy and humanity is what leads us to regard chaos as untenable and as a vice. If I contemplate the consequences for all other persons in my society of that state of chaos then it will cause me to feel pain as the result of the operation of the sentiment of humanity. It is this sentiment that leads to the approval of justice as a *virtue*. It is Hume's contention that his theory of justice and property rights indeed has this influence upon the sentiment of humanity and turns justice as he understands it into a virtue. So we need to investigate the factual claims which operate on the sentiment of humanity.

In Hume's view justice arises as an issue because of the circumstances in which human beings find themselves. They live in a world of scarcity. By cooperating together in society we are able to achieve far more than we can separately:

> By the conjunction of forces our power is augmented:
> By the partition of employments our ability increases:
> And by our mutual succor we are less exposed to fortune and accidents. 'Tis by this additional force, ability and security, that society becomes advantageous.[57]

Given that the goods produced by these forms of cooperation are 'both exposed to the violence of others and may be transferred without suffering any loss or alteration' and that they are subject to scarcity, it is necessary to have some rules governing the distribution and the rights of possession of these goods – 'to bestow stability on the possession of those external goods, and leave everyone in the peaceable enjoyment of what he may acquire by his fortune or industry'.

Such a convention regulating property rights is not to be understood as a restraint which runs against passion and sentiment, indeed, given Hume's theory such a convention could never have arisen if it were. It is only 'contrary to the heedless and impetuous movements'; indeed, the rules of justice are based upon sentiment, of reflection upon the deleterious consequences for all in the absence of such rules and it is this reflection which excites the appropriate sentiment which underpins justice:

> To the imposition then, and observance of these rules, both in general, and in every particular, they are first induced only by a regard to interest.... Thus self interest is the original motive to the establishment of justice: but a sympathy with the public interest is the source of the moral approbation which attends that virtue.[58]

Hume argues that justice is best understood as securing the existing structure of property rights in a way that seems to follow from the theory developed so far. Hume considers three possible models for distribution: desert, equality and present possession. He rejects desert on the grounds that the criteria of desert are morally controversial and cannot be enshrined in general rules because deserts would have to be assessed in particular cases; equality he regards as impracticable. Because individuals differ substantially in terms of talents and abilities there will always be a tendency towards inequality which can only be corrected by an authoritarian government and that the threat for equality would actually weaken the power of government, which Hume took to depend upon hierarchy, when paradoxically a regime of equality would require a strong government. Given the importance of justice to the stability of society, Hume concludes that there is no other viable alternative than for the rules of justice to secure to people what they already have as possessions.

Thus for Hume justice arises from sentiment and not directly from reason. Surely we do reason about justice, about the circumstances in human life which make such rules necessary, about the effects upon society of not having a secure system of property relations, and, as we have just seen about different conceptions of justice? But Hume's view is that unless justice is combined with the operation of a distinct sentiment it can have no motivating force in human life. For Hume justice is a central political virtue, indeed, as he says 'after the agreement for the fixing and observing this rule, there remains little or nothing to be done towards setting perfect harmony and concord', but without an account of the role of reason and sentiment in human nature we can never develop a proper understanding of this central political principle and its place in human life.

This is not the place to enter into a full evaluation of Hume's theory, but one issue can be briefly explored because it raises issues of general importance for this chapter and indeed in some respects for the general place of a theory of the human self in political philosophy. Hume does not have a very rich conception of the self, indeed the possibility of this is precluded by his own strict empiricism. There is no enduring self which can be the object of sense experience. For us to have a rich concept of an enduring self this concept or idea, to use Hume's own terminology, would have to be derived from a sense impression. A sense of self as a persistent identity 'must be some one impression ... But self or person is not any one impression'.[59] Our sense experience is varied and discrete, there is not particular experience which could yield the concept of an enduring subject or self: 'there is no impression constant and invariable.' We have a simple awareness that accompanies each of our diverse sense impressions and what leads us to an enduring sense of self is the resemblance, contiguity and constant conjunctions of our sense impression. There is therefore no self which transcends the manifold of sense impression.

> For my part, when I enter most intimately into what I call myself, I always stumble on some particular perception or other, of heat or cold, light or shade, love or hatred, pain or pleasure. I can never catch myself at any time without a perception and can never observe anything but the perception.[60]

However, this theory poses problems for Hume's account of sympathy just because his account of sympathy requires a strong sense of self, as Hume himself recognizes. As Ellen Wood has argued:

> the concept of sympathy elaborated in the same work seems to require a more 'real' constant and so-to-speak absolute self, distinct from particular sense impressions.[61]

As we shall see in the next chapter the subsequent development of liberal political thought has shared the position of Hume here, attempting to produce a rich theory of politics, based upon a principled but very insubstantial theory of the self.

Aristotle, Hobbes and Hume differ fundamentally in their account of the self and its relationships to political understanding and judgement, but they are agreed in seeing a conception of human nature as being crucial to a correct understanding of politics. However, given the disagreements at work between these thinkers and, of course, many others not discussed in this book, it might be tempting to argue that the basic problem with the doctrines held by these three writers is their philosophical approach, whereas we should now turn to psychology, rather than to philosophy for a theory of human nature. It might follow from such an assumption that the whole attitude to seeing politics in terms of moral categories, principles, ideas of right and wrong etc. is misconceived – that in fact these moral categories should be replaced by ideas relating to correct or adequate human functioning, or indeed in terms of mental health and illness, that is to say the search in politics would be towards envisaging an institutional environment within which human nature as revealed to us by psychology could properly flourish. While this may be a modern thought to be found in the work of Fromm and Marcuse (to be discussed below), it is really quite an ancient model which is to be found in Plato. The good state is the one in which the parts of the human soul are reflected in institutions.[62] First of all we shall explore this idea in the work of three modern psychological theorists – Freud, Fromm and Marcuse – and then go on to some general reflections on the place of psychological theories in an account of politics.

Fromm and Marcuse

In the 1960s and 1970s the work of Fromm and Marcuse was very influential and is particularly interesting in relation to the role of theories of human nature in political theory. Both thinkers were very much influenced by the growth of the psychoanalytical movement, particularly the work of Freud. In this sense, therefore, the views of human nature with which they operate are more clearly a part of the consciousness of the modern world than those thinkers discussed earlier. Before discussing Fromm and Marcuse we need to look briefly at the Freudian theory of human nature. Of course, it must be remembered that in discussing the work of a thinker as complex and as prolific as Freud any summary is inevitably going to be crude and neglect the different views of commentators.

In Freud's view there can be no civilization, no society and no form of political organization which can fully express and fulfil human capacities and powers, because the very existence of society depends upon the sublimation of certain instincts and even the repression of those instincts. Men and women in Freud's view are radically amphibious. They live in two dimensions: the realm of instinctual drives dominated by the pleasure principle; and social existence controlled and directed in the individual case by the reality principle. Under the rule of the pleasure principle, human beings are creatures of animal drives, particularly concerned with sexual gratification, seeking to maximize pleasure and avoid pain. These drives, Freud argues, 'strive for nothing, but for gaining pleasure; from any operation which might crave unpleasantness, mental activity draws back'. But as Hobbes argued, as we saw earlier, unrestrained pleasure-seeking and gratification is incompatible with the existence of an ordered society. In social life the full and painless gratification of human desires is impossible because in a situation of scarcity in the objects of satisfaction individuals are brought into conflict with one another. The realization of this, which in the individual case happens in early childhood, leads to a modification of the pleasure principle and the growth of the domination of the reality principle. This principle is embodied in the institution, mores and standards within which parents, teachers and others help the individual to accept. The growing ascendancy of the reality over the pleasure principle alters the conception of pleasure. Instinctual pleasures and drives are sublimated into socially accepted practices or are repressed in the name of the reality principle:

> instincts are induced to displace the conditions of their satisfaction, to lead into other paths. In most cases this coincides with that of sublimation of instinctual aims with which we are familiar ... Sublimation of instinct is an essentially conspicuous feature of cultural development: it is what makes it possible for the higher

psychical activities, scientific, artistic or ideological, to play such an important part in civilised life ... Finally, and this seems most important of all, it is impossible to overlook the extent to which civilisation is built upon the renunciation of instincts, how much it presupposes precisely the non-satisfaction (by suppression, repression or other means) of powerful instincts. This cultural frustration dominates a large field of the social relationships between human beings.[63]

Civilization has a value because the 'higher psychical activities' play a large and valuable role in human life, but these activities depend for their existence upon the sublimation or repression of much more powerful instincts of human beings. The kind of sublimation which Freud has in mind here is, for example, the sublimation of anal erotic desires into a group of socially acceptable, and even socially desirable character traits such as parsimony, a passion for order and cleanliness.[64] In place of the insecure, temporary and destructive pleasures to be gained from adherence to the pleasure principle, following the constraints of the reality principle brings a more certain gratification of socially accepted pleasures, or for the sublimation of unacceptable pleasures. This gratification is more restrained; it may not be so immediate, but it is more or less guaranteed. Clearly, however, obedience to the dictates of the reality principle involves more than a modification of man's instinctual life, it rather involves a fundamental change in it. Marcuse makes this point very forcibly:

> However, the psychoanalytic interpretation reveals that the reality principle enforces a change not only in the form and timing of the pleasure, but in its very substance. The adjustment of pleasure to the reality principle implies the subjugation and diversion of the destructive forces of instinctual gratification, of its incompatibility with the established societal norms and relations, and by that token implies the transubstantiation of pleasure itself.[65]

Freud argues that this repression and sublimation in the name of the reality principle, which is the very condition of social life, produces neurosis. He argues, for example, that the sexual life of man in a civilized community is severely impaired. Only heterosexual genital love has been saved from repression because such a mode of sexuality is itself a necessary condition of the continuance of the civilization:

> Present day civilisation makes it plain that it will only permit sexual relations on the basis of an indissoluble bond between one man and one woman, and it does not like sexuality as a source of pleasure in its own right and is only prepared to tolerate it because there is so far no substitute for it as a means of propagating the human race.[66]

It is this restriction of sexual activity which causes neurosis, creating a tension between inner drives and social requirements, which leads to problems in the individual's social functioning. This restriction of basic drives according to the requirements of the reality principle is, in Freud's view, endemic in any sort of society. There is always a tension between the one and the many, between man and society. It follows that only by some kind of self-deception can a man experience his society as a community, because being a member of a community involves a deep identity between the deepest springs of human action, and the standards and norms of the community, an identity which Freud seems to imply can never hold.

Given this Freudian view about the nature of political identity – the relationship between man and society – psychotherapy can come to have a political dimension. The need is for therapy, to help people to come to terms with their social reality, not so much for reform, because problems of social functioning are endemic in any society whatever. Thus there can be no ideal community to which all will feel deeply attached, which fully expresses and satisfies the ideals, desires and instincts of the individuals who live in that society.

The possibility of fundamental reform or revolution to adjust social organization more to the needs and potential of human beings pre-supposes the view that some societies are less repressive than others, that some forms of political organization may be better objects of human adjustment which can enable a human being to live in harmony both with it and his or her own inner drives and motivations. This possibility of liberation is apparently denied by the Freudian theory and in its orthodox form this theory seems to be intractably pessimistic and conservative. However, in the hands of Fromm and Marcuse, Freudian theory is put to serve an ideal of human liberation. Before moving on to discuss the way in which the Freudian theory of human nature can be used to underpin a theory of liberation, however, it is worth pointing out that this link between political theory and a psychoanalytical theory of human nature has led to a change in the language of political theory away from talk of good, bad, right, wrong, that is to say moral categories, towards a set of quasi-medical categories such as drives, impulses, sanity, neurosis and the pathologies of political life. This becomes very clear with the work of Fromm and Marcuse, and perhaps shows most clearly in Fromm's work *The Sane Society*, the title of which signifies this shift.

Human nature and political reform

Fromm rejects the rather pessimistic, quietist approach to social life and politics which, as we have seen, is implicit in the work of Freud. He argues rather that society can be changed in the interests of human development and the realization of all human capacities. He points out quite correctly that social and political life is for Freud irredeemable:

> Primitive man is healthy and happy because he is not frustrated in his basic instincts, but he lacks the blessings of culture. Civilised man is more secure, enjoys art and science, but he is bound to be neurotic because of the continued frustrations of his instincts unreformed by civilisation.[67]

Fromm argues that this theory, as it stands, is a distortion. Society is doubtless in conflict with the asocial aspects of man's being, in particular his demand for sexual gratification, but it can also be in conflict with man's most valuable human qualities which certain societies may repress and distort. Societies can be judged in terms of the harm and distortion which they inflict on these qualities. Fromm appears to reject the view that the content of human nature is totally given and structured by society. If it is not, if our conception of man transcends the social order, then a conception of human nature can be used as a critical standard by which society can be assessed. These essential, but not socially given human attributes are, for example, a desire for happiness, harmony, love and freedom; these desires are inherent in the very nature of man. Some societies provide the appropriate form of social experience for the achievement and the satisfaction of these desires, others do not and either distort or deny their satisfaction. Social problems related to these drives are endemic only in these societies. In Fromm's view contemporary capitalist societies belong to this latter category. They do not provide a community in which human beings can act out their deepest desires and instincts. Fromm argues that in such societies man is alienated:

> By alienation is meant a mode of experience in which a person experiences himself as an alien. He has become, one might say, estranged from the world. He does not experience himself as the centre of his world, as the creator of his own acts, but his acts and their consequences have become his masters whom he obeys, or whom he may even worship.[68]

Alienation is, in Fromm's view, a form of mental ill health. The neurotic personality is an alienated personality, in that the person is a stranger to his own actions. Liberal capitalism as a form of social organization does not merely suppress or cause the sublimation of the pleasure principle instincts – a feature of any society; rather it goes much further in that it distorts certain central human capacities. Notice here the important move linking the moralistic notion of alienation with that of the quasi-medical concept of mental illness. This comes out very clearly in the following passage:

> Sanity and mental health depend upon the satisfaction of those needs and passions which are specifically human and which stem from the conditions of the human situation: the need for framework of transcendence, rootedness, the need for a sense of identity, and the need for a frame of orientation and devotion.[69]

In order to manage society in the interests of mental health, to maximize the achievement of harmony, love and freedom, and to minimize alienation and estrangement, Fromm advocates various reforms. In a chapter in *The Sane Society* entitled 'Roads to Sanity' he puts forward fairly detailed proposals. While Fromm seeks to bring Freudian and socialist insights together, he argues that a purely economic change in the infrastructure of capitalism will not suffice. He argues that sanity and mental health:

> can be attained only by simultaneous changes in the sphere of industrial and political organisation, of spiritual and philosophical orientations, of character, structure and of cultural activities. The concentration of effort in any one of these spheres to the exclusion of others is destructive of all change.[70]

Fromm argues that these reforms include the control by the people of the commanding heights of the economy, worker participation in industrial decision-making in order to humanize work, political decentralization, a communitarian reform of education so that educational processes can generate the spiritual renewal required and a rediscovery of ritual and corporate acts in order that people can come together again as human beings. Fromm's aim is clearly to advocate a communitarian society, one in which people can feel at home because they are closely involved with one another at all levels. Again it is interesting to see that Fromm argues what is in fact a moral thesis in terms of what appears to be the specific concept of mental health. Common forms of experience are vitally necessary for the development of community:

> The transformation of an atomistic into a communitarian society depends upon creating again the opportunity for people to sing together, dance together, and admire together – together and not as members of a lonely crowd.[71]

Fromm visualizes this new community in the following way:

> What society corresponds to this aim of mental health and what would be the structure of the sane society? First of all a society in which no man is a means to another's end, but always without exception an end in himself; hence where nobody is used, nor uses himself for purposes which are not those of the unfolding of his human powers; where man is at the centre, and where all economic and political activities are subordinated to the aim of his growth. A sane society is one in which qualities like greed, exploitativeness,

possessiveness, narcissism have no chance to be used for greater material gain, or for the enhancement of one's own personal prestige. Where acting in acordance with one's own conscience is looked upon as a fundamental and necessary quality, and where opportunism and lack of principles is deemed to be asocial; where the individual is concerned with social matters so that they become personal matters, where his relationships with his fellow men are not separated from his relationships in the private sphere. A sane society furthermore is one which puts a man to operate within manageable and observable dimensions and to be an active participant in the life of society as well as in his own life.[72]

Fromm sees the prospect for social and political reform in the interests of mental health, a prospect which did not seem to be part of Freud's own theory. It seems that Fromm is still willing to allow that any society must involve the repression of certain sexual instincts, but he argues that contemporary capitalist societies distort and repress other basic desires, for example the desire for freedom, for love and for harmony. Whereas capitalist societies are atomistic, a society for strangers, the sane society will be a community with a political and economic structure with which people are deeply involved. However, it is difficult to avoid the cogency of Thomas Szasz's comment on this type of theory that 'mental health and illness are new ways of describing moral values' or Kenny's similar view in his lecture 'Mental Health in Plato's Republic'.[73]

The feasibility, and in the light of Szasz's and Kenny's comments, the scientific cogency of Fromm's proposals depend, of course, upon his being able to formulate a testable view of human capacities and potentialities which are not dependent upon society, since only then can we use such a conception as a critical tool in terms of which he can assess the repressiveness of a particular society. Only if one already has a conception of what is essential to the person can one use this conception to show that these essential capacities are denied realization in a particular society. If, on the other hand, the content of human nature is given by society, on the face of it, it is difficult to see how this could then be a critical tool in the analysis of society. Fromm clearly thinks that it is possible to formulate a conception of human nature which will give some orientation to programmes for social and political reform.

Human nature and surplus repression

This issue is most clearly confronted by Herbert Marcuse in *Eros and Civilisation*, in which he argues in the light of a theory of human nature that there is no middle way between adjustment and revolution. In Marcuse's view either the content of human nature and the paradigms of thought and action are socially given, or they have some completely transcending content in which case to operate within the given paradigms and to seek to modify them in terms of the transcending ones is impossible. Either an individual has to be helped to come to terms with what are considered to be socially accepted standards of conduct as they in fact exist, or these standards have to be done away with because they are inimical to the development of the individual's ideal personality – that conception of individual attributes and powers which is the negation of the one presupposed in the shared meanings of the society:

> Either one defines personality and individuality in terms of their possibilities within the established form of civilisation, in which case their realisation is for the majority tantamount to successful adjustment. Or one defines them in terms of their transcending content, including their socially denied possibilities beyond and beneath their actual existence; in this case self realisation would imply transgression beyond the established forms of civilisation, to radically new modes of personality incompatible with the prevailing ones.[74]

In a sense, therefore, Marcuse is denying that an interpretivist approach to political theory can be other than conservative because it operates within shared meanings and understandings, but given a different, external, transcending view of human nature these shared understandings may embody false consciousness about human nature, the real capacities and powers of human beings which may be distorted or misunderstood in a particular society. Any radical political theory in Marcuse's view presupposed some external critical view of human nature.

Marcuse argues that although the Freudian theory does appear to be conservative and pessimistic at a superficial level, it does contain within itself the seeds of a critical theory of society of the sort which Marcuse is after largely because Freudian theory is committed to a view of human nature which can be specific independently of the particular culture of a specific society and its political organization. In his argument in *Eros and Civilisation* Marcuse utilizes the Freudian view of repression and agrees with Freud that a certain level of repression appears to be necessary for the existence of civilization and culture, but he argues that the amount of repression present in contemporary Western societies cannot be justified or explained in terms of that degree of repression necessary for the preservation of society as such. In order to facilitate the analysis of this point Marcuse seeks to refine the concept of repression which is so central to Freudian theory. He argues that two sorts of repression can be distinguished: basic repression and surplus repression. Basic repression is the form of repression which it seems has to exist in order for there to be an organized society at all – on this view some modification of instinctual gratification is necessary for the existence of society. Contemporary capitalist societies, however, and their associated political organizations involve far more repression than is necessary to secure their existence, this is surplus repression. Surplus repression is needed not so much to secure the existence of civilized life as such, but rather of a society of a particular sort with a specific form of social and political organization. In Marcuse's view the kind of society which surplus repression is used to maintain is based upon class domination. In Marcuse's view surplus repression will disappear when class domination and the capitalist system which underpins it is abolished. In a society in which there is no surplus repression Marcuse argues that gradually basic repression will become unnecessary. Without the distortions imposed upon human nature by the surplus repression of what he sees as a sick society, basic human needs and drives will be transformed and instead of being egotistical and self-centred will become cooperative and creative. Consequently, a society without repression is possible, a society which wilfully satisfies human needs. Such a society, Marcuse argues, cannot be achieved without a revolution and in *One Dimensional Man* he argues that revolution is only possible insofar as there is some negative element in society which stands in contradiction to the generally accepted beliefs and standards, particularly as they relate to views of human purposes and capacities, of the society. Marx had argued that this negative element will be the industrial proletariat whereas Marcuse rejects this possibility – the proletariat has become reconciled to welfare capitalism, it is as much a part of the status quo as any other group pursuing distorted capitalist values of consumerism. The negative element in late capitalist society will consist of all of those who for one reason or another find themselves alienated from the distorted standards of society. One example of the growth and importance of this negative element is the growth of the women's movement. In Marcuse's view women, because of their marginality, have sustained human qualities and relationships which are to a great extent external to the dominant values of the society.

In Marcuse's view therefore a radical theory requires a transcending conception of human nature, one which challenges the prevailing shared understandings of society, but this is not just to be regarded as a metaphysical abstraction but is rather embedded in the activities and understandings of those who are marginalized by the dominant, shared but distorted understandings of society.

Again, however, we see in Marcuse's work a reluctance to state the argument in straightforward moral terms. The Freudian reference leads him to couch his argument in terms such as sanity, madness and pathology. Here is a good example of this drawn from *Eros and Civilisation*:

> Is not the individual who functions normally, adequately and healthily as a citizen of a sick society – is not such an individual himself sick? And would not a sick society require an antagonistic concept of mental health, and not a concept designated (and preserving) mental qualities which are tabooed, arrested or distorted by the 'society' prevalent in the sick society? (For example mental health equals the ability to live as a dissenter, to live a non-adjusted life.)
>
> As a tentative definition of sick society we can say that a society is sick when its basic institutions ... do not permit the use of the available material and intellectual resources for the optional development and satisfaction of individual needs. The larger the discrepancy between the potential and actual human conditions, the greater the social need for what I term 'surplus repression', that is repression necessitated not by the growth and the preservation of society but vested interests in maintaining an established society.[75]

This is about as clear a link as one could get between a theory of human nature and political morality but understood in quasi-medical terms.

An account of basic human needs in relation to the nature of persons is held to define norms of health and sanity which political reform should seek to implement. These needs are, however, not based upon some abstract metaphysical theory (although they can be theorized), but are implicit in the demands and self-consciousness of those who are rendered marginal by the sick and pathological requirements of the dominant culture.

Human nature and political argument

So far we have looked at several theories which utilize a conception of human nature to underpin a particular theory of politics. Of course, these views are radically different: Aristotle defends an account of the nature of the person on the basis of what the individual potentially is, and this potentiality is implicit in the already on-going life of the society; it is not an abstraction or a counterfactual. It projects an ideal of human nature and human organization from the nature of man and organization as it is already revealed empirically in the way of life of society. Hobbes takes a view of human nature which he regards as severely scientific and materialistic even if it conflicts with our own cherished illusion about ourselves. Our illusions are shattered by the use of a scientific method and the application of a sharp materialism to the understanding of human nature and its predicaments. Here we begin to get the idea of an explicit shift from moral to scientific categories for underpinning arguments about political organization. This tendency, albeit in a very different mode, becomes dominant in the writings of Fromm and Marcuse in which a 'scientific' theory of human nature, derived not as in Hobbes from physics but from psychoanalysis, is held to underpin a critical perspective on politics which allows us to categorize politics in quasi-scientific forms such as sanity and madness rather than the moral categories central to Aristotle and the classical tradition. Of course, it might be argued that this displacement of moral categories from political thought is inevitable at least insofar as political theory is predicated upon human nature, because after all, a theory of human nature should be precise and empirical not speculative and moral and in this regard the psychologist and the psychiatrist have superseded the moralist and the metaphysician. So can we look forward to the development of views about political organization which are rooted in empirical theories of human nature? Can we therefore expect a way through in understanding political organization from some empirical view of the fundamental needs of human beings or does our view of human nature itself rest upon our evaluative position so that what we take to be human needs and the fundamental capacities political organizations should seek to satisfy, depend upon our values rather than, as the empiricist suggests, the other way around. Having looked at examples of arguments about human nature we now need to explore the logic of these arguments in more detail.

The starting point in this controversy would be to try to set out as clearly as possible the positive argument. If we are able to specify clearly and empirically the nature, say, of a plant, then we should be able to derive from this some account of the treatment the plant should get if we want it to flourish. We can say how much water it needs, what kind of soil it requires, whether it needs pruning or whatever. That is to say we can derive a regime of treatment for the plant from an account of its nature and its needs and if we want the plant to flourish we shall follow this regime. By analogy the empirical theory of human nature might be thought to play some similar role. If we could identify the fundamental nature of the individual person independent of social and political contexts, we should then be in a position to say something definite about the form of politics appropriate to this nature. This would yield an account of the human good and of the institutions which would encourage, sustain and embody such a good. As such this perspective would endorse a highly unified theory of politics in which all the ends of human life, and what were taken in the theory to be the characteristic excellences of human beings, would be ideally sustained across societies by a common set of institutions underpinned by this common sense of values. If on the other hand the universalism and the unifying nature of this approach fails, so that there is no account of the human essence which could justify institutions, what would follow politically from this? One possibility on a pessimistic reading of the moral pluralism which would follow would be anarchy, with no agreement on the fundamental questions of how society should make public choices. As we shall see, however, there is an alternative view, a liberal view of politics which takes it as axiomatic that there is not and cannot be any such foundational agreement on the nature of humanity of the human personality and consequently of the human good both personal, political and social, and which therefore sees the aim of political organization and authority to be not so much the realization in the sphere of politics of one particular essentially contested conception of human excellence, but rather the securing of that framework within which human beings can pursue their own self-chosen view of the good, whatever it may be, so long and insofar as it does not conflict with the pursuit by others of their good. A great deal therefore turns on this argument about human nature for our conception of the deep and fundamental purposes of political life and institutions.

So can theories of human nature which are rich, specific and substantial enough to support theories about political organization be grounded in some secure reasoning? In the modern world, marked as it is by its great respect for scientific as opposed to metaphysical theories, the obvious place to start is by examining those accounts of human nature which appear to claim some scientific status based either in some account of the biological nature of man or in a psychological account of human nature. Of course there are many who would claim that this is possible. We have already seen that Fromm and Marcuse are prepared to give their own conceptions of the good life a kind of scientific legitimacy by talking about social and political institutions in terms of sanity and madness – using the language of psychopathology to make claims which in the classical tradition of political thought were made on moral grounds. However, these are not the only examples in the modern world. We can find other psychologists with rather different orientations making the same point, for example Maslow argues:

> We are working up what amounts to a scientific ethic based upon our knowledge of human needs.[76]

Other examples of the 'scientific' case for a particular set of political institutions could also be found in the writings of socio-biologists and those who argue on the basis of the nature of human genes and their relation to IQ. These latter theories particularly argue strongly on a 'scientific' theory of human nature that there are definite limits to political and social equality. Both theories would therefore restrict a particular set of political options grounding them upon the facts about human nature.

The first and perhaps the most obvious critical point which is likely
to be made is the extent to which we can really have confidence in the
political prescriptions of theories of human nature when these theories
have been so much in dispute not only within the classical tradition
with Plato, Aristotle, Hobbes, Locke, Rousseau and Marx offering us
radically different views of the nature of man but also within the modern
world in which there are major disputes about alternative theories of
human nature which purport to have some scientific status. One need
think, for example, not only of the radically different directions the
psychoanalytical movement has taken as we have already seen in Freud,
Marcuse and Fromm, but also of disputes between more behaviourally
minded psychologists. The disputes here are both substantive – in the
sense that radically different views of human nature and the needs,
purposes and excellences attached to it have been advanced – but also
deeply methodological, for example about whether a scientific theory
of the human mind should attempt to make reference to consciousness
and inner states generally or whether psychology should be concerned
with describing complex patterns of behaviour. We need only, for
example, compare Hull's *Principles of Behaviour* with Charles Taylor's
The Explanation of Behaviour[77] to see the depth and complexity of
these issues. One of the central issues at stake is the role of teleological
explanation in psychology which takes us back to the issues implicit in
Aristotle. It would be difficult to see how a psychology such as Maslow's
which puts need at the centre of explanation could be other than
teleological. It would be a mistake to believe that this is a purely
theoretical and methodological dispute without substantive pay-off.
Rather, what is at stake here as the result of these methodological
disputes are different views about the distinctive features of human life,
for example about the nature of purposive action which are bound to
have clear social and political overtones. For example, B. F. Skinner's
account of behavioural technology, control and modification in *Beyond
Freedom and Dignity* which are given a social and political substance
in *Walden 2*[78] depends entirely upon his rejection of the need for
psychology to pay heed to states of consciousness or inner states and
the necessity for psychology to take up a more 'scientific' view of human
nature. Skinner takes the view that politically salient notions such as
human freedom and dignity depend upon ideas such as intention,
purpose and motive being characteristic possessions of human beings.

These could be discarded if we took up a more 'scientific' view of human nature:

> Although physics soon stopped personifying things ... it continued for a long time as if they had wills, impulses, feelings, purposes of an unwilling agent ... All this was virtually abandoned to good effect yet the behavioural sciences still appeal to comparable inner states.[79]

If only we could stop looking at human beings in an anthropomorphic way, illusory ideas of human freedom and dignity which put moral constraints on how individuals should be treated could give way to a more rational and scientific form of social control and behaviour modification rather than an inefficient system based upon illusory moral constraints, illusory because based upon an inadequate account of the nature of the psyche.

As we shall see in chapter 8, the acceptance of a view such as this can and did have an enormous impact on politically salient activities such as punishment. Instead of the state sanctioning a penal regime in response to intentional wrongful actions we should institute rather a system of behaviour modification to change the variables which have elicited the wrongful behaviour. So, as we can see, methodological disputes about the nature of human psychology can have very profound effects upon substantive views about the nature of persons and the social and political organizations which would best suit persons understood in the methodologically preferred way. These disputes may well be intractable, but until they are shown to have a clear resolution we cannot place any more confidence in these theories than in more directly metaphysical theories of the human personality. Indeed the disputes about method in psychology are themselves metaphysical disputes which cannot be settled by scientific observation, because in fact, the disputes are themselves the result of deep-seated metaphysical differences about the nature of consciousness and how particular forms of consciousness, purpose, intention, desire, remorse etc., are to be understood and investigated. These issues are not capable of being arbitrated by straightforward empirical observation but are conceptual and metaphysical through and through.

We need thus to come back to the point at which this discussion started. The critic will say that theories of human nature are contestable in both form and substance and cannot play the foundational role which both classical metaphysical thinkers thought they could or more scientific modern thinkers believe they can. This point can be given additional emphasis if we consider the points made in the final chapter about the intractably context-relatedness and situatedness of human knowledge and our capacity for self-understanding.

However, there are also other arguments which go a long way towards casting doubt upon the idea that a theory of human nature of persons as they are or might be can provide political theory with some kind of external grounding. As we saw in the last chapter, one of the central arguments deployed by positivists against the objectivity of morals is that evaluative conclusions about the proper shape of social and political institutions cannot be logically derived from factual premises. This so-called fact/value dichotomy is the result of the logical principle that there can be nothing in the conclusion of a valid argument which is not already present in the premises. If this is applied to theories of human nature and their relation to political organization, then it follows that in so far as the theory of human nature is factual in content it cannot yield any conclusion about the morally desirable form of human organization. This would apply also to those theories such as Fromm's and Marcuse's which cast the argument for the appropriateness of political institutions on an account of human nature in terms of sanity and madness. As Kenny argues in his lecture on 'Mental Health in Plato's Republic':

> The moralistic concept of mental health incorporates a tech-nological dream: it looks towards the day when virtue is succeeded by medical knowhow. But we are no more able than Plato was to make ourselves virtuous by analysis or prescription: and renaming virtue 'mental health' takes us no further than it took Plato in the direction of that chimerical goal.[80]

In so far as theories of human nature are not merely factual, but describe human nature and human life as it could or might be under improved circumstances, then, of course, moral conclusions about social and political reform could be drawn but these only put the problem for political philosophy one stage further back because what would then have to be grounded would be the evaluative/theory-laden concept of human nature. So the dilemma is clear if the theory of human nature is factual, it is difficult to see how it will support a conclusion about political principle and morality, in so far as it is evaluative it may support the moral conclusion, but will itself need to be grounded in something other than a subjective preference for one set of views about human nature rather than another.

Notes

1   J. Habermas, *Communication and The Evolution of Society*, trans. by T. McCarthy, Heinemann, London, 1979, p. 201.
2   A. MacIntyre, *A Short History of Ethics*, Routledge, London, 1967, p. 268.
3   J. Habermas, *Communication*, p 201.
4   A. MacIntyre, *After Virtue*, 2nd edn, Duckworth, London, 1985, p. 148.
5   Ibid.
6   Aristotle, *Politics*, trans. Sir E. Barker, The Clarendon Press, Oxford, 1946, p. 1.
7   Aristotle, *Nicomachean Ethics*, trans. J. A. K. Thomson, Penguin, London, 1953, p. 28.
8   Ibid., p. 36.
9   Aristotle, 'Physics', in *The Works of Aristotle*, eds J. A. Smith and W. D. Ross, trans. R. P. Hardie and R. K. Gaye, The Clarendon Press, Oxford, 1910–1952, chapter 2.8.
10 Aristotle, 'The Parts of Animals', in *The Works*, 1.5 (645b15).
11 Ibid., 2.1. (646a25).
12 Aristotle, *Nicomachean Ethics*, p. 38.
13 See *The Parts of Animals*, 2.14 (658b2); 2.16 (659b27).
14 Aristotle, *Nicomachean Ethics*, p. 38.
15 Ibid.
16 Ibid., p. 38.
17 Ibid., p. 40.
18 Ibid., p. 65.
19 C. Taylor, *Sources of the Self*, Cambridge University Press, Cambridge, 1989, p. 125.
20 Aristotle, *Nicomachean Ethics*, p. 51.
21 Aristotle, *Politics*, p. 119.
22 Ibid.

23   Ibid.
24   See J. P. Sartre, *Existentialism and Humanism*, trans. P. Mairet, Methuen, London, 1948, p. 26.
25   Ibid., p. 28.
26   Ibid., p. 33.
27   Taylor, *Sources of the Self*, p. 125.
28   MacIntyre, *After Virtue*, p. 148.
29   J. MacDowell, 'Virtue and Reason', *The Monist*, 63, no. 3, 1979, pp. 331-50.
30   H. G. Gadamer, *Kleine Schriften*, vol. 1, J. C. B. Mohr, Tübingen, 1967, p. 187.
31   T. Hobbes, *Leviathan*, ed. C. B. Macpherson, Penguin, London, 1968, p. 167.
32   Ibid., p. 105.
33   Ibid.
34   See Part 1, Chapter 6 for a full and impressively terse list.
35   Ibid., p. 121.
36   Ibid., p. 120.
37   Ibid., p. 130.
38   Ibid., p. 186.
39   Ibid., p. 188.
40   Ibid., p. 186.
41   Ibid., p. 188.
42   Ibid., p. 189.
43   Ibid., p. 199.
44   Ibid., p. 271.
45   Ibid., p. 272.
46   D. Hume, *An Inquiry Concerning Human Understanding and The Principles of Morals*, ed. L. A. Selby-Bigge, 3rd edn, rev. P. Nidditch, The Clarendon Press, Oxford, 1975, pp. 83-4.
47   For a full discussion of this apect of Hume, see D. Forbes, *Hume's Philosophical Politics*, Cambridge University Press, Cambridge, 1973, ch. 4; D. Miller, *Philosophy and Ideology in Hume's Political Thought*, The Clarendon Press, Oxford, 1981.
48   For a focused discussion of this in Hume, see *Inquiry*, Appendix 1.
49   D. Hume, *Treatise on Human Nature*, ed. L. A. Selby-Bigge, The Clarendon Press, Oxford, 1888, p. 457.
50   Ibid., p. 468.
51   Ibid., p. 469.
52   Ibid., p. 467.
53   Ibid.

54 D. Hume, Essay XXIII on 'The Standard of Taste', in *Essays Moral, Political and Literary*, vol. 1, eds T. H. Green and T. H. Grosse, Longman, London, 1875.

55 Hume, *Treatise*, p. 472.

56 Hume, *Inquiry*, Book V. See *Treatise*, p. 385.

57 Hume, *Treatise*, p. 485. See J. Rawls's use of this material in *A Theory of Justice*, The Clarendon Press, Oxford, 1971, pp. 126ff.

58 Hume, *Treatise*, p. 499.

59 Ibid., p. 251.

60 Ibid., p. 252.

61 E. Wood, *Mind and Politics*, University of California Press, Berkeley, 1972, pp. 71-2.

62 See A. J. P. Kenny, 'Mental Health in Plato's Republic', Dawes Hicks Lecture on Philosophy to the British Academy, *Proceedings of the British Academy*, London, 1969.

63 S. Freud, *Civilisation and Its Discontents*, Hogarth Press, London, 1963, p. 34.

64 Ibid., p. 33.

65 H. Marcuse, *Eros and Civilisation*, Sphere, London, 1969, p. 30.

66 Freud, *Civilisation*, p. 42.

67 Ibid., p. 76.

68 E. Fromm, *The Sane Society*, Routledge and Kegan Paul, London, 1963, p. 120.

69 Ibid., p. 19.

70 Ibid., p. 271.

71 Ibid., p. 349.

72 Ibid., p. 276.

73 See A. J. P. Kenny 'Mental Health in Plato's Republic', p. 253.

74 Marcuse, *Eros and Civilisation*, p. 203.

75 Ibid., p. 203.

76 A. Maslow, *Motivation and Personality*, Harper and Row, New York, 1954, p. 366.

77 See C. Taylor, *The Explanation of Behaviour*, Routledge and Keegan Paul, London, 1964, and the discussion of Hull's *Principles of Behaviour* contained therein.

78 Skinner, *Beyond Freedom*, Knopf, New York, 1971; *Walden 2*, Macmillan, New York, 1969.

79 Skinner, *Beyond Freedom*, pp. 8–9.

80 Kenny, 'Mental Health', p. 253.

3

Liberalism: Rights and Justice

Men have different views on the empirical end of happiness, and what it consists of, so that as far as happiness is concerned, their will cannot be brought under any common principle, nor thus under an external law harmonizing with the freedom of everyone.

Kant, *Metaphysik der Sitten*

The unity of society and the allegiance of its citizens to their common institutions rest not on their espousing one rational conception of the good, but on an agreement as to what is just for free and equal moral persons with different and opposing conceptions of the good.

Rawls, *A Theory of Justice*

During the past two centuries liberal political theorists have sought to develop a theory of politics which accepts as a fact and as a principle radical and irresolvable differences over what the good for human beings is and what their ultimate nature is thought to be. In view of these disagreements there is no foundation to guide us to an understanding of the ultimate nature of the good and the bad in politics; these are personal values which cannot be objectively grounded. Those who believed to the contrary, for example Plato, Aristotle, Marcuse and Fromm, accepted that values could be given a foundation and this led them to a communitarian conception of politics, that is to say that the basic political project should be the building of a political community within which these basic virtues, which constitute the common human good, could flourish. However, the pressures which I have sketched in the two previous chapters have led to the widespread collapse of this as the basic project of Western political theory. Alasdair MacIntyre has made this point particularly clearly:

> The notion of the political community as a common project is alien to the modern liberal individualist world ... we have no conception of such a form of political community concerned as Aristotle says the polis is concerned, with the whole of life, not with this or that, but with man's good as such.[1]

When MacIntyre says 'we' in this passage, he means we in the West, because obviously the project has not been lost in large parts of the world. Communist states and Islamic fundamentalists may both be engaged in this project, underpinned in the one case by what is seen as the historical inevitability of the task of building socialism in which human nature will realize its full potential in an unalienated form for the first time in human history, in the other case it is based upon views about the will of God and his purposes for man. This kind of political thought is sometimes known as perfectionism – concerned with the institutional structure necessary to fulfil or to perfect, in the sense of complete, human nature. It is characteristic of liberal political thought, however, and particularly that version which has its roots in Kant, that it has abandoned the project of pursuing the idea of a political community in the sense described above. Moral pluralism has to be accepted and a political theory developed around this. Many of the major liberal political theorists' writings today are explicit on this point, abandoning the idea of an objective moral order which would define man's telos; they argue instead that liberal thought is neutral over fundamental moral issues.

For example, Ronald Dworkin, whose work will be discussed in detail below, claims that 'liberalism does not rest upon a special theory of the personality',[2] that 'liberals as such, are indifferent as to whether people choose to speak out on political matters, or to lead eccentric lives ...'.[3] John Rawls equally argues that the key assumptions of liberal political theory require 'no particular theory of human motivation'.[4] Bruce Ackerman, too, argues in *Social Justice and the Liberal State* :

> Liberalism does not depend on the truth of any single metaphysical or epistemological system ... In order to accept liberalism, you

need not take a position on a host of Big Questions of a highly controversial character.⁵

Similar themes are found in other writers too. Thus Richard Wollheim argues that:

> It has been characteristic of the civilised parts of Europe – their pride, some would say – to develop a theory of politics [which holds that] the identity and continuity of society resides not in the common possession of a single morality but in the mutual toleration of different moralities.⁶

John Gray argues that:

> recognition of the chronic character of normative and epistemic dissensus ... can provide the departure point for an endorsement of the basic values of a liberal civilisation.⁷

Joseph Raz echoes the same points:

> [Liberalism is] committed to moral pluralism, that is to the view that there are many worthwhile and valuable relationships, commitments and plans of life which are mutually incompatible.⁸

On the face of it, it would appear from this selection of quotations that some forms of liberal political theory thus abandon the idea of basing a conception of politics upon the good life, depending upon agreed truths about man's nature. It is rather concerned with *rules*, with those rules which will secure to each individual the greatest amount of freedom to pursue his own good in his own way so long as he does not act unjustly and infringe the freedom of others. The ethics of rules rather than goals or ends is the central characteristic of this form of liberalism and it is central to the coherence of the project that these rules can be justified by arguments which do not make specific assumptions about epistemology, metaphysics, human nature or the good life. If the aim of liberalism is, as Dworkin argues:

> that political decisions must be as far as possible independent of conceptions of the good life, or what gives value to life. Since

citizens of a society differ in these conceptions, the government does not treat them as equals if it prefers one conception to another.[9]

then the problem for liberalism becomes that of determining that set of rules under which government can treat individuals with equal respect and not seek to impose one particular conception of the good on individuals. Neutrality is a central value in liberalism and for its project to be coherent it has to show that the rules which define a liberal society can be derived from a position of neutrality in relation to differing conceptions of the good. Any form of legitimate state activity has to be undertaken within a set of rules which were derived in a neutral way, and be directed towards policies which are, as far as possible, neutral between different conceptions of the good life.

This has led to two major preoccupations in liberal theory. The first, which we shall explore in this chapter, is the importance of finding a set of rules to guide political action which are independent of a conception of the good and which do not require the illegitimate imposition of morality upon those who disagree with it; the second is a concern with individual liberty, of trying to determine the nature of the institutions which will give individuals the maximum opportunity to pursue their own plan of life independent of the constraints and interferences of others. Because this is a large and ramified topic discussion will be postponed until another chapter but perhaps just one point could be made at this juncture, namely that the conception of liberty favoured by liberal theorists is a negative one, in a sense to be defined later, and rigorously independently of any particular view of the values and positive ends which liberty can serve. To define liberty in terms of the pursuit of particular ends such that individuals can only really be free if they are following values X, Y, Z would be a positive conception, presupposing a theory of human good and fulfilment and would thus be incompatible with the basic assumptions of liberal theory.

If we go back to the first point about rules, we can see how natural it is that liberalism, committed to moral neutrality, should turn its attention away from the goals of human fulfilment just because these are contestable, towards specifying that set of rules which would allow individuals to pursue their own good, subject to not interfering with the similar rights of others. In recent years these issues have been at the forefront of liberal theory and have been central to the work of Hayek, Rawls, Dworkin, Ackerman and Nozick.

Before going on to discuss the nature of rules and their possible justification, however, it is important to attend to a distinction which is not well understood, but is nevertheless a central issue for liberal political theory. In the light of what has already been said, it might be thought that liberal political theory is merely a response to moral pluralism or moral scepticism. After all, the brief quotations given above from Rawls, Dworkin and Ackerman might be taken to imply this. If this is so, however, then liberal political theory is in a very severe difficulty, a difficulty implicit in a passage towards the end of Isaiah Berlin's essay 'Two Concepts of Liberty' which has been a central text in post-war liberalism:

> 'To realise the relative validity of one's convictions,' says an admirable writer of our time, 'and yet stand for them unflinchingly, is what distinguishes the civilised man from the barbarian.' To demand more than this is perhaps a deep and incurable metaphysical need; but to allow it to determine one's practice is a symptom of an equally deep, and more dangerous, form of political immaturity.[10]

If liberalism is seen only as a response to moral pluralism and scepticism, on what grounds should we stand for our convictions unflinchingly and on what moral basis can a liberal polity be based because its own moral basis can be only relatively true? That is to say, if the liberal concern with neutrality, or equality or, as we shall see later, with rights, is solely a response to moral scepticism, pluralism or more dramatically moral nihilism, than its own foundations are very insecure. It becomes the political response to a moral vacuum, rather than a principled theory which has strong arguments to defend its own basis – because on their view these arguments will be as insecure as any other moral views. It is a sign of the optimism of this approach to liberalism that it sees itself as the only response to radical moral pluralism and nihilism in the modern world, whereas there are other darker and anti-liberal responses to this, as Nietzsche's writings illustrate very clearly. In the presence of moral nihilism, morality has to be created by will and indeed only the strong, the *Ubermenschen*, will be able to create such a transvaluation of values. Certainly some liberal theorists, more notably in recent years Bruce Ackerman, have given some credence to this view of liberalism. In his book *Social Justice and the Liberal State*, he says that one of what he calls the four main highways to liberalism is 'skepticism concerning the reality of transcendent meaning' and in a paragraph with the heading 'Liberal Skepticism' he says the following:

> But can we know anything about the good? Sure, all of us have beliefs: but isn't it merely pretentious to proclaim one's knowledge on the subject? Worse than pretentious – isn't some loud fool typically the first to impose his self-righteous certainties upon others? ... The hard truth is this: There is no moral meaning hidden in the bowels of the universe. All there is is you and I struggling in a world that neither we nor any other thing created.[11]

As Ackerman himself realizes, however, liberalism is not the only response to this situation and most liberal theorists have sought to resolve a paradox: that liberalism does not presuppose a particular view of the good or of the human personality, while at the same time claiming that it has a secure moral base, but a base which could command moral assent despite first order moral disagreement and moral scepticism.

In this sense, therefore, grounding the rules of a liberal society in a way independent of an overall conception of human purposes is central to intellectual coherence of the liberal project of producing a compelling political philosophy for a morally pluralist society, one which all citizens could accept as legitimate and feel loyalty to irrespective of their particular conception of human purposes.

So what are these general rules and how are they to be established and the crisis of reflexivity in liberal theory overcome? The first point to notice is that there is quite a major dispute between liberal theorists about the nature of the rules in operation here. Hayek insists that truly general and unbiased rules cannot have any bearing on distributive issues, that is to say, they can have no bearing on issues of social justice, on the distribution of goods and services in society. A properly liberal society, the legislation of which is independent of views of human purposes, cannot be concerned with issues of social justice, whereas it is equally important to Rawls and Dworkin that state action to secure social justice is central to liberalism and that this can be pursued without infringing the purpose-independent nature of legislation in a liberal society. We shall now turn to a detailed examination of a range of liberal political theorists in order to identify their responses to these issues.

Hayek: justice in a free society

It is central to Hayek's theory of justice and law that the laws of a free society should be framed independently of a particular view of human purposes and goals. He draws a sharp contrast between society and an organization. An organization exists to secure particular purposes and within an organization the rules are devised to help the members secure their common purposes which is why the organization exists. In Hayek's view, however, as human society has developed the range of human purposes has become more diverse. With the collapse of small-scale societies based upon tribes and localized communities, human society has lost any sense of overall purpose or hierarchy of purposes and, as such, has grown into something quite different from a purpose-dependent form of organization. A tribal society or a modern organization which does presuppose a set of agreed purposes he calls a teleocracy (from the Greek *telos* – end, goal or purpose). There is, however, in a spontaneous order, a need for basic rules of conduct which will secure the framework within which individuals pursue their own purposes. A spontaneous order has to develop rules of conduct which 'must progressively shed their dependence on concrete ends' and such a set of end-free rules he calls a nomocracy. The common good of a free and spontaneous order does not consist in these agreed purposes of its members just because it is a consequence of modernity or civilization that there are no such overall agreed purposes. Rather, in a free society 'the general good consists principally in the facilitation of the pursuit of unknown individual purposes'. This common good consists in the rule of law.

In this idea Hayek draws inspiration from both Hume and Kant. Hume argues the thesis which Hayek endorses when he argues that the benefit of law:

arises from the whole scheme or system ... only from the observ-

ance of a general rule ... without taking into consideration ... any
particular consequences which may result from the determination
of these laws, in any particular case which offers.[12]

Equally Kant argues that the rule of law which is abstract and impartial
cannot be divised in terms of a specific purpose such as welfare.[13] In so
far as rules of conduct or laws serve welfare it is only in the sense of
facilitating the achievement of a wide variety of individual purposes,
the content of which will be unknown to the legislator. Given this view,
the tests for laws cannot be that they produce particular results for
individuals , but rather they have to be abstract and procedural tests
which, as Hayek argues, are based upon universality and consistency.
Justice is not therefore concerned with balancing interests in a particular
social context, it is not concerned with *results* at all, but rather with the
rules which will enable the largest amount of freedom to individuals to
pursue their own purposes. They are concerned not to secure the certainty that an individual *will* be able to secure his or her own ends, but
rather with that framework which will enable an individual to act
without the interference of others in the pursuit of his/her own purposes.
The point of justice is therefore to secure as large a space as possible
for each individual to act in his/her own way except when acting in a
way which will interfere with the secular freedom of others. It is not
about the distribution of goods and resources so much as securing a
framework within which individuals are free from coercion to make use
of opportunities which may come their way.

From these observations it should begin to become clear why Hayek
is antagonistic to the whole idea of social justice. Social justice typically
is concerned not with securing the freedom of the individual from
coercion and interference so that each individual can pursue his/her
own good, but rather with the specific results of human enterprises.
Usually theories of social justice are concerned with securing a particular
pattern of the distribution of the goods and services of society to
individuals, whether this is based upon needs, desert or any other
criterion. As such, patterned principles of distributive or social justice
as Nozick calls them are concerned with *results* rather than *procedures*
within which each individual will have the opportunity to secure the
results or goods that he or she wants. Social justice is teleocratic in that
the rules of distribution are related to procuring some overall social

end – namely the division of the social product according to some agreed pattern.

Given his view about the proper role of justice in society, Hayek argues that injustice attaches to the particular intentional actions of individuals. An injustice occurs when an individual interferes with the domain of freedom of another person when this is secured by just and universalizable rules. Because injustice is a critical term which can only apply to individual acts of coercion, it follows for Hayek that societies with such general rules cannot be characterized as just or unjust precisely because the degree of intention necessary is lacking. When society is seen as spontaneous, purpose-independent then the outcomes which result from each individual pursuing a conception of the good in his/her own way are not intended or foreseen by anyone. Social outcomes as a whole are not intended, but rather an unintended outcome of individuals intentionally pursuing their ends in their own way. So, for example, Hayek rejects the view that the outcomes of a free market can be criticized because the individual who experiences poverty as a result of its operations can be regarded as suffering an injustice. Poverty is not injustice because in a free economy bounded by the rule of law and justice as he understands it, millions of individuals pursue their own purposes in buying and selling and no doubt a particular outcome in terms of income, wealth, goods and services emerges from this, but this is not a 'distribution' of income and wealth because it is an unintended consequence of these processes of buying and selling. Social injustice implies a *maldistribution* but the idea of maldistribution itself pre-supposes a distributor acting in an intentional manner to produce such a maldistribution. However, this does not apply to market transactions. So to talk about the distribution of income and wealth, goods and services produced by a market economy is a category mistake, it pre-supposes a distributor whereas in a free market there is no such dis-tribution agency.

Hayek's point about the role of the idea of a distributor in the context of social justice can be put in another way. Take for example a congenital health defect such as spina bifida. If we exclude for the moment the idea of a malevolent God who distributes such handicaps, we view those with these handicaps as suffering from bad luck in the genetic lottery not from an injustice, just because the latter characterization would presuppose a distributor. Similarly we would regard those who suffer as the result of a natural disaster such as an earthquake as suffering from misfortune or bad luck rather than injustice. Injustice is an intentional action by an individual, or a group of organized individuals such as a government, but it cannot be used to describe the unintended outcomes of a spontaneous process. Hence socialist or social democratic critics of market processes who argue that free markets produce injustice for the poor are mistaken. The poor may suffer from misfortune, but they do not suffer from injustice unless they have been deprived, by intentional actions of something to which they had a right, but this is not the case when poverty is the result of the operation of a free market:

> It has of course to be admitted that the manner in which the benefits and burdens are apportioned by the market mechanism would in many instances have to be regarded as very unjust *if* it were the result of a deliberate allocation to particular people. But this is not the case. Those shares are the outcome of a process the effect of which on particular people was neither intended nor foreseen … To demand justice from such a process is clearly absurd, and to single out some people in such a society as entitled to a particular share evidently unjust.[14]

Hayek also identifies other problems with the idea of social or distributive justice which relate to the process of moral consensus in a pluralistic society – problems which relate to the possibility of agreement about the appropriate principles of social justice. We might think first of all about two rather general principles: those of desert and need. On the basis of these two possibilities we might say that the most socially just distribution of social resource is to be on the basis of desert or merit or alternatively on need. Clearly whichever principle we adopted would lead to very different distributions. So which should we take as the defining characteristics of just distribution? The fact of the matter is, or so Hayekians argue, that desert on the one hand and need on the other are parts of different moral outlooks. So, for example, what people might be thought to deserve will depend ultimately on different moral values and indeed different conceptions of the person and human nature. The same is true of needs. As John Gray argues in a powerful statement of Hayek's thesis:

Hayek's first observation is that not all needs or merits are com-
mensurable with each other ... Bureaucratic authorities charged
with distributing medical care according to need will inevitably
act unpredictably and arbitrarily from the standpoint of their
patients for want of any overarching standard governing choice
between such incommensurable needs ... The idea that distribution could even be governed by these subjective and inherently
disputable notions reflects the unrealism of such contemporary
thought ... Attempts to impose any other principle on the free
exchanges of free men involve imposing upon them a hierarchy of
ends and goals, a ranking and a code of judgements regarding
needs and merits, about which no consensus exists in our society
and which there is no reason to suppose can be achieved.[15]

So to choose between merit on the one hand and need on the other
is a moral choice, and having made that choice, there are still difficulties
because if we favour deserts there will be no consensual account of what
merit and desert consists in and similarly with need, there will be no
account agreed across society about the nature of needs. These terms
only make sense within a specific account of human nature and human
purposes and as such rules for distributing resources on these bases
would be purpose-dependent but, there is no agreement about such
purposes. Any attempt to secure distributive justice in society will
therefore, in Hayek's view, inevitably bring about two bad consequences
in a free society. First of all, to seek to secure a particular pattern of
justice will mean that one set of values related to human purposes will
be given a privilege over others in a society and this is incompatible
with a liberal and free society in which the diversity of ends is recognized.
Secondly, because there will be a lack of clarity and precision about
these values, reflecting social and moral diversity, to attempt to distribute
goods and income according to one or other of these criteria will be a
very indefinite enterprise and will have a very great deal of power in the
hands of officials who will of necessity have to exercise this power in a
discretionary way just because the ideas are so indefinite. There is, for
example, the case of medical needs. We can imagine an argument for
a government-funded National Health Service being based upon an
argument for social justice in relation to need – that these needs create
rights to social resources in order to satisfy them, and if they are not

satisfied then those who are ill will suffer an injustice. However, in the view of Hayek such needs cannot be identified with any determinacy and because of this we have no rational way of relating one person's needs to another's. Because medical needs are incommensurable – there is no way of weighing the importance of one set against another, and this has to be done in a situation of scarce resources: 'bureaucratic authorities charged with distributing medical care according to need will inevitably act unpredictably, and arbitrarily for want of any overarching standard governing choice between such incommensurable needs.'[16] The same would be taken of other needs in fields such as education, welfare and housing. Similar points too could be made about distribution according to merit. This has a bad effect upon society, making citizens' expectations subject to a high degree of uncertainty and conceding to bureaucracies considerable arbitrary powers. This arbitrariness is not accidental, it would be endemic to any attempt to secure social justice.

This argument can be generalized into a doctrine about the arbitrariness of government once the claims of social justice are accepted. Government, in such circumstances, would be seen to have the responsibility for securing the just status in society of individuals and groups and would also be involved in securing just rewards for individuals through, for example, incomes policies. However, given the earlier argument that there are no objective or determinate criteria for making judgements about social justice it will follow, on Hayek's analysis, that interest groups will dress up their claims in the language of social justice and the role of justice in society will become a matter of what Hume called private interests – a competition between interest groups to get their own subjective views about their deserts or needs as the politically accepted ones. In the absence of agreed criteria governments, like bureaucrats in the previous example, will act in arbitrary ways, responding to the pattern of interest group pressures. This is sometimes connected with theses about the growing ungovernability of societies marked by the pursuit of social justice. The argument here really makes explicit what is involved in interest group pressures. If we take the idea of interest group pressures on government then any group or coalition of groups which involved more than 50 per cent of the population would have an incentive to use its pressure on government to despoil the remainder, but even this overbearing position would be curtailed because the minority would equally have an incentive to try to form new coalitions with some of the groups temporarily in the majority to form a new majority coalition. So long as government is seen as having this role in social justice such strife between interest groups will be endemic and, as MacIntyre has put it, politics would become a matter of 'civil war carried on by other means'. In addition, government action would be resented by those who felt that their subjective deserts had not been properly recognized by government and would seek to break down the temporarily prevailing system of social justice:

> Society has simply become the new deity to which we complain and clamour for redress if it does not fulfil the expectations which it has created.[17]

Perhaps the clearest example of this for Hayek would be the operation of incomes policy in the British economy since the mid-1960s. In each case such policies have been unsustainable even when backed with the threat of legal sanctions. Groups of workers have sought to break through the system because they were thought not to be receiving what in their subjective view was their just reward. On this view we have no way of weighing in the political arena the just wage of a nurse compared with a teacher or a baker. To give in to one group's view that it should be a special case will merely open the way to other forms of resentment building up. In Hayek's view the attempt to determine income and status politically leads to arbitrariness in government and the possibility of ungovernability. Such 'decisions' are best left to the market mechanism in which the income and social position of individuals is an unintended, and thus neither fair nor unjust, outcome of spontaneous market processes. The role of government or politics is therefore to hold the ring and the place of justice in this is to prevent individual coercion and not a political attempt to secure a *just outcome* for groups and individuals.

Hayek argues that modern ideas of social justice threaten the transformation of the free order into a totalitarian organization. A liberal society with a state neutral between competing conceptions of the good, will therefore consist fundamentally of two points: on the one hand a set of abstract laws which will secure the maximum amount of individual freedom from mutual coercion and a free market unconstrained by distributive principles of social justice. All of this in Hayek's view follows logically from a recognition of the diversity and incommensurability of conceptions of the good and the range of human purposes in a modern society. The ideal of a political community committed to the enhancing of certain specific human virtues has to be abandoned in favour of the idea of a Great Society of free individuals pursuing their own good in their own way.

In Hayek's view the appeal of the idea of social justice is at the heart of socialism because he sees the impetus of socialism to be the demand that there should be a 'just' distribution of income and wealth. Within the socialist tradition this has taken two forms. On the one hand there has been the idea that socialism should be concerned with the social and public ownership of the means of production. However, Hayek sees the rationale of such a demand to be that it is only such a form of ownership which can secure a just distribution of the goods produced by productive efforts in society. The other dimension to socialism has been the idea that ownership is not so important – that a more just distribution can be attained by taxation and by the provision of government services such as welfare, rather than by a fundamental change in the pattern of ownership of the means of production. In each case though, the impetus to the process has been a commitment to social justice. In Hayek's view this has led to a major difference between the view of the role of government and politics within classical liberalism on the one hand and modern doctrines of government which have been influenced by socialism on the other:

> the former was governed by principles of just individual conduct while the new society is to satisfy the demands for 'social justice' – or, in other words, that the former demanded just actions by the individuals while the latter more and more places the duty of justice on authorities with power to command people what to do.[18]

Socialism based upon social justice has the prospect of restoring the idea of a substantive political community, but this is not comparable with the freedom and diversity of liberal society.

Hayek's solution to the problem is that we should abandon the pursuit of social justice and the growing interference in, and bureaucratization of, life which would accompany it and turn over the question of rewards, the 'distribution' of income and wealth and individual status, to the market. As an impersonal force, whose outcomes are unintended, Hayek believes that its outcomes would be regarded in Fred Hirsch's phrase 'in principle unprincipled'. In this way the market could not become the object of resentment in the way in which the intentional acts of government could.

> Our complaints about the outcome of the market as unjust do not really assert that somebody has been unjust; and there is no answer to the question of who has been unjust ... There is no individual and no cooperating group of people against which the sufferer would have a just complaint, and there are no conceivable rules of just individual conduct which would at the same time secure a functioning order and prevent such disappointments.[19]

Consequently, Hayek's thesis is a strong reassertion of the role of the market against government regulation and the politicization of economic life which has been a consequence of the pursuit of the mirage of social justice and this is based upon the impossibility of social justice in the context of moral pluralism.

A further argument about the superiority of the market mechanism as opposed to government in 'distribution' is that any system of social justice of matching resources to merit or desert will break the link between reward and services rendered which is necessary to economic efficiency. If people are rewarded for their merits or needs rather than the perceived value of their services to others then there can be no economic efficiency. It may be that A and B provide the same service to a client. A provides it very well, B very badly, but let us assume that B's deserts, or needs are greater than A's. If following one or the other rule of social justice B receives more than A, then this will lead to a decline in economic efficiency. So there are very practical as well as strong moral reasons for abandoning the search for just rewards and a patterned distribution which seeks to secure a particular view of justice.

The Hayekian view therefore sees the state which seeks social justice as illegitimate: it is pursuing a vague and ultimate goal about which there is no agreement in society and which cannot be founded on any rational basis and yet the pursuit of this goal requires the imposition on society of a view of ends and purposes only in which either merit or need find a definite place. The attempt to constrain the outcomes of free exchange in this way threatens to transform a free order into a totalitarian organization. However, in order to round out his theory Hayek has also to say something about the legitimacy of the market order and in particular in relation to the worst off members of society whose concerns were probably uppermost in the minds of those who think in terms of social justice. He therefore has to say more about the superiority of market allocations over political ones, particularly from the point of view of the worst off. His answer here is complex and relies upon a particular theory of economic growth and how the goods procured by growth are 'distributed' in a free market economy. Hayek holds to what is variously known as the 'echelon advance' or 'trickle down' theory of economic growth. He takes the view that a dynamic economy requires inequalities if it is to be innovative. Innovation requires rich people to provide demand for new products, but once produced these products do not remain the preserve of the rich. At one time it was only because the rich were able to provide a market – to take for example, air travel and refrigerators – that these things were developed to any extent, but once developed they trickle down gradually to the rest of the population. Because the rich have an incentive to demand new goods, new goods are produced and find their way into the rest of the economy. So there is an 'echelon' advance in consumption. What the rich consume today will be consumed by more and more people tomorrow.

Attempts to reduce inequalities in pursuit of the mirage of social justice will affect the capacity of the economy to grow and to innovate and this will be an advantage to welfare in the long run. A free economy will therefore have more inequality and indeed more relative poverty (these are closely related concepts for Hayek) than an economy constrained by criteria of social justice, but the economic position of the society will suffer in the long run, including the position of the worst off. They will be better off than they would be under any alternative to a free market, even though they may experience more inequality. The market assignment of rewards will be acceptable if the majority of people feel that they will be better off in the long run than they would under a more socialist and 'just' economy. Hayek's moral case for the market is almost the opposite of that put forward by socialists. Anthony Crosland, for example, argued for a socialist strategy of economic growth in which the tax dividends which would accrue to government could be used to secure a relative improvement in the worst off while enabling the better off to maintain their absolute standard of living.

Hayek is arguing that the relative position of the worst off does not matter; it is their standard of living compared with other alternatives which is important, not the degree of inequality, and on this basis, the worst off will improve their position if the rich are able to improve their relative position which would follow from the inequalities generated in the free market. So the legitimacy of the market economy is partly based on the defects of the socialist alternative and is partly derived because as the result of the echelon advance the poor will be better off in absolute terms even though inequality may increase but this will be required by economic growth.

Hayek does not reject the provision of a welfare safety net so long as its basis is clear. It is not there to secure greater justice or in response to some imaginary 'right' to welfare, but is provided at a minimum level to prevent destitution and social unrest, but Hayek is very clear that there is a clear difference between this and any attempt to develop social justice. He argues that security against severe physical privation and a given minimum sustenance for all should be clearly distinguished from:

> the assurance of a given standard of life, which is determined by comparing the standard enjoyed by a person or group with that of others. The distinction, then, is that between the security of an equal minimum income for all and the security of a particular income that a person is thought to deserve. The latter is closely related to the third major ambition that inspires the welfare state: the desire to use the powers of government to ensure a more even or more just distribution of goods.[20]

The latter, for reasons which we have already discussed, Hayek regards as 'bound to lead ... to socialism and its coercive and essentially arbitrary methods'. Obviously this view is only cogent if the two forms of welfare which Hayek distinguishes are in fact as capable of distinction as he clearly thinks they are.

How are we to assess Hayek's critique of social justice, the cogency of which has, it seems to me, to be acknowledged? In what follows I shall leave on one side the claims of social justice in terms of needs which I shall discuss in a later chapter, and ideas about merit and desert which will be discussed more fully in the context of a review of Rawls's theory. At this juncture I shall look more at Hayek's ideas about the role of intention in characterizing situations of injustice and his arguments about the legitimacy of markets. His argument is clearly vitally important in the light of the dominant theme of this book, namely the response to moral pluralism. It is central to Hayek's thesis that moral pluralism requires a shift away from political allocation of resources and values just because these are so contested in a free society, towards a market allocation, believing as he does that in a market individuals can define their own good in their own way coupled with the view that since the market is an impersonal non-teleocratic institution it is immune from moral criticism in terms of its outcomes. So this argument about the unintended nature of market allocations is central to his attempt to differentiate market allocations from political ones and to vindicate the superiority of the latter in a free society. Hence his arguments about unintended consequences here need careful scrutiny.

The first point to make in this discussion is that Hayek has to take the existing position of distribution of resources such as income, wealth and other forms of property as historically given. They cannot be given any formal moral foundation for exactly the same reasons as any argument for their redistribution cannot be given a moral foundation, given what he says about social justice. This means that in a free market economic agents will have very different resources to bring to bear in making their transactions. Against this background of existing and given inequality, the market will operate and individuals will buy and sell for all their multifarious reasons. At any particular time this will yield a 'distribution' of income and property which is for individuals neither intended nor foreseen and hence is not unjust.

Now in so far as this point concerns individuals, Hayek's argument seems to be well taken. We cannot predict in a free market what the economic outcome will be for an individual. However, this is not the only judgement we might want to make. We might, for example, want to consider the economic consequences not for an individual but for a group – in this case the position of those who, given the existing inequalities, enter the market with the least resources. Now it might well be the case that we can foresee that for this group as a whole, those who enter the market with least, are likely to end up with least. Of course, Hayek is correct in thinking that we cannot make this judgement with respect to any individual, but this does not mean that the judgement cannot be made for groups. If for the sake of argument it turned out on empirical research to be true that those who, at the start of the market transactions, started with least ended up with least and that this was foreseeable, would this make any difference to Hayek's claim that the market is immune from criticism on the basis of its lack of social justice? Hayek would still argue that it would not because even if this outcome for the least well off group were foreseeable, it is still not intended and injustice applies only to intentional acts. The position of the worst off groups is still the unintended consequence of millions of individual transactions in the market and even though, given inequalities of property rights, this might be foreseeable, it is still an unintended consequence and hence is not an injustice. In order to try to clarify this issue let us take another example from a small-scale interaction. If, for example, I am a doctor and I prescribe a massive dose of a pain-killing drug to stop the pain of a weak, terminally ill patient and it kills the patient, and that this is in some sense a foreseeable although unintended consequence to my action (my intention is defined in terms of relieving the suffering of the patient, not to kill the patient), is this sufficient to discount responsibility for the outcome? Clearly in this sort of case there are arguments both ways but, if we say that as a matter of routine my intended actions produce a foreseeable but unintended outcome for another person, then it is going to be disingenuous to claim that I am not responsible for the foreseeable but unintended consequences of my action. Indeed, if this were not so, there would constantly be a strong incentive continually to narrow down the characterization of intention so that it does not include the foreseeable consequences of action. In these circumstances there could be good reasons for saying that an individual is responsible for the routine, foreseeable consequences of an action, the intention of which is described in a different way. If we apply this analysis to the market context, we can argue as follows:

(a) if as an empirical fact those who enter the market with least will tend to end up with least (with exceptions for random individuals);

(b) if this is known to be the case as a foreseeable general outcome even though it is not intended;

(c) if there is an alternative course of action available, namely some redistribution in the interests of social justice;

then we can argue that those who support the market do bear responsibility for the least well off even though they do not intend that these people should be in this position and in this context the outcome of the market should not be accepted as in principle unprincipled. Hayek's argument rests upon the idea that there is not an intended 'distribution' and hence no injustice. The above argument would suggest, however, that where these consequences are foreseeable, as they may be for groups (this is an empirical question), then there can be a case for convicting the market of injustice.

We could, additionally, come to doubt the moral conclusions which Hayek claims from arguments about the irrelevance of justice to cases where there is clearly no intentional distribution, as for example in the case of congenital handicap. Here, Hayek's claim is that the handicapped only suffer from misfortune or bad luck and not injustice because their position if we look *back* at how they came to be in it is not the result of an intentional process. Thus, they have no claim on the resources of society in terms of rights and justice, so much as in terms of charity and humanity. There is a very large issue here about the place of the past in thinking about justice and injustice which will come to the fore more fully in the discussion of Nozick's theory later in the chapter, but we could argue against Hayek at this point that justice and injustice is not *only* a matter of how a particular outcome came about or arose but is rather a matter of our response to that outcome. Imagine that I am walking down a street and see a baby lying face down in a gutter full of water, the issue of justice and injustice here is surely not merely a matter of how the baby came to be there. If I can save the life of the baby at no comparable cost to myself and I fail to do so, then it could be argued that I am committing an injustice in not doing so. Certainly someone who was born with a genetic handicap does not suffer an injustice in terms of the genesis of his handicap, but justice and injustice can come in via our *response* to his position. If we fail to compensate him as far as possible when we could do so at no comparable cost to ourselves, then this is where at least one dimension of injustice lies. The same is true of those who suffer as the result of the impersonal forces of the market. We have not exhausted all the questions relating to justice when we have established that poverty is the result of an impersonal force. If we can change that person's position by a redistribution of resources at no comparable risk to ourselves – that is to say by creating for ourselves comparable poverty – then a failure to do so would be an injustice.

In these ways it could be argued therefore that the market can be made susceptible to a moral critique based upon some idea of social justice, and whatever difficulties there may be with this latter idea, these are not sufficient to abandon it. It may be that there are immense difficulties in the political assignment of status, income etc., but if the points made above have any cogency, then it follows that the market does not avoid these either. They are both implicated in the difficulties of making judgements of moral principle in a situation of moral diversity.

What can be said finally about Hayek's own arguments about the legitimacy of markets? Here two points are worth making. In a discussion of this topic in *Law, Legislation and Liberty*, Volume II, which is subtitled *The Mirage of Social Justice*, Hayek makes a very damaging admission. It is central to his thesis that markets do not 'distribute' according to any moral criterion, but he recognizes that many defenders of the market believe that they do, namely in a market people receive their just deserts. Hayek, of course, rejects this, but concedes that the very legitimacy of markets may well depend upon these widespread although false beliefs and he considers that it may be necessary to maintain the legitimacy of markets that such beliefs should exist because he thinks that a defence of markets as neutral between moral standpoints may not be sufficient to sustain their legitimacy. If the outcomes of markets are in principle unprincipled and if luck and windfall are indispensable to them, will this be a rich enough defence of markets to secure their acceptance? He says of the views that markets reward deserts:

> it bodes ill for the future of the market order that this seems to be the only defence of it which is understood by the general public ... It is therefore a real dilemma to what extent we ought to encourage in the young a belief that when they really try they will succeed ... and whether without such partly erroneous beliefs the large numbers will tolerate actual differences in rewards which will be based only partly on achievement and partly on mere chance.[21]

This point makes his positive defence of the market, that in the long run there will be a trickle down effect of the benefits of economic growth to large numbers of people in society even more important. The material value of the free market to most people in society would seem to be the only basis to its legitimacy if the rather paradoxical ethical defence of it as in principle unprincipled is likely to fail, at least in practice as he intimates above. In the discussion of this point, I shall refer to the thesis developed by Fred Hirsch called the 'social limits to growth'[22] as a way of throwing doubt on at least part of Hayek's claim in this context of market legitimacy. If, as Hirsch suggests at least for an important class of goods, the market cannot meet its promise of increasing prosperity for all, or at least for a majority, then its legitimacy may be very insecure. In the absence of a theory of distributive justice, the promise of increasing prosperity is central to the practical legitimacy of the superiority of the market over other sorts of distributive mechanism.

In Hirsch's view the argument about the echelon advance or trickle down effect of markets is seriously flawed because it assumes that all goods can trickle down to a wider group of consumers at the same level of economic value. Certainly this argument works for some goods, for example, electric fires or refrigerators, without changing their value for individuals. Your capacity to derive value from your electric fire does not decline if I too have an electric fire, but there are certain sorts of goods, what Hirsch calls positional goods, which cannot be consumed more and more widely without altering the value to those who consume them. The value of these goods depends on the fact that only a few people are consuming them and they decline in value the more widely the goods are consumed. An example will help to explain this. The paradigm case of a positional good might be standing on tiptoe in order to see a procession better. This, however, is a positional good in the sense that the value of doing it declines the more people take part in it. Similarly tourism and having the benefits of secluded beaches or cottages are positional in this sense. When only the rich could afford to travel, there was greater value to be derived from sitting in St Mark's Square in Venice than is available now with the overcrowding which comes from greater access to travel, through the trickle down effect. The trickle down effect may have worked, but as it has worked, it has changed the value which can be derived from the commodity in question. The positional economy, as Hirsch calls it, relates to those goods which are either scarce in some socially generated sense, or are subject to congestion and crowding through more extensive use. The material economy can continue to grow and be susceptible to a trickle down mechanism because there will be no deterioration in quality the more widely such goods are consumed, but this is not the case with the positional side of the economy.

It might be thought, however, that if the only goods susceptible to social scarcity are things like deserted beaches, holiday cottages, or enjoying cappucino in an Italian square free from tourists then we might be able to contemplate their discovery with equanimity just because they seem to be so marginal and unimportant in terms of basic life chances. However, education is also a positional good for Hirsch, in the sense that as an instrumental good, one that has a marketable value, as opposed to being a means of self-fulfilment in a non-material way, the value of education depends to a great extent on its scarcity value. It cannot be distributed more equally without changing its value to those who consume it. So, in fact, instead of individuals, as in the trickle down theory, being able to consume today the same educational goods which were reserved for the rich two generations ago, they do not consume the same sort of good; the good has declined in value the more people have come to consume it. Education is a positional good which cannot be distributed more widely at the same level of value. Far from increasing equality and lessening tensions the more equal distribution of education has led to the growth of credentialism, with more and higher qualifications being demanded for jobs which in previous generations may not have required qualifications at all. It would, of course, be comforting to think that the demand for qualifications was the result of the growing complexity of the jobs, but clearly in many cases this is not so. Credentialism is a function of the paper chase and not the cause of it. In so far as this is true it follows that a good deal of working-class demand for education is defensive in nature. Jobs which could be done in the past without qualifications now require them. The demand for educational expenditure could be seen as an attempt to secure access to the same jobs which in previous generations might not have needed publicly certified levels of educational attainment at all. As the American economist Lester Thurow has written:

> As the supply of educated labour increases individuals find that they must improve their education to defend their current income position. If they don't they will find their current jobs no longer open to them. Education becomes a good investment not because it would raise people's incomes above what they would have been

if no one had increased his education, but rather because it raises their income above what it will be if others acquire an education and they do not.[23]

In this sense education acts as a screening device for recruitment to unequal positions.

The argument about positional goods poses two questions for Hayek. The first is the clear limit to the trickle down effect on the basis of which he wanted to justify the legitimacy of the market economy in the absence of a principle of distributive justice. The second is that if there are such goods and some of them are very important in determining life chances such as education, then this raises very clearly the question of who is to consume such goods. Because of Hayek's rejection of distributive justice, his only answer can be: those who can get their hands on them first. If this is so, then we are really back with the question raised earlier about the necessary acceptance from Hayek's point of view of the given structure of property rights of income, wealth and power and we saw then that there were very good reasons for rejecting such an acceptance. The issue of positional goods puts the distributional question at the centre of the positional agenda which cannot be avoided by the argument about the trickle down and prosperity enhancing features of the market economy for material and non-positional goods. The centrality of the value of social justice cannot be displaced as easily as Hayek believes and it is necessary to wrestle with the problem of the nature of the social justice in a morally pluralistic society.

Other liberal thinkers have denied, however, that these are the only conclusions which can be drawn from the recognition of intractable moral pluralism. Such thinkers, among whom Rawls and Gewirth are the major examples, accept the positive side of Hayek's argument, that a liberal society will embody a framework of law to ensure maximal mutual freedom from coercion, but they reject the negative point of his argument that a liberal society has to eschew questions of social justice. However, in order to argue this in a manner consistent with liberal principles they will have to meet Hayek's claim that any such principles will be purpose-dependent and will rely on the illicit imposition of a particular conception of the good within which distributive criteria are given their place.

Rawls: contract and rules

In Rawls's book *A Theory of Justice* the answer to this central question
is given by two components of his highly complex theory: the theory of
primary goods and the argument about the 'original position'. Rawls
rejects Hayek's assumption that all accounts of the good are goal-
dependent and thus involve intractable disputes about human purposes.
Rather, he argues, it is possible to define a set of primary goods which
are wanted by any persons whatever their own conception of the good
might turn out to be, and which are independent of any particular
assumptions about human nature. Rawls uses a device called the 'thin'
theory of the good to explain the issues at stake here. All rational
persons have 'thick' or developed theories of the good. That is to say,
they have a plan of life, an idea of what they would like to be or what
they would like to achieve in life, and of their own nature, personality
and purposes. In a pluralistic society these plans of life will be different
and incommensurable. This does not mean, however, *pace* Hayek, that
we cannot arrive at an agreed account of some goods even in a radically
morally pluralist society. This agreement is what he calls the 'thin'
theory of the good, and it consists of that range of goods which will be
required by any rational person in order to frame and carry out his/her
plan of life whatever it might turn out to be:

> primary goods ... are things which it is supposed a rational man
> wants whatever else he wants. Regardless of what an individual's
> rational plans are in detail, it is assumed that there are various
> things which he would prefer more of rather than less.[24]

And:

> though one's rational plans all have final ends, they nevertheless
> all require for their execution certain primary goods, rational and
> social. Plans differ since individual abilities, circumstances and
> wants differ ... But whatever one's system of ends, primary goods
> are necessary means.[25]

These basic goods are the basic means for the advancing of any 'thick'
theory of the good, a particular plan of life. While plans of life may

differ radically they do not do so in terms of the necessary conditions for framing and executing such plans. In this sense we can arrive at a definition of basic goods to be distributed in society which is *neutral* in respect of specific human purposes because it is the same for all such purposes. What then in Rawls's view are these goods? They include rights and liberties, opportunities and powers, income and wealth and a sense of one's own worth. Rights and liberties are necessary conditions for pursuing a conception of the good because without various sorts of freedoms guaranteed by constitutional rights the individual will not be in a position to pursue his conception of the good in society (this is the point of agreement between Rawls and Hayek); without material resources the individual will not be able to implement his/her plan of life, without a sense of one's own self-respect a plan of life will be meaningless and the conception of the good will not seem important. So Rawls takes himself to have avoided Hayek's problem, which as we have seen was clearly defined by John Gray. However, this is only half the battle because he now has to explain how there can be a neutral principle of distribution of such goods. Surely the Hayekian will argue, any particular principle of distribution or 'social justice' will depend upon a particular conception of the good such as desert and will infringe the principle that a liberal state should be neutral between such principles?

Rawls's answer to this problem brings us to the second aspect of his theory relevant to the present discussion, that is his contractual conception of the original position and the veil of ignorance. The task of this theory is to produce an account of fair distribution of primary goods which again does not depend upon a particular view of the good. In order to do this Rawls constructs a hypothetical model of social choice. He asks us to consider what distribution of primary goods would be agreed upon by people in a position of moral equality, having the capacity to reason, but being ignorant of their own conception of the good and also their own particular qualities of mind and body which can be very important in advancing the interests of a particular group of persons. For example, if I have limited altruism, which Rawls assumes, and if I know that I have a high IQ, then in choosing a particular form of distribution of primary goods I would be likely to favour a distribution which enhances the life chances of people such as myself. So the requirement of neutrality entails that the choice has to be made by these hypothetical rational choosers under conditions in which they are all ignorant of their specific qualities and values. They do, however, know what the primary goods are and they are able to know any general facts about human psychology and human society. By imposing these conditions on the hypothetical model the requirements of neutrality are specified and the choices made under these conditions will be impartial.

So what choices will be made? In Rawls's view the answer falls into two parts. The first point will be an agreement of the most extensive basic liberty so that each individual will have the most extensive opportunity to execute his plan of life whatever it may turn out to be, subject to not interfering with a similar liberty for others. At this point Rawls and Hayek are in agreement. However, the disagreement comes in the second area of the choice made in the hypothetical position which articulates Rawls's now famous difference principle. This principle asserts that social and economic inequalities, this is to say in income, wealth and status, are only just if they work to the advantage of the most disadvantaged members of society and that these inequalities attach to positions which can be competed for under conditions of fair equality of opportunity. Thus inequalities of resources are therefore only legitimate if they work to the advantage of the worst off so that an increase in equality will actually make the most disadvantaged in society worse off than they would be under some degree of inequality.

The difference principle also allows Rawls to weight the primary goods which were mentioned earlier. Clearly merely to identify such goods is not sufficient, they have to be weighted in some way. Those primary goods which refer to civil liberties and rights are always equally distributed, and this can be achieved because the duties which correspond to such goods are negative ones of non-interference. As such there can be no scarcity over such goods because the corresponding duty is that of abstaining from action. Thus these primary goods do not, in Rawls's view have to be balanced against other sorts of goods. There is a difference, however, with income and wealth, which are clearly variable. In Rawls's view, however, the difference principle provides the way of weighting these goods. The benchmark here is the position of the worst off group and the distribution of income and wealth which would most improve their position. Hence these goods are weighted on the basis of what combination of such goods would be preferred by a rational individual representative of the least well off group in society.

It is central to the coherence of Rawls' strategy that the choice should be based upon purely rational consideration and should *not* involve any prejudgement about a conception of the good which gives some particular moral value to the worst off and that the theory does not presuppose some particular view of motivation. So how are the principles arrived at by the exercise of some wholly rational and non-moral specific considerations? The answer with regard to the first principle is obvious. Unless each person has the same equal freedom to pursue his/her conception of the good no one in the original position, behind the veil of ignorance, will have any confidence that he/she will have the opportunity to follow his/her view of the good life whatever it may turn out to be. The reasoning for the second principle is more complex and controversial and depends upon a view about decision-making in uncertainty. The view of ignorance ensures not only neutrality about 'thick' or substantive conceptions of the good but also injects a radical degree of uncertainty into the choices made. Because the decision-makers are ignorant about their basic qualities, they do not know in advance whether they will be advantaged or disadvantaged by the genetic lottery in the distribution of physical and mental capacities, or the advantages of a fortunate family environment. In such a situation of uncertainty, anyone not knowing how economic and social resources will affect his/her life chances, Rawls argues, will adopt a maximin strategy, that is to say they will choose those distributive principles which will safeguard the position of the worst-off members of society. In this way I will be protected whatever my conception of the good turns out to be and however disadvantaged I may be in terms of endowment and family background.

This then is the reasoning behind the second or difference principle. This principle secures the position of the least advantaged member of society because his or her welfare constitutes the benchmark against which the legitimacy of any inequalities is to be assessed. If there are to be any inequalities their size and scope is to be judged against the welfare of the worst endowed members of society and whether they will benefit from their inequality.

So Rawls's claims to have produced what Hayek denies can be produced, namely a theory of the basic goods of a liberal society and a neutral principle of distribution of these goods. This strategy is of the first importance to liberal theory, so how coherent and compelling is it?

There are perhaps two important lines of criticism which are relevant to the assessment of how far Rawls is able to maintain the idea that his theory of justice is neutral between different conceptions of the good. The first is the claim that his list of primary goods is in fact tendentious in two ways. The first criticism embodies a point which will be discussed in more detail later in the book, in the chapter on Liberty, namely that the distribution of social and economic resources such as income and wealth does not affect the *liberty* of an individual in seeking to implement his conception of the good. Liberty, on this view, is the absence of intentional coercion. I am only constrained when someone is intentionally coercing me, not when I lack resources as a result of the action of no one in particular – such as in an impersonal economic market. As we shall see later, this is an argument of central importance in liberal theory and a strict view of negative liberty can be used to cast some initial doubt on the cogency of Rawls's assumption that social and economic resources are necessary goods in the attempt to facilitate and execute a plan of life. The second point, more germane to the main features of the present discussion, is Rawls's claim that primary goods are necessary means to the fulfilment of any rational plan of life. The criticism here is that it is perfectly possible to think of plans of life which do not, for example, require income and wealth – the most obvious examples being those forms of life which involve various forms of self-denial and rejection of worldly goods – for example, in Western monasticism or Eastern mysticism. The difficulty with this approach is that there are some patterns of life conforming to specific conceptions of the good, which may not require wealth and income for their fulfilment. Certain primary goods may not be the appropriate benefits to distribute in all forms of society and hence primary goods are not neutral between different substantive theories of the good but in fact tacitly presuppose some objective theory of the good to provide for their privileged status. To concede this would invalidate Rawls's claim that his theory is not teleocratic in the appropriate sense. In so far as this criticism is cogent, it follows that Rawls is mistaken in regarding such goods as what all rational persons will need, whatever their conception of the good, and in this sense it might be argued that Hayek's claim that we cannot arrive at a neutral list of basic goods for distribution is vindicated. However, it is arguable that even Hayek is equally committed to some account of such goods in his account of monopoly as coercive. In *The Constitution of Liberty* Hayek argues that a monopoly in a good which is necessary for life is coercive, but it is not at all clear why this should be so unless there is a conceptual link between freedom and such goods (which his book by and large denies) and if we have an account of such goods. It might then be argued that liberal theory has to make use of some very general ideas about basic goods even in its most radical form, as in Hayek. Of course, if this is so, it shows that neutrality between conceptions of the good can only be relative and not absolute.

The second major criticism applies to Rawls's attempt to produce a neutral, rational procedure for distribution, in that it is frequently argued that far from the maximin strategy behind the veil of ignorance for securing the position of the worst off being a neutral and disinterested form of rationality, as Rawls claims, independent of any particular account of human motivation, rather it embodies a particular, substantive and controversial human characteristic, namely risk aversion. Why might it not be the case that in choosing behind the veil of ignorance I would choose the outcome with least risk, I could equally prefer a society with a much greater amount of inequality, and thus the possibility of a much larger gain for the successful, at a greater risk for the less advantaged, and then hope that I turn out to be among the advantaged? This point has been made tellingly by Brian Barry in *The Liberal Theory of Justice*:

> If a decision maker knows all the possible outcomes of each of the alternative choices before him but has no idea at all of the relative probabilities of these outcomes he will rationally take account only of the best outcome and the worst outcome that can arise from each choice. Since any outcome can occur with any probability it is obvious that any idea of maximising expected value is out of the question in such a situation and there is no point in looking at the outcomes between the best and the worst. But it should also be noted that this does not entail a maximin strategy. Some further argument would be required to get to the conclusion that it is rational in the circumstances to be a 'pessimist' rather than an optimist, and to take account only of the *worst* possible outcome.[26]

On this view, far from maximin being the definitive rational strategy to adopt in a situation of such radical uncertainty, it is a strategy which is tainted with a particular assumption about human nature – that human beings are averse to risk taking. This being so, there is no way in which maximin can be regarded as a value-neutral decision-making procedure.

One aspect of Rawls's theory which is important for us to consider in this context is his thoroughgoing rejection of desert as a criterion of distributive justice. As we saw earlier, Hayek rejects desert because we cannot know enough about deserts and the idea varies with different moral traditions so that in a modern complex society marked by pluralism it could never become a point of the rule of law, being both uncertain and teleocratic. Rawls is equally critical of desert as the basis of a particular distributive claim, but his grounds are rather different from those of Hayek. To take desert as the basis of a distributive claim would have to presuppose that the individual could claim some credit or responsibility for his possession of those superior talents which are the true basis of a particular distributive claim. However, any such claim for credit and responsibility is, in Rawls's view, difficult in two respects. In the first place we are not responsible for what might be called our native endowments, which are the result of the genetic lottery or the arbitrary distribution of nature. Nor are we responsible for our initial starting place in society, for example, that we have been born into a fortunate family background. Secondly, it is also problematic to claim that we are responsible for those qualities of character which enable us to capitalize upon and make use of our initial natural endowments because in Rawls's view 'character depends in large part upon fortunate family and social circumstances' for which the individual can claim no credit. Given then that it is always very unclear what qualities of mind and character we can claim responsibility for, it follows that moral claims to resources based upon desert cannot be sustained. It is important in this context to remember that, although under the terms of the difference principle there would be a basis for inequality – to pay rewards for scarce talent etc. without which the worst off members of society would be even worse off – these are, however, not paid on the basis of the moral deserts or worth of those with scarce talents but are rather paid as a rent of ability so that talents will be mobilized when they serve the common interest, not because the talented deserve them since 'the initial endowment of natural assets and the contingencies of their growth and nurture in early life are arbitrary from the moral point of view'.

Rawls clearly regards this theory as morally uncontroversial and he says that it is 'one of the fixed points of our considered judgements', and certainly in a theory which has to disclaim a substantive theory of human nature and the human personality it is clear why this would have to be so. However, his argument here has been disputed both in the sense that it does in fact presuppose a rather definite and controversial account of the nature of the human personality and the fact that it is incompatible with his own views about human worth and self-respect as a basic primary good. The issues here probably speak for themselves but it would be worth bringing them into the open. In the first place, it is not clear what role there is for autonomous choice by individuals in Rawls's theory in the sense that he regards how we choose to develop our talents as in some sense the product of nature and nurture, e.g., 'the effort a person is willing to make is influenced by his natural abilities and skills and the alternatives open to him'. In this sense, as Nozick argues,[27] almost everything noteworthy about an individual is related to some explanatory account in terms of nature and nurture, and the role of the autonomous human agent, which is central to the liberal tradition in political thought, becomes deeply problematic. Given what Rawls says about self-respect and a sense of one's own worth as a primary good, it is difficult to dissent from Nozick's verdict that 'one doubts that the unexalted picture of human beings Rawls' theory pre-supposes and rests upon can be made to fit together with the view of human dignity it is designed to lead to and embody'.[28] This is not to say that Rawls's account of the nature of character in relation to action is indefensible, only that it is a controversial conception which might lead one to suspect that Rawls's theory cannot get along without presupposing a substantive theory of human nature with all the attend-ant problems which the thesis was designed to avoid.

In a sense, however, there is a more fundamental issue to be posed for Rawls's theory given the general theme of this chapter, because even a sympathetic critic like Ronald Dworkin is sceptical about the value neutrality of the whole apparatus of the veil of ignorance and the original position. As Dworkin has argued recently:

The device of the original position ... cannot plausibly be taken as the starting point for political philosophy. It requires a deeper theory beneath it, a theory that explains why the original position has the features that it does and why the fact the people would choose particular principles in that position, if they would, certifies these principles as principles of justice.[29]

That is to say the original position is to be seen not only as productive of political principles but in some way predicated on other principles. The principle which Dworkin has in mind as being presupposed by the device of the original position is that of equality of concern or respect. The original position which enforces ignorance about the capacities, interests and goods of the contracting parties is designed to 'enforce the abstract right to equal concern and respect which must be understood to be the fundamental concept of Rawls's deep theory'.[30] This right to equal respect is not then a product of the contracting parties in the original position; rather the original position embodies an institutional device for securing equal concern and respect. So the centre of gravity would move to the justification of such a principle. It is in Rawls' view owed to persons in the light of their moral personality which expresses itself in being able to raise issues of justice and distinguishes men from animals.

Equality is therefore based upon a conception of moral personality or moral capacity. The possession of moral personality is a sufficient condition for equal justice. However, this issue is rather muted in Rawls's argument despite its crucial role in his theory, but the argument raises a fundamental question: is there an account of moral capacity which can be given independently of a substantial conception of the good, or a substantive theory of the personality? Is it possible to theorize about the capacity for moral agency as such independently of how this agency is realized in particular substantive moralities? Rawls assumes this to be so and the original position embodies this assumption.

If we turn to our next two authors, Gewirth and Dworkin we can see how complex these issues are. Gewirth concentrates his argument very much on what it is to be a moral agent and what is required for a moral capacity; Dworkin places the issue of equal concern and respect at the centre of his argument and approaches the question less obliquely than Rawls.

Before moving on to discuss these two figures, however, I want to make some final remarks about Rawls's theory. As I have presented it here it looks as though it is an attempt to provide some kind of objective and universal foundation for justice and certainly there is a good deal in Rawls's book which provides a basis for that assumption. One thing I have not discussed in this chapter, however, is his device of reflective equilibrium which is crucially concerned with the relationship between moral theory of which justice is a part and the ordinary moral judgements which people make in society. Consideration of this device makes the theory look a good deal less foundational than it is presented here. However, this will be considered in more detail later in the book, in the final chapter, when we return to general considerations about method in moral and political philosophy.

Gewirth on agent, action and generic goods

In his two works, *Reason and Morality* and *Human Rights*,[31] Gewirth concentrates his attention on the nature of moral action and agency and what its preconditions may be thought to be. The arguments of these books have been recognized for their stringency and are currently at the forefront of argument and controversy.[32] His argument, although it has complex ramifications, none of which can really be discussed here, is basically much simpler than Rawls's very complex theoretical edifice.

Gewirth begins from an assumption which is central to liberal practical theory and indeed might be regarded as presupposed by it, namely that citizens are deliberative moral agents capable of choosing values and seeking to act upon them. So we are committed to a view of individuals as rational moral agents. However, the capacity to be a rational moral agent is not one which exists in a vacuum, it presupposes a measure of freedom and well-being, in the sense that I cannot act with deliberate rationality if my behaviour is coerced either by the intentional actions of others, or by my lack of social and economic resources. In addition, the possibility of rational agency presupposes some level of well-being which goes beyond mere physical survival – I may for example survive in a vegetative state on a respirator but my capacity for rational agency is impaired. My rational agency is not therefore a kind of disembodied capacity but requires certain kinds of goods, what Gewirth calls generic goods. These goods do not presuppose a particular conception of the good, on the contrary they are necessary conditions for an agent coming to have a theory or a conception of the good at all as a rational activity. The ideas of rational action and agency are therefore seen by Gewirth as neutral between conceptions of the good, but equally as necessary presuppositions for any pursuit of the good. In Gewirth's view these goods of freedom and well-being require life, physical integrity and mental equilibrium and these goods are denied when a person is killed, starved, physically incapacitated, terrorized or subjected to mentally deranging drugs. In addition, related to these basic goods are *non-subtractive* goods which are the abilities and conditions required for 'maintaining undiminished one's level of purpose fulfilment' – they include things such as restrictions placed upon one's projected actions, and the utilization of resources relative to these plans; and *additive* goods – that range of goods and conditions required for increasing a person's capabilities for purpose and actional fulfilment. These goods constitute the generic goods of action which, as a rational agent, I have presupposed as necessary conditions of my own activity. So whatever purposes and view of the good life each individual may have, from the standpoint of each agent the following statement is affirmed: 'My freedom and well-being are necessary goods.' As such, generic or necessary goods are neutral between particular views of the good life.

Gewirth wants to go further than this, however, beyond each agent's appreciation of the necessity of his generic goods to the view that each agent has these generic goods, and that agents have rights to such goods, rights which the state has a duty to uphold and defend. In order to establish this final proposition, the intermediate one must be grounded that each agent must admit that all other human beings have these generic goods. The argument proceeds as follows:

(a)   The only ground that every agent must accept as the sufficient justifying condition for his/her having generic goods is that he/she is a prospective agent who has purposes to be fulfilled.

(b)   It follows from this that if I have generic goods in terms of my actual or potential agency then on pain of self-contradiction I have to admit that all other actual or potential agents also have these generic goods.

(c)   (b) follows (a) by the principle of universalizability. If I have the quality X (generic goods) only in virtue of Y (my potential/actual agency) then all other potential/actual agents also have these goods.

So far then, Gewirth claims to have produced an account of generic goods which are purpose-relevant, but independent of specific purposes or concepts of the good, and these goods of freedom and well-being can be filled out in specific ways. He then wants to go on to argue that there is an equal basic right to such goods and that it is central to the legitimacy of the state that such goods are provided. At this point we shall not enter this part of the debate because it will be taken up more fully in chapter 5 on needs. The main point though, is to see why the thrust of liberal thought should be in this direction. The collapse of the project of sustaining a political community in terms of shared goals of action has led liberals to attempt to situate the basis of social cooperation in the *preconditions* of action. This point has been made particularly clearly by J. L. Mackie:

> Aristotle went wrong in thinking that moral philosophy could determine that a particular sort of activity constitutes the good for man in general ...
>
> People differ radically about the kinds of life that they choose to pursue. Even this way of putting it is misleading: in general people do not and cannot make an overall choice of a total plan of life ... I suggest that if we set out to formulate a goal based moral theory, but in identifying that goal try to take account of three factors, namely that the 'goal' must belong to the category of activity, that there is not one goal but indefinitely many diverse goals, and that they are the objects of progress (not once for all or conclusive) choices, then our theory will change insensibly into a rights based one. We shall have to take as central the right of persons progressively to choose how they shall live.[33]

The attempt to decide what is involved in this right lies at the heart of modern liberal thinking about rights and we shall return to it later in the chapter on rights in general (chapter 7). However, to take up the point made at the beginning of this chapter, we can see very clearly that while Hayek, Rawls and Gewirth see liberalism as in some way a response to moral pluralism they do not take the view that it is itself morally groundless. What they are attempting to do is to produce a definite basis for liberalism coupled with a recognition of the pervasiveness of first order moral disagreement.

As Gewirth says at the start of his project:

Different modes of resolution [of moral dissensus] are of course possible. But if a principle for one such resolution can itself be rationally justified, while other possible resolutions cannot be, then the former resolution is to some extent more correct than the latter. The inevitability of conflicts among ideals taken unqualifiedly is hence no bar to the possibility of a supreme principle that adjudicates conflicts among ideals suitably modified.[34]

Gewirth sees his own work based on trying to trace out the implications of moral agency as securing such a principle.

Dworkin: neutrality and preferences

Dworkin is perhaps the modern liberal political theorist who has grappled most with these questions and in this section I shall consider his views on three issues – neutrality and preferences, equality, and the role of the market. In all of these cases I shall be concerned primarily with how he deals with the problems of political theory in the context of moral pluralism.

Dworkin is very clear about the role of the state in a liberal society marked by moral pluralism when he argues that a liberal society must be, as far as possible, independent of any conceptions of the good life or what gives value to life. Since citizens of a society differ in these conceptions, the government does not treat them as equals if it prefers one conception to another. However, he is very clear that this principle, which he takes to be constitutive of liberalism, is not just a response to moral pluralism or moral scepticism, but is itself dependent upon equality. That is to say the neutrality of the liberal state is not the result of the contingent fact that in the modern world we find it difficult to ground, and therefore privilege in politics, a particular moral conception. On the contrary, liberal neutrality is a consequence of a more basic moral principle, namely that of treating individuals with equal concern and respect.[35] For liberalism *has* a moral foundation if it can be shown that there are cogent reasons for equality of concern and respect which leads to neutrality. If this can be seen to be a coherent principle in operation, then liberalism would have a clear moral basis, but one which was sensitive to moral diversity.

We need therefore to look first at Dworkin's account of the abstract principle of equality and the sort of justification of which it might be susceptible. In his book *A Matter of Principle* he defines the principle of equal concern and respect in the following way:

> This form of liberalism insists that government must treat people as equals in the following sense. It must impose no sacrifice or constraint on any citizen in virtue of an argument that the citizen could not accept without abandoning his sense of equal worth.[36]

On the face of it, it could be thought that such a principle looks just like the response of liberalism to moral diversity about which he is so critical, because one form of reasoning behind the principle could be that my sense of my own worth is necessarily connected to my conception of the good, my projects and my values. Hence government should not act in such a way as to pursue purposes and goals which are (a) not my own, (b) cannot be rationally grounded. However, it is clear that Dworkin would reject such an argument, just because it would reduce liberalism to a response to moral scepticism. Nor in Dworkin's view can the principle of equal concern and respect be seen as being derived from the kind of contractual argument favoured by Rawls, because in his view, as we have seen, the Rawlsian contract *presupposes* a principle of equal concern and respect and does not itself justify it. How then is this constitutive principle of liberalism to be justified in the absence of some substantive moral and political outlook? In an important article he says:

> The principle is too fundamental, I think, to admit of any defense in the usual form. It seems unlikely that it can be derived from any more general and basic principle of political morality that is more widely accepted. Nor can it be established through one or other of the methods of argument popular in political theory, for these already presuppose some particular conception of equality.[37]

Clearly from the context Dworkin has Rawls in mind in making this final comment. Additionally, the principle cannot be derived from the idea that people deserve an equal share in resources, because taking this as the basic justificatory argument would depend, presumably, upon a substantive theory of the human personality which it is part of the aim of liberalism to avoid in his view. It would 'appeal to some contingent qualities or achievements in virtue of which individuals come to deserve something they are not otherwise entitled to have and so cannot be used to justify a principle taken to be both foundational and universal'. As we have seen in both the case of Hayek and Rawls, the liberal argument about desert is difficult because both its assertion and denial seem to involve a theory of the personality. Indeed so foundational is the principle of equality of concern and respect that it cannot be derived from any antecedent theory in Dworkin's view: 'But we have no duty *prior* to equality to treat all others with equal concern and respect, and so cannot argue from such a duty to the political ideal.'[38]

So, there can be no direct argument which would provide a foundation to the principle because *it is itself foundational*. Hence the only strategy open to Dworkin, and the one which he himself takes, is to consider whether there are any plausible reasons of principle for rejecting it. He considers three such possibilities. The first is that while it matters to me that my life has a value and to you, individually, that yours has value, it does not matter for the standpoint of politics whether anyone's life is good. The second reason is based upon a partial rejection of the first, namely that while it does matter that anyone's life is good, nevertheless there are other goods too which might be compromised by programmes particularly in the welfare field whose aim is to ensure that people have the resources to make sure that other lives go well. The final counter-argument to the abstract claim of equality is that while it matters to me that my life goes well and that I have the resources to ensure this, why does it matter to me that your life goes well and that you have the resources?

The egalitarian answer to the first counter-argument in Dworkin's view is to claim that we could not construct any justification of political action – whether this is positive action as in the provision of resources, or negative in the sense of putting strict limitations on the powers of government – unless we assume that 'it is important what happens in peoples' lives'.

Dworkin's answer to the second objection is to assume that the objection itself presupposes some idea of equal concern and respect. Consider two of the forms the argument might take. The first might be that if equal concern and respect require provision of welfare to all citizens, then it might be argued that there are other values in life such as cultural achievement which could be put in jeopardy by welfare expenditure. The second might be that individuals have rights and these rights, particularly to property, might be compromised by the taxation levels required to finance the welfare programmes, which we are assuming a concern with equality requires. In the case of the first argument Dworkin trades upon the view of vicarious success, namely that there is a connection between equality and the argument for culture in the sense that if cultural considerations matter in politics it is because culture is connected to people's interests. It matters to individuals and is therefore a matter of their interests whether their lives go well or badly and these factors will be concerned with culture as much as other things: 'it matters to many people what is achieved by other members of their family, or faculty or community, or nation or even race.' In this sense, therefore, culture is connected to interests and it is precisely with the interests of each person equally that equality is concerned.

In the counter-example for the case of rights the argument is more straightforward, at least at this stage, namely we want to know what the foundations of property rights are and in Dworkin's view a theory of rights is going to be *derived* from a principle of equal concern and respect and therefore presupposes exactly the principle which the example of rights is designed to undercut. The final counter-argument in some respects reveals a good deal about Dworkin's assumptions about how liberalism does not depend upon any particular theory of the good. What might justify the claim that it matters to me how my life goes, but it does not matter to me how yours goes? His argument here is as follows:

You might want to say, for example, that it is more important how your life goes because you are a more virtuous person. But your convictions about the importance of how your life goes are too deep, too fundamental – to permit this. Your belief provides you with a reason to consider whether to be virtuous, and where virtue lies, which means that you think it important how your life goes for some reason that in this way precedes your virtue. If so, you cannot say that it is more important how you live for any reason drawn from your merit or the merit of your life, and no

other kind of reason can plausibly distinguish you from anyone
else who has a life to lead.[39]

In this sense Dworkin affirms a point made by Rawls, which is central
to the liberal project in political theory and is to be found implicitly in
Gewirth too, namely that the self is prior to the ends which are chosen
by it and in this sense, because the self can be detached from its virtues
and goals, it cannot be the case that the life to be led by self X is
intrinsically more important than the life to be led by self Y because
that judgement can only be made in terms of particular "thick" goals
and values and this judgement has to be avoided at the political level.

Having therefore argued that the principle of equal concern and
respect cannot be given a direct foundation, but is to be found presupposed even in these arguments which seek to refute it, Dworkin goes
on to discuss the political and institutional consequences of taking the
principle of equality as the constitutive value of liberalism. Government
cannot treat its citizens as moral equals if its policies are based upon
some particular conception of the good life which some of its citizens
do not share, or some conception of human nature which might mean
that some citizens are inherently more deserving than others, perhaps
for example because of their racial characteristics. Given that this is the
constitutive principle of liberalism, what follows in institutional terms,
and in particular in terms of the distribution of the products which the
cooperative work of the community produces? These institutions have
to be compatible with different theories of the good and of what gives
value to life. One solution to the problem of equality of respect in this
context of disagreement is the market. In an efficient market, a price for
a product will be generated that reflects the opportunity costs of raw
materials, labour and capital; this in turn will determine for the *con-
sumer* how much his resources should be debited; it provides for the
producer a measure of how much should be credited to his account 'for
his choice of productive activity over leisure, and for one activity rather
than another'. Dworkin concludes that:

> If people start with equal amounts of wealth, and have roughly
> equal levels of raw skill, then a market allocation would ensure
> that no one could properly complain that he had less than others
> over his whole life. He could have had the same as they if he had

made the decisions to consume, save or work that they did.[40]

This is very abstract, so it is as well to be clear about the alternatives it rules out of court. Under planned allocation these decisions would reflect the personal moral beliefs of planners, beliefs that for the liberal ought not to influence policy decisions which should not be influenced by one conception of the good rather than another.

There is therefore in Dworkin's view a good reason in principle for seeing the market as reflecting preferences and being a neutral mechanism for distributing costs and benefits in an impersonal way in the light of the preferences so revealed. As Dworkin argues, however, the liberal has to accept that this idealized picture of the market is deeply flawed because the preferences involved in the market reflect antecedently existing conditions such as an unequal distribution of talent and ability, an unequal distribution of wealth, and special needs, for example, of the handicapped. Preferences do not reveal in a straightforward way the conceptions of the good life which people have. These conceptions will be deeply influenced by these antecedent conditions and thus what people value and prefer will depend upon what they take to be possible for themselves against the background of these other conditions. On the one hand the market is sensitive to preferences and conceptions of the good, but at the same time these preferences and effective demand reflect pre-existing inequalities of labour, wealth, opportunity and inheritance. A liberal commitment to equality will require some degree of redistribution and a set of welfare rights which will secure a fairer basis for preferences to be expressed in the market. The question then arises as to whether there is a scheme of redistribution which can itself be neutral between conceptions of the good. That is to say, are there principles of social justice which can be used to constrain the market and ensure a more equal distribution of the preferences expressed in the market, which is still the best mechanism, for reasons already outlined, for dealing with expressed preferences in a neutral way? In Dworkin's view there is and it turns upon the idea that some differences between human beings which are often taken as a basis for distribution are morally irrelevant; for example, the distribution of talent which is in some sense arbitrary and should not be allowed to influence individual life chances to the degree that it does. In Dworkin's view the liberal 'therefore considers that those who have less talent, as the market judges talent, have a right to some form of redistribution in the name of justice'.[41]

A system of redistribution which compensates for morally irrelevant differences such as talent will enable the preferences of the less talented to be given much more equal weight in the market. How then does this argument proceed, and can it be defended without references to some specific conception of the good or some substantive theory of the human personality, both of which are illegitimate for the liberal point of view? That is to say in this specific case, is it possible to defend a system of redistribution as a form of political right without reference to some conception of the political good? We have already met this problem in the case of Rawls and it is necessary now to look very briefly at Dworkin's own solution to the problem. In the essay on 'Liberalism' Dworkin seems to take the view, which Rawls also takes, that the inequalities which redistribution should rectify are those which are morally arbitrary and these include the genetic distribution of talent, special needs such as physical handicap, skill or luck, and inheritance. To some extent these points are summed up in the sentence:

> It is obviously obnoxious to the liberal conception, for example, that someone should have more of what the community as a whole has to distribute because he or his father had superior skill or luck.[42]

So it looks as though redistribution will seek to compensate for these inequalities, which are the result of arbitrary factors, based upon luck, and these factors are to include talent and skill. However, the problem which Dworkin faces in this context is the extent to which the claim that the initial distribution of talent, ability and skills can be regarded as arbitrary without presupposing a particular moral standpoint and without invoking, however tacitly, a particular theory of the personality – both features from which liberalism should be independent in Dworkin's view. A theory about the arbitrary nature of the possession and exercise of talent and skill might be thought to engage both of these considerations. While of course it might be readily agreed that talents and skills do depend to a great extent on an initial genetic endowment for which an individual can claim no responsibility, and that they are nurtured in a family and an educational setting which again is not the individual's responsibility, nevertheless to argue that such talents are not part of the individual's responsibility at all would seem to require a highly debatable theory of the personality in which personal qualities played little or no part.

Dworkin draws a distinction between endowment and ambition. A scheme of egalitarian redistribution has to be ambition-sensitive, that is to say, it has to allow for individuals to *develop* their talents and capacities, even though this may result in inequalities, and the market is the mechanism for achieving this; but the principle is not to be 'endowment-sensitive', that is to say, reward people purely in view of their *being* more talented, because these are arbitrary from the moral point of view, presumably because the individual is not responsible for them and therefore no claim for desert can be made upon these. The distinction between endowment and ambition leads Dworkin to put the point thus:

> The distinction required by equality of resources is the distinction between those beliefs and attitudes that define what a successful life would be like, which the ideal (i.e. of equality of resources) assigns to the person, and these features of body or mind or personality that provide means or impediment to that success, which the ideal assigns to the person's circumstances.[43]

Talents, skills and physical and natural handicaps fall into this second category, but it is very difficult to see how this distinction can be developed so that my skills and talents become part of my circumstances without some rather specific theory of the personality which liberalism is supposed to eschew – it does not in Dworkin's own words depend upon 'any special theory of the personality'. However, the distinction between those features of human life which are ascribed to a person and his/her preferences and those which are ascribed to circumstance, particularly when the latter involves differential talents, does seem to require such a special and controversial theory of the personality and in the light of that, what responsibility a person does or does not bear for talent and what claims to desert can be made on the basis of these. Dworkin tries to handle this sort of question by the idea of luck and an insurance market. For example, we would normally see our sexual preferences as part of what we are as a person rather than as a matter of unavoidable circumstance, but if these preferences, as in the case of homosexuality for example, are seen by the homosexual as disadvantages, then it might be thought that these should be classified under circumstances rather than choice. If so, then they could be the sorts of things which might be thought to be accidental and therefore the sorts of things which could intelligibly be thought to be capable of being insured against. Clearly my preferences are not accidental nor are they things which merely happen to me, and it would make no sense to think of insuring against having certain preferences; however handicaps or negative endowments are different, and a case could be made for thinking of those risks as insurable.

Hence the idea of a hypothetical insurance market is used to distinguish between preferences and ambitions which belong to me as a person, as an agent and chooses those other features of life which are seen as accidental and circumstantial and in this way we may avoid the view that the distinction between the self and its wants, preferences and ambitions on the one hand, and circumstances on the other, cannot be drawn in a neutral way, because they would have to invoke some specific theory of the personality. However, this project seems very implausible, partly because it is such a highly imaginary construction and it is much more direct to assume that the distinction between preferences and circumstances should be made much more in terms of a theory of personality, whatever problems this may pose for liberalism which seems to eschew such a theory.

The final aspect of Dworkin's view about how liberalism can be given a strong theoretical base without presupposing a conception of the good or a particular theory of the personality which I want to consider is the claim made by some critics that the neutral state plus redistribution, and equality of resources, coupled with the market economy in fact *favours* some values against others and thus cannot, in fact, vindicate its claim to be neutral. This point has been put very strongly by W. E. Connolly in *Appearance and Reality in Politics*:

> One might wish to live in a society where the extended family provides identity, security and subsistence for its members; but extensive labour mobility which is indispensable to the operation of a market economy, is inconsistent with such a way of life. One may wish to participate in a public life governed by shared religious

beliefs and principles, but the separation of church and state, must of course, nullify that possibility. One might wish to decrease the consumption of those goods oriented merely to oneself or one's family unit (e.g. cars and private homes) and increase those consumed in common with a larger collectivity (mass transit and housing collectivities); goods of the first set may be more compatible with a competitive market economy than goods of the second source especially if the market tends to undermine the durability of collective units needed to house the latter purchase.[44]

A rather similar argument is to be found in Richard Titmuss's *The Gift Relationship* in which Titmuss[45] argues that I may prefer to give my blood, but that the value and identity of my gift is somehow infringed if alongside a voluntary donor system there is a market in blood. I might therefore have preferences which cannot coexist with other people's preferences for other ways of life.

However, these arguments are not cogent objections to liberal neutrality as they stand, because Dworkin has tried to develop counterarguments in *Taking Rights Seriously* and he has done this through the notion of *internal* and *external* preferences. A personal preference refers to my own enjoyment of some goods or opportunities; an external preference is a preference for the assignment or the denial of goods or opportunities to others. In Dworkin's view it is illegitimate to count external preferences in political decision-making and this is so, as it seems for two reasons. The first is that to count external preferences is to indulge in a form of *double counting* in the sense that my own personal preferences and my external preferences are counted. The second is that to count my external preferences given that they relate to you and your goods and opportunities, is not to treat you as an object of equal concern and respect because *my* judgement about *your* goods is being weighed along with yours – this is inherently paternalist.

It is very important to appreciate exactly why Dworkin resorts to this device of distinguishing between internal and external preferences. If he is to be consistent in his liberalism, he cannot discount one set of preferences in terms of their *objects*, for example, if I wanted to live in an all-white society, because this would presuppose some substantive view of the good. If preferences are to be discounted it must be in terms of either a formal procedure – as in the idea of double counting – or in terms of a foundational value such as equal concern and respect which he sees as antecedent to other conceptions of the good.

The issues at stake here for the coherence of liberal theory are very deep. If we adopt what might be called a subjective view of the good which may be based, as we saw in the first chapter, on a philosophical critique of moral realism and objectivity, or which may just embody sociological reflection on the diversity of values in a modern developed society, then in politics it would seem that government should only value what individuals themselves value if it is to be neutral over conceptions of the good. To rule out one set of preferences or certain aspects of preferences a priori either has to depend upon a theory about what good or appropriate preferences are, and this is inconsistent with liberalism, or, alternatively, has to rule out some preferences on procedural rather than substantive moral grounds.

Some liberal theorists, notably Albert Weale,[46] have seemed to suggest that the issue can be solved within a morally subjectivist position without recourse to Dworkin's procedural response in terms of double counting. This argument proceeds as follows. We can imagine two sorts of external preferences. There can be altruistic preferences – supportive preferences where A, in addition to preferences about his own life, also has preferences in regard to B's life *which B also has* and which make a claim to be counted politically. At the opposite extreme, there can be negative or hostile external preferences, where A has preferences about his own life but also a hostile preference for B and his preferences.

Both of these positions can be illustrated with reference to proposals to reform the law on issues of personal morality. Let us assume in both the case of altruistic and hostile preferences that B is a homosexual and that there is at the moment a repressive homosexual law which prohibits sexual acts between homosexuals. In the case of altruistic preferences A (who is heterosexual) has an altruistic external preference for B: that is, he would like homosexuals to be able to indulge in the sexual practices of their taste and this is also B's preference for himself. In the case of a hostile external preference A wants to maintain the legal sanction against private homosexual acts.

If we were to adopt the double counting reason proposed by Dworkin for ruling out external preferences of any sort both altruistic or hostile, then if homosexuals, i.e. all the B's in society, were in a small minority, and government could only counter internal preferences, then since the reform of the law would only be an internal preference for the *B* group, it is difficult to see how the law in a liberal society which discounted external preferences on procedural grounds would ever be reformed. At the same time this would be rather paradoxical because the liberal state is supposed to be as neutral as possible between conceptions of the good. Of course Dworkin's obvious counter-argument here would be that the initial existence of the law is illegitimate because it involves antecedently counted external preferences on the part of those who wished to prohibit homosexuality. However, is there any other way of dealing with the issue without recourse to the idea of double counting which at the same time does not involve taking a particular stand on the conception of the good?

This issue has an importance outside Dworkin's own particular concerns and has exercised other liberal theorists of a more utilitarian persuasion, the basis of whose views will be discussed in the next chapter. For example, Samuel Brittan argues in *The Role and Limits of Government*[47] that government should disregard what he calls 'negative interdependence effects', that is, in his view, those external preferences which have a negative impact on liberty. If these are not discounted, then Brittan argues they will yield results which are incompatible with liberal theory. However, in saying this Brittan seems to come very close to saying that it is not the *externality* of the preference which is objectionable, but its *content* and this, it might be thought, involves taking a stand on a particular conception of the good. This may seem cogent on its own terms, but if it is accepted, it would seem to undermine at least an element in the liberal assumption that if preferences are to be discounted it should be in terms of a formal procedure rather than a judgement about the moral content of the preference.

The same point comes out very clearly in Harsanyi's contribution to Sen and Williams's book *Utilitarianism and Beyond*[48] in which he argues in favour of excluding what he calls antisocial or in the terminology above, hostile preferences, such as sadism, envy, resentment and malice. Again, the argument seems to be in terms of the *content* of the preferences rather than the form and Sen seems clearly right when he says that 'the motive for these exclusions seems to be a simple moral one, not to be captured by any formal constraint on the preference in question'.[49] Weale, however, develops an interesting argument which is rather different from Dworkin's double counting argument, but comes closer to his less developed idea about equality of concern and respect in relation to external preferences. Whereas Dworkin seems to be in favour of discounting *all* external preferences, both supportive and hostile because to count them would be double counting, Weale develops an argument for claiming that supportive preferences can be counted and hostile ones discounted in a way which does still embody a formal rather than a substantive moral principle and can thus be consistent in the liberal assumptions. If we combine the principles of equality of respect with a subjective theory of the good, it would seem that supportive preferences *can* be counted politically if A's supportive preference for B's interests accurately reflect B's own views of his interests. If all A is doing is helping to further B's projects and conception of the good A is *not* claiming the superiority of his view of the good over B's, which would be inconsistent with liberal assumptions. Of course, if A's preferences for B are not in fact in B's view in his interests, then this would be a claim on the part of A to have a superior view of B's good than B has. This would be an exercise of unjustified moral paternalism (at least if B is an adult), which is inconsistent with liberal views. However, in Weale's view hostile preferences can be discounted when they are held one sidedly by A against B because this would simply mean that A's view of the good is superior to B's and this would be incompatible with liberal assumptions about the factors which can count in public policy.

This approach seems to me more consistent with a liberal approach than the radical discounting of external preferences on the basis of double counting endorsed by Dworkin. It should be noted, however, that Dworkin argues that the best way to deal with external preferences is in fact to secure a set of rights embodying a principle of equal concern and respect which will act as trumps against any attempt to maximize welfare, counting external preferences.

Nozick: the entitlement theory of justice

In the final part of this chapter I want to consider some of the salient aspects of the work of Robert Nozick whose *Anarchy, State and Utopia* presents a fundamental challenge to the liberal theory of justice as found in Rawls, Dworkin and Gewirth and whose views, although very different from Hayek's, take us back rather more in that direction.

As we shall see, his theory raises deep problems about the nature of rights in general and the nature of property and there will be themes to take up in subsequent chapters, but again the same issues will arise: is it possible to develop a theory of rights without a specific account of the human personality and its purposes, and is it possible to develop a theory of property rights which does not presuppose some conception of the human good?

Nozick's theory of justice is based upon a conception of rights that in turn embody a view about the nature of human inviolability. Whereas in Rawls and Dworkin's theories justice was seen as a kind of end state, a particular pattern of social arrangements which would embody the claims of social justice, adjusting entitlements and resources according to the demands of the favoured principles which were supposed to be derived in as neutral a way as possible, Nozick's theory is almost the reverse of this. On Nozick's view individuals have rights which put constraints on how they may be treated without their consent. These rights and the constraints which they embody are not there to produce some further good, but are rather fundamental and should be respected whatever putative good might accrue to society by infringing such rights. Justice is not a matter of trying to organize society so that its institutions seek to achieve a distributive pattern such as 'From each according to their ability, to each according to their needs', but rather of respecting basic rights which as I have said limit what may be done to someone without consent, and the entitlements which such rights yield. In Nozick's view these rights are so fundamental and the constraints which they impose upon the actions of others are so strong that only a minimal state is justified, that is to say one which, as in Hayek, eschews any attempt to procure distributive justice. The type of state which would embody social justice is in fact incompatible with individual rights.

In order to make the discussion of this important book manageable I shall concentrate on those themes which are most important to the general theme of this chapter, namely the account of the functions of the state which appears most compatible with liberal, or in Nozick's view libertarian, values. Hence, I shall discuss the nature of rights in Nozick, how these relate to entitlement, his rejection of patterned and end state theories of justice and his own account of justice in acquisition, transfer and rectification. Nozick is insistent upon placing the right before the good in politics. He rejects entirely the position that what is right, or what one should or ought to do, can be defined in terms of producing good or the greatest good; the opposite is the case for Nozick, but there is no case for infringing rights in order to produce the greatest good. We need now to look into the basis of this claim together with the theory of the state and government to which it leads.

One basic problem is that Nozick does not give much of an argument in favour of his view of rights that place an absolute constraint upon what may be done to individuals, particularly by the state:

> Individuals have rights, and there are things no person or group may do to them (without violating their rights). So strong and far reaching are these rights that they raise the question of what, if anything, the state and its officials may do. How much room do individual rights leave for the state.[50]

These rights are clearly basic for Nozick, but equally there is no very clear argument for them, but he does refer to a range of considerations which in his view point in the direction of accepting what he takes to be rights as basic. There are two major interrelated considerations here. The first is the idea of respect for persons or inviolability; the second is what Nozick calls the fact of our separate existence. The non-violation of rights as a side constraint upon action reflects what Nozick calls the Kantian principle of inviolability or respect for persons, that individuals should be treated as ends in themselves and never as means to the ends of others. In Nozick's view what accounts for this liberal principle is just the fact of our separate existences. There is no value outside of individual human life. There is no good for an individual which goes beyond his view of his good whether this good is the good of others or some transcendental background of good which is supposed to make demands upon us. Each individual life has value for that individual and this is all that the human good can consist in. It follows from this in his view that there can be no moral balancing act between individuals, so that the good of one individual can be outweighed by that of others as of society:

> there is no social entity with a good that undergoes some sacrifices for its own good. There are only individual people, different

individual people with their own individual lives. Using one of these people for the benefit of others uses time and benefits the others. Nothing more.[51]

The idea of basic moral rights is based upon these considerations – they articulate in detail at least in the political realm what is required by the principle of inviolability; they express certain ways in which individuals may not use others and the side constraints involved are those which prohibit the violation of rights:

> This root idea, namely that there are different individuals with separate lives and so no one may be sacrificed for others, underlies the existence of moral side constraints.[52]

Because what is valuable in the world relates only to individual lives and not to some transcendental, metaphysical or social background or entity, it follows in Nozick's view that there can be no moral basis for someone to infringe the moral space of someone else without his or her consent. Such rights are basically concerned with non-aggression, with not killing, assaulting, interfering, coercing etc. That is to say, they are negative rights and the corresponding side constraints require that other individuals refrain from doing certain things, even, as we have seen, if they are done in the name of some social or national good. No one, private individual or government, has a right to force an individual to make any kind of sacrifice for the social good and the state must be neutral between its citizens. Nozick argues that these issues are related to the idea of the meaning of life, that it is possibly the capacity to shape one's life with one's own values that gives meaning to life and this is why the idea of inviolability is important and why the rights which define the nature of this inviolability are so central in Nozick's view.

   For Nozick most contemporary theories of social or distributive justice are incompatible with such rights in that they involve continual interference in and coercion of individuals. As Nozick sees it, most theories of social justice, such as distribution according to need or ability, are patterned principles, that is to say, the distribution of goods and services, benefits and burdens in society is thought to be just if the current pattern of distribution fits the formula, whether it be distribution according to need or desert. The question of justice is a matter of comparing contemporary holdings at a current time slice with the appropriate structural formulae, irrespective of how that distribution has *arisen* and whether in the processes of acquisition of property and income and through the processes of production people have acquired rights in what has been produced. This points to the contrast which is central to Nozick's work and to his conception of the relationship between justice and rights, between historical principles of justice and end state views of justice which embody a particular distributive formula. In Nozick's view the only theory of justice which is compatible with moral rights and the side constraints which have been mentioned is a historical one which is backward looking in that it sees the question of justice not in terms of whether a particular distribution of goods conforms to a formula, but rather how it came about, because it is only in this way that rights in acquisition, production, exchange and transfer can be recognized and protected. If we adopt a formula or patterned principle of justice this may well involve a sanction to infringe rights of ownership in order to bring the pattern of distribution of goods and services into line with the requirements of the formula:

> In contrast to end results principles of justice, historical principles of justice hold that past circumstances or actions of people can create differential entitlements or differential deserts to things.[53]

and:

> Whoever makes something having bought or contracted for all other held resources used in the process, is ... entitled to it. The situation is *not* one of something's getting made, and there being an open question of who is going to get it. Things come into the world already attached to people having entitlements over them.[54]

How does this sharp distinction between patterned or end state theories of justice on the one hand and historical or entitlement theories on the other relate to the earlier argument about rights? There are at least two aspects of the answer to this question which are important at this point: an argument about how liberty upsets any patterned principle of justice, and in more general terms a theory about rights and entitlements.

If we seek to impose on the distribution of resources in society a particular pattern, such as 'From each according to his ability, to each according to his needs,' then in Nozick's view the maintenance of that pattern will not be compatible with individual liberty. How could the pattern be maintained over time if people were allowed to transfer, exchange, give gifts, leave bequests and so on. All these actions will result in distributions which diverge from the approved pattern. To maintain the pattern, one would either have to prevent such actions or alternatively to intervene continuously to restore to the pattern the distributional 'distortions' which had occurred and the result of such free actions of transfer, donation and bequest. In either case the attempt to preserve a pattern will mean continual and illegitimate interference in people's lives and liberty in a way that is ruled out by the earlier points about rights.

However, before this last part of the argument will work, it has to be shown that Nozick's theory of rights does lead to entitlements of the strong and inviolable sort for which he has argued. What makes the interferences alluded to above immoral in Nozick's view is that they constitute an *illegitimate* interference with peoples' lives, but to show this he has to demonstrate the link between rights and entitlements which such interventions would undermine. The issue at stake here is actually much broader than Nozick's own treatment of it because any market based system of the sort that Nozick supports has to be concerned with property rights and their basis in the sense that in a market goods and services to which property rights are asserted are bought and sold, but in this sense the market only transfers property rights between individuals. Unless these property rights can be given some principled basis, then there could be an argument in favour of their political redistribution. Hayek, for example, gives no account of this. He accepts property rights and the inequalities which flow from these as given and he does not seek to justify them except to assume that existing property is probably held by those with the best opportunities to make use of it for the benefit of society as a whole. If, however, and argued earlier, the position of the worst off in a market could be foreseen, then if the better off have no principled basis to their goods, the redistribution in the interests of social justice could become legitimate. In this sense therefore Nozick's theory is much more thoroughgoing than Hayek's and the issue of property rights becomes very acute. So, how do Nozick's ideas about human inviolability relate to issues of property rights.

There are three crucial strands to the argument: the relationship between inviolability and the idea of self-ownership, the idea of self-ownership and property acquisition, and finally the relationship between an individual's ownership of property and others in the sense of how does my acquisition of property relate to the rights of other persons.

In Nozick's view, following the work of John Locke in the seventeenth century, each person owns his own body and the labour which consists of physical movements of his body; in 'mixing my labour which I own, with unowned resources I establish a property right in those resources as long as in doing so I do not in some sense worsen the situation of others'. If all of these arguments go through, this leads to a full theory of property rights and one which would legitimize unequal holdings of property at the stage of acquisition, and that these unequally acquired holdings can be traded in a free market and the unequal consequences of such transactions would be legitimate whether these inequalities were foreseeable or not.

> A distribution is just if it arises from another just distribution by legitimate means. The legitimate means of moving from one distribution to another are specified by the principle of justice in transfer. The legitimate 'first moves' are specified by the principles of justice in acquisition.[55]

So the question of whether a particular distribution is just depends upon how it came about and this inevitably takes us back to the question of the legitimate acquisition of resources.

In Nozick's view if persons are inviolable or if we seek to treat them as ends in themselves, then they have clear property rights in their own bodies. That is to say that I am able to use my capacities and powers both physical and mental as I choose so long as in using them I do not treat others as means or use my powers in an aggressive way against them. Any other alternative in which others are able to direct how I should use my powers and to the pursuit of which purposes would give others a kind of property right in my own person:

> If people force you to do certain work or unrewarded work for a certain period of time, they decide what you are to do and what purposes your work is to secure apart from you decisions. This

process whereby they take this decision from you makes them a part owner of you. Just as having such a partial control and power of decision by right over an animal or an inanimate object would be to have a property right in it.[56]

If a person is inviolable, then he has an absolute property right in his own person, his powers and capacities and in his labour, which consists of physical movements in his body. Given this point, Nozick next has to explain how using my powers and capacities through my labour I can come to have a private, unquestionable property right in unowned things. Nozick's answer here is a variation of Locke's labour theory of property – that it is the action of *mixing my labour* with unowned goods that yields the idea of a property right in those goods.

Nozick's arguments on this point are quite difficult to assess because in the course of his discussion of the Lockean theory which he endorses, he brings forward some cogent and amusing objections to Locke's theory which he then proceeds to ignore. The central issue to be addressed here is this: the argument runs as follows:[57]

(a)   Human beings are inviolable.
(b)   Inviolable persons own their persons and their labour.
(c)   Person *A* mixes his labour which he owns with *X* which is unowned.
(d)   *A* has a property right in *X*.

Assuming that there is a clear line of argument from (a) to (c), how do we get from (c) to (d)? On Locke's view it is because of some kind of incorporation of *X* into *A* through the process of labour. In some cases, this incorporation is exact and literal, as it would be in the case of using an animal for food as in Locke's own example of how the venison nourishes the 'Wild Indian'. In killing and eating the animal, the hunter incorporates it into himself and this becomes part of himself and on the argument about self-ownership, part of his property. However, most property is not literally incorporation of the unowned resource into oneself. Locke wants to argue that it is mixing one's labour with the thing which is analogous to incorporation. In a famous passage Locke describes this process whereby something which I undeniably own, my person and my labour, can give me a property right in that which I mix my labour with. Hence:

every man has a property in his own person. This nobody has any
right to but himself. The labour of his body and the work of his
hands, we may say are properly his. Whatsoever, then he removes
out of the state that nature has provided and left it in, he has mixed
his labour with it and joined it to something that is his own, and
thereby makes it his property.[58]

This argument as it stands, however, is not sufficient to justify the
idea that mixing labour creates a single property right in something.
Nozick is very good at specifying the sharp questions which can be
asked about this argument. They are as follows:

1   What are the boundaries of what labour is mixed with? We only
    labour on parts of objects. Why does mixing labour entail a right in
    the whole of the object?
2   Why does mixing my labour which I own with something which I
    do not own, lead me to own the thing rather than losing what I
    own, as opposed to gaining what I don't?
3   Why should mixing one's labour with something entitle you to the
    whole of that thing as opposed to the added value which one's
    labour has created. If my labour adds to the value of something I
    might certainly be thought to have a right to that added value, but
    why do I have a right to the total object rather than the added value?

Nozick raises these questions about the idea of mixing labour with
something leading to a property right, but he does not try to answer
them and in fact moves on to discuss the proviso that my original
acquisition of property should not worsen the position of others, or in
Locke's famous phrase, leaves as much and as good for others. The
reason why he moves on to this issue seems fairly clear. Given the
difficulties involved in the transition from A mixing his labour with X,
to A owns X, it then might seem plausible to argue that attention should
be moved to the question of how anyone could object to this move, and
in Nozick's view the only ground for objection is that in coming to own
X A worsens the position of others. To use his own example, if I
appropriate a grain of sand from Coney Island, leaving aside the question
of mixing my labour with it, the only real objection to my appropriating
it is whether it worsens the condition of others, which in his view it
clearly does not. So attention moves away from the metaphysical issue

of whether labour creates a property right by some mysterious process to the question of whether this appropriation worsens the position of others. If it does not, there can be no objection to the assertion of my property right however obscure the metaphysical basis of that might be.

So the problem becomes, does a system of private property rights worsen the position of others when there are few if any unowned resources in the world left to appropriate? In Nozick's view the proviso that property acquisition should not worsen the position of others can be understood in two ways:

1   It could be that as the result of my acquisition other people can no longer acquire that sort of property and those sort of resources.
2   It could mean that while others can no longer appropriate, they can still have access to and use those resources.

That is to say, is the position of others worsened if they are unable to appropriate, or if they are unable to satisfy their needs in relation to those resources? This second interpretation is the one proposed by Nozick and he argues that 'no one can legitimately complain if the weaker provision is satisfied'. The reason why Nozick takes this view is that while a system of private property rights may well mean that others have no longer the right to appropriate they can still benefit from being excluded from such ownership because private property will yield all sorts of advantages even to those excluded from the possibility of appropriation and according to the weaker criterion therefore their position will not be worsened and therefore no basic right is violated. The reasons why Nozick takes this view are the result of what he takes to be the beneficial effects of private ownership, which he argues are as follows:

1   Private ownership increases the overall social product by putting resources into the hands of those who can use them most efficiently and profitably.
2   Private ownership encourages experimentation because with separate persons controlling resources, there is no one person or small group whom someone with a new idea must convince to try it out.
3   Private property leads to expertise in risk bearing because such a system requires that each person should bear the costs of the risks they bear in business.

4   It protects future generations by leading some to hold back resources from current assumption for future markets.
5   It provides protection for unpopular persons in the labour market because in a private property system there are many different sources of employment.

In Nozick's view, therefore, a free market and the private ownership of resources will not run against the Lockean proviso so long as the proviso is understood as being that the position of others no longer at liberty to use the thing is thereby worsened. It will already be clear how close Nozick is here to Hayek's claim that the private market is superior to other forms of social organization because of the trickle down effect, or the benefit that all will receive over time in absolute terms from the operation of the twin institutions of private property and free markets. This argument is crucial to the defence of free markets as opposed to state redistribution. Indeed, as with much else in liberalism this argument too goes back to Locke when he argued in the *Second Treatise* that the day labourer in England is better off than the king in an American tribe. There may, of course, be more inequality in England than in the tribe, but what matters is not inequality, but the level of basic welfare. In the view of Nozick and Hayek following Locke the poor are better off in a private property/free market society than they would be under any other alternative and in Nozick's view this satisfies the requirement for the legitimacy of private appropriation, coupled with the fact that any other alternative – say, a state-directed system of redistribution and social justice – would violate rights and inviolability.

It should be made clear, however, that Nozick is not offering this argument as a utilitarian justification of a market structure as opposed to a socialist one. Rather the argument is designed to show that those who do not own property and are excluded from the opportunity of doing so by initial acts of appropriation cannot complain that their rights have been infringed.[59] This would be a legitimate argument only if their position had been worsened. However, the argument above is designed to show that under a private property and free market regime their position under the weak version of the Lockean proviso will not be worsened and will be better than it would be under any other alternative.

The important point at the moment, however, is the conclusions which Nozick draws from all these arguments about the proper role of the state in society. It is clearly not the function of the state to seek to secure some patterned or end state principles of social justice such that the goods and services in society should be distributed according to need or desert. Given the cogency, in his view, of the idea of rights to initial acquisitions then goods which are transferred from one person to another in market exchanges, or in what he calls 'capitalist acts between consenting adults', which are based upon legitimate property rights and entitlements, are justly transferred, donated, traded or bequeathed and any attempt by the state to impose on the result of such exchanges freely arrived at based upon legitimate rights would be incompatible with the basic rights which we have as persons, embodying as these rights do a sense of the separateness of our existence and our inviolability as persons. Compulsory state redistribution of resources to meet concerns of patterned principles of social justice is incompatible with individual rights. So the poor and the needy do not have any *rights* to welfare or to any particular set of resources. Of course, individuals may choose as an act of generosity, altruism, humanity or philanthropy to transfer their justly held property to those who are worse off than themselves, or they can choose to join groups or communes which go in for pooling and redistributing resources, but this is a matter for individual choice and not for the state. Justice for Nozick, therefore, is a matter of *how* a particular distribution came about, whether property was acquired justly and whether it was transferred freely and not whether a particular outcome satisfies some structural principle such as the claim of the need or desert. To argue this latter case would be equivalent to giving the needy and deserving property rights in the resources of others which, because of the relationship between property and labour, would be equivalent to giving these property rights in the actions and thus the persons of others. As he says, 'patterned principles of distributive justice involve appropriating the actions of other persons.'

Of course, there can be injustices. Property may have been acquired coercively and in a way that has worsened the position of others or transfers of property may have been compelled, and in these circumstances rectification of injustices is possible. Indeed, Nozick goes so far as to argue that since we lack the historical information to make informed judgements about these matters in the world as it is now, then some kind of attempt such as Rawls's difference principle might be legitimate to adapt as a kind of rule of thumb in relation to redefining the consequences of likely injustices in the past:

> Lacking much historical information and assuming (1) that victims of injustice generally do worse than they otherwise would and (2) that those from the least well off group in society have the highest probabilities of being the (descendants of) victims of the most serious injustice who are owed compensation from those who have benefited from the injustices (assumed to be those better off ...) then a *rough* rule of thumb for redefining injustices might seem to be the following: organise society so as to maximise the position of whatever group ends up least well off in society.[60]

On this basis an extensive state could be justified at least in the short run to rectify past injustices but this will be in the short run; 'although to introduce socialism as the punishment for our sins would be to go too far, past injustices might be so great as to make necessary in the short run a more extensive state in order to rectify them.'[61] However, this root and branch rectification is not to occur afresh in each generation because this would require a more extensive state which continually interferes with property rights. It is a once for all rectification to take society back to a kind of approximation to a past starting point after which only specific injustices in acquisition and transfer would be justified. Subsequent generations would inherit the consequences of previous acquisitions and transfers of holdings made by their pre-decessors except in cases in which these acquisitions or transfers trans-gressed the principles of justice in acquisition or transfer. The mere fact that for future generations this would yield sharp inequalities in holdings is no justification for seeking to iron out such inequalities unless they are the direct result of previous injustices.

Hence for Nozick there can be no grounds for interfering in rights which embody a source of inviolability in the interests of our conception of the human good or human welfare. Again the theory of right grounds claims which come before that of the good. As such Nozick's theory denies that it is the job of the political community to articulate any particular concept of the human good. Human goods in his view are so diverse that there is not just one way of life or one hierarchy of human goods which can meet the diverse range of goods which people have.

Hence not one community will serve as the ideal for all people. Rather in Nozick's view it is important to devise a framework within which individuals can be free to join with others or not, as the case may be, in advancing their conceptions of the good, and only this framework, which is not teleocratic at the state level, can possibly be consistent with the side constraints which rights yield. So the claims of the good, or a specific version of the good community or the good state, cannot override individual rights just because of the inherent diversity of human goods which is again a reflection of the facts of our separate existence. To require individuals to live their lives according to a specific conception of the good, therefore, is not compatible with the separateness of persons and the values which this entails and it would not be compatible with respecting persons as ends to require them to do so.

Nozick's theory is also incompatible with a naturalistic theory of politics which sees the role of the state as meeting human needs. This is so for two reasons: that an account of basic human needs is itself likely to embody a particular theory of the good, and partly because to have the state meeting needs would itself involve modifying property rights if A has a legitimate entitlement to what B needs. In order to pursue this question in more detail we have to turn in a later chapter to an examination of the claims of need in politics. For the moment, however, I want to move to discuss another issue, namely utilitarianism which seeks to reassert the priority of the good over the right in politics and in a sense is the counterpoint to all the arguments discussed in this chapter.

Notes

1   A. MacIntyre, *After Virtue*, 2nd edn, Duckworth, London, 1985, p. 156.
2   R. Dworkin, *A Matter of Principle*, Harvard University Press, Cambridge, Mass., 1985, p. 203.
3   Ibid.
4   J. Rawls, *A Theory of Justice*, The Clarendon Press, Oxford, 1972, p. 130.
5   B. Ackerman, *Social Justice in the Liberal State*, Yale University Press, New Haven, Conn., 1980, p. 361.
6   R. Wollheim, 'Crime, Sin and Mr Justice Devlin', *Encounter*, 13, 1959, p. 38.

7   J. Gray, 'On the Contestability of Social and Political Concepts', *Political Theory*, 5, 1977, p. 335.
8   J. Raz, 'Liberalism, Autonomy and the Politics of Neutral Concern', *Midwest Studies in Philosophy*, 7, 1982.
9   Dworkin, *Matter of Principle*, p. 191.
10 I. Berlin, *Four Essays On Liberty*, The Clarendon Press, Oxford, 1969, p. 172.
11 Ackerman, *Social Justice*, p. 368.
12 D. Hume, *An Inquiry Concerning the Principles of Morals*, quoted in F. A. von Hayek, *Law, Legislation and Liberty*, vol. 1, Routledge, London, 1973, p. 113.
13 I. Kant, *The Metaphysical Elements of Justice*, ed. and trans. J. Ladd, Bobbs Merril, Indianapolis, 1965, passim.
14 F. A. von Hayek, *Law, Legislation and Liberty*, vol 2, Routledge, London, 1976, p. 65.
15 J. Gray, *Hayek on Liberty*, Blackwell, Oxford, 1984, p. 73.
16 Ibid.
17 Hayek, *Law, Legislation and Liberty*, vol. 2, p. 69.
18 Ibid.
19 Ibid, p. 69.
20 F. A. von Hayek, *The Constitution of Liberty*, Routledge, London, 1960, p. 259.
21 Hayek, *Law, Legislation and Liberty*, vol. 2, p. 74.
22 F. Hirsch, *The Social Limits to Growth*, Routledge, London, 1977.
23 L. Thurow, 'Education and Economic Inequality', in *Power and Ideology in Education*, ed. J. Karable and A. H. Halsey, Oxford University Press, Oxford, 1977.
24 Rawls, *Theory of Justice*, p. 92.
25 Ibid., p. 93.
26 B. Barry, *The Liberal Theory of Justice*, The Clarendon Press, Oxford, 1973.
27 R. Nozick, *Anarchy, State and Utopia*, Blackwell, Oxford, 1974, p. 214.
28 Ibid.
29 R. Dworkin, 'What is Equality?', *Philosophy and Public Affairs*, Fall 1981, p. 345.
30 Ibid.
31 A. Gewirth, *Reason and Morality*, University of Chicago Press, Chicago, 1978; *Human Rights*, Chicago University Press, Chicago, 1982.
32 See Gewirth's *Ethical Rationalism*, ed. E. Regis, University of Chicago Press, Chicago, 1984.
33 J. L. Mackie, 'Can There Be a Rights Based Moral Theory?', *Midwest Studies in Philosophy*, 3, 1978, p. 354.

34 Gewirth, *Reason and Morality*, p. 15.
35 Dworkin has made his opposition to the idea that liberalism rests upon moral scepticism clear in 'What Liberalism Isn't', *New York Review of Books*, 20 January 1983.
36 Dworkin, *Matter of Principle*, p. 205.
37 R. Dworkin, 'In Defence of Equality' in *Social Philosophy and Policy*, 1983; Vol 1, No 1, p. 31.
38 Ibid.
39 Ibid.
40 Ibid.
41 Ibid.
42 Dworkin, *Matter of Principle*, p. 195.
43 Dworkin, 'What is Equality?'.
44 W. E. Connolly, *Appearance and Reality in Politics*, Cambridge University Press, Cambridge, 1981, p. 97–8.
45 R. Titmuss, *The Gift Relationship*, Penguin, London, 1970.
46 A. Weale, *Political Theory and Social Policy*, Macmillan, London, 1983.
47 S. Brittan, *The Role and Limits of Government*, Temple Smith, London, 1983, pp. 38ff.
48 J. C. Harsanyi, 'Morality and the Theory of Rational Behaviour' in *Utilitarianism and Beyond*, ed. A. K. Sen and B. Williams, Cambridge University Press, Cambridge, 1982, p. 39–64.
49 Ibid., p. 9.
50 Nozick, *Anarchy, State and Utopia*, p. ix.
51 Ibid., pp. 32–3.
52 Ibid.
53 Ibid., p. 155.
54 Ibid., p. 160.
55 Ibid., p. 151.
56 Ibid., p. 172.
57 I am indebted to O. O'Neill's discussion here in 'Nozick's Entitlements', in *Reading Nozick*, ed. J. Paul, Blackwell, Oxford, 1981.
58 J. Locke, *The Second Treatise of Government*, ed. J. W. Gough, Blackwell, Oxford, 1956, p. 15.
59 This point is well made in an excellent discussion by A. Reeve in *Property*, Macmillan, London, 1986, p. 135.
60 Nozick, *Anarchy, State and Utopia*, p. 231.
61 Ibid.

4

UTILITARIANISM

The fathers of utilitarianism thought of it principally as a system of social and political decision, as offering a criterion and a basis of judgement for legislators and administrators ... government in a secular state must be secular and must use a system of decision which is minimally connected beyond its intrinsic commitment to the welfare of its citizens.

Bernard Williams, *Utilitarianism*

As we have seen so far, one of the ways in which thinkers within the liberal tradition of political thought have sought to cope with moral diversity and moral subjectivism has been through a recourse to procedural notions of various sorts of which Rawls's original position is perhaps the most obvious and well known. Such recourse is natural in a moral world with a plurality of voices: a concentration on fair arrangements to allow each voice to take part in the decision, rather than a concern with the specific content of different moral points of view. A political concern with the latter would be thought to be illiberal except in circumstances in which the proponents of one moral outlook seek to limit the freedom of others with a different standpoint. Even in these cases though some attempt is made, as we have seen by Dworkin and others, to attempt to solve the problem on procedural rather than substantive grounds by means of the device of not counting external preferences when these preferences embody a concern not only with the way my own life goes, but also with the goals and purposes of others. There is, however, a second approach to the problem of political morality in a morally diverse society which has probably played a more crucial role in the development of political theory, namely utilitarianism,

138

a philosophical position associated with the great eighteenth- and nine-
teenth-century figures of Jeremy Bentham, John Stuart Mill and James
Mill and subject to controversy, debate, amplification, and attack ever
since.

Perhaps the easiest way into the utilitarian system of ideas is to
consider some aspects of its historical development in the light of the
issue of growing moral diversity and how the utilitarians saw the
solution to principled political authority and decision-making in the
light of this diversity. In his astute commentary on Bentham's work in
The Mind of Jeremy Bentham,[1] David Manning describes one of the
major sources of inspiration of Bentham's ideas in terms of finding some
sort of political response to the social changes which had been brought
about by urbanization and the industrial revolution together with the
growth of secularization. Earlier patterns of British society had been
smaller scale, in towns and villages where there had been a familiar and
settled way of life. There were clear expectations of people in particular
roles and having a particular status. Custom and tradition defined a
background corporate existence against which individuals identified
themselves. The changes which came about from the late eighteenth
century undermined this corporate, communal existence; people were
uprooted from settled moral communities and thrust into new relationships with strangers so that, as Manning says, quoting Bentham, the
most searching question of modern society is 'who are you and with
whom do I deal?'[2] Individuals confront one another without clear
expectations, they can no longer rely on the moral assumptions and
habits of a lifetime based upon now disrupted forms of identity and
corporate existence. In this sense the background to Bentham's work
mirrors in a sociological sense some of the issues about moral pluralism
and subjectivism discussed in the previous chapters. As Manning writes:

> ... it is the sentiment and understanding born of a shared experi-
> ence which enables man to co-operate and enjoy an identifiable
> pattern of thought and behaviour some of which will be political
> in character. In the absence of this common heritage the experience
> of man is divested of meaning and value. It becomes merely sub-
> jective.[3]

In response to this changing character of human relationships

Bentham attempted to devise a new moral basis for society, one which would, in his view, be based upon the 'facts' of human nature and human motivation and which would provide an *impersonal* way of arriving at social and political decisions in a world characterized by moral diversity. Again to quote Manning, Bentham sets himself 'to consider the effects of law upon men as men, without suffering his thoughts to fix upon any particular individual'.[4] There was a need for a new moral basis for political decision-making which would replace custom, tradition, Christian values and natural law. These things might survive for particular groups and in the case of Christianity be of paramount importance for individuals, but these things were not a *shared* inheritance, they were no longer what Hegel was to call a matter of *Sittlichkeit* – a shared set of moral values on which could be based all the important decisions of a society. This had to be replaced by something else which would not replace individuals' own subjective moral values, but which would allow for morally legitimate decisions to be made in a situation of growing acute moral diversity and this system was that of utilitarianism. Understood in this light, the salience of utilitarianism to the issues which have been central to the early chapters of this book could hardly be stronger. Utilitarianism is the doctrine that political and social decisions should be made on the basis of the greatest happiness of the greatest number in Bentham's formulation, or in more general terms, that political decisions should be based upon the consideration of which course of action will produce the greatest general welfare. Welfare is to be defined in terms of the satisfaction of the wants and preferences of each individual which are taken as given and incorrigible. Maximizing the welfare of the greatest number becomes equivalent to giving the largest number of people the greatest amount of whatever it is they happen to want.

In a sense, therefore, utilitarianism is a second order morality. First order moralities, religious or secular, require particular courses of action and the pursuit of particular values and these are construed by the utilitarian as the objects of citizens' wants and preferences, these different first order moral views will come into conflict and no single one can provide the moral basis of political society. Utilitarianism provides a second order way of resolving these first order moral conflicts. People may have a wide range of varied wants and preferences which will be influenced by their particular moral outlook. Utilitarianism resolves these conflicts by the neutral and impersonal rule that of all the policies available to government, the one which is likely in its consequences to procure the greatest amount of want satisfaction is the course which should be chosen. As Alasdair MacIntyre argues:

> No matter how ultimate our disagreements on absolute principle, the very continued existence of a coherent form of social life presupposes an agreement in practice. So the need to continually secure such agreement leads to a continual growth in the influence of utilitarianism ... The utilitarian criterion comes before us in many guises. 'Welfare', 'the public interest', 'the interest of the community' – all these phrases suggest a public and socially accepted criterion of action, extrinsic to the action itself used to judge effects and consequences.[5]

In order to do this utilitarianism has to make a number of assumptions which are basic to its whole project. In the first place just because it is an attempt to decide in a situation of first order moral disagreement it cannot of itself be a very rich conception of morality. If it were, it would become as contestable as first order moral views. It is in fact a single principle morality – that of maximizing happiness, welfare or utility, all of which are identical with the satisfaction of wants or preferences. If it were not a single principle morality it could not fulfil its own function because multi-principled moralities are (a) likely to be more contested and (b) have to provide a further way of resolving potential or actual conflicts between principles. In so far as it is a single principle morality it then has to operate either by dismissing alternative principles such as rights, justice or equality which might be thought to be alternative guides to political decision-making, or, and this is the strategy most frequently adopted, by showing that such principles are not independent of utility but are rather given meaning and substance only by being shown to be a part of a general utilitarian framework. In addition to this, utilitarianism has to show that it is only legitimate to evaluate actions by consequences or the calculation of hypothetical consequences – in terms of the creation of welfare or want satisfaction. A consequence of this assumption is that there must be some technical way of measuring (a) consequences and the welfare-producing qualities of actions and (b) different levels of welfare between individuals in the calculation. It has also to assume that sense can be given to the idea of the 'greatest happiness of the greatest number' as the welfare of the largest number of people in society or 'the interests of the community'. Finally it has to show that it is morally legitimate to take the wants and preferences of individuals as, in a sense, the bottom line of utilitarian calculation and thus of political decision-making. In what follows, we shall see how these assumptions are embedded in the work of Jeremy Bentham the first systematic utilitarian thinker, and then we shall go on to see how they were extended and modified by John Stuart Mill and finally we shall look at some modern versions of utilitarianism before moving to a critical evaluation of it, specifically in relation to the theme with which we started, namely the problem of determining a principle basis for political decision-making in a morally diverse society.

Bentham and the fabric of felicity

Bentham took the view that a conception of morality had to be based upon the bare facts about human nature as revealed by empirical experience. Whatever we ought or ought not to do has to be based upon our capacities as they are observed to be. In his view observation shows that human beings are motivated to pursue pleasure and avoid pain. Any intentional act, whether it is an action in pursuit of religious discipleship or physical indulgence is undertaken because we expect to find it pleasant. We could not undertake actions which in advance we knew to be outweighed by pain. If we do so, in fact, it is because we have miscalculated. In the famous first paragraph *An Introduction to the Principles of Morals and Legislation*, he argues:

> Nature has placed mankind under the governance of two sovereign masters, pain and pleasure. It is for them alone to point out what we ought to do, as well as to determine what we shall do. On the one hand the standard of right and wrong, on the other, the chain of causes and effects is fastened to their throne.[6]

This is the doctrine of psychological hedonism – that the only things which human beings desire for its own sake is pleasure or happiness or the absence of pain. Given these springs of human action, good and bad have to be defined in terms of them. What is good for an individual is what tends to produce happiness or pleasure in the individual; what is bad or evil is what brings pain and unhappiness. Bentham is not defining, as Aristotle does, as we saw in chapter 2, what it is that brings happiness or pleasure – these are wholly subjective – he is saying only that whatever good we pursue as individuals, it is because we expect it to produce happiness or pleasure and if it does not then it is a miscalculation. The greatest good for an individual is for that individual to get as much as possible of whatever he/she wants and that is what will bring the greatest amount of pleasure. A person's interests, therefore, are what will help to maximise happiness or pleasure; what is against a person's interest is what will promote more unhappiness. Human well-being consists in the pursuit of happiness and human welfare consists in living a life with a preponderance of pleasure over pain. If these are the facts about human nature in Bentham's view, they must be central to morality – there can be no basis for morality other than that which is found in the fundamental facts about human motivation. In this sense, therefore, Bentham stands between Aristotle and other thinkers who have a fully developed view about the content of human purposes and human flourishing and those liberal thinkers discussed in the previous chapter who believe that there can be no philosophically derived *content* to human flourishing. Bentham dissents from this latter view – we can assign a definite structure to human motivation, namely the pursuit of pleasure and in this sense political philosophy does presuppose a particular theory of the personality; on the other hand, Bentham does not seek to prescribe in what form an individual's happiness is to consist. The concept of utility emerges in all this to give content to the idea of utilitarianism in the following way:

> By utility is meant that property in any object whereby it tends to produce benefit, advantage, pleasure, good or happiness (all this in the present case, comes to the same thing) ... to the party whose interest is considered.[7]

The fundamental motivation for an individual is, therefore, the pursuit of utility and each individual defines the content of that utility for him or herself. Thus in terms of the background against which we started the discussion of utilitarianism, each individual will pursue his or her conception of the good, but that conception will have in all cases the same form, namely the attempt to maximize utility or happiness. This enables us to move towards a decision procedure in ethics for both the individual and society. The principle of utility in the individual case is that principle which means that for the individual the right action is that which for him maximizes utility under his own conception of it.

In Bentham's view there is no basis for moral beliefs and values outside of the motivations of individual men and women and it follows from this that at the level of society the utility and interests of the community are identical with the greatest happiness of the greatest number of people in the society:

> It is in vain to talk of the interest of the community without understanding what is the interest of the individual.
> ... A measure of government (which is but a particular kind of action performed by a particular person or persons) may be said to be comfortable to or dictated by the principle of utility when in like manner the tendency which it has to augment the happiness of the community is greater than any which it has to diminish it.[8]

The principle of utility is thus a neutral decision procedure for social choice which takes the desires of individuals for their own pleasure as given and incorrigible and recommends as the principle of choice that the right course of action is that which will lead to the greatest aggregate utility. Thus moral dilemmas in the sphere of public choice are to be solved by a rational calculation of the pleasure-bearing qualities of the consequences of different courses of action, in which the interests of each individual affected by the decision are to be considered equally – each, as Bentham says, is 'to count for one and not more than one'. The principle of utility on this conception of it provides an impersonal rule for resolving problems of public choice in a situation of first order moral diversity, that is to say in which individuals have different conceptions of what they find pleasant, therefore good and in their interests, and over which they have the final authority. Bentham had very strong views about the capacity of utilitarianism to produce a definitive and objective answer to problems of social choice and developed the idea of a felicific calculus as a mechanism for producing such decisions.[9] Although we may find the idea bizarre it is not wholly unconnected with the idea of cost benefit analysis used by present day economists in an attempt to make social choices, for example about the siting of airports, capable of rational resolution. Each individual is capable of calculating the value of prospective pleasures and pains relating to proposed courses of action and in Bentham's view there will be different dimensions to the calculation of value such as the intensity, duration, certainty and propensity of pleasures. The individual will in everyday life make rough and ready calculations between different courses of action, bringing to bear on his calculations implicit rules of thumb such as those for assigning value to pleasure in different respects. At the level of public choice the same characteristics of pleasure are to be calculated together with the extent of the distribution of the pleasure, that is 'the number of persons to whom it extends; or (in other words) who are affected by it'. There is therefore a technical resolution of conflicts over values which to speak somewhat anachronistically could be seen as the province of the social sciences, assigning values to utilities and performing the calculations required by the felicific calculus.

In discussing 'principle adverse to utility' in Chapter II of *An Introduction to the Principles of Morals and Legislation* Bentham makes some interesting comments on what he takes to be the consequences of rejecting utility as the principle of public choice particularly in relation to what might be called moral subjectivism. Without the principle of utility the moral subjectivist must either seek to impose his own values (which merely represent his own feelings of moral approval or disapproval) on everyone else, or alternatively he has to endorse the moral anarchy which will follow from the combination of moral subjectivism with the lack of an external criterion of conflict resolution such as that which the principle of utility endorses. Bentham does not mince his words over these two alternatives:

> In the first case, let him ask himself whether his principle is not despotical, and hostile to all the rest of the human race. In the second case, whether it is not anarchical, and whether at this rate there would not be as many different standards of right and wrong as there are men.[10]

So the principle of utility provides an impersonal way of resolving the problem of public choice which avoids the moral despotism of forcing one's own ungrounded values on others and the moral anarchy which would follow from moral subjectivism taken in itself without a criterion for conflict resolution.

The claim about the principle of utility avoiding moral despotism might look rather obscure, however, in the light of the formula about the greatest happiness of the greatest number. Public policy will be directed towards the production of the greatest aggregate utility, but what if there is a minority whose good is defined in a different way from that of the majority? That is to say, imagine a society in which seventy persons find their utility in X and thirty in Y. Clearly on the principle of utility X ought to be pursued, but what about the other thirty? If Bentham is right about human motivation they cannot in a straightforward way transfer their allegiance to X because they will still find Y pleasant and they have to pursue what they find pleasant or utility-producing. Without a resolution of this conflict the principle of utility looks as 'despotical' a principle as the imposition of one set of subjective values on others in society, which as we have seen, Bentham criticizes.

To put the point another way, why should I seek to maximize the general welfare? It is not only a principle of legislation that the general welfare or utility be maximized, but also that individuals should seek to maximize the general welfare. How are my interests to be squared with the interests of the community if and when they differ? There are two possible answers to this question within Bentham's theory. The first is just to assume that at least over the long run there will be some sort of harmony or convergence of interests. The other is to argue that there have to be sanctions in order to bring conflicting interests into an artificial harmony.[11] The first of these assumptions, while there seems to be some basis for it in Bentham's text, is a rather utopian assumption and certainly more space is given to discussing the creation of a harmony of interests through sanctions. In the social situation described above, it has to be accepted that those who prefer Y to X when X is in the general interest do so because they find Y prospectively more pleasant in all the dimensions of pleasure identified in the felicific calculus and they cannot be expected to change their motivation, which is to pursue their utility, just because the majority prefers X. The role of sanctions, however, is to change the basis of their calculation of pleasure and pain or utility and the role of sanctions on behaviour is to secure this.

We need not go too far into Bentham's views about sanctions, but broadly speaking they are of four sorts, physical, political/legal, moral /popular and religious. Physical sanctions are of three sorts: (i) calamities which occur as the result of accidents in the pursuit of what an individual takes to be his utilities; (ii) the result of an individual's own imprudence in pursuing a particular view of utility; (iii) a punishment inflicted by a political/legal authority. A moral or popular sanction is the disapprobation which accrues to pursuing a particular utility. The religious sanction is a constraint on behaviour felt because an individual takes himself to be under the judgement of God either in this life or the next. In each of these cases those who would prefer Y to X in terms of utility can be influenced in their calculation of utility by taking into account that in pursuing Y they will suffer one or more sanctions which will vary from the disapprobation of friends, colleagues and neighbours to the threat of legal punishment if Y is pursued once the community has adopted X as *its* utility. As MacIntyre argues:

> The only motive for obeying the rules necessary to social life is the pleasure to be found in obedience or the pain resulting from disobeying them.[12]

Sanctions play a crucial role in securing this conformity to the impersonal rule of utility, which in Bentham's view is the only way of avoiding moral despotism or moral anarchy.

John Stuart Mill and the dilemmas of utilitarianism

John Stuart Mill, the son of James Mill, one of Bentham's disciples and collaborators, was, as might be expected, the heir to the utilitarian position. He was educated in a way made famous or infamous by his father to become the leader of the utilitarian cause in the next generation. However, Mill was a much more subtle thinker than either Bentham or his father and, partly as the result of the mental breakdown which was caused by his education, was open to a much wider range of influences which made his utilitarianism at once more complex and sophisticated and less coherent than that of Bentham.

One of the major modifications which Mill made to utilitarianism was an attempt to move away from Bentham's rather crude quantitative approach to utility. As we saw, for Bentham problems of social choice were to be resolved on a quantitative basis by the use of the felicific calculus and if taken literally this would mean that the various dimensions of pleasure or utility could be assigned quantities. On this basis, as Bentham once briskly informed his readers, 'the quantity of pleasure being equal, pushpin is as good as poetry'. In a choice between any actions or legislative proposals, quantitative considerations should determine the pattern of utilities in question. To Mill, however, who during his nervous breakdown had been greatly influenced by the poetry of Wordsworth and Coleridge, such a quantitative view was too unsubtle. Qualitative considerations had to be taken into account as well as quantitative ones, and in the essay on *Utilitarianism* Mill draws a distinction between higher and lower pleasures because, as he argues, 'it would be absurd ... that the estimation of pleasures should be supposed to depend upon quantity alone'.[13]

If quantity has to be supplemented by qualitative judgements, how are such judgements to be made and how are they to be morally authoritative? Recall the issue at stake here: the Benthamite quantitative approach is supposed to yield an impersonal decision procedure which 'considers the effects of laws upon men as men, without suffering his thoughts to fix upon any particular individual'. To bring qualitative considerations into account would, it would seem, require the judgement of particular individuals and this is in fact the line, indeed, it is the only line, that Mill could take. Mill appeals to the judgement of those who have experience of all sorts of pleasures, both the higher pleasures of intellectual and aesthetic experience as well as those of physical gratification. In so far as those with these experiences choose the former, then these higher pleasures are qualitatively superior to those which are not chosen, the lower pleasures. So, of those with experience of both poetry and pushpin, if they habitually choose poetry then that is the higher pleasure, or produces greater utility understood in qualitative rather than quantitative terms.

It is very clear from the text that Mill did not intend that this test should be reinterpreted as some kind of quantitative test and he takes the view that it is possible to take 'the higher ground with entire consistency'. He goes on to say:

It is quite compatible with the principle of utility to recognise the fact that some *kinds* of pleasures are more desirable and more valuable than others. It would be absurd that while, in estimating all other things quality is considered as well as quantity, the estimation of pleasures should be supposed to depend on quantity alone.[14]

And in several places in the context of this argument Mill refers explicitly to the idea that the higher pleasures are intrinsically superior to the lower pleasures.

It is not at all clear, however, how this introduction of qualitative differences in utility is consistent with the basic assumptions of utilitarian ethics as enunciated by Bentham. There are two reasons for this. In the first place the introduction of qualitative factors seems to deal a fatal blow to the idea that the principle of utility is an impersonal and objective mechanism for choice which avoids the despotism or anarchy which is involved in basing the assessment of public policy on subjective moral values. If the assessment of higher and lower pleasures is to be included (how?) in the utilitarian decision then it would seem that it has to refer back to the judgements of individuals which are irredeemably subjective, and a policy outcome derived from these among other factors would bring back into play what Bentham calls the element of caprice. In addition, Mill's modifications would seem to imply a radical move away from the hedonistic base of the interpretation of utility given by Bentham:

If X and Y are identical in the *amount* of pleasure N which they produce, but X is preferred to Y then it would seem that the factor which governed *this* preference is something other than pleasure.

The idea of a quality of pleasure seems to be an evaluative one and in Mill's view if we take the 'higher ground' on this issue as he suggests, this normative criterion cannot be reduced to some notion of the quantity of utility.

There is a way in which Mill's argument can be made consistent with the more quantitative and objectifying assumptions of Benthamite utilitarianism but it does seem to be a way which the whole thrust of Mill's argument rejects. Mill's own criterion for accepting the view that the pleasures of intellectual and artistic endeavour are higher is that those with experience of all sorts of pleasure give a 'decided preference' for these. However, this could be interpreted in a quantitative way, viz. they have a stronger desire for or a stronger preference for these sorts of pleasures. If I desire something it must be because it is pleasant in Mill's view, if I desire X more than Y it must be because I find it *more* pleasant and this could still be a quantitative judgement. However, it is clear that this interpretation of the argument, which would make his position more consonant with utilitarianism, is not one which Mill himself puts forward. The tensions in Mill's arguments on this point are actually very instructive because they seem to follow from his recognition in one way of a wider set of ideas and values in human life than Bentham was prepared to accept, while at the same time attempting to bring all these values under the unitary standard of utility or pleasure. It was pointed out earlier that utilitarianism is a moral theory which has to embody minimal commitments and has either to reject other moral considerations or attempt to bring them under a unitary value. Mill's argument about higher pleasures gives an indication of the stresses within utilitarianism caused by the attempt to do this.

These difficulties are also revealed in Mill's famous proof of the principle of utility. While he takes the view that on matters of ultimate value direct proof is not attainable he nevertheless thinks that good reasons can in fact be given for accepting the principle of utility as the final arbiter in moral questions. The proof runs as follows:

> Questions about ends are, in other words, questions about what things are desirable. The utilitarian doctrine is, that happiness is desirable, and the only thing desirable, as an end; all other things are desirable as a means to that end. What ought to be required of this doctrine – what conditions is it requisite that the doctrine should fulfil – to make good its claim to be believed.
>
> The only proof capable of being given that an object is visible is that people actually see it. The only proof that a sound is audible is that people hear it: and so of the other sources of our experience. In the manner, I apprehend, the sole evidence it is possible to produce that anything is desirable, is that people do actually desire it. If the end which the utilitarian doctrine proposes to itself were not in theory and practice acknowledged to be an end, nothing could ever convince any person that this was so. No reason can be

given why the general happiness is desirable, except that each person, so far as he believes it to be attainable desires 'his own happiness'.[15]

The exact interpretation of this proof is unclear, but the very lack of clarity is itself instructive. It has been argued by G. E. Moore particularly that Mill construes the relationship between desired and desirable as a strict entailment.[16] That is from the fact that people desire pleasure for itself therefore pleasure is ultimately desirable. However, as Moore has no difficulty in showing, this argument is invalid because desirable does not mean 'is desired' but rather 'ought to be desired'. No observation of the facts of human desire can *entail* that these show what is desirable in the sense of ought to be desired. Because of the argument discussed in chapter 1 there can be no entailment relation between 'is' and 'ought' propositions and hence Mill's argument fails. He is misled into thinking that there is an analogy between 'visible' and 'desirable'. One can determine what is visible by showing what people can and do see; but one cannot, in the same way, determine what is desirable for its own sake by showing what people in fact desire for its own sake.

However, this is not the only way of reading the argument. The alternative is to deny that Mill is making an attempt to set up a logical entailment between 'desirable' and 'desired'. Rather, he is treating the argument as a factual assertion, the point that people desire pleasure for its own sake. But if this is a factual assertion, then the most that it can show is that a desire for pleasure is one of the possible objects of human desire. That is to say there is the possibility that there could be other objects of desire. Either Mill takes the view that pleasure is the name that we give to whatever people desire and then it becomes a necessary truth but both uninformative and lacking in explanatory power, or he takes it as a factual assertion in which case pleasure must be the name of one end among others. If the first assertion is the correct one then it can no more explain human behaviour to say:

A desired X because it is pleasant

than it is to say

A is a bachelor because he is unmarried

because on this interpretation the meaning of 'an object of desire' is equivalent to 'something pleasant' in the same way as the meaning of 'bachelor' is an 'unmarried man'. This would be a necessary truth but one which could not form the basis of an ethical system because it could not form the basis of an informative account of human nature and human motivation. It is only if '*A* desires *X* because it is pleasant' is taken as a factual and therefore possibly false assertion that it can be informative about *A*'s motivation, but then it can be false. Indeed there are many cases in which it is difficult to justify the claim that someone desires something because it is pleasant – martyrdom for example. We can only regard martyrdom as pleasant if we accept the equation of what is desired with what is pleasant but this would not be informative. This again reveals the deep difficulty in treating all human values as if they were reducible to one overriding value such as pleasure or utility. The cost of such a reduction is vacuity. In the next section we shall explain in some detail the question of whether utilitarianism is able to reduce to its own terms other basic political and social values, particularly those relating to justice, equality and needs.

Utilitarianism and the diversity of values

Before going on to discuss the relation of utilitarianism to other values it is important to take into account a further modification of the doctrine since Bentham and Mill. Because of the psychological theories on which Bentham's view is based, which are widely regarded as unsound, and because of the highly problematic ideas of pleasure and happiness used by Mill, subsequent utilitarians have tended to modify the doctrine so that the ends to be satisfied by utilitarian principles are no longer defined. Instead of defining utility in terms of pleasure or happiness, utility is defined in terms of want satisfaction, or the satisfying of preferences the objects of which are not further defined. The reason why they are not further defined leads us back to the issues discussed in chapter 3, namely that it is thought impossible either by means of a psychological theory or by a priori means of reasoning to specify in a substantive way what the specific goals of human endeavour are. People have wants and preferences which are revealed in behaviour and it is the aggregate satisfaction of these which is to be maximized, and whether or not the goals towards which these wants and preferences are directed can be defined in terms of some substantive good such as pleasure or happiness is left unresolved. Instead of the more substantive principle of social choice of pursuing the greatest happiness of the greatest number, the utilitarian injunction is now to maximize aggregate utility where utility just means the satisfaction of wants or preferences revealed in behaviour, or to put it in another way, first proposed by A. J. Ayer in his essay 'The Principle of Utility',[17] to give as many people as possible as much as possible of whatever it is they happen to want. In this sense this modernized form of utilitarianism is close to the assumptions of modern liberal thought as described in chapter 3, in which it is thought to be either impossible or undesirable to specify the goods which individuals seek. Each person is the best judge of his own good, but these goods are not to be defined in a specific way such as the attainment of pleasure or happiness. Liberal thought must be agnostic about the final ends which individuals have, and as Rawls argues 'all dominant end conceptions' must be rejected in attempting to determine criteria for social choice and in the institutional arrangements which would emerge from such criteria when applied. Although these changes in the structure of the classical theory are important, and indeed central to welfare economics, they still leave in place most of the philosophically central features of the classical theory, namely that there is just one decision rule – namely the maximization of utility – and also, in a way that will be seen as important later in the chapter on needs (chapter 5), the idea that interests are related to want satisfaction: that what *A*'s interests are is defined in terms of *A*'s revealed wants, or to put it another way, what is in *A*'s interests is identical to what *A* is interested in and this is to be shown behaviourally by attending to what *A* tries to get or what *A* wants.

As a one principle theory, whether the principle is to secure the greatest happiness of the greatest number or to secure the greatest amount of want satisfaction, utilitarianism has often been regarded by its critics as defective because it fails to find a place for other principles which are thought to be of great importance and in particular principles to do with justice and rights. As Mill himself acknowledges in *Utilitarianism*, critics 'find it difficult to see, in Justice only a particular kind or branch of general utility, and think that its superior binding force requires a totally different origin'.[18] In what follows, I shall consider a number of possible ways of thinking about distributive justice, namely in terms of deserts, needs, equality and basic rights, and we shall consider what sense if any utilitarianism can attach to these concepts. However, before doing this we need to see how the issue arises. If we take the principle of utility maximization as the basic criterion of utilitarianism in which the wants or interests of each person are to count as one and not more than one, to use Bentham's formulation, then we can see how the issue of justice or rights arises. We could imagine circumstances in which a larger overall level of happiness or want satisfaction could be achieved in society but it would be secured by severe discrimination against a particular group of individuals. This would be represented diagrammatically. Imagine two social situations A and B in which there are two groups of people X and Y. In situation A the goods of society, let us say income for example, are distributed reasonably evenly between these groups and the total amount of income in society is represented by the size of the circle. So we might have the following situation:

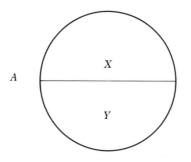

But it might be possible to imagine, as it is indeed argued by some economists, that the total amount of income could be increased by a much greater degree of inequality so that X who got a reasonably large share in A, got much less in B (see p. 155), but there the total size of the economy is increased.

On the principle that we should seek to secure the greatest happiness of the greatest number or the largest amount of want satisfaction we should prefer situation B to situation A (assuming that happiness is

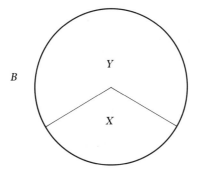

defined in terms of increase in income, or that in the second formulation, people want more income). Without other criteria such as justice, whether in terms of needs, deserts, equality or whatever, there could be no basis for challenging the utilitarian reasons for choosing B rather than A. So on this view not only does utilitarianism neglect justice, but without it it will fail to make determinate its claim to be a substantive principle of social choice. This criticism could be made in a number of ways:

1   That group X deserves more than it gets in B.
2   That if in B, the income of group X has declined so that they are no longer able to satisfy their basic needs, they have a moral claim to have their needs satisfied, that is to say, distributive justice requires that we should pay attention to needs.
3   That situation B is unjust because it neglects claims of equality in some respects – the most extreme case being that we should aim for the greatest degree of equality of outcome and this is a demand for justice in distribution.
4   That in moving from situation A to B the rights of group X are infringed.

Whichever of these views is taken, it is being assumed that in attempting to secure the greatest happiness of the greatest number some individuals may experience injustice in the distribution of social resources because the benefit either in terms of pleasure or want satisfaction to group Y outweights the disbenefit to group X. In this sense, therefore, utilitarianism is not sufficiently morally sensitive because it fails to provide a place for fundamental moral conceptions relating to desert, need, equality or rights or, in a word, to the strict moral claims of justice. The utilitarian seems forced to reject this. He has a conception of the good – the greatest happiness or the greatest net satisfaction of wants and the right thing to do in politics is to share this good. As Rawls puts the point:

> The appropriate terms of social cooperation are settled by whatever in the circumstances will achieve the greatest sum of satisfaction of the rational desires of individuals.[19]

Utility and distribution

Can utilitarianism cope with conceptions of justice in the sense of incorporating them within utilitarianism and giving them a plausible interpretation in terms of either happiness or want satisfaction? The issue here is of the very greatest importance for utilitarianism because the idea behind it of a unitary principle of social choice which does not have to achieve a balance between itself and other principles is one of the greatest sources of its appeal as a way of resolving issues of political morality in a situation of moral pluralism. If it cannot incorporate and interpret on its own terms other deeply held moral values, it will lose much of its appeal, a point which has been well made by Bernard Williams:

> A system of social decision which is indifferent to issues of justice or equity certainly has less to worry about than one that is not indifferent to these considerations. But that type of minimal com- mitment is not enticing. The desirability of a system of social choice can be considered only relative to what it can reasonably be asked to do, and the simplicity of utilitarianism in this respect is no virtue if it fails to do what can reasonably be required of government, as for instance to consider issues of equity. Certainly the simplicity that utilitarianism can acquire for neglecting these demands is not itself an argument for saying that the demands should not be made.[20]

What response, if any, can the utilitarian make to these criticisms? In the case of the argument about needs, desert and equality, I shall rely particularly upon the writings of Anthony Quinton, who has tried to answer this question from a utilitarian point of view. Quinton's basic principle in tackling this issue is that the utility accruing from the distribution of some good is in fact dependent upon the manner of its distribution and, adjoining this idea with that of diminishing marginal utility, he feels able to provide a wholly utilitarian interpretation of equality, needs and deserts in a way that does not require us to treat them as moral principles independent of utility. The two ideas which Quinton uses are highly abstract and I shall try to make this clear in relation to the three moral values using Quinton's own example, namely the distribution of oranges.

Equality

On Quinton's view the utilitarian is on strong ground in relation to the principle of equality if we imagine a society of 100 people with 100 oranges to distribute; on utilitarian grounds the distribution which is most likely to satisfy utility is an equal distribution (assuming that all members of society derive happiness from an orange, or they each want an orange, or that each sees having an orange as being in his/her interests). Why should this be so? Because of the finite satiability of human desire the consumption of oranges like most material goods is subject to the law of diminishing marginal utility, that is to say:

> If the desire for a given kind of thing within a given period is finitely satisfiable, there must be a finite amount of that thing which will wholly extinguish the desire for it and whose final or marginal portion will yield no satisfaction at all.[21]

That is to say, within the period of time relevant to the distribution of oranges a second orange will satisfy an individual less than the first, a third less than the second and so on. Hence, if a large number of oranges are distributed to a small number of people within a limited period they will derive correspondingly less satisfaction from these than would each individual in the group of 100 having an orange each. Assuming that for each individual the diminishing marginal utility of oranges decreases at the same time, then the greatest total utility will be achieved by a strictly egalitarian distribution of oranges rather than a distribution which gives more to some and leaves others without. Certainly this type of argument has been used by socialist economists to justify the redistribution of income – that an extra £10 per month of income to someone on £20,000 p.a. produces less utility to that inidividual than it does to someone on £5,000 p.a. on the assumption that income and wealth are also subject to diminishing marginal utility. On this view, therefore, greater equality of distribution of social resources can be justified on utilitarian grounds without our having to assume that equality is a value which has to be given some sort of meaning and significance independently of utilitarian considerations. Egalitarians have always been attracted by this argument. Hugh Dalton, for example, Chancellor of the Exchequer in the post-war Labour government, argued this case in his book *Some Aspects of Inequality of Incomes in Modern Communities.*[22] Christopher Jencks argues that:

... if we want to maximise the satisfaction of the population, the best way to divide any given amount of income is to make everyone's income the same. Income disparities ... will always reduce average satisfactions, because individuals with low incomes will lose more than individuals with high incomes gain.[23]

Similarly in *New Fabian Essays* Roy Jenkins argues as follows:

A modicum of redistribution would obviously have increased the total welfare of the individuals who made up the nation. The liberal view that every individual has an equal right to his own happiness and the Marshallian concept of diminishing marginal utility, amounted between them, to a very strong levelling case.[24]

See also I. M. D. Little:

If we assume a law of diminishing marginal utility of income, this implies that an egalitarian distribution of income will yield the most satisfaction.[25]

So the egalitarian position, so it is argued, can be accommodated within utilitarianism given the fact of diminishing marginal utility of goods and income and the possibility of making interpersonal comparisons of the utility drawable from such goods and income.

However, the appeal of strict equality has always been a limited one because it has often been thought that it has to be seen in relation to other legitimate moral claims upon social resources, claims based upon desert and need. On this basis departures from strict equality can be based upon the claims of desert and need as separate moral principles – so what can utilitarianism make of these values?

Desert

The argument here is that it is just to reward people in some way for their merits or deserts and that utilitarianism cannot account for this. Indeed in his discussion of the relationship between utility and justice John Stuart Mill regards desert as 'perhaps the clearest and most emphatic form in which the idea of justice is conceived by the general mind'. In Quinton's view this idea again is not an independent moral principle to be employed in distribution but rather something that can be interpreted in strictly utilitarian terms. Take again the example of the oranges and their distribution in society. If we concentrate our attention on the production of oranges for the moment, as opposed to their distribution, we can begin to see how utility would operate in relation to the concept. If in the society we envisage oranges are produced by individuals cultivating orange trees and this process of cultivation involves, as it must, effort and disutility on the part of the cultivator, then in arriving at a judgement about the distribution of oranges we have to take this disutility into account. So that if X's orange tree produces two oranges and X is interested in consuming both, it would not necessarily maximize utility to transfer the second orange to someone who had not cultivated them. X might see the consumption of oranges which he had grown as a compensation for the disutility and effort involved in the cultivation of them. In Quinton's view 'it would be no injustice if he were to eat both [of the oranges] and not give half of his crop to another man who happens to be passing by at the time when it becomes ripe ... To bring him up to the normal level of satisfaction, which the passer-by may be presumed to enjoy, he needs both oranges.'[26] In this sense desert is rather like entitlement. I have expectations about what I should receive based upon the effort and labour which I have contributed to the production and the demand of justice here can be interpreted in utilitarian terms.

Indeed, the issue here can be generalized so that on this basis utilitarianism could be used to justify in terms of a sense of justice the practice of a market economy. In a market economy it may be assumed that people are rewarded according to the effort which they put in. The larger the contribution they make to the total system of production, the larger their rewards will be. Because their efforts contribute to the growth of the economy and therefore greater aggregate satisfaction of wants, then their greater rewards are just or fair on a utilitarian basis even though this will lead to inequalities of various sorts. The departure from equality, which seemed initially to be the most natural utilitarian position, is justified with reference to a utilitarian idea of desert understood as compensation for disutility involved in producing a larger overall national product. If this is combined with the view associated, for example, with Hayek and other liberal economists that in a free market even the worst off members of society will be better off in absolute, although not relative terms, than they would be in an economy constrained by egalitarian ideals, then not only do utilitarian ideas about desert provide a powerful interpretation of desert, they can provide a very powerful defence of inequality.

Needs

As we shall see in a subsequent chapter, the idea of need is a much more complex than is usually realized but these complexities can be avoided at this stage of the argument. What kind of understanding of need can the utilitarian provide? Take again the society with 100 persons which has produced 100 oranges. The original assumption was that diminishing marginal utility would entail that each receive a strictly equal distribution of oranges. However, when the criterion of desert is brought into play we can see that the utilitarian can countenance departures from equality in order to compensate for the disutility originating from effort and contribution to the production of oranges. Let us assume, however, as a matter of objective fact that at the time at which the distribution of oranges is made there are five people each suffering from a shortage of vitamin C, which in this society can only be satisfied by the consumption of oranges, or at least their need for it can only be satisfied through the consumption of oranges. It is not just that they want oranges or have an interest in oranges, rather without oranges they will be objectively harmed. In this case we can correlate their need for oranges with the degree of utility which will accrue to them from the consumption of oranges and clearly *ex hypothesi* this utility will be large. In this case, the criterion of need will sanction a departure from equality, and not only that, may justify overriding the utility involved in the claim of desert. While as a producer I have a claim to two oranges to compensate for the effort of production, the fact is that I shall not be harmed to the degree that those who have a great need for vitamin C will be harmed, if I do not get my two oranges. In this case the degree of utility which will come from need satisfaction will, we may suppose, outweigh the utility which will come either from respecting strict equality or by distribution according to desert or productive effort.[27] Thus equality of satisfaction may be secured in three ways: equality of distribution, desert-based distribution or need-based distribution. Which will actually secure equality of satisfaction will depend on circumstances and the goods to be distributed – some may be 'luxury' goods, for example, to which a claim to need may be inapplicable, some may be goods which are produced in such a complex way that individual deserts or entitlements arising from the productive process cannot be disentangled. What is clear is that these issues cannot be settled for the utilitarian in an ethically a priori way insisting in advance upon the rightness of a particular type of distribution. Because we are concerned with the greatest possible satisfaction of wants we cannot settle a priori what should be the proper balance between equality, need and desert, the moral force of these claims will be different for different goods at different times. However, they are *not* independent moral principles, they are on this view internal to utilitarianism and utilitarianism is able to provide in a formal sense an account of their meaning and moral force together with an account of how they should be balanced in particular circumstances. Clearly, however, the force of these claims in all the three moral principles we have been discussing depends crucially upon the possibility of making interpersonal comparisons of utility so that we can *know* in some sense that my claim to desire two oranges as a compensation for disutility does not outweigh your claims based upon your vitamin deficiency.

Leaving aside this problem, which will be discussed shortly, some critics will find this position unsatisfactory because they will want to argue that the utilitarian is forced into the position of arguing that apart from the injunction to maximize utility there are no absolute claims of desert, equality or need, whereas some critics want to argue that these should in one or other respect be seen as absolute claims or rights: that I have a right to get what I deserve, or that I have a right to have my basic needs satisfied and that these rights cannot be overridden by my consequentialist considerations. As we saw in the discussion on justice, for example, in chapter 8, Nozick would reject the view that my entitlements which arise in the processes of production can be overridden on the basis of your greater need for the resources in question. Of course I may *choose* to give you the resources, but you have no right to them. They are mine by entitlement and there can be no moral balancing act between my and your utilities to determine where these resources should be in specific circumstances.

The concept of rights will be discussed in more detail in a later chapter, but what if anything can the utilitarian make of rights? Can utilitarianism make sense on its own terms of rights as categorical moral claims which cannot be overridden by calculating the beneficial consequences which might accrue from doing so? The cases we have been discussing about the distribution of oranges are in danger of trivializing the issue. Let me put it another way. Would it be right to expropriate people of what is their property to meet the needs of others because without doing so these people will be harmed? Is not a property right categorical, which ought not to be overridden even if some utility accrues by doing so? Or at the other end of the spectrum do not I have a categorical right to life which I am in danger of losing because my basic needs are not being satisfied? Can the utilitarian make sense of any of these categorical moral claims?

Utility and rights

Certainly in terms of the language they use utilitarians are antagonistic to the idea of natural, basic or human rights. Bentham in a famous phrase regarded the appeal to rights as 'nonsense on stilts'. Mill, in his defence of liberty in the essay *On Liberty*, says:

> It is proper to state that I forego any advantage which could be desired to my argument from the idea of abstract right, as a thing independent of utility. I regard utility as the ultimate appeal on all ethical questions ... [28]

Again we see the assertion of a unitary standard of political judgement which would seem to imply that any other legitimate moral principle would have to be understood in relation to it and we have already seen this strategy at work in relation to needs, deserts and equality – so what can be said about rights in this context?

The worry of the rights theorist in relation to utilitarianism is that because it sees the rightness of actions, and in the cases in which we are particularly interested this means government actions, as based ultimately upon the assessment of consequences in terms of utility, then it follows that nothing is *absolutely* wrong. There is no absolute prohibition obtainable within utilitarian theory in what may be done to persons, their lives and property if acting in a particular way will in fact maximize the net satisfaction of desire. Take a rather crude example from Alisdair MacIntyre:

> If in a society of twelve people, ten are sadists who will get great pleasure from torturing the remaining two. Does the principle of utility enjoin that the two should be tortured? Nothing could have been further from the thought of Bentham and Mill. But this only makes it clearer that they are not consistent utilitarians, that they rely on an implicit appeal to other norms ... [29]

Among the candidates for these other norms would be some idea of rights: that it is absolutely wrong to treat people in the way suggested irrespective of the utility to the majority in doing so. For the rights theorist rights and the rules of conduct to which they lead are basic; for the utilitarian if there are any settled moral rules at all, then they seem to be derivative from the assessment of consequences. However, this is far too sharp a division for the debate as it currently exists. While Bentham may have emphatically dismissed the idea of moral rights and did not seek to accord them a subsidiary place within his theory, many utilitarians, Mill included, have not been as rigid as Bentham and have attempted to formulate a consistent form of utilitarianism which could accommodate some basic protection for fundamental human interests. This has turned into the supposed difference between 'act' and 'rule utilitarianism', a distinction that I hope will become clearer later.

In Chapter V of *Utilitarianism* Mill tries to accommodate moral rights to utilitarianism in a way that preserves their substance as basic moral requirements while at the same time denying that they have any moral basis independent of utility and thus there is no need for the utilitarian to abandon the idea of a single principle basis for political morality and political judgement. In this Mill has a very different approach from Bentham. Bentham wishes to banish talk about rights which he denigrates and rejects. Mill takes rights seriously but believes that he can provide a place for them within utilitarianism. His argument is complex and subtle and only its main points can be noted here. However, it would be worth the reader comparing the arguments deployed by Mill in Chapter V of *Utilitarianism* with those of rights theorists who do see rights as independent of utility and whose arguments are discussed in a later chapter.

Mill basically has two arguments. The first is that talk about rights is designed to protect certain vital interests of persons and that these can be fully protected and understood within utilitarian theory; the second is that in disputes about the weighting of particular rights we have to appeal to utilitarian arguments as the only available means for resolving such disputes. In Mill's view, for an individual to have a right means:

He has a valid claim on society to protect him in the possession of it, either by the force of law, or by that of education and opinion. If he has what he considers a sufficient claim, on whatever account, to have something guaranteed to him by society, we say that he has a right to it. If we desire to prove that anything does not belong to him by right, we think this is done as soon as it is admitted that society ought not to take measures for securing it to him, but should leave it to chance or to his own exertions.[30]

So what is the moral justification of a right? Not in Mill's view the sorts of arguments usually deployed by rights theorists based upon, for example, natural law or contract theories, but rather on recognizing the *basic interests* of human beings which rights seek to protect. These basic interests are, in Mill's view, of two sorts: physical nutriment and general security of person and possession. These are necessary goods, or interests of all human beings, which can only be satisfied if 'the machinery for providing it is kept unintermittently in active play'. It is therefore the idea that we have a claim on our fellow citizens to 'join in making safe the very groundwork of our existence'. These are vital and necessary interests and it is on these that the idea of a right is based. But this emphatically does not mean in Mill's view that the grounds of rights are independent of and external to utility:

> To have a right, then, is I conceive, to have something which society ought to defend one in the possession of. If the objector goes on to ask, why it ought? I can give him no other answer than general utility.[31]

Because these interests are so vital to human life and happiness, the utilitarian has to preserve a central place for them because protecting these interests as rights will contribute to the greatest happiness of the greatest number. In the essay *On Liberty* when he argues that he foregoes any appeal to natural or abstract right and regards the appeal to utility as the final appeal on all ethical questions, he says 'but it must be utility in the largest sense, grounded upon the permanent interests of man as a progressive being'. Among the *permanent* interests must be those relating to physical security which requires the constant machinery of society to ensure it.

Mill goes on to argue that it is for psychological rather than logical reasons that we are tempted to want to make the basis of rights lie in something independent of utility. Because the interests, and hence for a utilitarian the desires are so basic here, he believes that they gather around them feelings which are much more intense, and that the difference in degree becomes a real 'difference in kind'. It is these feelings which account for the sense of the absoluteness of rights, but nevertheless in Mill's view this is a misleading psychological attitude if it leads us to believe that the basis of rights must lie in something independent of utility. Mill goes on to back up this assertion by claiming, through an extended discussion of punishment, entitlement and taxation, that when claims to right conflict, they can only be resolved by considering the consequences of different courses of action. He sums up his attitude to rights and justice in the following way:

> While I dispute the pretensions of any theory which sets up an imaginary standard of justice not grounded on utility, I account the justice which is grounded on utility to be the chief part, and incomparably the most binding part, of all morality. Justice is the name of certain classes of moral rules, which concern the essentials of human well being more nearly, and are therefore of more absolute obligation, than any other rules for the guidance of life, and the notion which we have found to be of the essence of the idea of justice, that of a right residing in an individual, implies and testifies to this more binding obligation.
> The moral rules which forbid mankind to hurt one another ... are more vital to human well being than any other maxims ...[32]

But, as he says, these rights are related to the furtherance of human well-being and cannot be justified in any other way.

Is this an adequate defence of rights? To some extent final judgement on this issue has to rest upon looking at the alternatives in a later chapter devoted exclusively to rights. What we are concerned with here is whether Mill's utilitarianism preserves itself as a unitary moral principle which can take on board rights as important but still subsidiary moral principles?

There are two difficulties with Mill's view, one from the perspective of utilitarianism, the other from the perspective of rights. From the utilitarian perspective the problem is: are what Mill calls rights wholly exempt from utilitarian consequentialist assessment once they have been set up? It is one thing to regard rights as generally morally binding because they contribute to well-being, quite another to imply that they can never be overridden by consequentialist reasoning. If Mill is arguing that they are exempt from this sort of reasoning, that is in particular cases, is it morally wrong to override rights even if in a particular case doing so would contribute to utility because overall the rule in question contributes towards general utility and well-being even though in this particular case the right does not. If so, then it is not at all clear how far his theory is utilitarian. It would seem to imply at the very least a move away from *act* utilitarianism, the view that the moral assessment of the action is to be judged by the good or bad consequences of *that* particular action, towards *rule* utilitarianism, that the rightness or wrongness of an action is to be judged by the good/bad consequences of a rule that welfare should perform such an action. There is a basic difficulty with rule utilitarianism which has been advocated by J. C. C. Smart. Why should the utilitarian advocate abiding by a rule – for example protecting rights when in fact we know that in a particular case utility will be increased by breaking the rule? For example, a rule utilitarian might justify a right not to be tortured because overall and in the long run this will further human well-being. But in a particular case we may be reasonably sure that to torture this individual will reveal information about where he has hidden a bomb in a city and that abiding by the general rule in *these* circumstances will diminish well-being. Smart asks why should the rule utilitarian 'advocate abiding by a rule when he knows that it will not in the present case be most beneficial to abide by it? ... Hence to refuse to break a beneficial rule in those cases in which it is not most beneficial to obey it seems irrational and to be a case of rule worship.'[33] Indeed argument can be developed to show that in fact in these circumstances rule utilitarianism has the same upshot as act utilitarianism or is extensionally equivalent to it. In the example which we are discussing we have a rule R which asserts a right not to be tortured. If in particular circumstances because of the calculation of consequences we are prepared to say that in circumstances of type E, where breaking the rule will save several lives, we should break the rule, then the rule becomes: follow R except in circumstances E. However, if we accept this then act and rule utilitarianism seem to be the same because circumstances E which lead the *act* utilitarian to break the rule, will be the same circumstances in which the *rule* utilitarian is prepared to modify the rule. In both instances, we are prepared to modify the rule in the light of the utilitarian consequences in particular cases. On this view then a rule for rights is either incompatible with utilitarianism if it is absolute, or in so far as it is not absolute it seems incompatible with a genuine accommodation of a theory of rights. The dilemma for Mill is well summed up by R. G. Frey:

If Millians keep their rights away from their consequentialism, they will fail to be act utilitarians; if they bring them into contact with their consequentialism, then the rights which they incorporate into their theory are going to be pale shadows of full blooded rights.[34]

We shall have to wait until a later chapter for a full discussion of the idea of 'full blooded' rights but in order to avoid the issues posed by utilitarianism here, it would appear to be necessary for all rights to be compatible. If rights, on the other hand, can conflict in the real world, then we are going to have to find ways of weighting rights and one way of doing this is by evaluating the consequences of weighting right X more highly than right Y and vice versa. It would seem that even a full-blooded rights theory might need some kind of consequentialist calculation if the weighting of rights is not to be *ad hoc* and intuitionistic. However, further discussion of this issue will be postponed until a full discussion of rights in chapter 7.

Wants, desires and preferences

I now want to turn away from the issue of whether aggregative utilitarianism can cope with issues relating to distribution to consider some of the issues relating to the basic data of utilitarian theory, namely the wants which have to be taken as incorrigible and the interests which follow from these wants, together with some remarks about the calculation of consequences. Utilitarianism is a want-regarding theory. In classical utilitarianism, as we have seen, the wants in question are thought to be desires for pleasure or happiness, in later forms of utilitarianism this assumption was dropped, but in both cases the wants, desires and preferences of individuals are regarded as basic and incorrigible data on the basis of which utilitarian calculation could proceed. This is very far from being the case, however, and there are major problems posed by the role of wants within utilitarianism, so that an injunction to maximize want satisfaction may be much more complicated and contentious than appears at first sight. From these complexities I shall select for discussion three important topics: the relationship between preferences and wants on the one hand and information together with a sense of what is possible on the other; problems to do with the interpersonal comparisons of utility; and finally issues to do with the estimation and calculation of the consequences of action.

In taking wants and preferences as incorrigible together with the associated view that the interests *of* a person are the same as what that person is interested *in*, the utilitarian makes a number of assumptions which are highly questionable and controversial. In the first place, of course, wants do not occur in a vacuum and politics is not just a matter of government seeking the greatest aggregate want satisfaction, taking wants as given and as in some sense formed before and independent of politics and all the pressures of our life in society. What I want, or certainly what I reveal as a preference, will always depend importantly on what is possible. If I believe that a particular group of satisfactions is out of any reach – higher education for example – then I am unlikely to reveal a preference for it. So, the narrower one's views about what the possibilities available in society are, typically the narrower will be the range of one's wants as an individual. It then becomes a very important question as to what are the sources of information and values which might restrict this range of possibilities in an individual's mind. As Bernard Williams argues:

> What one wants, or is capable of wanting, is itself the function of numerous social forces, and importantly rests on a sense of what is possible. Many a potential desire fails to become an express preference because the thought is absent that it would ever be possible to achieve it.[35]

It is perfectly possible to consider hypothetical desires and thereby hypothetical interests which might exist in the light of different information or on the basis of a different conception of what is possible. As we shall see in chapter 5 on needs, this becomes an important issue in the light of a radical view of needs and interests. It would be a case of trying to determine what X would want if he or she were better informed or had a broader grasp of the possibilities of a situation than is currently available to him or her. The problems of accommodating such a theory within liberal thought are severe because of the apparently inherent paternalism of the idea that someone in particular circumstances may not be in the best position to determine what his or her interests are, that is to say, on this view A's interests are not necessarily identical with what A is interested in because the latter may be limited by a shortage of information or a misconception of the possibilities of the situation. Within utilitarianism the most radical proposal here has emerged from Harsanyi's essay 'Morality and the Theory of Rational Behaviour'[36] in which he draws a distinction between 'manifest' preferences and 'true' preferences. Manifest preferences are those which are actually revealed in behaviour, but these preferences, he argues, may be based upon 'erroneous factual beliefs, or on careless logical analysis, or on strong emotions that at the moment greatly hinder rational choice'.[37] True preferences in contrast can only be identified counter-factually as the preferences which A would have without all the defects mentioned in the previous sentence and he goes on to argue that 'social utility must be defined in terms of people's true preferences rather than in terms of their manifest preferences'.[38] So what a person wants, what his interests are and therefore in Harsanyi's terms 'what is really good for him' may well be ascribed independently of avowed wants, although he does argue that we should always use an individual's own preferences 'in some suitable way as our final criterion in judging what his real interests are ...',[39] but the mechanism for this is left obscure. The ramifications of this argument that agents may experience false consciousness in relation to their interests are manifold and will be further considered in the next chapter, the important point to notice for the moment though, is that the utilitarian has no real mechanism for dealing with this general argument which at least in limited form has strong plausibility namely that individuals' conceptions of their wants are based upon information and views of possibility. But how are these to be dealt with by the utilitarian who believes in the ultimate and incorrigible nature of wants and the information that the greatest net satisfaction of a *given* set of wants is the object of public policy. There seems to be clearly room for at least the beginning of a critique of wants and preferences, as we shall see in some detail in the chapter on needs, but the liberal utilitarian finds it impossible to deal effectively with such a critique and in effect has to ignore it.

The second point of controversy over preferences concerns the possibility of interpersonal comparisons of utility. The centrality of this issue became very clear when we were discussing Quinton's attempt to show how the utilitarian could deal with distributive notions such as need, desert and equality. In each case, the possibility of taking the idea seriously and providing for some interpretation of it depended upon the probability of impersonal comparisons of utility. For example, the justification of egalitarian redistribution was in terms of comparing the utility of an extra £10 for a rich person and for a poor person, and the whole idea of the diminishing marginal utility of income depends crucially on this issue. However, there are very deep issues relating to this which can be no more than indicated here. The *locus classicus* for this controversy is to be found in Lord Robbins's essay *The Nature and Limits of Economic Science*, in which the types of comparisons proposed by Quinton are denied. The issue as Robbins poses it is particularly acute for utilitarianism's claims to be a scientific ethics in which there can be a calculative solution to moral problems because Robbins denies that there can be any scientific basis for the interpersonal comparison of utilities:

> It is a comparison which necessarily falls outside the scope of any positive science. To state that A's preference stands above B's in order of importance is entirely different from stating that A prefers N to M and that B prefers M to N in a different order ... Hence it is purely normative. It has no place in positive science.[40]

So, for example, if we go back to Quinton's argument to consider that A's need for X outweighs A's desert or entitlement in relation to Y cannot be a scientific judgement, it is itself an inescapably moral judgement. Robbins takes the specific case of diminishing marginal utility, which as we saw, was used by some socialist economists to argue in favour of equality:

> Suppose that we differed about the satisfaction derived by A from an income of 1,000 and the satisfaction derived by B from one twice that amount in magnitude. Asking then would provide no solution. Suppose they differed. A might argue that he had more satisfaction than B at the margin. While B might argue that on the contrary he had more satisfaction than A. We need not be slavish behaviourists to realise that here is no scientific evidence. There is no means of testing the magnitude of A's satisfactions compared

with B's. There is no way of comparing the satisfactions of different people.[41]

It is interesting to compare this sceptical remark with the confidence of Quinton's own formulation of the issue in explaining, as we saw earlier, that the utilitarian could sanction a move away from the equal distribution of resources which seems to be implied by diminishing marginal utility by taking into account needs and deserts. He takes a strong view about the rigour and scientific status of utilitarianism in answer to this question when he says of deserts and needs:

In these two cases then, there are differences between the satisfaction patterns of the individuals involved which, if the principle of utility is accepted imply precisely the departures from strict external equality that reflective moral intuition requires if just distribution is to be assured. Utilitarianism provides here a connected and systematic derivation of correctly recognised principles of justice that the intuitionist must it seems lay down as an unrelated set of axioms or dogmas.[42]

Utilitarianism has a stronger and more rigorous, more scientific and systematic approach to social choice than other approaches and as can be seen from the first sentence in the above quotation this is based upon comparing the satisfaction patterns of individuals. If, on the other hand, these comparisons cannot be made, then clearly the confidence expressed by Quinton in the capacity of a utilitarian scheme to resolve the dilemmas of public policy, particularly in a distributive context, cannot be sustained. It is worth pointing out that exactly the same problems seem to arise however sophisticated the argument becomes. Take, for example, Harsanyi's argument for determining utility levels: the utility level of person A in given material circumstances is the same as that of person B in his material circumstances if an impartial third party would be indifferent between the prospect of assuming A's material circumstances together with A's tastes and interests etc. and the prospect of assuming B's material condition together with *his* subjective outlook.

The issue is clouded in both obscurity and controversy. The first difficulty would seem to be that in order to produce determinate political results utilitarianism must presuppose that individual welfare is measurable in a cardinal and determinate way and that having done this there must be some way of comparing the scales based on cardinality between persons. Without this it is going to be impossible to say that gains for some outweigh losses for others in the calculation of utility. The difference between cardinal and ordinal measurement is crucial here and to the determinacy of the utilitarian project. That is to say, not only do we have to say when X has more or less satisfaction than Y which is the ordinal judgement, but also by how much X's satisfaction outweighs Y's. Without this it is not clear how one could make the determinate judgements between say needs and deserts which Quinton seems to imply are possible and certainly the cardinality issue seems to be presupposed by Bentham's idea of a felicific calculus. A great deal depends upon the degree of exactitude which the utilitarian believes can be brought to bear on making these judgements.

As John Rawls has pointed out,[43] many of the arguments advanced by critics of interpersonal comparisons of utility tend to be too strong and veer on scepticism about other minds, in this case scepticism about being able to make judgements at all and in principle about similarities between people's desires and their well-being. If I am convinced that my desires are quite different from yours, that what my well-being consists in has a different meaning from yours, then in effect I am sceptical about other minds in the sense that I have no confidence that the concepts in terms of which I describe and identify my own psychological states of desire or well-being have the same meaning for you as they do for me.[44] As Ian Little argues, the doubt that one can compare well-being between A and B in an everyday commonsensical way is really a doubt about the existence of other minds, because nothing short of denying their existence can entitle one to say that other minds cannot be compared.[45] If this is the basis for scepticism about interpersonal comparisons of utility then it is clearly too strong because such a degree of scepticism would in fact undermine the whole enterprise of political philosophy because it seems inescapable that in political philosophy some social judgements have to be made about gains and losses and well-being. These may not be the same as those proposed by the utilitarian, but nevertheless scepticism about other minds would destroy the whole enterprise. This strong version of the argument, however, is and has been subject to considerable philosophical attack over the past few years. Assuming that we do believe that the meaning of the concepts of desire, preference, well-being etc. are the same between individuals, the question is not so much whether they can be compared in principle, but how determinate those judgements can be in practice. We do in fact make such interpersonal comparisons all the time and the real issues are perhaps twofold: can they be rendered determinate enough to produce a calculative and objective sort of answer of the sort which seems to be required by utilitarianism; the second is whether they can be made without invoking other values. If comparisons are as much normative as they are calculative, this would undermine utilitarianism's claim to be a one principle morality. If interpersonal comparisons are ineradicably normative, as Professor Robbins argues that they inevitably are, then rather than such comparisons underpinning our interpretation of normative concepts such as desert and need, it would be normative ideas of this sort which would enter into the making of interpersonal judgements. One argument to this effect is that in making interpersonal comparisons we usually in fact, at least in public context, make reference to basic goods of various sorts such as basic needs or some other norms of human behaviour. We feel confident in saying that X is richer or better off or has a greater level of well-being than Y if his basic needs for food, shelter, health etc. are obviously satisfied. We do not need detailed cardinal measures of these differences, rough and ready ordinal judgements will do, and this is so because we do appear to have an agreed basis namely basic needs, on which to make the judgement. If all wants are taken as equal then clearly the basis on which wants are ranked is much more obscure and would demand cardinality for a secure outcome. If we limit the basis of the comparison, however, the judgements seem to be better grounded and to make fewer demands about the nature of the measurement. This position, though, is bought at considerable cost to utilitarianism because it requires us to privilege in the calculation some idea of basic needs or primary goods as an independent principle, whereas the typical utilitarian view as represented by Quinton is that the comparison of utility is what yields a theory of basic need and not the other way around. This issue will have to be pursued further in a subsequent chapter on the detailed nature of needs, but for the moment the issue is whether an ordinary basis of making comparisons of utility does not in fact presuppose some perhaps intuitive antecedent scaling of utilities to reflect some idea of basic human needs, rather than, as the utilitarian would have it, the other way around that our view of needs comes from the intensity and urgency of our preference and desires.

Ian Little has a very good summary of the utilitarian dilemma here. Having argued that we can say '£1 would make more difference to Smith than it would to Jones', he argues that it is wrong to assume that there is a theoretical basis for such judgements which can be brought out and rendered wholly precise:

> The conflict, which one may go through between thinking that utilitarianism is nonsensical and thinking that there must be something in it, results from the endeavour to make it too precise. So long as it remains vague and imprecise and avoids the use of mathematical operations such as 'adding', and 'sum total', there is something in it; but it becomes nonsensical if it is pushed too hard in an attempt to make it an exact scientific sort of doctrine.[46]

Perhaps, as I have suggested, attention should be turned away from the idea that the possibility of making common or garden judgements that 'A has greater well-being than B' is based upon some deep theory about the cardinal measurement of utility, to the idea that a particular community within which the assertion will be made has certain types of norms about basic needs and well-being and the possibility of making the judgements rests upon these rather than mathematical precision, but this does require a considerable move away from utilitarianism.

There is a final area of controversy about preferences which is salient to political philosophy and which should be mentioned, and it takes us back to an issue that was originally raised in chapter 3 in the discussion of Dworkin's arguments about external preferences, that is to say, A's preferences about how B should live his life. In the context of that discussion it will be recalled that the issue at stake was the supposed agnosticism on the part of liberalism about conceptions of the good. Dworkin, it will be remembered, had to consider a purely formal or procedural way of ruling out A's preferences about B's life and as we saw then, this runs into severe difficulties and it becomes clear that it was difficult to avoid ruling out preferences in terms of their content rather than their form. This problem reappears in two recent essays on utilitarianism which were mentioned briefly in the earlier discussions. Samuel Brittan[47] argues that the utilitarian decision-maker at the public

policy level should disregard external preferences – the preferences that
A has about the way B should live his life – on the grounds not of
procedure or double counting, but rather in terms of their content, what
Brittan calls the negative interdependence effects, that is to say those
that have an adverse effect on liberty. In this argument Brittan is clear
that he is taking liberty as an independent value and is clear that this
means in his view, a move away from the idea of utilitarianism as a one
principle morality. Similarly, Harsanyi in his contribution to *Utilitarianism and Beyond* argues a similar thesis and his argument is worth
quoting in some detail because it raises some basic issues about the
nature of utilitarianism:

> Some preferences, which may well be their 'true' preferences under
> my definition, must be altogether excluded from our social utility
> function. In particular we must exclude all clearly anti social
> preferences, such as sadism, envy, resentment and malice ... Utili-
> tarian ethics makes us all members of the same moral community.
> A person displaying ill will towards others does remain a member
> of this community, but not with his whole personality. That part
> of his personality which harbours these anti social feelings must
> be excluded from membership, and has no claim for a hearing
> when it comes to defending our concept of utility.[48]

In a very revealing footnote to this argument he goes on to press the
case that 'a really satisfactory theory of legitimate and illegitimate
interests would be a major step forward in utilitarian moral philosophy'.
It is very clear why he should take this view because it is often taken as
an argument against utilitarianism that it would sanction the persecution
of a minority – say the Jews – if this would maximize social utility.

To try to rule out of the utilitarian calculation the anti-social preferences which could lead this to happen would clearly be a step forward.
As we saw earlier in the discussion, one way of trying to do this would
be to try to develop a utilitarian view of rights of the sort intimated by
Mill in Chapter V of *Utilitarianism*. However, Harsanyi's attempt to
resolve the problem is more radical. Rather than having a sort of rule
utilitarian theory of rights, he proposes to restrict preferences. This
proposal raises two difficulties. In the first place it marks a distinct move

away from the idea that individual preferences, whether for pleasure or for a less determinate form of utility, should be taken as the basic datum in ethics because in this case preferences are being ruled out of court in the utilitarian calculation. Secondly, as Sen points out,[49] this restriction seems to be based upon some antecedent conception of the good rather than some formal constraint such as the externality of the preference or double counting of preferences. However, where does this antecedent conception of the good actually come from? After all, the social good is supposed to be generated out of the aggregate utility rather than a substantive theory of the good being used to rule certain preferences out of court. Harsanyi argues that utilitarianism makes us members of a moral community, but in fact he seems to be trading upon some kind of pre-existing values in a community to restrict what is to count as a legitimate preference. What seems to be at stake here is the implicit appeal to other norms, which cannot be given a straightforward utilitarian meaning since the basis of the utilitarian calculation is being constrained by these norms. If these remarks are combined with his earlier views discussed above (p. 170) about social utility only counting 'true' preferences, those arrived at with the best possible information, careful logical analysis and free of irrational emotions, it can be seen how far utilitarianism has moved from the ideas that utilitarianism should be driven by people's actual wants which are taken to be basic and incorrigible. It is difficult to see how true preferences and anti-social preferences are to be identified independently of some substantive theory of the good which is antecedent to the aggregation of preferences and thus of utility itself.

Finally, I want to turn to another area of controversy and difficulty with utilitarianism, that is, its account of consequences. While not all consequentialist theories need to be utilitarian, all forms of utilitarianism are consequentialist and therefore it is crucial to the theory that there is a proper account of how consequences of action are identified and estimated. We shall be concerned with the following issues: the identification of the consequences, comparing the consequences of action and inaction, and the range of consequences in question – that is to say, in assessing consequences how broad should the range of interests to be counted be and how far in time should they extend, e.g. the relation of consequences to future generations? These issues are problematic for any political theory, but they are particularly troubling to utilitarianism because of its claims to the determinacy and objectivity of the outcome of its procedures.

Obviously, before the consequences of actions can be evaluated on some sort of utilitarian scale they have to be identified and this is by no means as straightforward as it looks. Work on the philosophy of mind over the past thirty years or so has tended to support the view that any human action is identifiable under more than one description and that secondly, and partly following from the first point, it is difficult to separate out the action in itself, as it were, from the consequences. So if actions can be described in different ways, so might consequences. If they are described or identified in different ways, then valuation might well differ. The calculative assumptions of utilitarianism seem to imply that consequences and actions are definite and determinate, in a sense like natural events, and that assessment is not rendered problematic by their identification. If this is not so, then it certainly makes utilitarianism a more complex and, on any view a more problematic theory; complexities and problems which are increased if the selection of *the* identifying description of action and consequences cannot be divorced from values and norms.

The problem arises in the following way: is there any description which is *the* description of an intentional action given the intentional action occurs? An example made famous by Elizabeth Anscombe illustrates the complexity of answering this question. Imagine that a man is pumping water to a house in which live the representatives of an undesirable government; that the water in the cistern has been contaminated with poison; that the movement of the man's arm casts interesting shadows on the rocks behind him; that the movement of his arm creates a rythmical clicking noise from the pump; that in doing all this the man's muscles are moving in a particular way and that certain chemicals are getting distributed in the nerve fibres of his body. Now, in Professor Anscombe's words, we ask 'What is *the* description of the action? Is he pumping water? Is he poisoning people? Is he contributing to a revolution? Is he creating aesthetically pleasing shadows and sounds? Is he exercising his muscles in a particular way? Is he interested in stimulating various nerve fibres?' So there are other possibilities too relating to the action: the man is earning his wages, supporting a family, wearing out his shoe leather, sweating, contributing towards better government etc. so is there just one description which is *the* description of the action, given that *all* of these are in fact *true* descriptions of it. Given that for the utilitarian the value of an action must be related to and indeed dependent upon how we identify and understand it, a definite answer to the question of what is *the* description of the action is vital. If action is always under a particular description, it is important for utility that there should be a determinate answer to the question of which description it is under. Perhaps the most obvious answer here is to make *the* description of the action the one which the agent himself would give. After all, it is the agent's preference which makes the action intentional so surely his description of it is *the* description of it as an *intentional* act although, as we have seen, there are other true descriptions.

There are three difficulties with this view, two of which are inter-related. The first is that an intentional action is an action which it is assumed will bring something about: that is to say, that there is for the agent a foreseeable consequence of what he is doing and in some sense there is an idea of a causal relationship between the action and what it is assumed will be brought about. Anscombe puts this point in the following schematic form: 'In order to make sense of "I do P with a view to Q", we must see how the future state of affairs Q is supposed to be a possible later stage in the proceedings of which P is an earlier stage.'[51] Unless this condition is satisfied by the agent's account of his own intention then we are likely to question either the sincerity of the avowal or the intelligibility of the description – so in Anscombe's own example to say that I am going upstairs to get the book from the cellar, without any explanation of how these two are related is a basis for saying either that the identification of the action is insincere or that it is unintelligible.[52] The point is, however, that whichever judgement we make we do not suppose that the agent is in all cases the final authority on what is being done in action. The second issue related to this is that the scheme used by Anscombe presupposes that the agent foresees in some sense the effect or consequence Q which his action is supposed to bring about, but there are complexities about this. There might be effects or consequences which the agent does not foresee but which in some sense he might have been expected to foresee, or could have foreseen. In this case again we might wish to modify *the* description of the action to accommodate this. If I do action P to bring about Q but a foreseeable consequence of Q is X and I do not see this although others might, this could lead us to want to change or at least extend *the* characterization of the action to indicate this consequence. So in identifying *what* the action is, which is then to be assessed in terms of its consequences, we are clearly faced with two difficulties. Finally, there is the point that the agent himself may entertain more than one description of the action and how in this case do we determine the description and thereby the identification of the action under which it falls? This lack of clarity about the identity of action is particularly important for utility, partly because it is consequentialist and is to do with the utility assessment of the consequences of different actions and partly because the utilitarian view seems to imply that there is a determinate outcome of the assessment. However, if the criterion of identity of the action is itself a matter of dispute, so will be the utilitarian assessment. In addition, in disputed cases an assessment of what is the real identity of the action may not be easily separable from issues of valuation, of what we take to be important – so in the case of Anscombe's example of pumping water the political *values* of those involved may be crucial to determining the identity and hence the utility of the action.

A final problem with the identification of action is the relation to consequences and perhaps this point is only to make explicit what is implicit in the above. It is sometimes difficult to separate out action and consequences. On the basis of what has been said, and in particular if we reflect on the pumping water example, we get different identifications of the action if we include different consequences in the characterization of the action itself. Thus 'I was pumping water' gives one characterization which excludes one aspect of the consequences – namely, that as a long-term result, the people in the house die; 'I am poisoning the people in the house' incorporates the consequence in the action. Davidson has called this aptly enough, 'the accordion effect' of action.[53] If in intentional action we bring about certain things, then these things can become incorporated into a more complex description of the original action. Take the following example:

Luther nailed a piece of paper to the door of his church to draw attention to the abuse of Indulgences.

Luther started the Reformation.

In the latter case the more remote consequences of an action are incorporated into the identification of it. In Davidson's view, the extent to which consequences become built into the identification of the action is 'without clear limit'. One such clear limit would be the extent to which the agent foresaw the consequences, but as we saw earlier, this is not as straightforward as it looks because we might always want to refer to what he ought to have foreseen or something like that. Again, take the first of these lines and assert that in the application of utilitarian principles we must confine assessment to those consequences 'that the agent could reasonably be expected to foresee'. Obviously after the event we might identify the action differently, as in the second proposition about Luther, but as a *moral* guide, we have to take the former course. As we have seen, however, there are difficulties relating to this and there are others too, namely the scope of interests over which we believe that a proper assessment of consequences is supposed to range. The utilitarian is clear that each person's interests should be counted as one and not more than one, but whose interests are crucial here, because it can lead to a different assessment of consequences. There are at least two dimensions to this. The first is an inter-state or inter-society one. In calculating, at the level of public policy, the utility consequences of actions A and B should we take into account only the consequences for our own society or the consequences for other societies? These are real political issues – for example, to protect declining textile industries at home by imposing import duties may well impoverish people in other countries who depend upon such exports. Secondly, should we count inter-generational effects? We might consider a utilitarian policy about extracting scarce mineral resources which are not renewable and, so far as we know, are not substitutable. Should we take into account the consequences for future generations of citizens or not? Earlier, in a quotation from Harsanyi, reference was made to utilitarianism and the idea of a moral community, but to *which* moral community across space and time should the calculation of consequences over interests range? Without some kind of antecedently justified notion of what is the appropriate community of interests, utilitarian calculation lacks determinacy, but it is unclear whether the boundaries of such a moral community could be derived from utilitarianism itself.

Notes

1   D. Manning, *The Mind of Jeremy Bentham*, Longman, London, 1968.
2   Ibid., p. 4.
3   Ibid., p. 3.
4   Ibid., p. 5.
5   A. MacIntyre, 'Against Utilitarianism', in *Aims in Education*, ed. T. B. Hollins, Manchester University Press, Manchester, 1964.
6   J. Bentham, *An Introduction to the Principles of Morals and Legislation*, ed. W. Harrison, Blackwell, Oxford, 1967, p. 125.
7   Ibid., p. 126.
8   Ibid., p. 127.
9   Ibid., Ch. IV.
10 Ibid., p. 130.
11 See Chapter 3 of *Principles of Morals and Legislation*.
12 A. MacIntyre, *A Short History of Ethics*, Routledge, London, 1967, p. 235.
13 J. S. Mill, 'Utilitarianism', in *Utilitarianism*, ed. M. Warnock, Collins, London, 1962, p. 259.
14 Ibid., p. 258.
15 Ibid., p. 288.
16 In G. E. Moore, *Principia Ethica*, Cambridge University Press, Cambridge, 1959, p. 67.
17 A. J. Ayer, 'The Principle of Utility' in *Philosophical Essays*, Macmillan, London, 1954 (reprinted 1963).
18 Mill, 'Utilitarianism' p. 297.
19 J. Rawls, *A Theory of Justice*, The Clarendon Press, Oxford, 1972, p. 25.
20 J. C. C. Smart and B. Williams, *Utilitarianism*, Cambridge University Press, Cambridge, 1973, p. 137.
21 A. Quinton, *Utilitarian Ethics*, Macmillan, London, 1973, p. 76.
22 H. Dalton, *Some Aspects of Inequality of Incomes in Modern Communities*, Routledge, London, 1925, p. 10.
23 C. Jencks et al., *Inequality*, Allen Lane, Penguin Press, London, 1974, pp. 9–10.
24 R. Jenkins, 'Equality', in *New Fabian Essays*, Turnstile Press, London, 1952, p. 70.
25 I. M. D. Little, *A Critique of Welfare Economics*, Oxford University Press, Oxford, 1957, p. 11.
26 See Quinton, *Utilitarian Ethics*, p. 77.
27 Ibid.
28 J. S. Mill, 'Essay On Liberty', in *Utilitarianism*, ed. Warnock, p. 134.
29 MacIntyre, *Short History of Ethics*, p. 238.

30   Mill 'Utilitarianism', p. 309.
31   Ibid.
32   Ibid., p. 315.
33   In Smart and Williams, *Utilitarianism*, p. 10.
34   R. G. Frey, 'Act Utilitarianism' in *Utility and Rights*, ed. R. G. Frey, Blackwell, Oxford, 1985, p. 64.
35   B. Williams, in *Utilitarianism*, ed. Smart and Williams, p. 147.
36   J. C. Harsanyi, 'Morality and the Theory of Rational Behaviour', in *Utilitarianism and Beyond*, ed. A. K. Sen and B. Williams, Cambridge University Press, Cambridge, 1982, pp. 39–64.
37   Ibid., p. 55.
38   Ibid.
39   Ibid.
40   L. Robbins, *The Nature and Significance of Economic Science*, Routledge, London, 1932, p. 122.
41   Ibid., p. 124.
42   Quinton, *Utilitarian Ethics*, p. 77.
43   Rawls, *Theory of Justice*, See also Little, *Critique of Welfare Economics*, ch. IV; Harsanyi, 'Morality'; D. Jay, *The Socialist Case*, Faber and Faber, London, 1937, ch. 2.
44   For further reflections on these issues in the philosophy of mind see the final chapter of the present work.
45   Little, *Critique of Welfare Economics*, p. 51ff.
46   Ibid., p. 53.
47   See Brittan's fine discussion in his *The Role and Limits of Government: Essays in Political Economy*, Temple Smith, London, 1983.
48   Harsanyi, 'Morality', p. 56.
49   A. K. Sen, Introduction to Sen and Williams, p. 10.
50   G. E. M. Anscombe, *Intention*, 2nd edn, Blackwell, Oxford, 1963, p. 37.
51   Ibid., p. 36.
52   Ibid.
53   D. Davidson, 'Agency', in *Agent, Action and Reason*, ed. R. Binkley, R. Branaugh and A. Marras, The Clarendon Press, Oxford, 1979.

5

The Claims of Need and Politics

Human need priorities must be the ultimate basis for distinguishing legitimate from illegitimate public policies. Do these policies serve the most pressing needs better than any other, possibly available alternative politics? In principle the same kind of test must determine how legitimate, how deserving of loyalty and support, is a government, or a regime.

C. Bay, 'Needs, Wants and Political Legitimacy'

The word 'need' ought to be banished from discussion of public policy, partly because of its ambiguity but also because . . . the word is frequently used in arbitrary senses.

A. Williams, 'Need as a Demand Concept'

As we have seen, one of the central problems of modern politics and of the theory of modern politics is how can there be a clear political morality which will enable us to determine which sorts of human action ought to be subject to coercion and which should not, without this morality being based upon the convictions of just one particular group in society. Given the earlier use of the theological and metaphysical background which enabled previous theorists such as Locke or the framers of the American Constitution to take certain basic political truths – in these two cases about rights – to be self-evident and to be the moral basis of government, what can be put in the place of these metaphysical convictions and can whatever is put in their place be reconciled with the convictions of the vast bulk of citizens given their diverse values and moral traditions? Without some kind of criteria for

184

political judgement it seems as though political life will be anarchic and unprincipled and there will be no clear and morally compelling account of the range of activities which ought to fall under the aegis of the state. As we saw earlier, liberal theorists such as Hayek, Rawls and Dworkin each attempted to produce some morally neutral answers to these questions which, while being neutral between conceptions of the good, were also morally relevant to the basic questions of political morality by defining a set of basic political goods and in the case of Dworkin and Rawls, criteria for their distribution. In this way therefore they have all sought to articulate something which has long been a preoccupation of political theory, that is to say an account of the common good between citizens. For Hayek the common good is formal and abstract, a set of rules defining mutual non-coercion; for Rawls the common good is defined in terms of the two principles of justice; for Dworkin a set of neutral rules together with an endowment-neutral, but ambition-sensitive form of redistribution based on the principle of equal respect and concern. In each case the attempt is to be nomocratic rather than teleocratic, to place the right before the good, or to provide an account of basic political principles which is as far as possible neutral between conceptions of the good.

In this chapter I shall be concerned with trying to determine the claims of needs in politics in the light of these general considerations. Are there basic human needs and if there are what are the obligations of citizens and the state in respect to them? Can these needs be identified on an empirical basis and in what sense does the ascription of need presuppose some sort of expertise? How do we distinguish between needs and wants and what is the relation of each of these to interests? We have, of course, met some of these questions before, particularly in the discussion of Fromm and Marcuse, but the aim of the present chapter is to try to disentangle the nature and claims of need in a more direct and rigorous way to assess whether a moral basis for politics can be provided on the basis of needs as Christian Bay argues in one epigraph to this chapter, or whether the concept is so ambiguous that, as Alan Williams suggests in the other epigraph, the whole notion should be dropped. In this discussion I shall again be concerned with the question of how far needs might provide us with some kind of objective benchmark for political morality and judgement of political principle. Some theorists have taken a very positive view here. Abraham Maslow, a psychologist with a particular interest in needs, argued in his *Towards a Psychology of Being* that a theory of needs would provide the basis for a 'scientific ethics, a natural value system, a court of ultimate appeal for the determination of good and bad, right and wrong'.[1]

Needs and welfare

There is one area of modern society in relation to the nature and limits of state action to which the theory of needs is directly and acutely relevant and that is the welfare state. Without the idea of need and the nature of the claims on society which needs make, it would be very difficult to understand the nature and normative underpinning of the welfare state just because it is often thought that needs characterize the sphere of welfare independently of the sphere of markets. If one looks at contemporary writing on the welfare state it is littered with the use of 'need' discourse not just to describe particular social services as meeting needs, but the whole point of the welfare state. Some examples will perhaps illustrate the truth of this.

The definition of need presents a central problem for the social services, since this defines the objectives of these services.[2]

The concept of social need is inherent in the idea of social service. The history of the social services is the history of the recognition of social needs and the organisation of society to meet them.[3]

It is this concept of need, so it is argued, that marks off the welfare function of the state from its other functions. Radical social theorists have been very keen to emphasize this. In 1958 in the *New Reasoner* Dorothy Thompson argued that the social recognition of need and state actions to meet needs was profoundly antipathetic to the capitalist market. In a capitalist society the welfare state and the recognition of the claims of need have marked the extent to which socialist ideas have become important in the organization of that society:

The range of benefits are provided partly on the basis of need and not of cash payment or any abstract conception of social value. This conception is a profoundly anti capitalist one.[4]

Similarly emphasizing the importance of need for radical social policy George and Wilding argue:

> The fundamental principle of radical social policy is that resources whether in the field of health, education, housing or income should be distributed according to need.[5]

On this view, therefore, need satisfaction is the *internal goal* of the social services and criteria of need are the only appropriate grounds for distributing welfare goods; merit, desert, moral worth, or the ability to pay are irrelevant. Such an approach to welfare presupposes two things: (i) that needs are clear and determinate; (ii) that needs, once discovered, create obligations on others, the performance of which can be legitimately coerced through the tax system and the welfare state to satisfy such needs. If needs could be fixed in an empirical way then the aims of the welfare state could similarly be fixed and its performance monitored. The welfare state would not rest upon a dubious moral basis. On the contrary, the needs which it is supposed to meet would be clear and determinate and the moral claims which would arise from the definition of need would be compelling. The sphere of need would, in addition, mark off the area of welfare and state responsibility, from that of the market. Whereas the market is concerned with the satisfaction of individual preferences, the sphere of welfare is concerned with common and basic human needs. Each of these claims needs careful scrutiny and on this scrutiny may depend our conception of the moral legitimacy of state action in the sphere of welfare. The aim will be first of all to try to clarify the concept of need in relation to wanting and desiring, before going on to discuss the moral claims which might be based upon needs and to try to answer the question posed in a previous chapter by Hayekians and some libertarians such as Nozick and Mack that the welfare state is based upon some particular view of the good and is an illicit imposition of a substantive set of values upon a diverse, morally pluralistic society. Or whether the idea of a welfare branch of government responding to need can be seen as compatible with this moral diversity.

Needs and wants and psychological states

In ordinary language, there are perhaps two aspects of talk about needs and wants which are worth remarking upon. The first is that we do draw a distinction between needs and wants in the sense that we can quite ordinarily be said to need what we do not want and want what we do not need. Let us take the first case. Assume that there is a correct account of how much vitamin B12 the body requires in a day to remain healthy and let us further assume that this amount is contained in a food – say, a breakfast cereal which a child does not like. In these common circumstances it would be quite rational to say to the child who did not want to eat the cereal that he or she needed to eat them. Or again I may not at the moment know that I am a diabetic, so if I were asked for a list of even my most considered wants a dose of insulin would not be among them and yet I could be said to need it.

Three things emerge from these entirely commonsensical reflections which could be varied with a wide range of examples. The first is that claims to need appear to be objective and impersonal related to some kind of objective standard (particularly clear in the vitamin and the insulin case); secondly and related to the first, the ascription of need can take place independently of and indeed in opposition to the agent's own avowals about his/her own psychological states. The third point follows from these two, namely that if needs are objective and if one is unaware of them in the sense that they can be ascribed independently of avowals, then this appears to sanction expertise over needs. Someone – say, in the cases discussed the nutritionist or the doctor – is able to ascribe to an agent needs of which he may be unaware. It might be argued from this that similar expertise can apply in more general political contexts, so that political authorities or professional experts can ascribe needs to citizens independently of their own wants or preferences. It can be seen I think in the light of the discussion of the fundamental assumptions of the liberal tradition in political philosophy, that any such expertise on the part of government or welfare professionals which runs counter to wants actually expressed in the political or economic market place is highly illiberal.

These points can also be made by looking at the other side of the coin. So far the examples have been of needs which I may not want, but it works the other way too: I may want what I do not need. Take another nutritional example. It is possible to buy flavoured vitamin pills for children which contain all the recommended daily intake of these vitamins. Having eaten one and liked the taste the child may say that it wants another but it does not need one, it has had the recommended dosage for the day. Again the examples could be multiplied and would support the conclusions drawn above. Indeed even very young children soon become aware of the apparent authority, the objectivity, the impersonality and indeed the urgency of need statements when, for example, being taken around a shop and expressing a strong desire for an expensive toy, in desperation the child's desire is seemingly turned into a more authoritative form by saying 'Daddy, I really need it' which even young children realize is much more compelling and authoritative than 'Daddy, I really want it'. Need statements seem to embody much more authority and to imply a claim which has to be taken seriously or countered by argument in a way in which refusing to countenance a claim to want does not.

In the sphere of politics these features of needs have often been seen as the cause for a deep suspicion, well summarized by Ross Fitzgerald:

> Prescriptions phrased in terms of 'needs' are such that they appear to be not merely the demand of one person but one that applies to all human beings whether they know it or not. Thus talk in terms of 'needs' appears to get the theorist out of the problem of imposing one's value preference upon others. Needs talk has a scientific ring about it when the concept is used as if it were non-normative: it seems to open the way to objective expertise. If one talks as if a theory of needs were empirically established it gives the appearance of scientific utterance. This is especially important in a society where the language of science has considerable public authority and prestige ... Looked at in this way the revival of need theory is part of the search for certain political values and an objective political morality.[6]

The salience of the discussion of needs to the problems which were discussed in the previous chapters could not be greater, and we have to look further into the characterization of needs.

As we have already seen, needs seem to be able to be ascribed to individuals independently of their psychological avowals and indeed on occasion in opposition to such avowals. This has led some philosophers to argue that needs are not psychological states at all, as the following examples from recent literature make clear. In *Social Justice* David Miller argues as follows:

> Want is a psychological state which is ascribed on the basis of a person's avowals and his behaviour . . . Needing on the other hand is *not* a psychological state but rather a condition which is ascribed 'objectively' to the person who is its subject.[7]

In his essay 'Let Needs Diminish that Preferences May Flourish' David Braybrooke argues that:

> In a case where there is evidence that N does desire something and equally weighty evidence that he doesn't, his testimony will decide the issue, provided at least that we have grounds for thinking him habitually sincere. But in a case where there is evidence both ways about N needing something, his saying so only begs the question. It carries no more weight than the opinion of any one else equally observant.[8]

These arguments rest upon the points which have already been made but there are other arguments too for trying to draw a sharp distinction between needs and wants/desires/preferences.

One very important point deployed by philosophers in this context is called the argument from referential opacity. This will be an obscure idea to students of political philosophy and it requires some elucidation before being applied to the context of need. In all of these complexities, however, we should keep in mind a very important point, namely that if needs are different in logical type to psychological states then the way is prepared for the potentially illiberal argument that an individual may be in a state of need about which he or she is unaware and this state can be ascribed with authority independently of an individual's own preferences.

It has been argued that one of the defining characteristics of a mental or psychological state as opposed to a physical state is that verbs which one used in psychological statements are referentially opaque or are subject to indirect reference, whereas the same is not true of verbs which describe physical wants, actions, processes and performances. If this in fact turned out to be a feature of the verb 'to want' and not of the verb 'to need' then this would provide very strong evidence for the non-psychological character of need as recent philosophers have argued. The criterion of indirect reference has been put as follows:

> Let E be a sentence of the form $A = B$ (where A and B are names) If P is a sentence containing A and if Q is a sentence containing B which is otherwise the same as P except for the substitution of B for A, then sentence P is intentional, or describes a psychological state if P and E together do not imply Q.[9]

So in applying this criterion to the objects of wants or needs we arrive at something like the following analysis which is taken from Professor Alan White's *Modal Thinking*.[10] Under item E in the above schedule let us say

$E =$ The person who is blocking my path is my son (i.e. $A = B$)
$P =$ I want to kill the person who is blocking my escape.
$Q =$ I want to kill my son.

P here is referentially opaque and therefore psychological because E and P do not entail Q. I may want to kill the person blocking my escape, but this does not entail that I want to kill my son. That is to say, psychological states are always under a particular description, as is shown in the analysis above. However, if we replace 'want' in the above analysis, with the verb 'to need', then we can see that the sentence is *not* intentional or subject to indirect reference. If I need to kill X and X is my son, then I need to kill my son. As White puts the point:

> What one needs, one needs whatever its description. If, in order to escape, one needs to kill the man blocking one's way, then one needs to kill one's own son.[11]

White goes on to make an interesting point in relation to animals. He takes it as clear that we are able to ascribe needs to animals in a clear and straightforward way because these needs are objective and relate in some sense to the physiological facts about the animal. However, because of the complication that wants are always avowed under a particular description, or are referentially opaque, we have very considerable difficulty in ascribing wants to animals. Because we have no way of getting access to the description under which an animal perceives objects in its environment, it is a very difficult matter to ascribe wants and desires to animals with any degree of determinacy.[12] So on this basis philosophers have wanted to argue for a sharp distinction between wants, desires and preferences as psychological states and needs being objective states of the world. As Griffin has argued:

> Needs are not a sub class of desires. They are not say strong, or widespread, or central desires. While 'desire' is, need is not, an intentional verb; I can only need a thing if I need anything identified with it.[13]

The point can be put as Wiggins does: 'I can only need to have X if anything identical with it is something that I need.' This is not so in the case of wants. Wiggins's important analysis is that:

> What I need depends not on thought or the workings of my mind (or not only on these) *but on the way the world is.* Again, if someone wants something because it is F, one believes or suspects that it is F. But if one needs something because it is F, it must really be F, whether or not one believes that it is.[14]

This point is also supported by Professor White when he argues in support of Wiggins's point:

(a)   one can want something because one believes that it possesses certain characteristics, whether it does or not, but one can need something only because it actually does possess certain characteristics.

(b)   To explain my action by reference to my wants may be to explain them by *my* reasons; to explain them by reference to my needs . . . can only be by *the* reasons.[14]

These considerations support the view that needs are not psychological states, but objectives states about a person about which others may have more knowledge than the subject of the needs – a point which Galston makes in a stark way when he argues 'since the need for food is not grounded in subjective desire, an alleged "psychological need" for it is an abuse of speech and a misleading causal analysis'.[16]

In a sense all of these arguments are about the relationships between wants, needs and beliefs, the point being that what I can be said to want depends upon my beliefs, whereas what I need does not depend upon beliefs in the same way, as the example of the man whose son is blocking the passageway shows. This point can be made in an alternative way, again following the attempt by philosophers of mind to discover criteria for diagnosing the difference between psychological and non-psychological verbs. One formal criterion for a psychological state is that it can be directed towards a non-existent object in the sense that the presence of the psychological state does not entail the real existence of the object towards which it is directed. So while I may want to have experience of God, this does not entail that there is a real object of such experience. This criterion can be formalized as follows:

A simple declarative sentence is psychological if it uses a substantival expression – a name or a description – in such a way that neither the sentence nor its contradictory implies that there is or that there isn't anything to which the substantival expression truly applies.[17]

On this criterion:

'I want experience of God' is psychological.
'I sat in a pew' is not psychological.

Now once again this applies to the distinction between needs and wants. As we have seen, the experience of wanting does not entail that the object wanted exists, whereas in the case of needs because, so it is argued, what I need is independent of my beliefs, what I need depends upon the real character of the object, not upon my beliefs about it. Hence it if is true that I really need X then the question of the character of X must depend, as Wiggins says, on the way the world is rather than on my beliefs about it.[18] Thus these points once again tend to confirm the view that wants are psychological states whereas needs are not and can be ascribed objectively and authoritatively to an individual.

This distinction between need as an objective non-psychological state and desire as a psychological state is supported by three further considerations which White brings to bear in his analysis. He claims that need is not an emotional state because he argues an emotion logically involves a want or inclination whereas needs do not because one may have needs such as an objective need for insulin for which one has no inclination. The second point is that the observation of behaviour is the best basis for discovering what a subject wants, whereas he argues that there is no such close connection between what someone needs and what behaviour he exhibits. For example, if an individual is not disappointed at his failure to get X, this may give a basis for saying that he did not really want it, but it would not be a ground for saying that he did not really need it:

> The way in which biological or psychological reactions are related to needs is not logically different from the way in which e.g. the reactions of an engine to certain tests show whether it needs more oil.[19]

The third point is that wants are logically related to what an agent is capable of understanding and expressing, partly because, as we have seen, objects are always wanted under a particular description, whereas needs may be related to things about which the subject has no conception. My body may be in a condition that it needs an injection of X which has a highly complex molecular structure of which I currently have no conception. I can still be said to need such a thing, whereas it would be difficult to make sense of a want directed towards such an object.

There do therefore seem to be good grounds for distinguishing between wants as psychological states and needs as physiological ones. In an earlier work on this issue I made the mistake of arguing from the case of psychoanalysis that the distinction was not as clear cut since in psychoanalysis there is talk about unconscious wants and wishes which seem to be ascribed in a diagnostic way independently of the agent's avowals, otherwise they would not be 'unconscious' and thus be more like needs.[20] However, this was mistaken because the analyst will call an 'unconscious' want only something which the patient will be able, with the right therapy, to come to admit as a want or a desire, but as

White argues, 'there is no reason to insist that something can be a need of which one was unaware only if we can be brought to acknowledge that it was withheld'.[21]

These points, when taken together, have, as Fitzgerald suggests, very profound political consequences. There is a suggestion that when confronted with fundamental questions of political morality we are presented with two quite diverse sets of facts about a person: (a) a schedule of wants revealed in behaviour and in avowals about which in general the subject has final authority; (b) a set of needs which are not psychological states, which depend upon 'objective facts' on the way the world is rather than on avowal and behaviour, on reasons about which there can be expertise. This account of needs legitimizes a role for expertise in politics and for determining what a person's real interests, connected with needs of which the subject may be unaware, are considered to be. These points are made very cogently by Alan White and, because of their political salience, are worth considering in some detail. In political thought and argument we frequently refer to interests and use this expression when we talk about a particular policy as being in the interests of a group or set of individuals, or in the public interest. How is the idea of interests related to wants or needs?

Needs and interests

If we hold to a want-regarding view of public policy then it is the duty of the state only to pursue those policies which respond to the expressed wants of individuals, which do not try to 'second guess' those wants or pursue policies which are supposed to represent the 'real wants' of individuals and groups. Here we are construing 'interest' as 'A is interested in X' and the criteria for making this judgement will be exactly the same criteria as we use when determining whether A wants X – psychological avowals, attempting to get X and so forth. However, talk about objective needs sanctions a radically different view of interests in which we speak not so much of what A is interested *in* but more of what is *in* A's interests, where these interests are based upon an account of A's needs about which A does not necessarily have the final authority, needs not being psychological states. So what A is interested in and what is in A's interests can be radically different. We can see this clearly in the case of children, when among Richard's interests, in the sense of things which he is interested in, would not figure a list of particular vitamins he should consume in a day to meet his needs, and yet, while vitamin B12 is not something Richard is interested in, a particular consumption of it is in his interests. On a strong version of theories about the objectivity of need this kind of judgement is ubiquitous in politics and sanctions a view of public interest which is not directly want-regarding. Here it is useful to put together some remarks by Alan White which are politically crucial and are derived entirely from his arguments that needs are not psychological states:

> Deciding in favour of public or private interests is deciding in favour of needs not wants ... Just as someone may not know what he needs, so he may not know what is in his interests; though he will as surely know what he is interested in as he knows what he wants ... Whitehall may know better than we do what is in our interests. There is therefore, no inconsistency in the political suggestion that someone's true interests may be elsewhere than in his own wants or inclination. It is because modern industry needs a large body of consumers that joining the Common Market may be in our interests even if we do not want to join.[22]

On this view a theory of needs will provide us with a definite set of goods on which to base political morality and one of the problems with which this book started is then solved. What are we to make of this argument that what is in the public's interest is more dependent upon needs and real interests than upon what individuals and groups want? One way of assessing this argument would be to probe more deeply the argument that needs are not psychological states like wants and desires but this would take us into some very intractable and highly rarefied discussions in the philosophy of mind. There is, however, a more direct way, which is perhaps more politically salient and concerns the relationships between needs and goals, ends or purposes.

Needs and ends

It can be argued that the objectivity of needs is quite spurious and this is so for a simple reason which has complex ramifications. The simple idea here is due to Brian Barry in *Political Argument*,[23] in which he argues that a simple need statement such as *A needs X* is elliptical since we can always ask what is it needed for? To answer the question 'what is it needed for' is central for two reasons: (i) it secures the intelligibility of the need claim; (ii) it is a basis for arguing for the justification of the claim. In accordance with (i), if I assert a claim to need *X* but am at a total loss to explain what I need it for, my need will appear strange, or unintelligible and possibly pathological. More importantly for the present discussion, however, citing the goal or purpose for which this is needed will be a basis for *justifying* the need. The need is only justified *if* the end for which it is needed can be justified. As Barry then says 'the only interesting questions arise in connection with the ends'. For example, 'I need a crow bar' is made intelligible and justifiable if the end is to open a window when I have locked myself out of my house; it is intelligible but not justified if I need it to break into your home. Needs are, therefore, on this view, normative, they are logically related to ends which have to be evaluated for the claim to need to be amenable to justification.

However, this argument has been subjected to criticism by Alan White and it is very important to take note of the points he makes and why they fail, at least in relation to need in a political context. White takes the view which, as we have seen, follows from Barry's argument that needs are normative and rejects it:

> It is the existence of the end state, not its value or desirability, that makes something needed. A batsman on 99 needs one more run for his century, whatever one thinks about getting a century. Children need to understand addition in order to manage multiplication, whatever the value of either ... The confusion between the existence of and the desirability of an end state has arisen from a confusion between specifying the end state in virtue of which the need arises and justifying it. One cannot decide whether *A* needs *X* unless one knows what the alleged need is for; but one does not have to pronounce on the merits of the latter.[24]

Of course, what White says here is true up to a point, but has no real bearing on the political context in which need claims arise. Needs have to be identified by *specifying*, rather than *justifying* the end, but in politics we are concerned not just with the identifying of needs but satisfying what we take to be the important ones. And it is this that leads us to the question of the justification of the ends. It is only those needs which are related to the most important human ends which political action is called upon to satisfy. Hence, we have to be involved in questions of justification of these ends and securing claims to need satisfaction in relation to them. Many thinkers have argued that, in Simone Weil's comment, 'Needs create obligations', but strictly speaking they do not; it is rather because we see the importance of certain ends or goals in human life as being important and worth enhancing that it can be argued we see an obligation to satisfy those needs which are means to such ends.

On the face of it then, these simple observations deal the death blow to the view that claims about needs are objective and empirical and that they could support in an unproblematic way political prescriptions. The ends for which things are needed have to be specified and justified before the claims which they embody are in turn justified. This brings us back, however, to the problem with which we have been wrestling since the beginning of the book, namely the justification of values. Since needs have to be considered in relation to ends, they look as though they will vary in a pluralistic society just as conceptions of ends or the good differ in such a society. On this view there can be no scientific basis for needs, there can be no authority for need claims because such authority would have to depend on accepting certain values as foundational and as we have seen this is difficult to argue. It also follows from this that in so far as the welfare state meets needs it must be involved in imposing a particular normative conception on citizens – the conception which renders the needs justified, as opposed to a free market in which free individuals express their wants. This point has been very well made by John Gray in a recent discussion of poverty:

> The objectivity of basic needs is equally delusive. Needs can be given no plausible cross-cultural content, but instead are seen to vary across different moral traditions. Even where moral traditions overlap so as to allow agreement to be reached on a list of basic

needs, there is no means of arriving at an agreed schedule of urgency among conflicting basic needs ... There is an astonishing presumptiveness in those who write as if dilemmas of this sort can be subject to morally consensual resolution. Their blindness to these difficulties can only be accounted for by their failure to take seriously the realities of moral pluralism in our society or ... to their taking as authoritative their own traditional values.[25]

If needs vary in relation to ends, and if, in a pluralistic society, ends differ, then needs will differ systematically too. As the ends cannot be grounded to anything other than the normative preferences of agents, then the needs relative to these ends are also preference-dependent.

There are, however, many thinkers who operate with the idea of need who would reject the relativistic consequences which appear to follow from this argument. Philosophers of this more objectivist persuasion have linked the idea of need with that of harm or ailing.[26] The link is best illustrated in the following way: if we want to answer the question 'Are there any basic needs?' then, because of the link between needs and purposes, this becomes 'Are there any basic human purposes which would then specify a set of needs as the means to the attainment of these purposes?' It is then suggested that basic human purposes are those which, if not fulfilled, would cause harm to the individual. So if a person has a need then he/she will be harmed by his/her not satisfying it, and getting what he/she needs will provide a remedy for the condition of harm. On this view, if needs are related to harm, we can overcome the relativism central to the pluralist's critique and the claim of need can become categorical and compelling in politics if we can find an objective account of harm. This argument and its categorical nature have clearly been set out in an essay by David Wiggins on 'Claims of Need'.

> I need (absolutely) to have X
> if and only if
> I need (instrumentally) to have X if I am to avoid harm
> if and only if
> It is necessary things being what they actually are, that if I avoid harm, then I have to have X.[27]

The assumption here is that there is a state of human flourishing or welfare and if a person fails to achieve this state then he will ail or be harmed. Needs are what are necessary to achieve this condition of flourishing, and getting what one needs to flourish or to improve one's welfare will act as a remedy for one's condition. The necessary means to flourishing or welfare that are needed on this view might be called basic goods. So are we able to specify in a non-normative, neutral and empirical way what basic harm or ailing consist in, and by implication what a minimum level of human flourishing or welfare is, understood just in the sense of not being harmed? If we can do this, then we shall be provided with a non-contestable account of human needs which can then be made the object of social policy and a non-contestable list of primary or basic goods that are the objects of such needs – both lists being generated by the basic human ends or purposes in question. If our set of needs turns out to be contestable, that is to say, if the idea of harm is held to differ between individuals and groups then it would seem that any individual would be able to classify any demand as a basic need so far as he/she is concerned just by arguing that he/she would be harmed by his/her position if the 'need' is not satisfied. We would then be back with relativism. We can see how easy it would be to deploy such an argument if we allow a sphere of psychological harm, because then an individual might well argue that the frustration of a particular desire would cause him harm, this desire would then become a need and there would then be a prima-facie obligation on the part of others to meet this need and thus prevent harm from befalling him/her. So can we say that there is an uncontested state of human flourishing, so that the failure to achieve this state constitutes objective harm to the person, and that there is therefore a set of needs in relation to this, based not upon subjective preferences, but rather in Wiggins's phrase 'on things being what they actually are'?

This ancient question has been discussed a good deal in recent moral and political philosophy. Some philosophers, Philippa Foot and Elizabeth Anscombe particularly, have argued that there are some things which will be seen as harm and as a failure to flourish whatever one's ideological or moral standpoint and the most obvious example is physical injury. This argument is, of course, Aristotelian in its inspiration because needs are being related to a substantive norm of flourishing and harm is defined in terms of a failure to flourish and might thus be thought to require some substantive view of human nature: a theory about flourishing and a theory about harm and the failure to flourish. However, this assumption has been attacked by Philips and Mounce in their influential paper 'On Morality's Having a Point' and they cite two examples to show that even physical injury cannot be considered an incontestable harm and therefore that physical health could not be seen as a basic need. One example they discuss is the case of Brentano, the philosopher who regarded his blindness in later life as a blessing because it allowed him to concentrate on philosophy. Here, a physical disability is not seen as constituting harm – what harm consists of on this view is going to depend crucially upon what one takes to be important in life. In the second case a Catholic mother resists the claim that she will be harmed by having further children because in her view ultimate harm cannot accompany the birth of the children of God.[28]

These cases do seem to give some substance to the idea that harm is so indeterminate a concept that any unsatisfied state could be thought to result in harm and thus could generate a need, and the point is given particular weight by the fact that both of these examples show how elastic and value-dependent even the case of physical harm might seem to be, which of all possible examples of harm seems to be the most concrete and determinate. If needs are to be seen in terms of harming or ailing then, given the value-dependence of these concepts, anything might in principle become a need. Conversely then, a person to whom a need is ascribed, because it is thought that he/she lacks something and therefore ails, may well be able to resist the ascription of the need on the grounds that he/she does not believe he/she is being harmed. In some cases it will of course be possible to convince the person by factual argument because his/her belief about not being harmed is based upon false belief, e.g. the person not knowing that he is a diabetic resisting the assumption of a need for insulin. If we convince him that he is in fact a diabetic then the need for insulin is likely to be accepted. Other cases though are much more intractable – perhaps the most realistic example is that of a badly injured Jehovah's Witness who is quite clear that he/she will die without a blood transfusion, but rejects it because of operating with a different conception of harm.

The central point here is that a theory of human needs does not provide an objective basis for moral beliefs; on the contrary our conception of what are fundamental needs depends upon our fundamental moral beliefs and not the other way around. A consequence of this argument would be an endorsement of the point made by MacIntyre in a passage cited above in chapter 1. Given that a theory of human needs will be in some sense a theory about human nature in at least its basic aspects, it would follow from the argument just considered that I cannot:

> look to human nature as a neutral standard, asking which form of social and moral life will give it its most adequate expression. For each form of life carries with it its own picture of human nature. The choice of a form of life and the choice of a view of human nature go together.[29]

If this is so, then Christian Bay's argument cited at the head of the chapter embodies an illusory approach to the deep questions of political morality. It is important to be clear about exactly the point that the critic is making, it is not that the connection between the conception of needs and morality is being denied, rather what is being argued is that from the fact that something is regarded as a basic human need must logically be regarded as good, it does *not* follow that anything in particular has to be regarded as a need. On this view what we take to be a need or a set of needs is a matter of our choice or our particular moral standpoint, rather than inescapable facts of human nature.

Considerations of this sort would lead one to suggest as pluralists do, that the concept of need is essentially contestable because it is related to a conception of harm which is essentially normative and is going to vary from morality to morality, both inside and outside a particular society. In the case of welfare institutions which exist to satisfy needs it would follow from these considerations that when the social services recognize needs, these needs are not being 'discovered' as empirically detectable states that people are in; rather a norm of harm is being assumed and people are regarded as being in need relative to this norm which may in fact be contested within a society as much as outside it. This dispute will be of two sorts. Libertarians will argue that since welfare needs are related to a set of disputed values about human flourishing, it is incompatible with the minimal morality of a free society to have a compulsorily financed welfare system based upon a particular conception of need, harm and flourishing, rather than having a private insurance system within which individuals will be able to take steps to insure themselves against harms which they themselves define. If they choose not to insure this will either be because they do not see a particular position as being harmful or because they do not realistically expect to experience these harms. On the Left, however, the argument is likely to be that within contemporary welfare states needs and the associated conceptions of flourishing are being conceived too narrowly and that the welfare system should be expanded to cater for new needs related to wider views of harm.

Thus, if our ideas about human flourishing and harm are going to vary from one moral code to another then our ideas about needs are going to be equally morally contestable and there will be very little room within the morality of a liberal society for having state institutions related to the satisfaction of need which will uncritically impose one view of human flourishing on society.

Moral agency and needs

These considerations might therefore lead one to argue that the idea of need should have at the very most a residual place in politics, if indeed it has a place at all. However, this claim can be doubted if we consider the arguments which have been developed by Alan Gewirth in *Reason and Morality*[30] and *Human Rights*[31] and which were discussed in the previous chapter. According to this argument we can still identify basic needs while at the same time recognizing the facts of moral pluralism, even pluralism about flourishing and harm. Rather, these needs are not related to a particular morality and specific accounts of harm and flourishing, but are rather needs relating to the capacity for moral agency as such whatever the values of the particular moral tradition within which agency is exercised. Any moral code is going to have to find a place for the role of action and in Gewirth's view action itself presupposes certain needs: those of well-being and autonomy. Action presupposes that individuals are capable of deliberation and choice, forming plans of life and the desire to live in the light of particular views of human flourishing. This requires some defence of autonomy and in this sense autonomy is a need related not to particular moral views but to the very possibility of moral agency. It also presupposes not just physical survival but more than this, it requires a level of well-being because mere physical survival is not a *sufficient*, although it is obviously a *necessary* condition of action. If people have no relief from physical needs, if their whole life is bound up with meeting their basic subsistence requirements they will have no opportunity for pursuing plans of life or thinking about the kind of choices which they would like to make, or the kinds of life they would like to live. Gewirth argues that the basic generic goods of well-being and autonomy require both additive and non subtractive goods. Non-subtractive goods are those abilities and conditions required to maintain undiminished 'one's level of purpose fulfilment'; additive goods are those which enhance purpose fulfilment.

As we have seen the most ardent moral pluralist in relation to the concept of needs is disposed to argue that needs do not arise from the facts of human nature or the facts of human flourishing, but rather arise from the moral choices which we make in relation to regarding something as a need. However, just because this line of argument links the very nature of morality with agency and choice, it is vulnerable to Alan Gewirth's argument. Even if our conception of basic needs depends in some respects upon our moral outlook, we cannot neglect the fact that to be a moral agent at all requires that certain needs, those to do with the necessary conditions of agency, have to be satisfied.

It is, of course, difficult to know exactly what this argument shows. I believe that it does provide us with a basic groundwork for thinking about the moral claims of need which could be agreed as basic across different moral outlooks just because they are needs required for action as such not in pursuit of this or that particular view of flourishing, which as we saw is problematic for cross-cultural views of needs. However, there are very clear problems remaining. The first is a practical difficulty, because it could be argued that a high degree of relativity will be brought back into the argument if we cannot specify in a morally neutral way what are the types of goods which will satisfy these generic needs. The concepts of well-being and autonomy do not really seem to be specific enough to enable us to determine the types of goods to satisfy generic needs. If this is so, then it could be argued that well-being and autonomy play a similar role in this argument to flourishing in the previous argument. In so far as our conception of well-being and autonomy is inexact and may again vary between different moral standpoints then the recognition of this will weaken the foundational objectivity which Gewirth regards his argument as supplying to morality and politics. This does not entail that claims of need are irrelevant or dispensable; on the contrary the needs of agency will be present in any society and in any moral code but what is taken as an adequate level of goods, intuitions and forebearances to satisfy these needs will differ and will be subject to political negotiation. This does not mean, however, that the recognition of basic needs is irrelevant: far from it. It can provide us with a kind of basic mark or critical standard in terms of which a society can be assessed, even if there is political disagreement about what satisfies these needs. Indeed, this is how the issue has in fact been presented by Michael Walzer, perhaps the most self-conscious pluralist, in his recent book *Spheres of Justice* in which he argues that needs operate at two levels, a basic level at which we can elucidate philosophically the general nature of a need and then its particular mode of satisfaction, which is a matter of history and politics.

> People don't just have needs, they have ideas about their needs; they have priorities, they have degrees of need, and their priorities and degrees are related not only to their human nature but also to their history and culture. Since resources are always scarce, hard choices have to be made. They are subject to a certain philosophical elucidation, but the idea of need and the commitment to communal provision do not by themselves yield any clear determination of priorities or degrees ... The question of degree suggests even more clearly the importance of political choice and the irrelevance of any purely philosophical stipulation ... But it would be wrong to suggest therefore that need cannot be a distributive principle. It is, rather, a principle subject to political limitation; and the limits (within limits) can be arbitrary, fixed by some contemporary coalition of interests or majority of voters.[32]

He goes on to argue, however, that these need claims in specific cases, such as the need for security, would embody certain understandings more or less widely shared, controversial only at the margins, of what constitutes 'enough' security within a particular community and this reference to the community's own understanding and negotiation of such terms is vital since in Walzer's view the attempt to stipulate or elucidate the nature of need philosophically is in some sense anti-political, it embodies a lack of confidence in democratic political processes: 'Any philosophical effort to stipulate in detail the rights or the entitlement of individuals would radically constrain the scope of democratic decision-making.'

Nevertheless, it is precisely this point which marries the radical pluralist perspective of a need-oriented approach to politics and political claims. The views of John Gray, for example, provide a good counter-point to Walzer's argument and a lack of confidence in the possibility of doing, in a morally diverse society, what Walzer claims can be done in the absence of a philosophically watertight definition of needs and the sorts of goods which would satisfy them. Thus Gray argues in a quotation cited earlier but which bears repetition at this point:

> Needs can be given no plausible cross cultural content, but instead are seen to vary across different moral traditions. Even where moral traditions overlap so as to allow agreement to be reached on a list of basic needs, there are no means of arriving at an agreed schedule of urgency among conflicting basic needs ... There is an astonishing presumption in those who write as if hard dilemmas of this sort can be subject to a morally consensual resolution. Their blindness to these difficulties can only be accounted for by them failing to take seriously the realities of cultural pluralism in our society or at what comes to the same thing taking as authoritative their own traditional values.[33]

Where an interpretivist such as Walzer sees the possibility of such a set of needs as a critical standard or bench mark which will act as a standard in democratic decision-making over what is to count as a sufficient level of satisfaction of such needs, Gray can foresee no democratic consensus emerging, or if it does, its consequences will be illiberal because, given the relationship between needs and ends and thus basic values, any government, even with majority backing, which uses a principle of need as a distributive principle will be imposing some moral consensus on the rest of society. The issue at stake between Walzer and Gray over the nature of needs goes again to the heart of the problem which has so far been a major theme of this book, namely how to ground basic political judgements in a situation of deep moral pluralism.

Needs and obligations

Given all of these complexities, what are the claims of need in politics? It is no longer enough to say with Simone Weil that needs create obligations, because as we have seen the concept of needs is very elusive and the obligations which relate to needs might be thought to vary with the particular interpretations of the concept which I have discussed. However, let us concentrate upon the connection between needs and moral agency for the moment. Let us assume that there are some needs which moral agents have in common and let us assume that there are certain generic goods which a moral agent has to have if he/she is to act at all. Why should I pay any attention to the needs of others? What is the source of the obligation to seek to satisfy the needs of others and can such an obligation be put in a universal and morally cogent form? Or does it apply only to those towards whom I choose to believe that I have such an obligation – my family, my friends, neighbours, city, state or whatever? One way of attempting such a justification is through the idea of respect for persons. As we have seen in the earlier chapters of this book, it is a central idea of liberal political morality that citizens should be shown equal respect both by fellow citizens and by the state. If we apply such an idea to the issue of the needs which all moral agents are thought to have, what do we find?

The idea of respect for persons is usually justified with reference to distinctively human capacities such as rationality and the capacity for moral agency. That is to say, with reference to the capacity of human beings to form projects and pursue purposes as the result of deliberation and choice. It is because human beings are able to pursue such things that they are sometimes, since the time of Kant, regarded as ends in themselves: human beings are the source of values and purposes in the universe and each person who has this capacity deserves respect. Now, if respect is owed to other individuals because of their moral capacities what does this mean in relation to the needs of a moral agent? Does respect for another moral agent require that I should seek to meet his needs?

The issues at stake here go back to Kant's discussion of benevolence in *The Groundwork to the Metaphysic of Morals* and attention to the Kantian argument throws a good deal of light on the issues here. Kant puts the issue in terms of whether the principle of respect for persons requires us to be benevolent in the sense that those in need have a right to have their needs satisfied and therefore have a definite moral claim upon the resources of others. In this context Kant takes first of all the following case of a man who is himself flourishing:

> but he sees others who have to struggle with great hardships (and whom he could easily help; and he thinks 'what does it matter to me . . .'). But although it is possible that such a law of nature could subsist in harmony with this maxim, yet it is impossible to *will* that such a principle should hold.[34]

A rational man may pursue ends that require cooperation of others with him if he is to secure those ends, and if so he has to will the means to those ends – the help of others. If this is universalized then he will require that men help one another to achieve those ends, which requires cooperation. On this kind of basis then, it would seem inconsistent with the Kantian premise to argue that a man has no duty to help those in need because in a similar situation he might be so deprived and needy that he could not achieve whatever ends he might have without the help of others to satisfy his needs. The principle of respect for persons, as an alternative formulation of the Categorical Imperative, would be consistent with such a principle of social cooperation. However, it does not actually require it, because the position need not be the only one open to a rational man. As Robert Wolff points out,[35] it would be possible for a man never to set for himself an end whose achievement appears to require cooperation with others and to forswear any ends he had adopted as soon as it turns out that such cooperation is needed. In addition, the actual upshot of Kant's discussion is unclear – it does not imply that such help in realization of ends should be seen as a *right* as opposed to a *claim*; that it should not necessarily be seen as a strict obligation rather than as a matter of beneficence. Certainly it is possible to read Kant as implying a principle of help in the satisfaction of need as a right, but in the case of Goldman's commentary on this passage this goes beyond the text:

> We undoubtedly not only would want to be helped or to be answered favourably when begging for help, but would want to be able to demand help as a right so that the need for begging with

its additional degradation would not arise. We would want not to await the beneficence of others as a dog might do but to be able to demand satisfaction of basic needs as a right of human beings ...[36]

Nevertheless, there are reasons for going beyond Kant's own formulation of this issue which would push the principle of need satisfaction as a right justified by the principle of respect for persons. The basic question here is whether I can really respect a person as an end in himself, as being capable of action in pursuit of self-chosen goals and be indifferent to the question of whether he has the means in the sense of the generic goods or basic needs to pursue such goals whatever they may be. As a moral agent I am aware from my own case that I need certain things to pursue any goals at all, the problem is what if anything does this mean in terms of the obligations of others to meet these needs, or alternatively knowing that I have such needs why should I pay attention to similar needs in others. Kant is ambiguous on this point and its relation to the principle of respect for persons:

Now humanity could no doubt subsist if everybody contributed nothing to the happiness of others, but, at the same time refrained from deliberately impairing their happiness. This is, however, merely to agree negatively and not positively with humanity as an end in itself unless everyone endeavour also, so far as in him lies, to further the ends of others. For the ends of a subject who is an end in himself must, if this conception is to have its full effect in use, be also, as far as possible, my end.[37]

But what is it that grounds the superiority of the positive as opposed to the negative interpretation of the principle of respect for persons? Why should respect for persons require provision of resources, to meet needs as rights, rather than merely obtaining forbearance from interferences of various sorts? It would seem that the argument would have to proceed as suggested by Alan Gewirth. Any moral agent must accept in his own case a basic premise such as:

1   The satisfaction of the basic needs of autonomy and well-being are necessary for me to act as a moral agent.

Therefore

2   I must have freedom and well-being, i.e. the satisfaction of those
    basic needs if I am to act as an agent.[38]

If I have to have freedom and well-being as a necessary condition of my
own action then I must judge that I must have these things which ensure
my freedom and well-being as basic needs and broadly speaking these
will be of two sorts:

1   The absence of interference.
2   The provision of those basic goods which are necessary for my
    freedom and well-being.

Given that from my own point of view these are things which I must
have to act as a moral agent at all, the point could be argued in terms
of a *right*: from my own point of view I have a right to the absence of
coercion, and the provision of those basic needs without which I cannot
be a moral agent. In my own case, this assertion of my right to these
things is prudential – it is in my interest to have them, but why should
they extend to others? Why, in Alan Gewirth's view, should an agent
'take favourable account of the purposes and interests of others besides
himself'? The only reason here is to do with rationality and universalizability. If some predicate Q belongs to some subject A because
A has quality X then in all other similar cases where there are other
subjects who have quality X then they have Q too. In the case we are
now considering A is myself the agent, the predicate Q is the fact that
I must have my basic needs satisfied, and X is my capacity for agency.
From this it will follow that any other subjects B, C, D . . ., who have
the quality X, namely that of being a moral agent, then they must also
claim the requirement that their needs have to be satisfied too. These
are difficult arguments which will come up again in the chapter on
human rights, but for the moment it can be argued that if in my own
case I assert the necessity for certain goods to act as a moral agent and
for both the acts of abstinence (from interference) and provision (of
those things making for well-being) on the part of others, then I have
to recognize a similar claim by all other moral agents and it is this that
gives rise to the idea that need satisfaction is a political right. This is a
disputable claim, however, for as Bernard Williams argues, Gewirth's
argument implies that

> Each person's basic needs . . . commit him to stepping into morality, a morality of rights and duties, and someone who rejects that step will be in a kind of pragmatic conflict with himself.[39]

This is Gerwirth's view and implicitly it was Kant's also, as we saw in the last passage cited from the *Groundwork*. However, Williams rejects this view on the ground that if I see myself as making moral rules about the framework of rational agency, then the argument might go through, but Gewirth has not explained why I should see myself as engaged in this enterprise at all: 'it is not a persuasive list of what you should reasonably do if you are not already concerned with justice.'[40] It is only because I am already committed to the moral enterprise, whose roots must lie elsewhere, that Gewirth's argument looks persuasive, but this enterprise cannot itself be grounded on rational agency. We cannot derive an account of why I should be bound by the consideration of such rights and duties merely from an account of the generic goods or needs of a rational agent.

An equally severe difficulty, and one which brings us back to the heart of the issue about whether basic needs ground certain rights to resources, is that is that to concede a right to need satisfaction might itself involve invading the very domain of autonomy, which is a basic need. If, for example, we take the view that the basic needs imply a person's right to resources of others, this will constitute a categorical moral claim upon those resources, a strict obligation to help those who lack the means to life. Furthermore, as a categorical moral claim on others the state would have a duty to perform these strict obligations which such a claim would embody. However, in the view of the critics of government as providing positive aid, and particularly Robert Nozick, the imposition of such an obligation on all persons would limit their autonomy. The poor or the sick have no claim in terms of rights upon the resources of the better off unless the better off have actually chosen these people as recipients of generosity. It will have interfered intentionally with their negative rights. Nozick puts the argument thus:

> Side constraints upon action reflect the underlying Kantian principle that individuals are ends and not merely means; they may not be sacrificed or used for the achieving of other ends without their consent. Individuals are inviolable.[41]

Why may we not violate persons for the social good? Individually, we each sometimes choose to undergo pain or sacrifice for a greater benefit or to avoid a greater harm ... why not similarly hold that some persons have to bear some costs that benefit others more for the sake of the overall social good. But there is no social entity with a good that undergoes a sacrifice for its own good. There are only individual people with their own individual lives. Using one of these people for the benefit of others uses him and benefits the others. Nothing more.[42]

Social and economic rights requiring state-enforced redistribution to secure such rights therefore infringe the principle of inviolability of negative rights and as such they are infractions of the sphere of autonomy which rights are there to protect. Indeed, Nozick argues that social and economic rights would constitute such a fundamental invasion of autonomy and negative rights it would be best to see such rights as conferring property rights on another person. For example, the tax system of a redistributive state seeking to secure economic and social rights would be in this position because if:

People force you to do certain work or unrewarded work for a certain period of time, they decide what you are and what purposes your work is to secure apart from your decisions. This process whereby they take this decision from you makes them a part owner of you. Just as having such partial control and power of decision by right, over an animal or an inanimate object would be to have a property right in it.[43]

Hence social and economic rights and the state powers and functions required to secure these rights are therefore incompatible with the basic protection of autonomy with which rights are concerned. Of course, I may choose to give my resources away to the poor, but this is a gift and there is no corresponding right to receive. Or I may draw up a contract say with a charity to make over part of my monthly salary, here the charity does have a right to receive the money but the right is created by an autonomous act of contracting.

Can social and economic rights be defended against this attack – that they strike at the heart of the values which rights are supposed to sustain and protect? The only way in which such a defence could be mounted would be by showing that the interference with autonomy was justified by something equally foundational and this argument will be discussed in the context of the fuller account of rights in chapter 7.

Needs and false consciousness

In the final part of this chapter I want to discuss more directly an issue which was implicit in the earlier discussion about whether needs were to be constructed as psychological states or whether they were 'objective' features of human life or nature which could be ascribed to a person independently of that person's own avowals by an 'expert' of some sort. This kind of argument can also be used to claim that an individual could in principle be mistaken about his or her beliefs about their needs or real needs and the interests associated with them. That is to say, if needs are grounded in something other than wants over which the individual might be thought to have final epistemic authority, then there are grounds for saying that a person could be held to be suffering from false consciousness about the nature of his or her needs in that either they are not recognised as being needs or that false beliefs are entertained about them. This idea, as we saw implicitly in the context of the discussion of Fromm and Marcuse in chapter 2, is vital for some forms of critical political theory, particularly those inspired by Marxism, and in this section we shall explore the logic of arguments about false consciousness.

What is being envisaged here is that an individual can be systematically misled about the nature of his beliefs and among these beliefs will be ones about needs and interests. Marx saw false consciousness about real interests and needs to be related to class structure and domination in capitalist society. The beliefs which people hold about themselves and their position in society do not arise in a vacuum but are moulded by the major social forces at work in a society which in a capitalist society will be forces based upon the power of the capitalist class, those who own the means of production. The ideological nature of the general beliefs in capitalist society therefore means that individuals and groups will have distorted views about their needs and interests, that is to say they will experience false consciousness in relation to them. Herbert Marcuse takes up this point particularly clearly in his *One Dimensional Man*:

False needs are those needs which are superimposed upon the individual by particular social interests in his repression: the needs which perpetuate toil, aggressiveness, heresy and injustice. Their satisfaction might be most gratifying to the individual, but this happiness is not a condition which has to be maintained and protected if it serves to arrest the development of the ability (his own and others) to recognise the disease as a whole and grasp the chance of curing the disease.[44]

Obviously such arguments rely very heavily upon the idea that the critic of the prevailing view of needs and interests has some kind of expertise which allows him to see through the ideological distortions so that now in the circumstances in which an individual is happy and contented with his life, as in Marcuse's example, that individual can still be said to have false needs. So what is the logic of the argument about false consciousness and what is the nature of the expertise? We saw earlier in the discussion about whether needs were or were not psychological states that the fact that they are not is taken to give a licence to some sort of expertise in the ascription of need independently of avowals. In many cases we are prepared to accept such claims without controversy. There are experts who can tell us that:

> This plant needs fertilizer if it is to flourish.
> This engine now needs two pints of oil.
> This child needs more vitamin B12.
> This man needs insulin.

In all of these cases the needs are ascribed on the basis of expertise and real knowledge of the nature of the plant, the engine and the human organism, but even in these cases, there is a reference to ends, although because they are so widely assumed in the context it would seem pedantic normally to spell this out. Nevertheless, the plant only needs the fertilizer *if* you want it to flourish, the engine needs the oil *if* you want it to run efficiently; the child needs the vitamin *if* he/she is to be healthy; you need the insulin again only *if* you want to be healthy. These are goals, ends or values, which have to be presupposed if the claim to need is to be justified. However, we usually assume in the case of the plant grower or the car owner that they want the plant to grow and the engine to work, or in the case of the child and the diabetic we assume that they want to be healthy. However, the important point remains that the expertise and the authority of the ascription of need presupposes this background of shared values. If we assume the values in question in these examples we can see how an individual can, in specific cases, be mistaken about his needs or interests. He wants the engine to run, the plant to grow, the child and himself to be healthy, he is just mistaken in not recognizing that the goods in question are necessary means to these ends. In politics, however, arguments about false consciousness are not of this limited sort. It is not a limited failure of knowledge or information in a specific case which causes a person to mistake needs, but rather if a person, or a class systematically mistakes needs, or if a whole society is geared, as in Marcuse's view of capitalism to meeting false needs, then either the failure of knowledge and awareness is more persuasive, or alternatively individuals or the society as a whole are mistaken about the values and are pursuing needs, perhaps with full knowledge, but in relation to wrong or false values. So the critical theorist who wishes to operate with the idea of false consciousness is making either a conjecture about false belief or a moral claim about mistaken values. The first claim is that there is nothing wrong with the values which individuals, or a society, are geared up to pursue, they are just systematically mistaken about the needs and associated goods which are necessary to pursue these values and goals. The moral claim is more radical, that the values which the individual has or which are embodied in the standard objects of desire in that society are false. It is typically this latter claim which critical theorists are making and this is clearly found in the writings of Fromm and Marcuse discussed in chapter 2. However, it is just this claim which is dubious because, as we have seen, it is difficult to see what the truth conditions are of such authoritative judgements about values, but without these truth conditions being satisfied, it is very difficult to see how the claim that needs are *false* as opposed to being related to a *different* set of ends and thus merely *different* needs could be vindicated. The idea of false consciousness as a *moral* claim requires some kind of moral vantage point which is regarded as being objectively valid from which to make the judgement that the pursuit of needs in relation to a set of ends or values which from the vantage point are regarded as *false* can be made. Typically, as we saw in the case of Fromm and Marcuse, this will depend upon the acceptance of a substantive theory of human nature, but there are strong reasons for believing that such theories have great difficulty in being objectively grounded, at least with sufficient cogency to be regarded as a basis for the ascription of *false* consciousness and the paternalist politics to which this could give rise.

The obvious claim in all of this from the radical critic's point of view is that in ascribing systematically false beliefs, perhaps also linked to false values, to individuals in the society of which he is critical, is that it appears to be a very paternalistic or authoritarian approach which seems to be painfully at odds with the very *emancipation* from falsehood and the creation of greater autonomy which appears to be the aim of the radical critic. So is there a way of making the argument about false consciousness in relation to needs and interests which does not carry with it these implications? In short is there an account of false consciousness which is more consistent with the humanistic aims of the radical critic rather than the very structural approach adopted by Marx and Marcuse?

In recent political philosophy attempts have been made by W. E. Connolly in *The Terms of Political Discourse* to endorse a view of interests such that what is in *A*'s interest is not necessarily the same as what *A* is interested in. What are *A*'s interests may be two different things. Connolly makes this point in a more elaborate way in trying to get close to a definition of real interests, or to a set of circumstances which would provide the truth conditions for such arguments:

> Policy *X* is more in *A*'s interest than policy *Y* if *A*, were he to experience the results of *X* and *Y*, would choose *X* as the result he would rather have for himself.[45]

This way of making the point is really very important. In discussing the relation between needs and wants I pointed to the possibility of being presented with two rather different sets of facts about an individual. His wants and an account of what he is interested in on the one hand, and his needs and what is in his interest on the other. There are obviously highly authoritarian overtones in ascribing the latter to an individual independently of the former, the assumption being based upon the authority vested in some kind of knowledge or external vantage point in relation to needs and real interests. The great merit of the Connolly proposal is that it brings back an account of interests to the person concerned – what he or she would chose under certain conditions – and moves it away from the claims of the expert. So a schedule of real interests would finally be determined by the individual whose interests they are by means of Connolly's account of choice in a hypothetical condition.

However, are the benefits of this proposal more apparent than real? The problems in the approach are fairly obvious. There is an indefinitely large range of policies in relation to A about which he might have to judge and it would seem to have to be the external observer or analyst who has the role of deciding which among the range of alternatives will be counted in the decision. In addition, these choices are hypothetical or counterfactual; how could they be operated? Does not the device in fact become a basis on which the radical critic would have to construct speculatively what he believes citizens *would* choose, if they were able to experience the range of policies in question. In order to construct an answer to this hypothetical question he will again be driven back to speculation about human nature and the way in which different social and political forms do or do not go to realize human nature and human flourishing. Again, it is very difficult to avoid the conclusion that one set of values are being privileged and that this is inconsistent with the equality of respect and the concern for courtesy which are at the very heart of liberalism.

This does not mean, however, that there are no grounds for arguments about false consciousness in relation to need. If it is in fact true that there are generic goods or basic needs related to the necessary conditions of agency as such which can be defined, at least in broad terms, without reference to a particular moral outlook, then there might be a very limited place for arguments about false consciousness focused on the idea of agency. As I have argued, this concept may be a central pre-supposition of any particular moral outlook even if it is not directly recognized as such within that moral position. Not to be responsive to the needs which relate to agency, which are needs both for goods and for forbearances, would be a form of false consciousness, and it would in fact be a case of willing the end but not the means, that is to say, endorsing the values of a particular morality but being indifferent as to whether individuals had the necessary means in the sense of the sat-isfaction of basic needs to pursue these goals and values. In this sense there could therefore be a form of false consciousness, but the vantage point from which it is ascribed is not based upon a particular substantive moral standpoint, nor is it based upon the claim to be in possession of a developed 'scientific' social theory; rather it is based upon what are taken to be the generic, primary or basic goods of agency and thus is concerned with a presupposition of morality rather than being drawn from one specific moral standpoint.

However, this claim is still vulnerable to Williams's argument discussed earlier, at least in so far as it is being used to provide some kind of philosophical grounding for a theory of rights and duties. This type of position does not provide an adequate explanation of why one should engage in the moral enterprise at all.

Notes

1   A. Maslow, *Towards a Psychology of Being*, 2nd edn, Van Nostrand, Princeton, NJ., 1968, p. 4.
2   A. Forder, *Concepts in Social Administration*, Routledge, London, 1974, p. 39.
3   J. Bradshaw, 'The Concept of Social Need', *New Society*, 1972, p. 640.
4   D. Thompson, 'The Welfare State', *New Reasoner*, 1958, 1, no. 4, p. 56.
5   V. George and P. Wilding, *Ideology and Social Policy*, Routledge, London, 1976, dust jacket.
6   R. Fitzgerald, 'The Ambiguity and Rhetoric of "Need" ' , in *Human Needs and Politics*, ed. R. Fitzgerald, Pergamon Press, Oxford, 1977, p. 211.
7   D. Miller, *Social Justice*, The Clarendon Press, Oxford, 1976, p. 129.
8   D. Braybrooke, 'Let Needs Diminish that Preferences May Flourish', *American Philosophical Quarterly Monograph*, University of Pittsburgh, Pittsburgh, 1968.
9   I have taken this formulation from A. J. P. Kenny, *Action, Emotion and Will*, Routledge, London, 1963, p. 198. See also R. Chisholm, *Perceiving: A Philosophical Study*, Cornell University Press, Ithaca, NY, 1957.
10 A. R. White, *Modal Thinking*, Blackwell, Oxford, 1975, p. 112.
11 Ibid.
12 Ibid.
13 J. Griffin, *Well Being*, The Clarendon Press, Oxford, 1986, p. 41.
14 D. Wiggins, 'The Claims of Need', in *Morality and Objectivity*, ed. T. Honderich, Routledge, London, 1985, p. 152.
15 White, *Modal Thinking*, p. 114.

16 W. A. Galston, *Justice and the Human Good*, University of Chicago Press, Chicago, 1981, p. 163.

17 Chisholm, *Perceiving*, ch. 11.

18 Wiggins, *The Claims of Need*, p. 152.

19 White, *Modal Thinking*, p. 115.

20 R. Plant, H. Lesser and P. Taylor Gooby, *Political Philosophy and Social Welfare*, Routledge, London, 1981, ch. 2.

21 White, *Modal Thinking*, p. 115.

22 Ibid., p. 119.

23 B. Barry, *Political Argument*, Routledge, London, 1965, p. 48.

24 White, *Modal Thinking*, p. 121.

25 J. Gray, 'Classical Liberalism, Positional Goods and the Politicisation of Poverty', in *Dilemmas of Liberal Democracies*, eds A. Ellis and K. Kumar, Tavistock, London, 1983, pp. 181–2.

26 See, for example: R. S. Peters, *The Concept of Motivation*, Routledge, London, 1958, p. 17; R. Wollheim, *Need, Desire and Moral Turpitude*, Royal Institute of Philosophy/Macmillan, London, 1976, pp. 162ff. There is a good discussion of these themes in G. Thomson, *Needs*, Routledge, London, 1987; and in Griffin, *Well Being*, p. 43.

27 Wiggins, *The Claims of Need*, p. 154.

28 D. Z. Philips and H. O. Mounce, 'On Morality's Having a Point', *Philosophy*, 40, 1965.

29 A. MacIntyre, *A Short History of Ethics*, Routledge, London, 1967, p. 268.

30 A. Gewirth, *Reason and Morality*, University of Chicago Press, Chicago, 1978.

31 A. Gewirth, *Human Rights*, University of Chicago Press, Chicago, 1982.

32 M. Walzer, *Spheres of Justice*, Martin Robertson, Oxford, 1983, p. 66–7.

33 Gray, 'Classical Liberalism', p. 181.

34 I. Kant, *Groundwork for the Metaphysic of Morals*, trans. H. J. Paton, Hutchinson, London, 1974, p. 90.

35 R. P. Wolff, *The Autonomy of Reason*, Harper Torchbooks, New York, 1973, p. 171.

36 A. Goldman, 'The Entitlement Theory of Justice', *Journal of Philosophy*, 73, 1976, p. 831.

37 Kant, *Groundwork*, p. 98.

38 Gewirth, *Reason and Morality* and *Human Rights*, passim.

39 B. Williams, *Ethics and the Limits of Philosophy*, Collins, London, 1985, p. 60.

40 Ibid., p. 64.

41 R. Nozick, *Anarchy, State and Utopia*, Blackwell, Oxford, 1974, p. 30.

42 Ibid., pp. 32–3.

43   Ibid., p. 174.
44   H. Marcuse, *One Dimensional Man*, Routledge, London, 1964, p. 5 and pp. 245ff.
45   W. E. Connolly, *The Terms of Political Discourse*, D.C. Heath, Lexington, Mass, 1974, p. 64.

6
Liberty, Interests and Morality

There could be no true liberty if a man was confined and oppressed
by poverty ... To be truly free he must be liberated from these things
also. More law has quite often meant more liberty.
Herbert Samuel, *Liberalism*

Poverty is not unfreedom.
Keith Joseph, *Equality*

The problems in analysing and providing a foundation for liberty
mirror many of the concerns which have dominated this book so far,
particularly the extent to which it is possible to provide a morally
neutral account of the concept of liberty and an account of the nature
of the associated idea of coercion which does not depend upon a highly
contestable social and economic theory.

There is also the question of how far different views of liberty imply
different accounts of the role of the state. On a negative view of freedom
which sees freedom in terms of the absence of coercion, the role of the
state in respect of liberty is limited to securing laws which will define a
framework of mutual non-coercion and staying its own hand in respect
of coercion. On a positive view of freedom which sees freedom as self-
determination, the state might be thought to have a wider role in securing
the conditions, powers, resources and opportunities for individuals to
become autonomous and self-directing. On what I shall call the minimalist view of positive freedom the role of the state would be not only
to secure the framework of mutual non-coercion, but also the resources

which are necessary for us to pursue general sorts of ends. On the maximalist view, the role of the state would be either to embody or to secure the embodiment of those goals and purposes in the pursuit of which alone individuals can be seen as free.

The attempt to provide a neutral and objective account of individual liberty usually issues in what has come to be called a negative view of freedom in which freedom or liberty (I shall use the terms interchangeably) is understood as the absence of coercion. The alternative conception appears to be more moralized and contestable. It is based on the idea that freedom involves realizing some specific human capacities, abilities and powers. The implication of this is that if these powers and capacities are not being realized then the individual is not free even if he or she is not subject to external coercion. It seems clear why this claim should be thought of as moralized and therefore tendentious because it seems to presuppose a theory of human nature out of which is developed a set of ideas about those abilities and capacities which bear most directly on freedom. In this sense, it may be argued, a positive conception of liberty depends on two evaluative assumptions: first of all a theory of human nature; secondly, an account of the important capacities and abilities in human life which bear most on human freedom. Neither of these assumptions can be regarded as other than deeply evaluative. In the view of liberal critics of positive liberty therefore, the negative view is to be preferred, partly because it is neutral between conceptions of the good and theories of human nature and secondly because only a de-moralized conception can play a role in political science and particularly in comparative judgements about the relevant degrees of liberty in different societies.

On the other hand, it is claimed that the negative view of liberty is not a moralized one. It is concerned with the absence of coercion of which an objective account can be given, not with the ends, goals, values, capacities and powers which it is believed a free individual should seek within the 'space' provided by the absence of coercion. The negative libertarian does not seek to prescribe the goals which an individual should have in order to be free. This is a matter of subjective moral preference. To be free on the other hand is to be free from coercion and we can provide a clear and objective account of this. Coercion, on this view, is a clear and identifiable state of affairs which can be determined independently of any particular normative or ideological position. Hence, on the negative view, freedom does not pre-suppose any particular view of human nature or any particular framework of values. Of course, the free person will pursue goals and values of all sorts, but this is not logically linked to freedom which is the absence of coercion. Hayek argues that:

> Our conception of liberty is merely negative. This is true in the sense that peace is also a negative concept or that security or quiet or the absence of any particular impediment or evil is negative. It is to this class of concepts that liberty belongs: it describes the absence of a particular obstacle – coercion by other men. It becomes positive only through what we make of it. It does not assure us of any particular opportunities, but leaves it to us to decide what use we shall make of the opportunities in which we find ourselves.[1]

It should therefore be clear that the negative view of freedom seems to fit most closely with the position which might be called liberal neutrality which it has been part of the aim of this book to explore. As we have seen, such an approach to political theory eschews a commitment to any specific theory of the good and any account of human goals and purposes. Positive liberty on the other hand has had a place, for example, in the works of Rousseau, Kant, Hegel and T. H. Green, who were clear that cogent political theories could only be achieved if they sought to answer what Ackerman calls the 'big questions', that is to say those that bear upon a metaphysical account of human nature, human purposes and interests. There is clearly a fundamental dispute here and in order to unravel some of its complexities we shall need to look seperately at the notions of negative and positive freedom and the related concept of coercion.

Negative freedom

The concept of negative liberty depends very heavily upon attempts to draw a sharp distinction between freedom on the one hand and ability on the other, such that freedom is to be understood as the absence of coercion, rather than a power or capacity and the associated resources and opportunities. It is freedom from rather than freedom to, and this view is then coupled with a stringent account of the nature of coercion. It will therefore be necessary to look at these features in some detail.

If freedom and ability were the same then the negative libertarian will argue that we would only be free if there was no limitation on our ability. Thus we could only be free if we were able to do all that we are free to do. However, the critic of positive freedom regards this as absurd. First of all it would, as Hayek argues, equate, freedom and omnipotence.[2] Perhaps only God would then be free in this sense because only God would able to do all that he is free to do. Secondly, the argument neglects the fact that there are many types of inability which it would be absurd to regard as a restriction on freedom. So, for example, inabilities may be of the following broad sorts:

1 Logical: I am unable to draw a round square or be in two places at once.
2 Congenital: As a male I am unable to bear a child.
3 Episodic: Since the wind is blowing today I cannot ride my cycle up that hill.
4 Dispositional: I cannot do complex mathematical calculations.
5 Decision-based inabilities: I cannot now run a marathon because of my physical condition which is the result of previous decisions which I have made.
6 Social and resource based inabilities: I am unable to fly on Concorde; unable to dine at the Ritz; unable to have a holiday; unable to eat three meals a day . . . and so on because I lack the resources to fulfil these desires.

In these different cases it might be argued by the critic I am free to do these various things because no one is preventing me or coercing me. If someone were physically to prevent me from running in a marathon or from riding my cycle then I would be unfree, but in all of the above cases my inabilities are not related to the coercive power of another. Clearly there are big differences between these inabilities. Some might be called natural in that they cannot be altered by human intervention; others are social in that they could be altered, as, for example, the resource cases show. This might lead us to want to say that where an inability is both natural, that is to say not induced by human arrangements, and not alterable by human arrangements, then the question of freedom does not arise. J. P. Day has argued this case. He takes the view that:

'*A* is able to *D*' is a necessary condition of both the truth and also of the falsity of '*A* is free to *D*'.[3]

That is to say, if someone is unable to do something, in a rather strict sense of unable, namely when that inability has not been caused by the alterable action of another person, then the question of freedom does not arise. I say a rather strict sense because the example which Day gives is of whether someone is free to fly before the invention of aeroplanes. Such a thing was clearly an impossibility somewhat like squaring a circle or a male bearing a child in my list. Given that such an action was impossible to perform were we free to perform it? Day argues that the question does not arise. So I am neither free nor unfree to bear a child or to draw a round square. However, this is a stringent sense of inability. Clearly Day's formulation is more general and would apply broadly to non-socially alterable inabilities. In which case something like Hayek's thesis would have to be modified to apply only to alterable inabilities.

Nevertheless, the strict negative libertarian view is that ability is not logically or conceptually linked with liberty. Freedom is the absence of coercion and that is all. None of the different sorts of inabilities cited above is the result of coercion and this leads Oppenheim to argue in the case of whether the poor person is free to dine at the Ritz that:

> Being free to do what one cannot do is usually of no value to the actor; but having a freedom is not the same as valuing a freedom that one has.[4]

In passing it might be noted that Oppenheim disagrees with Day on this point. In terms of non-alterable constraints on ability Day wants to argue that the question of freedom does not arise. However, Oppenheim argues slightly differently, namely that if one cannot perform an action such as fly before the invention of an aeroplane then while one is free to do it, it is a freedom of no relevance or value. However, taking Oppenheim's statement alone there are two crucial points about his argument. The first is the distinction between negative liberty and the value of liberty. The tramp is negatively free to dine at the Ritz, it is just that this freedom is of no value to him since he cannot exercise it. The second point is that the definition of liberty has to be kept seperate from the value of liberty. If liberty were to be defined in terms of the value of liberty then this would mean immediately that liberty was involved in subjective valuations of its worth and would lose any role that it might have in providing an objective criterion of a free society.

In order to avoid a moralized conception of freedom, negative libertarians need a stringent and verifiable definition of freedom and a similar account of coercion. By way of example let me take some definitions of freedom from the works of the leading negative libertarians.

Hillel Steiner argues as follows:

An individual is unfree if and only if, his doing of any action is rendered impossible by the action of other individuals. That is, the unfree individual is so because the particular action in question is prevented by another.[5]

Isaiah Berlin says:

I am normally said to be free to the degree that no man or body of men intereferes with my activity. Political liberty in this sense is simply the area within which a man can act unobstructed by others. If I am prevented by others from doing what I could otherwise do, I am to that degree unfree ... Coercion implies the deliberate interference of other human beings within the area in which I could otherwise act.[6]

Hayek argues in *The Constitution of Liberty* as follows:

By 'coercion' we mean the control of the environment or circumstances of a person by another such that in order to avoid greater evil he is forced to act not according to a coherent plan of his own but to serve the ends of others.[7]

Thus there is no reference in these definitions to ability or capacity. Liberty connects with ability only through the idea of coercion. Defenders of negative liberty are at pains to point out this fact, as for example Partridge does:

The linking of 'being free to' with 'having the capacity or power' deprives the word 'free' of its essential and unequivocal function, which is to refer to a situation or state of affairs in which a man's choice of how he acts is not deliberately forced or restrained by another man.[8]

The third argument which is used to distinguish between freedom and ability is an appeal to the ideal of equal freedom. On the negative view of liberty, equal freedom makes sense because being equally free from objectively identifiable coercion is a coherent notion; whereas on the positive view, so it is argued, equal freedom has to disappear because how could we equalize the ability of people to pursue the goals which they are free to pursue? So, for example, John Gray argues that:

modern classical liberals reject the Hegelian version of positive liberty, because as F. A. Hayek has pointed out, it results in the end in the equation of liberty with the power to act – an equation inimical to the liberal ideal of equal freedom because power by its very nature cannot be distributed equally.[9]

This is in fact where part of the practical political rub in these arguments comes from, in the sense that if freedom and ability/power/resources are seen as identical then this becomes a powerful argument for the redistribution of resources in the mistaken attempt of trying to equalize freedom under this false definition of it:

The confusion of liberty as power with liberty in its original meaning inevitably leads to the identification of liberty with wealth; and this makes it possible to exploit all the appeal which the word liberty carries in support for a demand for the redistribution of wealth. Yet though freedom and wealth are both good things which most of us desire and though we often need both to obtain what we wish, they still remain different. Whether or not I am my own master and can follow my own choice and whether the possibilities from which I must choose are many or few are two entirely different questions.[10]

So it follows from this that the concept of freedom does not bespeak a concern for welfare or the redistribution of resources. Freedom is different from power and ability and it is also different from the question of the range of opportunities which are open to someone. The question of what range of options is open to someone is not the issue; what counts is the extent of coercion. So, for example, this would mean that we could make reasonably objective judgements about the degrees of freedom across particular societies. Paraphrasing an example which Hayek gives in *The Constitution of Liberty*, it would then be argued that the tramp sleeping under Waterloo Bridge is in fact more free than the average citizen in the USSR because although he has few options to choose from he is not subject to the degree of legal coercion which characterizes the life of an average citizen in Russia.[11]

The final argument against the claim that there is a conceptual link between freedom and ability is that if we do link them then the degree to which an individual is free will depend on whether that person is able to fufil his or her desires. However, this has paradoxical consequences. First of all it makes freedom variable between individuals. I may have limited desires and the ability to fulfil them, you may have more ambitious desires but lack the ability. The degree to which each of us is free then turns upon the relationship between our desires and our abilities which is a subjective matter, rather than the objectivity which comes with the idea of coercion as an intentional action, rendering it impossible for someone to have done what he or she would otherwise have done. In addition, if freedom is our capacity to satisfy our desires, then this could mean, as Isaiah Berlin has argued, that one could become free by eliminating or reducing a set of desires which one did not currently have the capacity to fulfil.[12]

It is clear, therefore, that the idea of coercion is going to play a major role in the defence of negative freedom because it is this idea which rescues the negative view according to its defenders from the inherent subjectivism of the positive account. In general the argument here is twofold. First, that I may be prevented by natural and unchangeable inabilities, as for example the fact that I have now reached an age when it is impossible for me to entertain the possibility of becoming a long-distance runner. The second sort of preventing condition is an external impersonal force such as the weather: for example, the fact that it is raining prevents me from sunbathing; it is a fact that in Britain I cannot cultivate pineapples in my garden. These again clearly restrict what I am able to do but they are not restrictions on liberty because in both cases they are the result of impersonal forces – the ageing process and the climate which are beyond human control (coupled with Day's argument mentioned earlier that if I cannot do something as the result of an impersonal force then the issue of my being free to do it does not arise). Coercion requires the idea of intentional and organized constraint. However, the concept of coercion is complex and we need to consider several different examples, among which are:

1   Intentional coercion.
2   Threats and offers.
3   Structural and indirect coercion.

The first example on this list is usually taken as the definitive one by defenders of negative liberty and it certainly seems to be the paradigm case and fits definitions such as that proposed by Steiner and quoted earlier, namely that 'an individual is unfree if and only if his doing of any action is rendered impossible by the action of another person'. On the face of it this would seem to rule out threats and offers and forms of indirect interference as genuine cases of coercion. However, the argument has to be pursued further before these points become fully obvious. Physical violence or control of an incapacitating sort seems therefore to be the paradigm of coercion, and other sorts, if they are to be genuine, must be seen to have a close relationship with this core meaning. Certainly my rendering it impossible for someone to do X appears to imply some such concept of coercion. Such a stringent definition of coercion has one outstanding merit in terms of the issues discussed elsewhere in the book, namely that it appears to refer to palpable physical occurrences so that there is in fact no room for an evaluative element to creep into the account of coercion and thus the negative conception of freedom which depends upon it. This is at the same time a potential weakness, however, in that on a strict reading of the definition it implies that an action has to be literally impossible, that is to say not impossible in relation to the agent's interests or values but physically impossible. This is a very strict sense of impossible as opposed to saying, for example, that X was coerced because the action of another put, for example, his integrity or his religious beliefs or some other basic interest in jeopardy. However, if we move to this looser sense of impossible in which a person's valuation of his interests makes it impossible for him to do what he would have done before the intervention of the other person, then we lose the benefit of a non-normative interpretation of the idea of coercion. It would make coercion and therefore the nature of freedom depend ultimately on the agent's preferences or desires for certain goals, values or interests.

This point can be seen more clearly if we move to the question of whether threats and offers are coercive. While physical violence or close imprisonment is a core case of coercion, it may be argued that most cases of what is usually called coercion are not like this. In fact a coercive act is one in which threats are made or more broadly in which the coercer attaches to the options open to the agent costs which were not present before his intervention and thus deters the agent from doing what he would otherwise do. A choice or an option which was previously open is now no longer realistically available. The usually discussed example is the Highwayman's injunction 'your money or your life'. Prior to the threat the individual was able to keep both his money and his life; now he has to choose and the costs attached to keeping his money are insupportable i.e., losing his life.

However, there are difficulties with this. The first and perhaps the most philosophical is that it becomes very difficult to define an act which stops short of clear physical control as coercive without some view of human interests such as the value of life, or religious integrity which it would be difficult for a person to abandon. If this broader sense of coercion is allowed then the negative libertarian is giving an implicitly normative account of freedom and coercion because the account of coercion will depend upon a view about basic human interests. This could take two forms. On the one hand it could be argued that such interests are a matter for the individual to determine and will ultimately reflect his/her subjective preferences; or alternatively the view will depend upon some conception of what the objective interests of human beings are. The costs involved in the first alternative are obvious. It would mean that the idea of coercion would vary with individual preferences and this would make issues relating to the identification of coercion and thus of liberty irreducibly subjective. However, within the liberal tradition, at least as it has been interpreted since the Second World War, the costs of the second alternative are equally high because the identification of coercion would depend upon some objective characterization of interests and the difficulty with that is that this would be impossible to attain without some theory of the human person and associated capacities and interests which the negative libertarian wishes to avoid and which he criticizes the positive libertarian for holding.

That this is so can perhaps be seen by reflecting on an interpretation of the threat/offer situation. Consider the following case:

P offers a reward to R for doing X.
P threatens a penalty if R does not do X.

The first example, it may be argued, is not coercive because R can still be free to abstain from doing X and forgo the offer however tempting it is This may be widely agreed although it might depend upon R's antecedent situation. So if R were in poverty and X was the offer of more resources, then it could be argued that doing X is a coerced act because getting out of poverty is such a basic interest which R could not give up and his not doing X was therefore rendered practically impossible. The second case might be regarded as more obviously coercive depending on the nature and credibility of the threat. However, Steiner, who as we saw adopts the stringent view of coercion as a non-normative notion, says the following:

Interventions of an offering or a threatening kind effect changes in an individual's relative desires to do certain actions. But neither the making of threats nor that of offers constitutes a diminution of personal liberty.[13]

This again preserves the independence of coercion and liberty from what might be called philosophical anthropology, that is a theory of basic desires and interests, but at the cost of making the definition of coercion and liberty very narrow.

Take another example which brings out the difference: H threatens to kill T unless T hands over his money. Is this coercive? John Day and presumably Steiner argue that it is not. This is what Day says:

We can predict that T will almost certainly hand over his money, because we know that this is what almost everybody does in such a case. But it neither follows nor is it true that T is unfree to keep his money in this situation, as he would be if H forced him to hand it over.[14]

Here again we see this physicalist conception of coercion at work in Day's terminology of forcing the individual to hand over the money as opposed to the threat of death which, because it depends upon his desires, does not make the person unfree to hand over his money. However, the example is given a different interpretation by Oppenheim in that he argues that assuming the threat is credible then this becomes a threat of the 'severest kind of deprivation' and one that makes it 'practically impossible' for the person to resist and that 'makes him unfree to do so'.[15] Here we have a clear example and two radically different interpretations of liberty: one which trades upon a strict physicalist interpretation of coercion; the second of which recognizes the example as one of coercion because it recognizes a link between a basic human interest and practical impossibility. However, once this latter point is conceded then we really need a theory of basic interests which when threatened make it 'practically impossible' for someone not to do what the coercer wants. These could go way beyond just the maintenance of human life or ones's own life. Imagine a religious person who is faced with the desecration of an object important in his religious practice unless he does X. In this case a religious interest which impinges on what the individual regards as valuable and sacred in life would make a refusal of the action certainly physically possible, but practically impossible. We are therefore faced with a stark choice here: between a narrow and incontestable view of coercion which leaves everything other than coercion through total control of an action or the physical impossibility of performing an action within the realm of freedom. Or a view of coercion as embracing practical impossibility, which as Steiner clearly recognizes has to be linked to either the agent's own desires or preferences, which then seems to commit us either to a Protagorean relativism in respect of freedom and coercion, or to a theory about real or basic interests which would draw the boundaries of practical impossibility. The second of these seems more realistic, but it does commit the theorist to doing what has been so vigorously resisted, namely resting a theory of liberty on a defensible, but normative view of human interests reflecting a conception of human nature. As we shall see, a similar issue comes back to haunt the negative libertarian in relation to two other issues: namely an account of the relation between options and freedom and an account of the value of liberty in human life. However, before turning to these matters we need to look at some other issues in relation to coercion, but we need for the moment to draw out an important consequence of the preceeding discussion. That is, that except on the restricted basis proposed by Steiner and Day there is no sharp line at this stage to be drawn between the negative and positive concepts of liberty in terms of the latter requiring and the former not requiring a specific conception of human nature to support it in the sense of requiring an account of what fundamental human interests are.

So far we have been concerned with intentional or deliberate coercion whether through direct control or through threats and offers, but the issues relating to coercion go further than this and indeed are related to some of the sharpest political controversy over the nature and scope of freedom and coercion. All the definitions of negative liberty which were quoted earlier from Steiner, Berlin and Hayek presuppose an identifiable agent or agents in the process of coercion and in the case of Berlin and Hayek there is a clear commitment to the view that such coercion must be intentional. These definitions therefore rule out what might in relation to agents be called structural coercion, and, in relation to intention, indirect coercion. This is a politically acute issue in trying to determine whether the outcomes of a free market infringe liberty for those who end up with fewest resources. There are two issues here for the negative libertarian, although for the moment I only want to take up the second. The first is that the negative libertarian will argue that because freedom and resources are not the same thing the relative lack of resources of the poor is not an infringement of their liberty. It would only be such if an individual, either through physical force (Steiner) or threats (Oppenheim) actually dispossessed someone of resources. Only then would we be able to say that they had been coerced in relation to their possession of resources. The second argument, which is the one I wish to discuss at the moment, is due to Hayek and denies that coercion can result from market processes because of their lack of intentionality. Remember that freedom is infringed only by intentional coercion. As Dryer argues in his defence of negative liberty:

Someone who makes it impossible for another to do certain things

is not said thereby to impair another's freedom, unless it is his
intention to make it impossible to do them.[16]

In Hayek's view the outcomes of markets are not intentional in the
relevant sense. To be sure, in a market individuals buy and sell and we
may assume that each does so intentionally. As the result of all these
intentional actions a particular distribution of goods and services, benefits and burdens emerges. However, this outcome is an unintended
consequence of all these individual decisions. Because the distribution
of resources in a market is an unintended outcome in this sense, it
follows that markets cannot be coercive in relation to the resources of
the worst off. Coercion requires the intentional actions of identifiable
agents. This condition is not satisfied and hence markets are not coercive.
Market outcomes are also unforeseeable for individuals.

How cogent is this argument, because it is worth remembering that
quite a lot hangs on it politically in the sense that one traditional
justification for state intervention in markets was to compensate for the
loss of freedom which the worst off would suffer under a free market.
Quite a lot of the case has to be conceded, but not the conclusion.
Hayek is right about market outcomes being unintended and unforeseen
for individuals, but is this enough to show that they are not coercive?
Two considerations would weaken this view.

The first turns on the issue of foreseeability. Clearly market outcomes
are foreseeable even if not for specific individuals. If this were not so
the defender of the free market such as Hayek would in fact be completely stymied because he and those who support him want to argue
in favour of market rather than collective or state solutions on the
grounds that the foreseeable outcomes of markets will be preferable to
those of state provision. So, for example, market theorists might advocate the abolition of rent control by the state in order to increase the
supply of private rented accommodation through the market. This
judgement is based on the assumption that market outcomes are foreseeable.

The second point which has to be considered in relation to this is the
distribution of property rights against which the market operates.
Hayek, for example, has to take property rights as given because any
attempt to change them would be an illegitimate exercise in social justice
(see chapter 3). Given that such property rights are distributed very

unequally then the critic of the market could argue that it is foreseeable that those who enter the market with least will end up with least. Given the existing structures of property rights, this is one of the more obviously foreseeable effects of markets. Clearly this outcome is not intended, but is this sufficient to make it non-coercive to the worst off? It is arguable that the answer is no, for the following reason. In our individual lives we can be held responsible for the unintended but foreseeable consequences of our actions. If this were not so there would be no crime of manslaughter. In this sense, therefore, the idea of individual coercive action needs to be broadened to include non-intentional actions but whose consequences for others can be foreseen. If, therefore, like Hayek we support the spread of markets against a background of unequal property rights, and if the consequences of this are as I have suggested, then we bear responsibility for those outcomes, even if they are unintended. On this view an action, whether performed by an individual or by an organization like a market, can be coercive if its forseeable even if unintended effect is to make it practically impossible for people to do what they would have been able to do had the intervention not taken place or had it been different. This kind of point may lie behind Berlin's argument on a similar point:

> If my poverty were a kind of disease, which prevented me from buying bread or paying for a journey round the world or getting my case heard (in the law courts), as lameness prevents me from running, this inability would not naturally be described as a lack of freedom, least of all political freedom. It is only because I believe that my inability to get a given thing is due to the fact that other human beings have made arrangements whereby I am, whereas others are not, prevented from having enough money with which to pay for it, that I think myself a victim of coercion or slavery.[17]

The crucial phrase here is 'human beings have made arrangements'. I think Berlin means to imply that these arrangements have these effects intentionally,[18] in which case a pro-market critic such as Hayek can reject his argument because of his characterization of markets. However, if the arrangements had the foreseeable if unintended consequence of producing this outcome, then I am arguing that the moral position remains as Berlin states it.

Clearly such a view will not fit what I have called the stringent definition of coercion, but it can fit others if we argue that the possession of basic resources is a basic human interest or need; that coercion can occur as the result of the foreseeable if not the intended consequences of action; and finally if there is some alternative policy or arrangement subject to human control or alteration which could have produced a different consequence more favourable to these basic interests.

Freedom and desire

It will be recalled that Hayek argued:

> Whether or not I am my own master and can follow my own choice and whether the possibilities from which I must choose are many or few are two entirely different questions.[19]

The former is the crucial one for liberty the second is not. The crucial question for liberty is what is the degree to which I am coerced, not what options and opportunities are available to me. If liberty meant the latter then there would be no categorical distinction between negative and positive freedom because freedom would become linked to the idea of resources and opportunities. It would also be linked to desires and moral considerations because if liberty had to depend on the range and quality of the options open to a person then again the difference between negative and positive freedom would become very hazy just because some forms of positive freedom, as we saw earlier, are linked to the idea that freedom implies pursuing some goals and not others – usually those goals which are linked to some account of what is important in human life. On the face of it, Hayek's point might appear to be implausible in the sense that the options open to me may be ones which I am uninterested in and have no desire to choose. Take again the example of the tramp and whether he is free to dine at the Ritz, which I discussed earlier. In Hayek's view the range of alternatives open to him does not matter from the standpoint of liberty. It is important that the options he now has are not reduced by coercion or that he is otherwise interfered with. But the fact that he has limited options in relation to his resources does not restrict his freedom. However, what if none of the options available bear upon his desires? That is to say he has options 1 to 7 none of which he desires to do. What he really wants to do is 8, which he does not have the resources for. On Hayek's view the fact that he is only free to do what he does not desire to do or has no resources to do what he does desire to do has no bearing on his freedom. If Hayek is correct, then freedom would be independent of desire and interests. Again, such an approach would entrench a stringent and non-normative view of freedom because it would be independent of either the individual's actual desires and interests and also independent of any 'objective' account of what options a theory of real interests or needs would regard as fundamental to freedom. This view is also defended by Steiner who argues that:

> To ask whether an individual is free to do *A*, is not to ask a moral question. It is, rather, to ask a factual question the answer to which is logically prior to any moral question about his doing *A* . . . Thus it is mistaken to imagine that our conception of freedom is bounded by our notions of what might be worthwhile doing . . . It follows from these considerations that statements to the effect that '*X* is free to do *A*' do not imply or presuppose statements to the effect either that '*X* wants to do *A*' or that '*X* has no obligation to do or not do *A*'. Nor therefore do they imply or presuppose statements about what *X* 'really' wants or about what is in his 'real' interests to do or have done to him.[20]

Freedom, therefore, has no logical link with desires, interests, needs or with any view of what makes life worthwhile and particular actions valuable. It is clear that such a view will preserve a very sharp distinction between negative and positive liberty just because different accounts of positive freedom turn precisely upon such ideas.

One of the strong arguments in favour of a divorce between freedom and desires is presented by Berlin. If freedom were the same thing as my being able to satisfy my desires so that I would only be free if the options open to me linked up to what I desire to do, then a paradox could be engendered. I could extend my freedom by limiting my desires or shaping and adapting my desires to fit the options available to me:

> If degrees of freedom were a function of the satisfaction of desires,

I could increase my freedom as effectively by eliminating desires as by satisfying them; I could render men (including myself) free by conditioning them into losing the original desire which I have decided not to satisfy.[21]

Therefore the link between desire/ interests/needs etc. and liberty has to be cut, otherwise freedom could be attained not by expanding the options open, but by eliminating desires, interests and needs. Berlin concludes from this that 'it is the actual doors that are open that determine the extent of someone's freedom and not his own preferences.' On this formulation freedom would still be an objective state of affairs because it would not be linked to preferences, and the range of options which were not restricted by deliberate action could be counted. However, this objectivity becomes clouded by other formulations by Berlin when he argues in another place that freedom is measured by the number and importance of the doors and the extent to which they are left open and some doors are more important than others – the goods to which they lead are far more central in an individual's or society's life.[22] However, this makes the attempt to divorce liberty from preferences very obscure in two ways. In the first place these passages refer to the importance of the doors which are left open and the question then arises as to how this importance is to be determined. Either it is determined by desire and preference, in which case we are back with the position which Berlin criticizes earlier, a point which is strengthened when he talks about the relative importance of these 'doors' in my life, or it is some non-subjective sense of importance. We need a mechanism, however, for determining how this judgement is to be made and clearly it cannot be made without answering some of the questions about what basically matters in human life – which on the whole negative libertarians want to avoid because it will make liberty a normative and contestable concept linked to some idea of needs or interests. The point at issue has been well made by Charles Taylor when he argues that:

Freedom is no longer just the absence of external obstacles *tout court*, but the absence of external obstacle to significant action, to what is important to man. There are discriminations to be made; some restrictions are more important than others, some are utterly trivial. About many there is, of course, controversy. But what the judgement turns on is some sense of what is significant for human life. Restricting the expression of people's religious and ethical convictions is more significant than restricting their movement around uninhabited parts of the country; and both are more significant than the trivia of traffic control.[23]

The issue then becomes whether such judgements about importance can be grounded. As we saw in the first chapter and subsequently, there are three alternative answers to this question. One is to take broadly the emotivist line and take the view that what is important in human life is a matter of subjective desire and interest; the second is to take what might be called the foundationalist stance and seek a secure basis of judgement about what is important in life in some rational procedure; the final alternative is to argue that what matters in human life cannot be fixed in some kind of objective and timeless way, but equally is not based upon subjective desire, but is rather connected with the way of life of a particular society and what is seen as important within it.

Each of these alternatives has deep difficulties, but before discussing them further later in the book, we need to take brief stock of where we are in the argument. It could be argued that the issues at stake here fall between two basic intuitions about liberty:

1   If I live in a society where the options available to me overlap little, if at all, with what I want to do then it would be perverse to say that I had a great deal of freedom (*pace* Hobbes, Hayek and Steiner).

2   On the other hand if we accept a definition of freedom in terms of my being able to satisfy my wants which is what (1) implies then freedom could be increased by eliminating the wants which are difficult for me to fulfil.

It seems therefore that the focus, if (1) is to be preserved, must shift to a critical discussion of the nature of desire and interest. Such a discussion, it seems, would have to draw upon the three grounds mentioned above – subjective, foundational or communitarian. What is clear is that we cannot produce a coherent answer to the problem posed in (2) unless we identify a set of wants which are so linked with freedom that we could not see freedom being maintained by the elimination of those wants.

If we take a subjective view of the wants in question, that they are the desires and preferences which people happen to have, then two basic difficulties arise. The first is that it would conflate being free with feeling free and the latter would be a wholly subjective state. From this it would follow that freedom could not be used as an objective term in political science and it would be impossible to make comparative judgements about the degree of freedom enjoyed between individuals or societies which went beyond aggregating preferences. The second difficulty is related to the issue of false consciousness. If my freedom is related to my ability to meet what I take to be important in my life and this is to be determined on subjective grounds then what about the case where what I take to be important is severely limited by what I take to be the possibilities for my life? My sense of what is possible and therefore the range of what I may see as important may be limited by two things: impediments and limitations arising from within my own character and nature; the second could arise from the external culture of society which operates in such a way as to limit what people regard as a feasible set of options for themselves. In this sense, to accept people's preferences as an incorrigible basis for determining what their important interests are, and therefore their freedom, would neglect the possibility of increasing their freedom by extending their idea of what other options there might be in their lives in the light of a changed view of what they might regard as important. In each case practical consequences could follow from these critiques. The first, where the limitation on possibility is to be found within the individual, might indicate a role for consciousness raising or some form of psychoanalysis as a basis for liberating an individual from impediments in realizing a new conception of importance in life. The central issue here with taking preferences as an incorrigible basis has been well defined by Bernard Williams, and we saw parallel arguments in the chapter on utilitarianism:

> What one wants, or is capable of wanting, is itself a function of numerous social forces, and importantly rests upon a sense of what is possible. Many a potential desire fails to become an express preference because the thought is absent that it would ever be possible to achieve it.[24]

This argument, when coupled with the idea of the relativity of preference and its damaging consequences for an objective theory of liberty, leads us naturally enough to the search for a more foundational approach to the issue of trying to determine the most important human ends as a means of determining which satisfactions of which desires in life are important for liberty. It seems that broadly speaking there are three possible approaches to this issue. The first would be to adopt the kind of view which we considered in chapter 2, namely to work out an answer to this question based upon a fully developed theory of human nature. Clearly something like the Aristotelian view in which there is a clearly developed idea of the human telos and ergon would allow us to make definite judgements about human life and to allow for a critical standard for individual preferences to be examined against. As we saw in the earlier part of this book, however, there are major difficulties in establishing such a view and making it cogent in a pluralist culture. As a matter of sociological fact, it will be argued, what is taken to be important in human life will depend upon ideas about human nature which will differ within different moral traditions and our own society embodies this diversity. In the absence of first order consensus in society we have to turn to a philosophical vindication of a particular theory of human nature and as we saw earlier such an approach is fraught with difficulty and makes acute epistemological demands.

The second alternative would be to adopt a Rawlsian approach and argue that what is important in human life can be determined not from within a particular substantive theory of the good but within what might be seen as a thin theory of the good. Such a view would argue that what is of fundamental importance in life are the primary goods which are necessary conditions of achieving any other substantive goal at all. These are civil and poltical rights, income, wealth, the bases of self-respect and so on. A similar kind of argument could be derived as we saw in chapter 4 from Gewirth's argument about generic goods – those basic goods of agency which are necessary goods of action *per se*. On these views there can be an objective account of what is of shared fundamental importance in life and liberty would be connected analytically with the opportunities open for such goods.

There are difficulties, however, in establishing the objectivity of such goods in themselves and more so in trying to determine in an analytical manner what such goods require in terms of opportunities and resources. The second difficulty which is particularly relevant for the consideration of liberty is that such a view would ground a set of basic liberties to do with primary goods or basic goods, but unless we want to restrict freedom to these goods, then a broader definition of freedom will be linked still to other ideas of important interests which are part and parcel of substantive and incommensurable moral traditions.

The final alternative within the foundationalist model would be to argue that the important interests in human life are to be linked to the idea of what an autonomous agent would choose if he or she were fully informed and could experience life in terms of the realization of these interests. This assumption is in a sense implicit in Williams's remarks about preferences cited earlier. It is an idea which goes back to ideal observer theories in ethics developed particularly by Adam Smith and has been used a good deal recently by philosophers. Elster, for example, in *Sour Grapes*, seeks to solve this problem in relation to liberty with such a procedure, but his proposal is rather stymied because he cannot give a proper characterization of autonomy.[25] As we saw in relation to Connolly's argument in the chapter on needs, this is a very complex issue, but for the moment it is worth remarking that if we argue that a set of preferences are important to life because they are what an autonomous agent would have chosen in a free and unconstrained situation, then we need to question whether this judgement is possible without privileging a particular set of values above others, namely the values which form the background to his/her judgements in relation to what an autonomous person would choose to do. Is it possible, in addition, to give an account of the conditions of autonomy without invoking disputed values? In some ways Rawls's argument, which could even be seen as a rather elaborate attempt to determine the conditions for impartial and autonomous judgement, might lead one to be doubtful about this possibility.

The final alternative is to take the communitarian or hermeneutical approach to this issue and say that the basis for the judgement about what is important in human life certainly goes beyond individual preference, but is not capable of being given some kind of metaphysical or transcendental basis. Rather judgements of this sort are bound up with the identities which people acquire because they are part and parcel of a particular way of life. This goes beyond the arbitrary nature of individual preferences, but equally a way of life is not the sort of thing that it would make sense to see as having grounds of a philosophical sort outside of itself. On such a view judgements about what is important would depend upon the way of life of a particular society, as Berlin intimates in the passage quoted earlier (p. 238). It would follow from this that, given the putative link between accounts of important interests and freedom, the conception of freedom would differ between societies depending on what was counted as important within such societies. However, this would make the concept of freedom difficult to use in making comparative judgements between societies. Taylor, for example, wants to argue that without a view about what is of fundamental importance in human life it would be possible to argue that Albania was freer than Britain because while Britain tolerates religious differences and Albania does not one could still say Albania was freer than Britain because there are fewer traffic lights there and thus overall fewer specific infractions of freedom. Assuming for the moment that as the result of forty years of militant athiestic rule the Albanians have indeed lost any sense of the role of the numinous in human life, then given that what is important in life has to be seen against the background of life in particular societies on the model we are discussing, then it would be difficult to accept Taylor's case against the Albanians' being regarded as free because their basic interests as they conceive them are not being undermined by religious restrictions.

The other argument at stake here is one which is discussed in more detail in the final chapter, namely that the communitarians operate with two rather different conceptions of community: one a broad one in which not much more is required than an agreement on language and all that this implies; the other a strong one in which it is assumed that there is substantive agreement about specific judgements of what is important. The first is insufficient to address itself to the question of whether there are common judgements in society about what is ultimately important in human life as a basis for a substantive view of freedom; the second is far too strong in the view of critics because it assumes that there are such substantive judgements which could ground a theory about important freedoms and human desire whereas the critic will argue that, in a sense, political controversy arises just because we lack such agreement.

There is, therefore, a central dilemma here. On the one hand it does appear that only a normative theory of freedom can do justice to our intuition that it would be odd to argue that a person was free because he had a range of options which were a matter of indifference to him.

We do seem to need to link liberty to an idea of what is important in terms of human needs, desires and interests, but there are at the same time difficulties in grounding judgements about such things so as to produce if not an objective, at least a consensual theory of freedom for use in political science. For the moment perhaps the important aspect of the discussion to note is that it does not seem possible to draw a distinction between negative and positive liberty in the context of the former being objective and non-normative and the latter relying upon some disputed conception of the good. This issue of whether there is a clear distinction between negative freedom and at least some version of positive freedom can be pursued in another way too, in terms of the idea of the value of liberty.

The value of liberty

On the negative view of freedom we are offered a characterization of it in terms of the absence of intentional coercion by an identifiable agent and the question may be asked why do we regard this as valuable to us? What is particularly valuable about being free from coercion? It is possible that we might live lives with a higher level of material well-being and comfort without having liberty in this sense, so why do we invest it with such importance? Some thinkers have wanted to keep the issue of the correct analysis of the nature of freedom as a seperate one from the question of what makes liberty valuable. The former is capable of an objective and non-normative answer; the second naturally implies some account of the interests in human life which freedom serves. Before discussing the appropriate way of dealing with this question, we shall consider three potential answers to the question of what it is that makes freedom valuable.

The first is given by Hayek. In *The Constitution of Liberty* Hayek argues that the case for freedom in the sense of the absence of coercion depends upon the fact of the relative ignorance of individual human beings:

If there were omniscient men, if we could know not only all that affects the attainment of our present wishes but also our future wants and desires, there would be little case for liberty. And, in turn, liberty of the individual would, of course, make complete foresight impossible. Liberty is essential in order to leave room for the unforeseeable and unpredictable; we want it because we have learned to expect from it the opportunity of realizing our aims. It is because every individual knows so little and, in particular, because we rarely know which of us knows best that we trust the independent and competitive efforts of many to induce the emergence of what we shall want when we see it.[26]

The virtue of this answer from the perspective of negative liberty is that it provides what appears to be a non-moralized answer to the role of liberty in human life. This is important because if there is a close connection between the meaning of liberty and the worth of liberty then Hayek's account of the latter will not, as it were, spill over into the former. Thus Hayek's account of the role of liberty in human life is to stress that it has instrumental value in terms of the contribution that it makes to our ability to solve a basic feature of the human condition, namely our mutual relative ignorance. Even so it can still be doubted whether this answer can be detached from questions about the goals and purposes in human life when it is considered in the context of Hayek's broader philosophy which stresses the idea of human progress and the achievement of a particular kind of abstract society which he favours. So although his account of the role of liberty certainly draws from what might be regarded as an objective feature of the human condition, nevertheless it is difficult to argue that it is entirely cut off from moral considerations.

The second argument is to be found in J. S. Mill's *Essay on Liberty* in which there are broadly two sorts of answers to the question of what makes liberty valuable. The first is in some ways similar to Hayek's in that it draws upon epistemological considerations about the nature of truth. Mill argues that truth is many-sided and that it needs the freedom of expression and opinion whch negative liberty guarantees if the truth in its fullness is to emerge in human life. He also argues that to stifle dissent from prevailing opinions either through legal sanctions or the moral coercion of public opinion is an assumption of infallibility in respect of orthodox knowledge and values, an assumption which the history of human discovery shows that we have no right to make. Again, rather like Hayek, the instrumental value of human liberty is related to the nature and limits of human knowledge. However, there is a second type of argument in the essay which relates much more directly to a normative perspective. Mill argues in favour of negative freedom because out of such a society of mutual non-coercion will arise an experimental, self-confident, independent type of individual who constitutes his ideal of human life. In this sense freedom is justified because Mill argues the moral case that freedom will contribute to the development of a certain kind of character and it is obvious that this is a normative commitment. However, this still leaves open the question which we asked earlier, namely whether or not there are two separate issues here: that is, the meaning and nature of liberty on the one hand and the value or worth of liberty on the other. In the case of Mill it seems that these cannot be taken as two separate things because part of what he means by individuality and which gives liberty its worth is the capacity for exercising uncoerced choice. In this sense, therefore, his conception of liberty as negative freedom and his normative idea of individuality are logically related, that is to say related in terms of the meaning which he attaches to the concepts in his theory. If this is the case, however, then again the concept of negative liberty cannot be detached from an account of what makes life valuable and once again an attempt to differentiate between positive and negative liberty in these terms becomes highly dubious.

The final example of this sort of argument which I want to consider is to the effect that what makes liberty valuable in human life is that if I am free from coercion then I am able to live a life shaped by my own purposes and values, by my own projects and ideas of what is worthwhile. It is the opportunity of living such a life which makes freedom worth having. If, however, this is so, then a number of things follow. First of all it reinforces the points made earlier about the links between freedom and desire and interests. If the value of freedom resides in my ability to live a life shaped by my own desires then opportunities which do not overlap with these desires will not embody freedoms worth having. However, at the moment two other implications of the argument are worth pursuing. The first is that again the link between the nature of freedom and what makes freedom valuable is internal or conceptual. These are not separate or separable issues. Living a life shaped by my own purposes rather than those imposed on me by others both accounts for the worth of liberty and sees freedom in terms of non-coercion. Hence again there are moral issues at the heart not only of what makes freedom valuable but at the heart of what we take as characterizing freedom. The second point about seeing the value of liberty in this way is that again it makes it quite difficult to see a sharp division between a negative and positive theory of freedom in that if this is why freedom is valuable then there has to be some concern not only with what opportunities and options are available to me as seen by the strict negative view but the extent to which I am able to live such a life in the sense of whether I have the appropriate resources and practical opportunities to live such a life. At least part of the meaning of a positive theory of freedom is that it is concerned with freedom as a capacity concept, with the types of capacities and resources which are necessary to achieve the opportunities which negative liberty secures.

We have now concluded our review of negative liberty and it seems that two things are arguable:

(1) The distinction between negative and positive freedom cannot rest upon the objective character of the former and the normative character of the latter. If both are normative then issues about basic needs, capacities, interests and resources are going to be common to both.

(2) That when we consider the nature of the worth of liberty it is quite difficult to argue that the value of negative freedom can be judged to be independent of the resources necessary to secure the goals which within negative freedom will be open to me. Is a lack of capacity to achieve the opportunities open to a person a restriction of freedom or not? Even negative libertarians argue in different ways here. As we saw earlier (p. 235), Isaiah Berlin argues that it is a very plausible view to argue that the lack of opportunities and resources is a restriction on freedom. On the other hand, in the Introduction to *Four Essays on Liberty* he appears to reject this view:

> If a man is too poor or too ignorant or too feeble to make use of his legal rights, the liberty that these rights confer is nothing to him, but it is not thereby annihilated.[27]

In the first passage he argues that lack of opportunities can plausibly be regarded as restrictions on freedom; in the second he denies this claim. There he argues that it restricts the worth of liberty, but not liberty itself. However, we have looked at reasons for doubting the conceptual sharpness of the distinction between liberty and the worth of liberty. The clearest example of this is to be found not only in Charles Taylor's argument which we discussed earlier, but in Berlin's own work when he argues that the extent of liberty (not the worth or value of liberty) depends upon the possibilities open to me and the valuation which I place on these and 'what value not merely the agent, but the general sentiment of society in which he lives, puts on the various possibilities'.[28] If the extent of liberty depends upon these then it is unclear how negative liberty can be a non-normative account of liberty, and how criteria for recognizing its presence or absence can be other than morally based. Clearly the thrust of the argument developed so far in this chapter is that the lack of resources and opportunities are restrictions of liberty in so far as these capacities are either limited by social arrangements or are changeable by social arrangement, and in so far as they bear upon basic interests. The issue of how far we regard these things as being caused by social arrangements and alterable by them will depend upon the nature of the social and economic theory held – so, for example, Hayek's view of the nature of markets would not make the distribution of resources a restriction on liberty since market outcomes are unintended, whereas a socialist would because of their forseeability and alterability. Interests are also central in that not having the resources for a loaf of bread would, in terms of its relation to basic interests, stand in a different relation to liberty to the lack of resources for a journey around the world. However, we have to bear in mind this distinction between natural and social capacities. Those things which we are unable to do because of a natural limit to our ability, it might be argued, make freedom irrelevant. It is only when they are alterable by human action that freedom becomes a relevant category.

Positive Freedom

We need now to turn to a shorter examination of positive freedom and to consider some of the strictures on the concept posed by negative libertarians and to consider whether there is a defensible concept of positive liberty. In the same way as Berlin argued that there are two concepts of liberty, namely positive and negative, it could equally well be argued that there are in fact two concepts of positive freedom:

one minimalist, one maximalist. I will try to illustrate the difference reasonably informally and to argue in favour of the minimalist position.

Using the kind of terminology current in the debate about liberty, negative freedom is seen as 'freedom from' and positive freedom as 'freedom to'. So let us concentrate on what 'freedom to' might mean. It is arguable that broadly speaking it may mean two things. It could mean that X was only positively free if he was able to realize certain specific goals which, as it were, define what self-realization actually consists in or what human fufilment really is. Only in so far as a person is realizing such goals is he really free. In so far as he pursues other goals then, even if he is doing this in the absence of coercion, then he is not really free. This would be what I would call the maximalist view of positive freedom. Freedom is the fulfilment of a specific set of goals or ends. As such it is a highly normative account and is criticized by negative libertarians because it would appear to license some individuals imposing their values, i.e. their views of what these values of human fulfilment consist in, on to others in order to secure their liberty. In this sense positive freedom is both paradoxical and dangerous. Paradoxical because it can justify the use of coercion to secure someone's freedom, or in the famous phrase of Rousseau 'to force someone to be free', and dangerous because of the licence which this gives to one group who believe that they know what the good for man is to force these values on others in the interests of freedom. In discussing needs in chapter 5 we looked at some of the epistemological issues involved in providing rational grounds for such judgements about people's real interests. Whatever the cogency of these strictures, however, the difference between this and negative liberty cannot, as we have seen, lie wholly in the idea that one concept is moralized and the other is not.

The second view of what 'freedom to' might mean would be much more modest and would relate to the socially conditioned needs and capacities, opportunities and resources which someone has to have to pursue a conception of the good whatever it might turn out to be. In the first case positive freedom prescribes the goals to be pursued by a free agent; in the second case the minimalist account of positive freedom leaves the goals unprescribed and is concerned with means only. Of course, this is not to say that moral issues do not arise because how we define these necessary means to liberty will probably involve moral considerations as we saw earlier in relation to the arguments of Gewirth

250 Liberty, Interests and Morality

and Rawls and in the context of arguments about needs. It may well be impossible to give a non-normative account of these things; however, such an approach would remove the dangers of the maximalist account in relation to coercion in terms of ends. In this sense the minimalist account of positive freedom is in much the same position in relation to normative issues as negative liberty, in that both have to make some judgements about what needs, desires, capacities and so forth are of basic and fundamental importance, but they may be able to develop these ideas without having to be committed to some fully elaborated conception of human nature and the ends which have to be pursued by human beings if they are to be fully free. Given all the deep problems which we have considered in relation to such ideas about human purposes, it would seem that the minimalist view of positive freedom is the one to endorse, and the central issue here is located as that of trying to elucidate more fully the ideas of agency and autonomy.

All of this perhaps goes to support the idea that we are not presented with a straightforward choice between negative and positive freedom and pushes the argument in favour of the formula proposed by Gerald MacCallum, which is as follows:

X is (is not) free from y to do (not do) become (not become) z.[29]

That is to say, freedom is a triadic relation in which we have to identify the agent (X), the preventing conditions which may be constraints, restrictions, interferences and barriers (y) and actions or conditions of character and circumstance (z) which the agent wishes to achieve or values. As we have seen, however, it is going to be difficult, except on the most stringent view of negative liberty which does not really accord with our intuitions about the place of liberty in human life, to believe that there is not this triadic connection and that normative issues are central to all three components.

In the next chapter we shall take up some of the issues discussed here in the context of rights. On one view of rights, the role of rights is to protect liberty and such rights can be construed as negative rights, securing a space within which individuals are to be free from interference. The alternative view of rights has more in common with positive liberty, in the sense of securing the resources and opportunities necessary

for agents to achieve general sorts of goals. Such rights will be positive
rights to resources.

Notes

1 F. A. von Hayek, *The Constitution of Liberty*, Routledge, London, 1960,
p. 19.
2 Ibid., p. 16.
3 J. P. Day, 'Threats, Offers, Law, Opinion, and Liberty', *American Philosophical Quarterly*, 14, 1977, p. 260.
4 F. Oppenheim, *Political Concepts: A Reconstruction*, University of
Chicago Press, Chicago, 1981, p. 67.
5 H. Steiner, 'Individual Liberty', *Proceedings of the Aristotelian Society*,
1974, p. 33.
6 I. Berlin, *Four Essays on Liberty*, The Clarendon Press, Oxford, 1969,
p. 122.
7 Hayek, *Constitution of Liberty*, p. 20.
8 P. H. Partridge, 'Freedom', in *Encyclopedia of Philosophy*, vol. 3, ed. P.
Edwards, Macmillan, New York, 1967, p. 222.
9 J. Gray, *Liberalism*. Open University Press, Milton Keynes, 1986, p. 56.
10 Hayek, *Constitution of Liberty*, p. 17.
11 Ibid.
12 Berlin, *On Liberty*, p. 135.
13 Steiner, 'Individual Liberty', p. 43.
14 Day, 'Threats, Offers...', p. 264.
15 Oppenheim, *Political Concepts*, p. 63.
16 D. P. Dyer, 'Freedom', *Canadian Journal of Economics and Political
Science*, 30, 1964, p. 447.
17 Berlin, *On Liberty*, p. 122.
18 Coercion implies the deliberate interference of other human beings within
the area in which I would otherwise act: Berlin, ibid.
19 Hayek, *Constitution of Liberty*, p. 17.
20 Steiner, 'Individual Liberty', p. 35.
21 Berlin, *On Liberty*, p. xxxviii.
22 Ibid.
23 C. Taylor, 'What's Wrong with Negative Liberty?', *Philosophy and Human
Sciences: Philosophical Papers*, vol. 2, Cambridge University Press, Cambridge, 1985, p. 218.
24 J. C. C. Smart, and B. Williams, *Utilitarianism*, Cambridge University
Press, Cambridge, 1973, p. 147.

24   J. Elster, *Sour Grapes*, Cambridge University Press, Cambridge, 1983, p. 128.
25   Hayek, *Constitution of Liberty*, p. 29.
27   Berlin, *On Liberty*, p. liii.
28   Ibid., p. 130, n. 1.
29   G. C. MacCallum, 'Negative and Positive Freedom', *Philosophical Review*, 76, 1967.

7

Rights and the State

Political Philosophy ... is mainly the theory of what behaviour
legitimately may be enforced and of the institutional structure that
stays within and supports these enforceable rights.

R. Nozick, *Philosophical Explanations*

So far we have been concerned in this book with the possibility of basing
political principles on some sort of secure foundation. The collapse of
the Aristotelian project of founding a view of the nature, role and
purposes of government on an account of human nature and its corresponding virtues has led to a retreat from a goal-oriented approach,
or a teleological approach to this problem, to one based much more on
the consideration of the state as a guarantor not of *particular* human
goals, but rather of the possibilities for human beings acting as agents
pursuing goals and values of diverse sorts. That is to say, the centre of
gravity in political theory in the modern liberal tradition has moved
away from regarding state legitimacy as a matter of whether the state was
able to secure fundamental goals for human beings to a consideration of
those conditions which have to be met for individuals to pursue their
goods in their own way: that is, it has moved from a concern with goals
to a concern with rights.

On this view, which has been important to the liberal tradition since
the time of Locke, the proper range of the state's responsibilities and
functions is defined and limited by the basic or natural or human rights
of citizens. These rights are thought to give rise to enforceable claims
between citizens on each other and the basic function of the state is to
protect these rights and to enforce these claims. Any attempt to go
beyond protecting these rights is to extend to the state an illegitimate

253

range of functions for which there is no fundamental moral justification. However, so far these issues have been defined only formally – that is, if there are such rights then the legitimate role of the state, what it might be thought to have a duty to enforce, is defined in terms of them. Clearly the content of the list of rights in question is going to be fundamental in the sense that the more narrow the list, the less extensive the legitimate sphere of government will be. Before discussing this point, which is the subject of sharp controversy, two prior questions have to be answered. First of all, what is the point of talking about rights at all, as opposed to the interests, needs, welfare or utilities of citizens? That is to say, what is the particular moral and political force of talking about rights? Secondly, any coherent theory of rights looks as though it is going to have to be based upon a moral theory which provides the list of rights with some sort of moral foundation so that the list is not arbitrary, and which will also say what it is about human beings which makes them bearers of rights.

In order to answer the first of these questions, we need to draw the distinction between the idea of natural, basic or human rights on the one hand and positive, or actually existing legal rights on the other. Positive legal rights are those rights which a person has and can exercise under the legal rules of a particular society. In these circumstances to ask about a person's rights is to ask a question to be answered by referring to the legal system under which the person lives as a citizen. That is to say, the answer is an empirical one, to do with the description of aspects of a specific legal system. However, this is *not* the way in which the question of rights is posed by political theorists. They are interested in asking what rights a person *ought* to have, or what rights the state *ought* to protect and enforce. On this view, questions about rights are questions about how a person ought to be treated and about the state-based legal and other institutions which would underpin and sustain the morally proper way of treating someone. In this sense therefore, theories of natural, basic or human rights are attempting to pose the critical question: What rights ought a person to have under the law? Of course, this question does not admit of a directly empirical answer, although this is not to say that empirical evidence is irrelevant to answering it, as we shall see later in the argument. The point of theories of human rights is therefore to set up a critical standard whereby the moral legitimacy of a set of existing legal rules and the political institutions which back these with the use of threat of force should be assessed. There is, therefore, a clear difference between answering the question 'What are the rights of a person?' in this abstract morally foundational sense and 'What are the rights of an English citizen?', a question which is to be answered by looking at a specific legal code. Fundamental human rights are supposed to answer the question of how *any* human being ought to be treated and what kinds of actions can legitimately be enforced by the state to ensure that persons are treated in this proper manner.

Political and international history in the West has, over the past 200 years, thrown up many attempts to set up and codify such fundamental rights, the purpose of which is to set down absolute standards of political morality by which the actions of states can be judged. The most recent political examples of these are, first of all, the Universal Declaration of Human Rights adopted by the United Nations, which in its preamble is supposed to set 'a common standard of achievement for all peoples and all nations' and which in its final article denies that any state group or person has any right to engage in any action or to perform any act aimed at the destruction of any of the rights and freedoms set out in the Charter. In addition to this fundamental Charter, there is also the UN International Covenant on Economic, Social and Cultural Rights; the UN International Covenant on Civil and Political Rights, and the European Convention for the Protection of Human Rights and the European Convention for the Protection of Human Rights and Fundamental Freedoms agreed by the member states of the Council of Europe, which also sets up a European Court of Human Rights. This latter example reveals clearly the distinction made earlier between natural, basic or human rights and the rights which a citizen may or may not have under the laws of a particular state. So far as the United Kingdom is concerned, for example, the government has been obliged to introduce a Bill into Parliament which gives parents the right to have their children exempted from corporal punishment in schools as the result of a judgment delivered by the European Court that corporal punishment without such consent infringed the rights defined by the Convention, whereas this form of punishment without consent was compatible with previous English law. In this sense, therefore, we can see that the European Convention defines, in this case, how a person ought to be treated, whereas existing English law contravened this provision. As such, doctrines about human rights set up standards of political morality which go beyond what may be embodied in the law or the custom and practice of particular political communities. Indeed, it is precisely this aspect of rights which many political theorists have found objectionable because it makes political morality turn upon a set of abstract principles, codified sets of rights which must be abstract, because they refer to the rights which human beings bear in virtue of their humanity, or human essence rather than the rights which they have as the result of the specific and concrete life of the political community of which they are a part. This attitude is a specific case of an issue which I raised about the nature of political theory in the first chapter: namely whether it is properly the aim of political theory to ground the political morality of the state upon a set of abstract principles based upon some hoped-for objective standpoint founded on reason; or whether it is the task of political theory in a sense to bring to rational and critical self-consciousness the principles and values which are embedded in the practices, conventions, laws and institutions of a particular society. Indeed this matter is not just one for a proper account of political theory. It is articulated in a good deal of traditional conservative political practice of the sort which both eschews theorizing about abstract principles and also involves a strong sense of loyalty to existing institutions and the nation state as defining the boundaries of political morality, a point really summed up in Enoch Powell's pithy comment about a case taken to the European Court of Human Rights when he claimed that he would prefer to suffer injustice from the Queen's courts than gain justice from the European Court.

Rights are therefore currently politically important on both the domestic national political scene but also in the international sphere. The very fact that the UN Charter exists and provides an agreed transnational framework for political morality is a matter of great significance in the development of international politics. Despite all the ambiguities of the Charter and the obvious problems of enforceability, the Charter nevertheless provides a bench mark for arguments about the political morality of states and their moral legitimacy. Indeed, during certain periods since the Charter was promulgated these rights have played an important part in policy-making processes in the foreign relations of states. For example, President Carter attempted to make a commitment to these rights a cornerstone of his policy-making in foreign affairs. In addition, human rights provisions played an important part in the formulation of the Helsinki Agreement. There is also another way in which questions of human rights have figured in world affairs. Do human rights mean primarily or even solely civil and political rights, such as the right to free speech, the right to due process of law, freedom from torture, the right to vote, the right to free association and so forth, or do they also encompass social and economic claims against governments such as the right to work, the right to education, the right to welfare etc.?

As we shall see, there are sharp disagreements among political theorists about whether social and economic rights can genuinely be regarded as rights and this theoretical disagreement is mirrored in practical political disagreement between the right and the left in both domestic and international politics. Within domestic politics, for example, the moral force of social and economic rights would seem to require an extensive state with those powers and functions necessary to secure the social and economic rights of citizens; whereas the protection of civil and political rights would seem to require the existence of a state whose powers are much more limited. Internationally too this issue is contentious between East and West. When the West has criticized the communist bloc for failing to protect civil and political rights, the East has frequently pointed to what it regards as the failure of the West to protect the economic and social rights of citizens and in fact regards these rights as incompatible with the maintenance of a capitalist economy. This kind of issue at both the theoretical and practical political level has led one prominent theorist of rights to write as follows:

> I believe that a philosophically respectable concept of human rights has been muddled, obscured and debilitated in recent years by an attempt to incorporate into it specific rights of a different logical category. The traditional human rights are political and civil rights such as the right to life, liberty and a fair trial. What are now being put forward as universal human rights are economic and social rights, such as the right to unemployment insurance, old age pensions, medical services and holidays with pay. There is both a philosophical and a political objection to this. The philosophical objection is that the new theory of human rights does not make sense. The political objection is that the promulgation of a confused

notion of human rights hinders the effective protection of what are correctly seen as human rights.[1]

As we shall see, there are complex issues at stake here, but no one can really deny the centrality of conception of rights in both national and international politics.

Before going on to examine the issues and complexities at stake here, however, we still need to account for the function and importance of talk about rights. Why talk about rights of citizens as opposed to their interests, welfare, utility, preferences or needs. What is added to a political claim by making it in terms of rights? A practical clue to the proper theoretical answer to this question is to be found in the preamble to the UN Universal Declaration of Human Rights which states that:

> Disregard and contempt for human rights have resulted in bar-
> barous acts which have outraged the conscience of mankind, and
> the advent of a world in which human beings shall enjoy freedom
> of speech and freedom from fear and want has been proclaimed
> as the highest aspiration of the common people.[2]

Obviously the contracting parties to the Declaration signed in the immediate aftermath of the Second World War had in mind the way in which the rights of minorities had been overridden in fascist states and the subsequent holocaust in which millions of Jews, gypsies and the mentally retarded or the physically unfit were either actively killed or callously allowed to die. This leads us to the fundamental judgement which lies behind rights claims, namely how human beings ought to be treated and how others ought to be treated with regard to their behaviour towards other human beings. As such, claims to rights are categorical in that they define what human beings are entitlted to do and how they ought to be treated irrespective of the overall utility which may arise if their rights are transgressed, however much transgressing these rights may reflect the preferences of the majority, or the ruling party or whatever is the dominant decision-making group in a polity. The idea that the decisions of majorities may override all other claims was well caught in ex-Vice President Agnew's point that the concern for individual rights was a 'headwind blowing in the face of the ship of state'. A theory of rights is an attempt to provide some sort of basic moral foundation for the proper treatment of individuals by the state such that to infringe such basic rights is wrong irrespective of the utility-bearing consequences of infringing such rights. In this sense, rights are supposed to define the fundamental inviolability of persons and as such act as trumps in political argument and decision-making, so that the assertion of a basic right may trump or override the interests or the welfare of the majority. As it stands this argument is too crude and will have to be modified when we look in some detail at the complexity of rights, but it does capture something essential about the moral force of rights claims. It is in their opposition to a wholly instrumental, utilitarian, calculative view of political morality that theories of rights become distinctive and this accounts for their moral force.

Having said something about the purpose of rights in political argument it is time to move to analysis of claims about rights and to consider some of the complexities associated with these claims. If it is part of the function of claims about basic human rights they should, prima facie at least, trump claims about overall welfare, utility or the preferences of the majority and thus be foundational for a theory of political morality and the proper functions of the state, then it is important that rights claims are not merely invoked. They have to be grounded in some basic principle or set of principles which are thought to involve more than preferences or commitments. If they are not, then it is difficult to see how claims about rights are more than an oblique way of talking about one set of preferences over another. That is to say, we have to be able to base rights claims upon some basic principle which is thought to be rationally compelling. This principle will be able to explain why people ought to be treated in the ways in which specific human rights claims demand that they ought to be treated. Such a principle will be about those features of human life which support or underpin treating people in ways defined by rights rather than some other way. It could be said that rights protect human dignity and therefore we have to ask what it is about human beings that gives them the kind of dignity which rights are supposed to protect.

In order to bring some coherence to this discussion, I shall follow the lead of Alan Gewirth who, in his book of essays *Human Rights*, has proposed a kind of formula which claims of rights have to satisfy. A fully developed moral theory of rights will have to provide an account of at least four things:

1   The agent to whom the rights are ascribed.
2   The features of the agent which justify the ascription of such rights.
3   The nature of the objects, resources, states of affairs, forbearances
    and the performance of duties which rights are rights to.
4   The range of individuals or institutions who have duties or obli-
    gations which correspond to the rights of other agents; that is to
    say, who or what has the duty to respect, implement or satisfy the
    rights which individuals have.

Following Gewirth's lead,[3] these features can be put into a formula
which would go something like this:

A has a right to Φ against B in virtue of Y.

So, we have to give an account of the agent (A): what it is that grounds
the right (Y); the nature of the right asserted (Φ) and against whom it
is asserted (Y). Is there an account of rights which can fill out this
formula and provide us with a definite list of rights with a secure moral
foundation?

We can now turn to the problem of characterizing the elements A
and Y in the formula, namely the nature of the agent who bears the
rights and what it is about him/her which grounds the conception of
rights. What principles are relevant here? Such a principle appealing to
such features or characteristics of persons will have to fulfil three logical
requirements. First of all if the rights claims are universal then the
features of human life which make individuals bearers of rights will
have to be universal – that is, features which all persons everywhere
share – and not be culturally, racially or nationally specific. Secondly,
these features will have to be rich enough in content for us to be able
to derive definite rights claims from them. Finally, these features will
have to be morally relevant, that is to say, not just any universal features
of human life will do, they will have to have a clear logical bearing upon
how people ought to be treated and thus what rights they ought to have.
So, for example, while it may be both a distinctive and universal feature
of human life that all human beings have earlobes this is not a morally
relevant feature in the sense that it is difficult to see how any principled
conception of how people ought to be treated could be based upon such
a feature! The requirement in question at this point corresponds to the

formula cited earlier. A has a right to Φ against B in virtue of Y. What is at stake here is the nature of Y – what it is about human beings in virtue of which they can claim some basic, universal form of treatment by others such that states have a duty to enforce on all others such standards of treatment and dealing, and this feature must satisfy the requirements set out above. Only if rights claims can be based upon such a rationally compelling principle which will satisfy the criteria cited above will the claims be non-arbitrary and escape the charge that theories of rights are attempts to privilege one set of preferences against others.

Of course, positivists will argue, as we saw in the first chapter, that this search for a ground for rights in some morally relevant feature of all persons is bound to fail and that any attempt to found a theory of rights upon some such a priori philosophical anthropology is specious. The reasoning here will be twofold. The positivist will point to the fact that if the feature of persons in terms of which we ground our view about how we ought to treat them is an empirical feature, to be established by observation, then this feature, whatever it may be, will be of no direct moral relevance without further moral assumptions just because we cannot deduce an 'ought' from an 'is'. No strictly empirical feature of human personality can itself be a ground for treating individuals one way rather than another and codifying this treatment in terms of rights. On the other hand, if the moral relevance of some particular feature of what it is to be a person and to be treated in a morally legitimate way is established it must be based upon a moral major premise such as, for example, 'All beings capable of reason must be respected', which, with the empirical observation that human beings are capable of reason yields the conclusion that all human beings deserve respect. In the positivist view, however, the moral nature of the major premise means that it cannot be objectively grounded and is to be understood as either an expression of an emotional attitude or regarded as embodying some fundamental preference, in which case the scaffolding of human rights is really only attached to one set of basic preferences or attitudes compared with another. In this sense, as Habermas has argued, human rights arguments depend upon world views, that is to say, frameworks of moral values.[4]

Before this blocking argument is admitted as being decisive, however, we need to look in more detail at specific arguments designed to answer the question. In view of what features of human life are human beings to be regarded as bearers of rights? Or in virtue of what features do human beings have a dignity, a worth or a value which should be protected by rights?

One ancient answer to this question and one which indicates the requirements which any answer to it has to fulfil is the Christian one embedded in the natural law tradition, which takes the view that individual human beings have an inherent dignity and worth in the sight of God. This dignity and worth is not based upon the contingencies of race, nation, class, education, upbringing or any other contingent cultural factors about a person. While these factors are important and enter very deeply into the character of an individual there is still an aspect of a person which transcends these cultural contingencies and which is not fundamentally modified by them. So whatever a person's empirical circumstances may be, and however much his fellow human beings may disapprove of these features, nevertheless that person has an inherent and invariable dignity and worth not ultimately modified by these features, and as such he should not be treated in ways incompatible with this basic human dignity and a theory of rights and corresponding duties encapsulates this. I may vehemently dislike your character and what you do, but I must respect your dignity as a human being. This dignity does not require me to like you or love you but it does require that I respect you and do not infringe your rights. This argument does have the virtue of securing the idea that the feature in virtue of which human beings are bearers of rights has to be both universal – not modified by cultural contingency – and morally relevant – it is the basis of human dignity and respect. However, its force as an argument is confined to those who have the appropriate beliefs in the theistic position which secures the rights which would follow from human dignity. In this sense the situation will confirm the positivist critique of rights theories and Habermas's strictures – they turn upon convictions and commitments which cannot be rationally grounded and as such are arbitrary.

Whatever may be the difficulties of making the Christian argument here, it does give the rights theorist a clue about where to look for the basis of ascribing rights to persons. What is needed many have thought is some kind of secular analogue to the Christian soul – a feature common to all human beings which is not modified by empirical contingencies, but which is morally relevant. There are in the history of moral philosophy perhaps two general answers to this problem. The first is to posit universal rationality (or at least the potential for it) as the basis on which rights are ascribed; the second is to emphasize the ways in which human beings are distinctly beings who consciously pursue some conception of the good, whatever it might be, and it is in terms of self-determining moral endeavour that human beings have a claim to dignity and worth. For a theorist like Kant, both of those features are distinctive of a person and they are these features which all persons share at least potentially and which give life its intrinsic value and worth.

In the case of rationality the case is usually made in the following way. It is a distinctive feature of human beings that they are capable of ordering their lives, their thoughts, feelings and actions according to principles which they have reflected upon and deliberated about. Because of this capacity for what we might call rational volition or rational will, human beings live a distinctive life, each pursuing his or her own purposes, based upon some rational conception of the good for them, and are not therefore trapped within a circle of interests as animals are (so it is argued). Given this view, human beings' lives are not merely reactive, the passive receptors of external stimuli; nor are they directed by their own physiologically based desires and drives. Rather external stimuli and physiological drives can be harnessed by the use of reason to pursue some conception of a plan of life or a project. Since human beings have this distinctive capacity to follow purposes and projects of their own rational choosing, they have a basic dignity and worth based upon this potential. This implies, so the argument runs, that since human beings all have the potential to follow projects of their own choosing, they have a basic dignity or worth which is the basis of the respect which each person owes to another. Or to use the Kantian terminology, each person is an end in himself. From this it follows that individuals should not be treated in certain ways, e.g. they should not have this distinctive freedom eroded by actions or institutions which diminish their autonomy. The state should therefore enforce certain types of action – that is usually by prohibiting those actions by others which would diminish the freedom or autonomy of an individual to live his own life in his own way except, that is, in circumstances in which the exercise of freedom by one person will restrict the similar freedom of others. Treating a person as an end in himself and thus capable of rationally following purposes of his own choosing will require the state to secure a set of rights which put constraints upon the ways in which one individual can interfere with another.

This theory looks as if it can meet the tests which any theory about the basis of respect between human beings has to meet. The first test is universality – here the claim is that individuals have at least the potential for rationality and as such therefore a feature which is abstracted from cultural contingencies. Questions can be raised, however, about how far this is so. In the cases where claims about rights are most salient it is often the potential and not only the achievement of rationality which is in question. For example, in our own society several moral problems about rights have been raised by abortion, by the selective non-treatment of severely physically/mentally handicapped people, and the treatment of those in irreversible coma. In all of these cases the right to life, if we want to talk in terms of rights, is what is at issue and yet they are precisely cases in which we are very unsure about the ascription of the potential to reason, or to develop full self-consciousness. For Kant the capacity for reason was transcendental and noumenal and was not therefore in his view fundamentally modified by the empirical circumstances of an individual. However, if we take a less abstract view of human rational capacity, it is precisely in areas in which the conception of this capacity is so controversial that an objective answer about the rights involved is important, but because of the controversy about the ascription of rational capacity the value of the rights in question becomes very contorted. At the very least, therefore, a rational capacity basis for rights would seem to require us to be much more specific about the nature of this capacity so that its ascription in particular cases can be made a much more determinate judgement.

The rational capacity theory does seem to be able to meet the requirement that the feature in terms of which rights are ascribed should be morally relevant. If human beings were incapable of deliberation and choice, of living in accordance with their view of the good, it would not be at all clear what the role of morality and moral discourse would be in society. In this sense, therefore, the exercise of this rational capacity is not just an accompanying contingent feature of morality; rather it may be, as indeed Kant argued it was, a foundational presupposition of morality. In this sense, therefore, the positivists could be wrong. The possession of reason is an empirical characteristic of human beings which is intrinsically morally relevant because we could not explain the role of moral discourse unless this rational capacity to deliberate and choose were presupposed. In this sense, therefore, the capacity for rational deliberation is a bridge concept. Its ascription can be related to empirical criteria while at the same time it is a presupposition of morality. Therefore it can provide a basis for judgements about how persons ought to be treated.

Is it enough, however, to generate a theory of rights? On the face of it, it is, for reasons which I have already suggested. If this rational capacity is distinctive of the human person, then it would give us grounds for non-interference and putting constraints upon other people's action in relation to an individual. What is not at all clear, however, is how extensive those rights should be if based upon reason. This is particularly acute in the dispute about social and economic versus civil and political rights which I have already mentioned. I have already suggested that a theory of rational capacity could underpin a theory of rights which prevented various types of interferences with people, but it is ambiguous about social and economic rights. Does the exercise of a rational capacity for autonomous action in pursuit of one's own ends require the provision of social and economic resources? As we saw in chapter 5 on needs, Kant's own argument in the *Groundwork to the Metaphysic of Morals* is highly ambiguous about this. He clearly considers that treating a person as an end himself requires various types of forbearance and non-interference, which we could codify into a set of negative rights restricting interferences in free speech, free association etc. which would, so long as the individual conceded similar freedom to another, allow an individual to live life in his own way. However, Kant does argue that this is to agree negatively and not positively with the principle of respect for persons; a more positive or wholehearted commitment to the principle would, he seems to imply, require the provision of resources and aid, not just an absence of interference, and as such would provide a basis for a justification of social and economic rights. If the principle of respect for persons based upon a theory of rational capacity cannot of itself settle this dispute, however, then it clearly needs to be supplemented by further argument.

Part of this further argument, which is due to Gewirth, is to concentrate upon the value of human action in pursuit of moral values whatever they may be. The argument here is that we can recognize both moral pluralism and moral subjectivism and still be able to develop a compelling theory of rights. On the face of it this claim is paradoxical because surely, it might be argued, if what is regarded as moral value differs from culture to culture or even person to person, how could there be an agreed moral foundation for rights? The answer to this question proposed by Gewirth and others is to consider the necessary pre-conditions for the pursuit of any moral goal whatever it may turn out to be. These conditions, in Gewirth's view, will be autonomy and well-being. Autonomy is a necessary condition for action understood as the conscious pursuit of a self-posited goal rather than impulsive bahaviour. Well-being is necessary not just in physical survival, which is obviously also a necessary condition of the pursuit of any action. No, something more than mere survival is necessary – namely the ability to pursue one's conception of the good in the way required by that conception. So, for example, someone whose life depends upon a respirator survives but does not possess that range of abilities which will enable him to pursue his good. Autonomy and well-being in Gewirth's view can be the foundation for a theory of rights in two respects. First it grounds negative rights – all that range of rights connected with non-interference which are necessary to live a life shaped by one's own choices and dispositions – but it also requires having a range of abilities and resources. In this view the argument stresses the positive side of liberty, which was discussed in chapter 6, and as such would define the range of positive rights to these resources necessary for well-being and thus action.

In a sense, therefore, this argument could be interpreted as saying that there are two fundamental needs for human beings to be able to act morally: the first is autonomy, the second is well-being. Both of these support positive as well as negative rights and these fundamental needs define the basic necessary conditions for moral action whatever the conception of the good posited by individuals and cultures. In this sense it provides the moral foundation for a theory of rights. These rights should be equally possessed as a basic moral title by all individuals. The crucial thing, therefore, is the nature of action, which Gewirth takes to be the subject matter of all moralities:

Morality is a set of categorically obligatory requirements for action that are addressed at least in part to every actual or potential agent, and that are intended to further the interests or the most important interests, of persons or recipients.[5]

If this is an adequate characterization of the presuppositions of morality, namely action in pursuit of a categorical requirement within any particular moral outlook, whatever it might be, then reflection on what are the necessary conditions of acting could provide the foundation for rights. If in my own life I recognize these as necessary conditions for action, then I am committed to regarding them as necessary conditions for any agent acting in the pursuit of goals.

These ideas about human agency and its necessary conditions enables the political theorist to provide a more detailed moral foundation for rights than is usually provided in codes and charters which codify these rights. For example, if we turn to the preamble of the UN Charter we read a lot about the inherent dignity and worth of all members of the human family in which rights are grounded – but we need to explain the basis of human dignity more clearly and relate specific rights to these ideas.

Having therefore discussed the moral foundation for rights in relation to the agent – the ideas of autonomy and well-being – we now need to go on and see how these ideas relate to and indeed generate specific rights and in particular take up the question raised earlier about rights to non-intervention and interference compared with social and economic rights.

If the emphasis is placed upon autonomy, as in the first argument derived from Kant, then it is frequently argued such a basis for rights only justifies a range of rights to non-interference rather than rights to the provision of resources such as health, education and welfare. In recent moral and political theory this argument is most clearly present in the writings of Robert Nozick where the idea of autonomy is linked with that of inviolability. Respecting the domain of human autonomy is defined in terms of putting side constraints upon how other human beings may behave towards me and me towards them, and these side constraints as Nozick calls them will define the class of rights which I have to protect my domain of autonomy. Similarly you have a duty in respect of these rights – to forbear from a range of actions which have interfered with the domain of autonomy. On this view then rights are defined in terms of non-interference – the rights not to be interfered with so long as one is not interfering with anyone else. Traditional civil and political rights can therefore be interpreted in this way; for example, freedom of speech is the right not to be interfered with so long as my freedom does not infringe upon others' rights and the corresponding objection on others is to abstain from action, i.e. to forbear from interfering with my right. Freedom of speech is *not* the positive right to resources like newsprint or access to the media, nor is it the positive right to have someone listen to what one has to say. The right to life is the right not to be killed, *not* the right to the means to life – to resources, to food, health and medical care.

In this sense, therefore, arguments about negative rights are parallel to arguments about negative freedom and in fact may be said to presume the negative conception of freedom in the account of what the recognition of a domain of autonomy requires. For the same way as for the negative libertarian I am free if I am not the object of intentional coercion, so for the negative rights theorist my autonomy is secured by a structure of rights which require as their corresponding duties various forms of forbearance from intentional acts of killing, torturing, manipulating, shouting down etc.

It follows from this that if the fundamental role of the state is the provision of rights and enforcing the corresponding duties, then the state's proper duties do not extend to securing to individuals positive rights of various sorts – to health, education and welfare. The state has discharged its moral duty to protect the domain of autonomy if it secures the structure of negative rights. This point is frequently combined with an explicit critique of positive rights and we need now to analyse the basic elements of this critique.

The first and perhaps the most important point relates to the idea of forbearance. It is argued that if a set of rights is to be a coherent basis for political morality and for a theory of the state then the claims which the rights embody and the duties which correspond to these claims must be practicable. This follows from the Kantian dictum that I ought implies I can, that is to say, if I have a duty then it must be the case that I am able to discharge it. On the view of negative rights theorists there are both logical and practical difficulties to the idea of positive rights to resources. The practical objection is fairly obvious – if there is a universal right to welfare then it just may be the case that, given scarcity, it may not be possible to fulfil the claims embodied in the positive right. So Cranston argues, for example:

> The Government of India, for example, simply cannot command the resources that would guarantee each one of over 500 million inhabitants of India 'a standard of living adequate for the health and well being of himself and his family' let alone holidays with pay.[6]

Scarcity on this view makes nonsense of the claim to positive resources as a right. It may of course be an aspiration, but a right is different from an aspiration. 'Rights are', as Charles Fried argues, 'categorical moral entities such that violation of a right is always wrong.'[7]

In this respect, it is argued, negative rights are in a different position from positive rights. Positive rights as rights to resources are always claimed against a background of scarcity and therefore there are limitations on satisfying them; whereas, and it is at this point that the practical objection to positive rights turns into a theoretical objection, negative rights as rights to various kinds of non-interference are not asserted against a background of scarcity and are, therefore, always capable of implementation. The relevant duties corresponding to negative rights are duties of abstaining from actions of interference, and as such, because they imply *not* doing certain things, do not suffer from a scarcity limitation. Fried makes the point very elegantly:

> A positive right is a claim to something – a share of a material good or to some particular good like the attention of a lawyer or a doctor, or perhaps to a result like health or enlightenment- while a negative right is a right that something not be done to one, that some particular imposition be withheld. Positive rights are always asserted to scarce goods and consequently scarcity implies a limit to the claim. Negative rights, however, the rights not to be interfered with in forbidden ways do not appear to have such natural, such inevitable limitations. If I am let alone, the commodity I obtain does not appear of its nature to be a scarce or limited one. How can we run out of not harming each other, not lying to each other, leaving each other alone?[8]

As such negative rights, securing the protection of the domain of autonomy, are always possible to implement and are thus compossible, the claims embedded in such rights can be realized by all who have them simultaneously because the corresponding duties are costless duties of forbearance.

> It is logically possible to treat negative rights as categorical entities. It is logically possible to respect any number of negative rights without necessarily landing in an impossible and contradictory situation ... Positive rights, by contrast, cannot as a logical matter be treated as categorical entities because of the scarcity limitation. It is not just that it is too costly to provide a subsistence diet to the whole Indian subcontinent in time of famine – it may simply be impossible. But it is this impossibility which cannot arise in respect of negative rights.[9]

In this sense therefore negative rights are always compossible. They can be claimed by all rights holders simultaneously just because they are not claimed against a background of scarcity. They are categorical in a way that positive rights are not.

There is an obvious and standard reply to this argument, however; namely that the protection of negative rights *is* costly. In the world as we know it there may not be the requisite degree of forbearance to guarantee negative rights. There are in fact all sorts of interferences with the rights-protected domain of autonomy all the time. That is why we need the police, penal system and indeed government itself in order to impose the duty of forbearance. However, the negative rights theorist will typically reject this commonsense answer and he will do so by moving the argument to a conceptual distinction which can still be maintained despite the way in which the protection of negative rights in modern society requires costly forms of defence. He will argue that if we were a community of saints and had an unlimited degree of forbearance, institutions for engineering respect for negative rights would not be required and would thus not involve claims to resources.[10]

If the critic of positive rights can be allowed such a counterfactual in order to preserve the conceptual distinction, however, the defender of positive rights could equally claim that the distinction had no substance, by invoking his own counterfactual – a world without scarcity. If there were no scarcity of material goods the rights of such goods would not then be susceptible to the critics' strictures. There is nothing in this counterfactual that is more incoherent or far-fetched than the earlier one. Both arguments are basically about scarcity: in the case of negative rights it is a real world scarcity of human motivation which puts a limit on forbearance, in the positive or welfare rights case, a scarcity in material resources. Thus a sharp distinction between the two sorts of rights cannot be made out on these grounds. It might be argued that this way of making the point about the similarity between negative and positive rights is based on a confusion between the right and the means of its implementation. Obviously implementation is costly, but considered in the abstract the claim embodied in the right is costless. However, this seems to be a dubious distinction since it would be then unclear how rights could be distinguished from other sorts of claims. Rights are closely linked to the idea that they require special recognition and protection. If this is so then it is not clear that the costs of protection can then be turned into a contingent feature of negative rights.

However, other arguments have been used by negative rights theorists to claim the incoherence of positive rights. One of the most commonly invoked arguments is originally due to Maurice Cranston when he attacked the universality claim in positive/welfare rights. His argument here trades upon the idea of universality in a theory of rights. As we saw earlier human rights are supposed to be ascribed to a person in virtue of some characteristic or set of characteristics which that person shares with all other human beings. Universal rights are not therefore ascribed on the basis of the specific characteristics a person has in fulfilling a particular role. There may, of course, be rights in a particular society attached to performing a particular role which may be specific to that society, e.g. the Queen of England, but role-based rights cannot be universal human rights. Cranston wants to argue, however, that social and economic rights are role-based and cannot be universalized. That is to say, a right such as that of social security or holidays with pay can only be claimed by people filling the roles of the poor, or the employed respectively. In this sense, therefore, they are not universal because not all individuals are in that position or share that characteristic. However, there are two answers to this point. The first is that it is not at all clear how this argument distinguishes negative and positive rights. For Cranston the right to a fair trial or due process of law is a negative right in the sense that there is a claim that others shall not intervene in this process unfairly. However, this right too seems to apply only to those who at a particular moment fill the role of the accused. Of course, it will be pointed out that any citizen could be accused and therefore the right is a universal one, because it does attach to circumstances in which any individual could find himself. The difficulty though, with this perfectly plausible answer, is that it applies with equal force to positive rights – any individual *could* come to fill the role of a poor or an unemployed person. We might say then that both the negative right to due process and the positive right to social security are equally universal in that they will be concerned with how a person ought to be treated in circumstances in which any individual *could* find himself.

A more severe difficulty, and one which bring us back to the heart of the dispute between negative and positive rights theorists, is the claim by the negative rights theorist that to concede positive rights will itself involve invading the domain of autonomy which rights are designed to protect. If, for example, we take the view that the right to life implies a right to the means to life, this will constitute a categorical moral claim upon the resources of others, a strict obligation to help those who lack the means to life. Furthermore as a categorical moral claim on others the state would have a duty to perform these strict obligations which such a claim would embody. In the view of the critics of positive rights, however, and particularly Robert Nozick, the imposition of such an obligation on all persons would limit their autonomy. The poor or the sick have no claim in terms of right upon the resources of the better off. Unless the better off have actually chosen freely to give their resources to these people, it will have interfered intentionally with their negative rights.

Social and economic rights limited to state-enforced redistribution to secure such rights therefore infringe the principle of inviolability or negative rights and as such they are invasions of the sphere of autonomy which rights are there to protect. Indeed, Nozick argues that social and economic rights would constitute such a fundamental invasion of autonomy and negative rights it would be best to see such rights as conferring property rights in another person. For example, the tax system of a redistributive state seeking to secure economic and social rights would be in this position.

Hence social and economic rights and the state powers and functions required to secure these rights are therefore incomptible with the basic protection of autonomy with which rights are concerned. Of course I may choose to give my resources away to the poor but this is a gift and there is no corresponding right to receive. Or I may draw up a contract – say with a charity – to make over part of my monthly salary, here the charity does have a right to receive the money but the right is created by an autonomous act of contracting.

Can social and economic rights be defended against this attack – that they strike at the heart of the values which rights are supposed to sustain and protect? The only way in which such a defence could be mounted would be by showing that the interference with autonomy was justified by something equally foundational. The background to this argument is in the points developed earlier in relation to the idea of characteristics in lieu of which rights are held and the writings of Alan Gewirth in this context.

Nozick and others correctly see autonomy as foundational to rights because autonomy is a necessary condition of someone who can pursue values. Autonomy here is understood by the negative rights theorist both as a necessary condition for moral activity and is also understood negatively – being free from intentional coercion. A justified theory of social and economic rights would have to show that autonomy can be restricted by other than intentional interference – e.g. by economic deprivation – and that therefore the provision of economic resources was as foundational for rights as freedom from intentional coercion. Corresponding to this claim is the thesis that well-being in some form is a necessary condition of human agency. The basis of these arguments was rehearsed earlier and need not be repeated now in detail. Two points can be made, however. As we saw in chapter 6, there is a strong argument for the view that human liberty as autonomy does require access to the satisfaction of certain basic resources and needs and that this argument can be put through while stopping well short of the problems of full blown conceptions of positive liberty. The second point, which refers back to Gewirth cited earlier, is that if I recognize that my own agency as a person requires that I have command over resources as well as freedom from interference then I am committed to regarding all other persons with this characteristic of agency as having similar needs. Hence the argument for social and economic rights would depend upon regarding the provision of the resources claims in these rights as an aspect of agency upon which theories of rights are based. Hence the restriction of autonomy of which Nozick complains in the case of social and economic rights is justified by the following principles:

1   The provision of social and economic resources rests upon the same moral foundation as the claim for autonomy as non-interference, namely the necessary conditions for agency.
2   If these resources are not supplied then the autonomy of others deprived of these necessary resources will be infringed. The defender of social and economic rights will claim that these rights do not conflict with the principle of autonomy defined here. Complete autonomy for X to buy and sell as he will may well have the foreseeable although unintended effect (see chapter 6) of impeding Y's capacity for agency and in these circumstances the autonomy of X can be legitimately restricted on a principle as foundational as the one which ascribes autonomy understood as non-interference to X.

Having said that, it still remains the case that since both negative and positive rights are asserted against a background of scarcity of both motivation and material goods there may have to be procedures for dealing with priorities to claims to rights. If these are not to be dealt with on a consequentialist/utilitarian basis, which might undermine ideas of rights, then a rights-based theory has to be able to produce a decision procedure and a way of prioritizing rights claims which will avoid utilitarian calculation. This is a very difficult theoretical issue but it is one which affects negative as much as positive rights if my arguments above are accepted as cogent. If the rights in question are supposed to be absolute, then clearly to refer to consequentialism or utilitarian considerations to prefer one to another will be ruled out. However, this seems unrealistic since if all rights involve costs, there may have to be choices made. On the other hand, if the rights are thought of as prima-facie rights which can be overridden by consequentialist calculations, then in what sense are they rights at all? Jonathan Glover in *Causing Death and Saving Lives* has argued this point:

A doctrine of absolute rights goes further than this and excludes the possibility of ever justifying killing by its consequences. But the claim that we have only a prima-facie right to life does not exclude this possibility.[11]

So is there a decision procedure within rights theory which could avoid the collapse of absolute rights into prima-facie rights and these into utilitarianism? I certainly cannot construct such a procedure here, but if one could be constructed it would have to satisfy two criteria. First of all it would have to be developed out of a further elaboration of the grounds in virtue of which rights are ascribed in the first place. In terms of the theory offered as an exemplar here, namely that of Gewirth, this would be a development of the theory of needs and agency. If these needs can be described in greater detail than I have attempted in this book, then they could perhaps be put in order of priority in terms of the urgency of their satisfaction. So, for example, the need for survival would come before that of well-being and autonomy. However, there are difficult issues beyond this, but without confronting these, both negative and positive rights run the risk of collapsing into utilitarianism. The central difficulty is that it might be very difficult to put needs, for example, into any sort of hierarchy without having at least implicitly some idea of human excellence which gives the needs the place in the hierarchy that they have. This has been a complaint about the need hierarchy developed by Abraham Maslow in his *Towards a Psychology of Being*. However, the difficulty then is that the decision-making procedure in terms of priority of rights would turn upon a rather specific account of human goals and purposes which a rights-based theory has to avoid. It would seem that within this strategy only the idea of urgency in needs could do the work on a neutral basis, but this is not likely to take us very far.

The other strategy is to claim that rights can only be overridden by rights:

A theory of prima-facie human rights could be to the effect that any rights, and never other values or consequences, can override rights. Such a prima-facie rights theory would have no affinities at all with utilitarianism other than having a maximising calculus. However, it would be a calculus about maximising satisfactions of rights and only that. Such a theory could be one in terms of a hierarchy of rights, such that, solely by reference to the rights involved and their place in the hierarchy, we could determine what rights were absolute.[12]

No such theory has in fact been produced, however, and until it has been, given the assertion of rights theories of both the negative and positive sort against the background of scarcity, this strategy will be unproven. This seems to me to be perhaps the most urgent but soluble problem outstanding in theories of rights. This could not be marked out in a wholly abstract way and would have to relate to the specific values of a society to see what agency in that society requires. Only an appeal to such background values can solve this problem.

There is a further difference between the nature of the right in negative and positive rights claims, which is often used by critics of welfare rights to assert that there is a categorical difference between the two sorts of rights. It is argued that the sorts of resources to which positive rights are asserted are vague and indefinite so that it is difficult to specify the corresponding duty with any precision whereas in the case of negative rights the duty is clear and precise – it is abstinence from action, interference, killing etc. In the case of welfare rights these rights are asserted to physical well-being, education etc. If there is a corresponding duty to satisfy these rights, based as they are upon an account of the needs of a rational agent, then it is very unclear how extensive this duty is and any attempt to define the duty with more precision will be arbitrary. So, on this view, there is a basis here for a conceptual distinction between a negative and positive theory of rights. For example, if we take the right to life on the negative view, it is the right not to be killed and this duty is plain and categorical; whereas if the right to life is taken to imply a right to the means to life then it is much less clear how far this duty extends – do I have a right to all those medical interventions and technologies which will keep me alive? If not, then the cut-off point will be arbitrary, probably based upon utilitarian calculation and will be inconsistent with the general theory of rights in question. This point is often made with reference to the idea of needs, which, in the kind of example of the basis of rights I am discussing, provides us with the basic criteria in terms of which rights are ascribed. The argument here is twofold. First of all there is a claim that needs are insatiable and they are essentially culturally relative, so that in the light of these two considerations it is impossible for a theory of needs to provide a basis for a clear duty corresponding to the rights claimed on the basis of such supposed needs. These features of need yielding such unclear duties will mean that institutions and authorities seeking to satisfy such needs as rights will be forced to act in an arbitrary and discretionary way just because a theory of needs cannot provide us with a watertight account of corresponding duties. Such arbitrariness and unpredictability in relation to rights makes a nonsense of the whole idea of rights. In so far as needs are culturally relative and relative to subcultures within a society similar problems of corresponding duties will arise.

The argument, as it has been developed here by way of example, is that there is some objectivity of basic needs as a ground for rights and this object content will be generated by arguing not about what are the necessary conditions for pursuing a view of the good as seen within this, that or the other moral code, but rather by arguing that there are certain basic needs which will have to be fulfilled if *any* conception of the good is to be pursued. These needs will be both negative and positive, i.e. freedoms from intentional coercion and interference are necessary for agency but so also are certain resources such as physical well-being and education. Now it may well be that what is thought to be appropriate in the way of resources to provide well-being and education may vary from society to society but nevertheless the right to some standard in these cases provides a bench mark to assess the social responsibilities of government. It has, however, to be accepted that the exact content of these responsibilities in terms of the possession of goods and services cannot be settled in advance by reflection on the conceptual structure of the rights involved. Although this is a concession to the critic, how serious is it and does it mark a difference between positive rights to resources and negative rights? If we accept the argument deployed earlier that, in the world as we know it, negative rights cannot just be based upon non-coerced forbearance but will have to involve positive protection by government in the way of police, courts, prisons etc., then it becomes very unclear that the concession does make a difference. The degree of protection that may be required to secure negative rights cannot be excogitated from the nature of the rights in question any more than it can in the case of welfare rights. These are matters for policy and politics but nevertheless a right such as the right to privacy does not lose its force as a bench mark against which to assess governments, any more than a right to welfare – but the extent of the institutional provision to protect a right to privacy is a contingent matter not a conceptual one and, furthermore, one which, like medical needs, will change with technological advances. Computers and information technology pose a range of threats to privacy which could not have been foreseen two or three decades ago and the degree of protection needed to secure such rights will therefore vary with technological advance. Very similar kinds of arguments can be made about the nature of political and legal rights, assuming as I argued in principle earlier that such rights do require institutional forms of provision. Such forms will then be a matter of political negotiation and cannot just be 'read off' the nature of the rights in question, as we saw Walzer arguing in the case of needs in chapter 5.

This point can only be resisted if we were to take a purist view of negative rights, that they do not in fact require as I have suggested they do a positive form of protection by government. This point is argued in the following way by Charles Fried:

> My right to freedom of speech is not a right to be heard, much less a right to have my views broadcast and applauded. If my right implied these things, then certainly it would be equivalent to a positive right, and would run up against the limits of scarcity ... But what if others would deprive me of my freedom of speech – a hostile mob for instance? Surely it is the case that in asking for protection against the mob I make an affirmative claim upon the scarce resources of the community. But this objection misses the point too, for the fact that I have a right to freedom of speech against the government does not also mean that I have a right that the government protect any exercise of that right.[13]

Fried goes on to argue that this type of argument which he is here criticizing neglects the distinction between what is done to a person and what is allowed to happen. This point is crucial and, as we shall see, it has salience not only for the object of the right in Gewirth's formula, but also for forming a coherent idea of against whom a right is asserted.

The point at stake in Fried's argument is that a negative right can be wholly satisfied by forbearance. The right to life is satisfied by not being killed, the right to privacy by not having any mail tampered with, the right to freedom of speech by not interfering with my exercise of it. The forbearance in question is a duty which is always capable of being discharged. Thus Trammel argues as follows:

It is an empirical fact that in most cases it is possible for a person not to inflict serious physical injury on another person. It is also an empirical fact that in no case is it possible to aid everyone who needs help. The positive duty to love one's neighbour or help those in need, sets a maximum ethic which never lets us rest except to gather strength to resume the battle. But it is a rare case when we must really exert ourselves to keep from killing a person.[14]

To extend rights to resources and aid extends our responsibilities in an irrational way and makes the duties connected with rights difficult to characterize and thus to discharge.

Clearly part of the answer to these claims rests upon what has gone before, namely that a theory of rights based upon needs is bound to imply that even so-called negative rights are going to imply the commitment of resources, and therefore the sharp distinction made by Fried and Trammel cannot be maintained. However, the more serious criticism of this view is about the definiteness of the duties of negative rights based upon the idea that we have a very clear idea of forbearance and omission and the responsibilities connected with these. However, particularly in the case of not killing, this can be doubted and in doubting this we shall be forced to look briefly at the ethical issues of killing and letting die. The assumption of the argument is that there is a categorical moral distinction between the two; that the former involves the infringement of rights, whereas the latter does not, and that responsibility in the former case is clear and unequivocal, in the latter case vague and extensive. However, there are a number of reasons for coming to doubt the view that there is a simple moral distinction at stake here. The issues are very complex and cannot really be dealt with in sufficient detail, but I hope to be able to say enough for it to become clear that there is no easy and sharp distinction here and that the acts and omissions assumptions upon which the argument rests are not sufficient to account for a difference in the rights at stake in each case. If killing and allowing to die are, in certain circumstances, morally equivalent then these acts and omissions cannot be correlated with rights in terms of forbearance and the provision of resources, because the failure to provide resources for life could then be regarded as morally equivalent to killing and thus an infringement of the right to life. A more general way of putting the point is this. If the fundamental duty implied by a negative right is the duty not to harm, then this may well imply positive duties because the failure to act (to forbear) can itself produce harm, and indeed a degree of harm which is morally equivalent to the intentional infliction of harm. Certainly John Stuart Mill held this view when he argued in the 'Essay on Liberty' that 'a person may cause evil to others not only by his actions but by his inaction and that in either case he is justly accountable to them for the injury.'[15] If this argument is accepted then it is difficult to maintain the idea that infringing a right is always an intentional action and that the right can always be rejected by the appropriate form of forbearance.

One way in which critics of positive rights attack this idea is by arguing that harm can only be caused by omission if there is an antecedent duty towards the person or if the omission is performed by an agent who leaves some special responsibility towards the individual in question. So, for example, if there is a contractual relation between X and Y so that if X omits an action he may say that Y has been harmed. Thus if a doctor has assumed responsibility for the care of a patient and then fails to fulfil his obligation we can say that his inaction has caused harm. Similarly if a parent neglects a child, this inaction causes harm because there is an antecedent obligation to aid and care for one's children. In an example used by Gewirth in *Reason and Morality*[16] he discusses the case of a signalman whose failure to pull a lever causes the train to crash and thus the harm to those involved. However, while it may be true in these cases that inaction causes harm and maybe infringes the rights of the people concerned, this is only because there is an antecedent duty based upon contract (in the case of the doctor); a conventionally accepted set of expectations (in the case of the mother); or a rule book (in the case of the signalman). In these cases the individual who fails to act stands in a special relationship of duty with the person harmed and it is in this case that we can say that the inaction and the forbearance causes harm. However, the critic will go on to argue that this provides the basis for rejecting such an obligation between people generally in society. Unless there is an antecedent basis for a duty which creates a corresponding right to benefit from the performance of such a duty, there can be no basis for accepting the rights in question.

Hence the argument here turns upon two factors. The first is whether omissions can only cause harm if there is a specific contractual or quasi-contractual relationship between individuals; the second is whether the theorist of positive rights has a cogent argument for saying that there is an antecedent duty to meet the needs not just of those to whom we stand in something like a contractual obligation but rather people more generally, but if so which people and who generally? On a positive rights theory does our failure to do all that we can possibly do either as individuals or governments to alleviate starvation in the world mean that we are infringing the right to life of those anonymous others whom we could help but do not?

The first question raises some deep problems in not only political theory but also the philosophy of science because the issue is about negative causal responsibility: namely that a failure to act causes harm. This way of putting the point should alert us to the potential weakness in the critic's position. If X, in failing to act, is negatively causally responsible for the harm which befalls Y, then presumably, as with all cases of causation, this will depend upon the state of the world. Yet how can X's *moral* relationship with Y, which for the critic is crucial, make a difference to the sequence of causation? The critic is prepared to say that in certain circumstances in which X and Y stand in a moral relationship then X by his inaction may cause harm to Y and infringe Y's rights. However, assuming that he does not stand in such a relationship to Z the same failure to act does not cause him harm and does not infringe his rights. If this is so then we have to be prepared to argue that a conventional relationship of the sort that a contractual relationship is, may make a categorical difference to whether X causes harm to Y. Take the following example: in the first instance a lifeguard fails to rescue a child at no possible risk to him or herself from drowning in shallow water. In this case we would have to say that his or her failure to act caused harm and that he or she infringed the rights of the child because, given the moral relationship in question, the child had a right to expect protection in both positive and negative senses from the lifeguard who had a clear contractual duty in this case. In the second case imagine that a total stranger failed to save a child in similar circumstances knowing that he is the only person in a position to save the child. If he fails to save the child he has not caused it harm because there is no antecedent relationship between the child and the potential rescuer. Saving the child would be a meritorious act, but to fail to save the child does not mean that he has negative causal responsibility for the harm which befalls it. However, in each case the child ends up dead as the result of two forms of inaction and what is not clear, and what is vital to the critic's case, is how the issue of the moral relationship or the lack of it between the parties concerned makes any difference to the causal circumstances. These are obviously very large issues but I doubt whether a theory of antecedent moral obligation can enable us to draw the distinctions required in the categorical way assumed by distinction between negative and positive rights in the way the critic takes to be central. If as Jan Narveson argues, criticizing Gewirth, the signalman's 'inaction is a cause because there is an antecedent basis for the positive duty . . .'[17] we need to have a theory about how obligations can make a difference to causation. Contracts are marks on paper and it is not clear how these can make a difference to causation on which the ascription of moral responsibility is based.

The second crucial question is whether the positive rights theorist can in fact provide a basis for the obligation to aid. The negative rights theorist will argue that we only have a positive duty to aid when we stand in a specific moral, contractual or professional relationship with another individual and that we cannot generalize from these to other cases. So if the positive rights argument is to go through we need to have antecedent grounds for the obligation to aid others even when we do not stand in such a self-assumed relationship with them. Part of the argument to be deployed by the positive theorist here will be to claim that part of the answer has already been given in terms of needs and the resource preconditions of rational agency. However, the critic of positive rights can still argue that this argument is insufficient, we still need arguments on which my supposed obligation to meet the needs of others as a right can be based. It may be true that rational agency requires these needs to be satisfied but that does not of itself yield a right to the resources of others. Why should I pay attention to the needs of others even though I recognize them? So what moral force if any do needs have and how do they relate to the claim that they can act as the basis of rights?

We have already considered these arguments in the chapter on needs and found that it is difficult to see that Gewirth has answered this question effectively, for as we saw Bernard Williams argues that one cannot get from my acknowledging the necessary conditions of rational agency to an acceptance of my moral obligations to others. However, MacIntyre makes the same point in *After Virtue* and in a way which connects more closely with our current concerns. He argues as follows:

> One reason why claims about goods necessary for rational agency
> are so different from claims to the possession of rights is that the
> latter in fact presuppose, as the former do not, the existence of a
> socially established set of rules. Such sets of rules only come into
> existence at particular historical periods, under particular social
> circumstances. They are in no way universal features of the human
> condition. . . . Lacking any such social form, the making of a claim
> to a right would be like presenting a check for payment in a social
> order that lacked the institution of money. Thus Gewirth has
> illicitly smuggled into his argument a conception which does not
> in any way belong, as it must do if his case is to succeed, to the
> characterisation of a rational agent.[18]

MacIntyre's point brings us around full circle, however. Only within specific communities with shared values would claims to rights of any sort, negative or positive, make sense and of course the whole movement for human rights assumes that humanity as a whole shares certain values which would provide the antecdent conditions for us to be able to talk about universal rights and corresponding universal duties. This raises again the whole issue of the thrust towards universalism in the political theory of modernity, against the idea that the task of political theory is the explication of the values of particular communities. We shall not take up this theme further here, but will attend to it as the main theme of the final chapter of the book, although to anticipate one of the conclusions of that chapter, it can be argued that political philosophy of even the most communitarian kind has to make some use of universalistic principles, a point which will be pursued and defended later.

We have to turn now to the final aspect of Gewirth's formula namely the person, persons or institutions against whom or which the right is claimed. On the face of it, if human rights are generally universal then they should be held equally as claims against every other person. In the case of the negative interpretation of rights it is argued, sense can be made of this requirement. The reasoning here is parallel to the cases discussed earlier – that forbearance and abstaining from action is sufficient to satisfy negative rights. So, in so far as I am not actively killing, assaulting and interfering with the rights of others, I am respecting their rights. So if we take the case of an individual who is poor and destitute, in so far as I did not intentionally cause his poverty I can respect his right merely by abstaining from action and this is as true for a destitute member of my own society as it is for any other society. Hence, the idea of each having a duty to respect the rights of all other right holders individually is capable of fulfilment on this basis. However, it is not at all clear against whom social and economic rights are claimed. It would seem clear that while I have a strict duty to respect the negative rights of all other individuals simultaneously and given the nature of those rights this can be done in a costless way, nevertheless no single person can have a duty to fulfil the economic and social rights of other persons. As Narveson says:

> One could work twenty-four hours a day at the relief of suffering and could impoverish oneself contributing to charity, but it is felt that to require one to do this would be going rather too far.[19]

While I have a general moral duty not to harm and interfere with the lives of others and others have a right to claim such forbearance from me, I cannot have a general and strict moral obligation to provide resources to relieve the suffering of all who suffer, and they in turn have no right to my resources for such relief.

If this is so, then it would seem that welfare could not be a right just because the right could not be claimed against any particular person; no particular individual could be blamed for the non-fulfilment of the right, and no specific individual would be responsible for any claim to compensation falling due as the result of the failure to implement that right. It would seem that again it would be best to see welfare as a matter of humanity, generosity, altruism and therefore imperfect duty, to which there would be no corresponding right.

It might be thought that the answer to this from the point of view of a positive rights theorist would be that the right to welfare is a right to be claimed not against individuals, but rather against society as a whole, or more specifically the government, and this is in part the answer that Narveson gives in his interesting utilitarian discussion of this question. However, this still does not go quite as far as the welfare right theorist wants to go. As Narveson himself says, this move would still make the right in question an imperfect one, because if we go back to Mill's distinction – an imperfect duty is one that is directed against no particular person – the case we are now considering is closely parallel to this, and the right to welfare would become a right against no one in particular and thus would by parity of reasoning be an imperfect right. In the same way as no specific right corresponds to an imperfect duty, so an imperfect right could not imply a specific duty on the part of anyone. To be forced into this position would be just about the same as having to recognize that there is no right to welfare.

It is possible, however, following the lead of Narveson, to take matters further than this. Consider what Narveson says:

> But a duty has to be someone's duty. It can't just be no one's in particular. Consequently the thing to do is to make it everyone's duty to do something, even if that 'something' is a matter of seeing that someone else does it. Those who are put on the business end, such as the police, medical people, firemen, etc. should, of course, be compensated for going to the trouble of performing these activities. The simplest solution is simply to make these professions supportable by the public.[20]

If this is accepted, and I think that there are good reasons for accepting it, then the strict or perfect duty of individuals would not be that of the personal provision of resources to deprived individuals, but rather the support of institutions, welfare agencies, social workers etc., that attempt to meet social needs. As a strict duty this could then be required by government through taxation to support the meeting of social need. In this way we could still see the welfare state in terms of rights and duties rather than in terms of institutionalized altruism. To see the human right to welfare as implying a duty to support government welfare measures would be equivalent to seeing due process of law as a human right. A specific individual has not the duty to provide such due process, indeed it would make little sense to say that he had such a duty, but rather the duty to see that the procedures of due process are in fact carried out and to support this through the democratic process. The perfect duties corresponding to the rights of welfare are not then the personal provision of resources and services to individuals, but rather the duty to support governments and institutions that are organized to meet such needs. Hence my argument has been if there are rights at all then there are positive as well as negative rights and that a positive theory of rights can be developed in such a way as to satisfy the cogent demands of Alan Gewirth's formula. Certainly the most cogent objection is the one entered by MacIntyre discussed earlier, but that is an objection to negative as well as positive rights, so the case for both sorts of rights stands or falls together.

Even if this approach to rights is accepted there are still some controversial issues to settle, particularly relating to the place of rights in international relations. At the beginning of this chapter the issue of rights was raised partly in an international context through the UN Charter on Human Rights. In a sense such a declaration of rights attempts to set a normative background for international relations (*pace* MacIntyre). Obviously nations and different societies differ over their goals and within societies individuals too will differ over their conceptions of the good, nevertheless a theory of rights is an attempt to define the minimum conditions of morality based upon some assumptions about common humanity and human nature which no state should infringe whatever its national goals and which no individual should infringe in relation to other individuals whatever his goals might be. As such, human rights doctrines aim to provide a transnational background of moral principle. As we have seen, however, rights theories and assumptions are very much more complicated than they initially appear to be and now we shall go on to consider how these complexities relate to international relations between states.

The first point to notice which has emerged from the previous discussion is that from the point of view of the West human rights violations which call for comment and sanction are usually in the sphere of civil and political rights. That is to say, we protest when torture, false imprisonment or the failure to follow due process of law occur. The thrust of the argument so far, however, has been that there is no very clear distinction to be drawn between civil and political rights on the one hand and economic and social rights upon the other. If these arguments are valid, then it follows that concern should be with the failure to observe positive as well as negative rights. But the issues at stake go very much deeper than this obvious consequence of the earlier argument because, in addition, we have to address ourselves to the question of who or what has the responsibility to make sure that rights of all sorts are in fact observed, that is to say who bears the moral responsibility when they are not observed? This can only be answered by considering the question of against whom rights in general are held. The second issue relates to the extension of responsibility which would follow from the earlier argument for the idea of moral responsibility in relation to negative causation. That is to say, if we are responsible for the bad forseeable consequences of inaction as well as of action, then our sphere of responsibility is considerably widened and no more so than in the international sphere.

We need now to discuss these issues in more detail. In the case of against whom are rights claimed there seem to be two plausible candidates: the first is against the state in which the right holder happens to live; the second answer is that they are held against all other human beings. In the first case we say that the state has responsibility for implementing rights and if they are not implemented then that state bears the moral responsibility for its failure. In the case of negative rights, so it is argued, this is fairly straightforward: after all, on this view, negative rights consist of forbearances of various sorts so that the state abstains from action – from torture, assault etc. Since respecting these rights requires a limitation on action they are costless and any state has it in its power to abstain in these ways and is therefore always fully responsible for the failure to protect civil and political rights. Because the duty is categoric, clear and costless the moral responsibility which accompanies the failure of observance is to that degree clear and obvious and can thus become the object of protest in the international arena. If rights are extended to include welfare rights, as well as negative rights, however, then these issues become completely vague in the view of critics. Because such rights always involve costs and the provision of resources the duties on government in relation to those rights are much more indeterminate and hence the standard of failure to observe rights may be contested and with it the degree of responsibility for failure. Nevertheless, as we have seen, these sharp distinctions between negative and positive rights are very difficult to justify and the indeterminate and contested judgements are in principle as applicable to negative as much as positive rights. Although clearly there are disputed political judgements involved, a state on this view could be held morally responsible for its failure to meet welfare rights such as the need for food and subsistence, particularly when famine and the lack of food may well be more the result of a maldistribution of resources and entitlement rather than a sheer failure of the amount of food available.

This argument assumes an issue which is itself controversial, namely why rights should be seen to be held against the state and not against all other human beings. If these rights are genuinely universal is the responsibility which we usually assign to the state to meet them anything other than a kind of convenience – why should my rights not require respect from all other human beings rather than just from my fellow citizens and the society in which I am situated? After all the whole thrust of the argument of rights was against specificity, of culture, citizenship, race, gender, or class. If rights are rights of individuals as such why should they not be held against all other individuals, who have a duty to respect my rights?

The negative rights theorist has a plausible response to this claim. He can argue, so it seems, that there is such a duty to all humanity and that it is capable of being discharged. In so far as I am abstaining from killing, assaulting, raping, torturing etc. I am respecting the rights of all other human beings. The duties corresponding to the rights of all other people are duties of abstinence and in abstaining in the ways mentioned above I am respecting rights. However, in the view of such theorists the same cannot be said for positive rights, because it makes no sense to talk in terms of respecting the positive rights of all humanity. Surely, the negative rights theorist will argue, there is an absurdity in thinking that economic and social rights and duties cannot go beyond frontiers, whereas negative rights can be respected beyond frontiers because this involves doing nothing. Negative duties are perfect duties; because they involve abstaining from action they are always capable of being performed. Thus Narveson argues:

It is interesting how quickly 'everybody' tends to become 'one's fellow countrymen' when enthusiastic proponents of positive rights present their ideas. Consider for example, the matter of equal opportunity. For whom, we may innocently ask? Interestingly enough it seems that equality of opportunity has to stop at the border . . . Equally qualified foreigners do not have an equal chance at the job. If equal opportunity is a human right, then why is it that only some men are able to get it?[21]

If we did take what Narveson assumes is the absurd view that positive rights extend beyond frontiers, then the issues raised earlier in the chapter about scarcity and the necessity of utilitarian or consequentialist calculation would become magnified out of all proportion. If the provision of resources to meet positive rights to welfare within one's own society runs into scarcity problems and this requires consequentialist arguments to resolve, surely this is going to be much more so if individuals have a strict duty to meet the needs of all others. This scarcity constraint will be met much earlier and arguments about priorities will be impossible to resolve. Once again this argument depends upon the overdrawn distinctiveness of negative and positive rights, but apart from that issue, it is possible to argue the case in the following way. For the reasons given, I cannot have a strict duty to support these forms of collective action which most effectively, in the best judgement I can make in the circumstances, do most to meet needs. In this respect, therefore, individuals have both positive and negative responsibilities in the field of rights. They have duties of abstinence which would correspond roughly with respecting negative rights; but they also have indirect positive duties of provision of the sort which I described earlier (p. 285). There are therefore duties beyond frontiers and borders because the whole thrust of arguments about rights is to recognize duties based upon an abstracted idea of common humanity, and not merely the duties which arise naturally in the context of family, friends, neighbourhood and nation. But as was the case with individual duty in terms of resource provision for both negative and positive rights within a society, the individual's duty is primarily a supportive one to use his or her voice in a democratic society to encourage governments to do as much as they are able both to protect negative rights in other societies and to do what they can to provide resources for meeting positive rights too.

However, the issue of negative moral and causal responsibility also arises in this international context too. It was argued earlier that it is difficult to see how inaction can in certain cases fail to cause harm. Critics of this view, such as Narveson, have argued that such assumptions of responsibility for the failure to act on the part of agents is the result of an illigitimate attempt to take the idea of negative causal responsibility out of the area in which it is appropriate, say where there is a contractual, or other rule-governed relationship between A and B so that we can properly say in these circumstances that B's failure to act, as in the case of *B*'s failure as a doctor to honour his contract to care for his patient, causes harm to *A*. However, outside of such rule-governed frameworks there is no such harm. Theories of rights beyond frontiers are an attempt to move beyond specific rule-governed relationships to the idea that there are antecedent moral duties to human beings as such, so that the failure to act in accordance with the rules governing such duties would constitute doing harm to those to whom these spurious duties are owed. However, there are no such positive duties to humanity as such and the failure to fulfil such duties does not cause harm because I do not stand in such a relationship to some anonymous other potential beneficiary of my failed act, as could justify the ascription of harm. This is particularly so in those cases where I am unaware of the good which an action on my part might do. I certainly cannot be held to have done harm if I am unaware of a good which I could have done. This provides a philosophical justification of the idea that ignorance is bliss and would provide a strong incentive to avoid looking at charitable advertisements in newspapers.

I argued earlier, however, that it is difficult to see how negative causation can solely depend upon some kind of antecedent moral relationship. The fact is that the argument looks as if it should work the other way around, namely that the ascription of moral responsibility ought, on the face of it, to depend upon an analysis of causal responsibility rather than vice versa. If this is so, then it would clearly increase the range of responsibility which, as an individual, I owe to other bearers of rights. The failure to support collective action to meet the economic and social rights of all would, on this view, mean that such a failure implies moral responsibility for the harmful consequences which such a failure to act would produce.

All of this is controversial and debatable in a way that respecting rights within a national community is not, but as I have argued, the whole thrust of human rights theories is that the boundaries of nations are not the boundaries of moral concern. A positive rights theory has to see these concerns in terms of a strict obligation, and not as others do as a matter of selective benevolence and charity. The problem is that this could lead to the idea that the moral agent becomes irrationally overloaded with obligations, strict duties to meet the needs of others, unless these obligations are mediated through collectivities such that our strict obligations consist in supporting the collective provision to meet needs, and not in direct personal response to need, although, this is always open to the individual.

Human rights therefore provide foundationalist political philosophy with what is probably its greatest intellectual challenge. How to provide a moral rationale for a theory which is universal in scope, rich enough to underpin specific duties, but at the same time transcends the national, ethnic and cultural boundaries of political discourse. Some reject the whole project; traditional conservatives because they see obligations as nurtured in specific relational contexts which cannot just be left behind in an appeal to an abstract principle; Marxists because moral values ultimately represent not free-standing moral concern, but rather part of the ideology of a particular class or group; and others who may share the assumptions of rights-based political theorists, but who regard the whole attempt as intellectually barren. Thus R. G. Frey argues:

> We gain nothing in clarity, precision and understanding by trying to discuss moral issues in terms of rights, among other reasons, because we lack a method of arguing about them, certainly with any degree of finality ... rights actually get in the way of the issues: our attention is diverted from the important business of working out principles of rightness and justification of treatment in cases of the sort at hand, to the wholly speculative tasks of making something of (competing) rights claims, of their (often many) alleged grounds, and of the vast number of competing criteria for rights possession currently on offer.[22]

Frey argues as a utilitarian and, as we saw earlier, that moral system is not without deep problems in a morally pluralist society. In the next chapter on punishment we shall look *inter alia* at how rights- and utility-based theories actually deal with a specific moral and political issue. Whatever may be the intellectual cogency of rights-based theories – and it is my belief that if they are based upon a theory of need, it is quite high – the language of rights has bitten very deeply into the political discourse, particularly of the West, and any political philosophy has to take account of this language and its purported universal scope.

Notes

1 M. Cranston, *What Are Human Rights?*, Bodley Head, London, 1973, p. 65.
2 Ibid., p. 65.
3 A. Gewirth, *Human Rights*, University of Chicago Press, Chicago, 1982.
4 J. Habermas, *Communication and the Evolution of Society*, trans. T. McCarthy, Heinemann, London, 1976.
5 A. Gewirth, *Reason and Morality*, University of Chicago Press, Chicago, 1978, p. 45.
6 Cranston, *What Are Human Rights.*, p. 67.
7 C. Fried, *Right and Wrong*, Harvard University Press, Cambridge, Mass., 1978, p. 108.
8 Ibid., p. 110.
9 Ibid., p. 113.
10 I owe this argument to a conversation with Hillel Steiner.
11 J. Glover, *Causing Death and Saving Lives*, Penguin, London, 1977, p. 233.
12 H. J. McCloskey, 'Respect for Human Moral Rights', in *Utility and Rights*, ed. R. G. Frey, Blackwell, Oxford, 1985, p. 132.
13 Fried, *Right and Wrong*, p. 110–1.
14 R. Trammel, 'Saving Life and Taking Life', in *Killing and Letting Die*, ed. B. Steinbeck, Prentice Hall, New York, 1980, p. 168.
15 J. S. Mill, 'Essay on Liberty', in *Utilitarianism*, ed. M. Warnock, Collins, London, 1910, p. 74.
16 Gewirth, *Reason and Morality*, p. 222.
17 J. Narveson, 'Negative and Positive Rights in Gewirth's *Reason and Morality*', in *Gewirth's Ethical Rationalism*, ed. E. Regis, University of Chicago Press, Chicago, 1984, p. 99.
18 A. MacIntyre, *After Virtue*, 2nd edn, Duckworth, London, 1985, p. 68.
19 J. Narveson, *Morality and Utility*, Johns Hopkins University Press, Baltimore, Md, 1973, p. 235.
20 Ibid., p. 235.
21 Narveson, 'Negative and Positive Rights', p. 105.
22 R. G. Frey, 'Act Utilitarianism', in *Utility and Rights*, ed. R. G. Frey, Blackwell, Oxford, 1985, p. 64.

8
Justice, Punishment and the State

The injury, the penalty which falls on the criminal is not only morally implicitly just – as just it is *eo ipso* his implicit will, an embodiment of his freedom, his right.

G. W. F. Hegel, *The Philosophy of Right*

Usually discussions of punishment raise the deepest questions in social and political philosophy because in the practice of punishment we come up against one of the most concrete expressions of the coercive power of the state. Both the institution of punishment and the kinds of arguments which are devised to justify it are going to reflect general philosophical views about the role of the state *vis-à-vis* the citizen, the nature of law and the relationship of its procedural rules to the wider society, and about the nature of persons and how they should be shown respect. For these reasons questions about punishment should always be debated. They concern every citizen and, because of the deep nature of the ethical issues involved, these questions cannot be entirely made over to experts – criminologists, penologists, social workers etc. Although facts about different types of punishment and their effects on offenders are of course relevant, nevertheless such facts are always going to underdetermine values. To see punishment as a purely technical issue to be settled by expert opinion is an evasion of responsibility by the citizen. It is in the name of the political community that certain persons are deprived of their liberty, made to suffer pain and not infrequently death, and it is surely our responsibility as citizens that the institutions which have such a dramatic effect upon the lives of our fellow human beings should be

kept under review and the values on which such institutions finally
rest should be subjected to the most rigorous analysis. However, the
analytical basis of punishment cannot be divorced from the wider
questions concerning the moral values and principles held within the
political community, and must not ignore the degree of moral diversity
which may be found in the community. As we shall see later on in the
chapter, the importance of this connection between punishment and
morally pluralistic society may have been ignored by those holding
the retributive theory of punishment. Because there are problems in
determining the acceptability of retribution, there is always likely to be
a call for utilitarianism in the philosophy of punishment just because
utilitarianism, as we have seen, is often regarded as a very attractive
basis for morality and for providing an account of the purposes of
institutions in a pluralistic society. Equally, however, the utilitarian
position has considerable difficulties in coping with some of the principles which many people have felt should be within the ambit of ethical
theory. The attractiveness of the theory in a pluralist society is its
deceptive simplicity.

Rehabilitation

In Western societies since the Second World War penological thinking
has been greatly influenced by the so-called 'rehabilitative ideal' – that
is, in some sense the notion of punishment should be replaced by that
of rehabilitation and that a preference for punishment and retribution
should be replaced by an approach based upon the idea of seeking to
rehabilitate the criminal. In its most extreme forms this idea assimilates
the question of punishment to a medical model based upon treatment
and seeks to displace a moralized view of punishment based upon justice
or retribution. This development relates to themes discussed in chapters
1 and 2. First of all, if morality is pluralistic and subjectively grounded,
can punishment possibly be based on a firm moral foundation? Do we
have an agreed view of its social purpose? Secondly, in these circumstances, there is great pressure to turn ethical questions into technical
ones, to be solved by experts – in this case psychologists, criminologists,
social workers, probation officers etc. For example, Karl Menninger, a

noted rehabilitative theorist, has argued in his famous book *The Crime of Punishment*:

> The very word 'justice' irritates scientists. No surgeon expects to be asked if an operation for cancer is just or not. No doctor will be reproached on the grounds that the dose of penicillin he has prescribed is more or less than justice would stipulate. Behavioural scientists regard it as equally absurd to invoke questions of justice in deciding what to do with a woman who cannot resist her propensity to shoplift, or with a man who cannot resist an impulse to assault somebody.[1]

This could not be more explicit in its attempt to demoralize the issue of punishment and make the issue as of professional concern to the psychiatrist and the social worker. The function of the court would be restricted to determining whether an individual has committed the crime; therapy is to be decided by 'a psychiatrist, a psychologist, a sociologist or cultural anthropologist or educator and a judge'. Clearly this professionalization of the process of punishment or rehabilitation will side-step many moral problems about the justification of more traditional forms of punishment, justifications which in general, as we have seen, have become more difficult in a situation of moral pluralism. It is therefore extremely important to discuss the strengths and weaknesses of the rehabilitative case and to consider the assumptions about the nature of human behaviour on which it rests.

The rehabilitative ideal makes assumptions about the nature of persons, the nature of social science and what, in the light of a social scientific approach, an appropriate attitude of respect towards a person should be. This model, which might be called a medical or psychiatric model, has a lot in common with those themes which were discussed in chapter 2 relating to how concepts of action, and the moral categories of right and wrong used in evaluating it, tend to get displaced by more scientific or medical categories drawn from psychology and psychiatry. As we saw then, the pressures for a medical model of the person, in the context of moral diversity, are very powerful. I shall argue that it is precisely what is implied by the principle of respect for persons which marks the moral difference between rehabilitation, deterrence and the 'justice' model. The rehabilitative ideal is clearly influenced by assumptions about the nature of human behaviour drawn from the social sciences, and these assumptions seem to be as follows:

1   Human behaviour is explicable in causal terms, that is to say that behaviour is to be seen as an effect of a nexus of antecedent causal circumstances. These causal circumstances will be sought either in the physical and psychological make-up of the individual whose behaviour is to be explained, or in the environment within which the individual lives or, more plausibly, in some combination of both of these. In the case of criminal offenders their law-breaking behaviour is to be seen as the *effect* of causal factors of this sort. This is clearly represented in the following passage from Menninger's work:

There is today an utterly new psychiatry, a new understanding of abnormal and normal behaviour, as different from those held before Freud as the principles of modern physics differ from those in use before Einstein and even before Newton. For the first time in history we have a logical and systematic theory of personality, an explanation of what human behaviour is and how behaviour is determined and modified. This enables psychiatry to graduate from a science dealing with the recognition and handling of crazy people to a science of understanding the behaviour of all people, the so called normal and the so called abnormal ones, with increasingly less distinction between them.[2]

2   This had the effect of shifting the emphasis away from such notions as responsibility and personal desert. If behaviour is the result of antecedent causes then it is at least plausible to suggest that the individual is not responsible for his actions and if this is so, it is not at all clear in what sense he deserves anything – good or bad, punishment or reward – on the basis of his action. One can make claims for desert only on the basis of what one is responsible for; and precisely this factor is missing if we grant that human behaviour has a sufficient causal explanation. However, criminal behaviour will still need to be controlled or changed, but the justification of this is independent of otiose considerations about desert. Although B. F. Skinner is perhaps an extreme example, his book *Science and Human Behaviour* brings out both this feature of responsibility and the previous feature about the nature of social scientific explanations:

We do not hold people responsible for their reflexes, for example, for coughing in church. We hold them responsible for their operant behaviour – for example, for whispering in church or remaining in church while coughing. But there are variables which are responsible for whispering as well as coughing and these may be just as inexorable. When we recognise this we are likely to drop the notion of responsibility altogether and with it the doctrine of free will as an inner causal agent.[3]

3 In natural science prediction and control are closely related features and are central both to the aims of science and to the kinds of explanations of phenomena which natural science yields. A law-like generalization such as all gases expand when heated which can be represented as $(x)\varphi x > \psi x$ allows us in a particular case to say $(\exists x)\varphi x > \psi x$. We shall be able to predict the occurrence of ψ from the occurrence of φ and, of course, with prediction goes control. If we wish to produce that state of affairs π, i.e. the absence of ψ then we shall try to prevent φ from occurring. Similarly, in social science if we believe that it is or will be possible to produce analogous generalizations about human behaviour such a view would lead us to think that it ought to be possible to intervene in the causal antecedents of such behaviour and either prevent its occurrence or modify it to some degree. This kind of intervention is presumably the basis of rehabilitation. For example, Karpman says:

> Basically criminality is but a symptom of insanity, using the term in its widest generic sense to express unacceptable social behaviour based on unconscious motivation flowing from a disturbed instinctive and emotional life . . . If criminals are products of early environmental influences in the same sense that psychotics and neurotics are, then it should be possible to treat them psychotherapeutically.[4]

In this passage the model cited above is clearly at work. Criminal behaviour has a sufficient causal explanation which makes notions like responsibility and guilt redundant, and such behaviour can be modified or controlled by intervening in the causal circumstances – childhood conditioning and the like - which has led to its development. In Menninger's view we now have for the first time in history 'a logical and systematic theory of the personality, an explanation of what human nature is, and how behaviour is determined and modified'. In addition to this, the predictive element in the explanation of criminal behaviour is used as a basis for indeterminate sentences for those offenders whose prognosis is that they are likely to be of danger to society in the future. On such a basis individuals are 'punished' for what it is predicted they *would do* as much as for what it has been found out they *have done*. To quote Menninger again:

> Indeterminate sentencing will be taken for granted, and pre-occupation with punishment as the penalty of the law would have yielded to a concern with the best measures to ensure public safety, with rehabilitation of the offender, if possible, and as economically as possible.[5]

Also, indeterminate sentencing allows the therapeutic regime to take place. There is no reason as there is on the 'justice' approach to treat like cases in like manner, since the causal circumstances which led one person to commit a crime may be very different from those which led another, and the rehabilitative needs may be different and thus indeterminate sentences such as between one and five years for a particular offence would be appropriate.

4   The language of social science and the explanation of criminal behaviour in terms of social science generalizations has constituted the basis for the kind of 'clinical' terminology which is frequently used in the literature on rehabilitation. Notions such as responsibility, desert and punishment drop out in favour of notions such as cause, treatment, prognosis etc., and I have already cited examples of this.

5   Finally, there is the assumption that the rehabilitative approach is humanitarian. Treatment patterns are tailored to individual needs and problems. Investigations are made into the circumstances and psychological state of the offender – in short the whole process of treatment is individualized. Instead of being dealt with according to some kind of impersonal procedure the *particular* person is taken as a unique individual with his own needs, interests, desires and problems and this individualization, so it is argued, is central to the principle of respecting persons – at least as it is understood by social workers and

probation officers etc. Biesték for example, argues as follows – that individualization implies:

> The recognition and understanding of each client's unique qualities and the differential use of the principles and methods in assisting each towards a better adjustment. Individualisation is based upon the right of human beings to be individual, and to be treated not as *a* human but as *this* human being with his personal differences.[6]

In the rehabilitative model we are presented with a tangled skein of beliefs and moral attitudes: beliefs about the nature of human behaviour generally and about the explanation of criminal behaviour in particular; about the possibility of the scientific modification and change of such behaviour and also the consequences of these beliefs for our overall moral outlook, particularly a shifting away of emphasis from notions like responsibility, guile and desert, towards a more impersonal clinical view of human behaviour, a view which is well captured in the following section from Karl Menninger's 'Therapy Not Punishment' printed in *Harper's Magazine*:

> We, the agents of society, must move to end this game of tit for tat and blow for blow in which the offender has foolishly and futilely engaged himself and us. We are not driven as he is to wild and impulsive actions. With knowledge comes power, and with power there is no need for the frightened vengeance of the old penology. In its place should go a quiet, dignified therapeutic programme for the rehabilitation of the disorganised one, if possible the protection of society during the treatment period and the guided return to useful citizenship as soon as this can be effected.[7]

However, many of the assumptions behind this approach have broken down – or at least there is no longer this simple faith which Menninger has in either the knowledge or the power which social science is supposed to bring into penology. But in addition to this, there has been a moral crisis over the replacement of punishment by rehabilitation. Is rehabilitation and its assumptions in fact consistent with well-entrenched moral beliefs we have about respect for persons and similar practical attitudes towards persons?

Perhaps the first point to notice here is that the scientific background to the rehabilitative model is somewhat threadbare. In the first place, of course, many would argue that such faith in the predictive and explanatory power of social science is quite misplaced;[8] but leaving this argument on one side for a moment it is clear that the assumptions made by those who hold to the rehabilitative model are highly normative. Rehabilitation always has to be *to* something or other and in the present case presumably something like consensus expectations and social norms. This point is well made by Herbert Morris when he outlines what he takes to be the major presuppositions of the rehabilitative notion:

> In this world we are now to imagine, when an individual harms another, his conduct is to be regarded as a symptom of some pathological condition in the way a running nose is to be taken as a symptom of a cold. Actions diverging from some conception of the normal are viewed as malfunctions of disease in the way we might today regard the arm and leg movements of an epileptic during a seizure. Actions conforming to what is normal are assimilated to the normal and healthy functioning of the bodily organs.[9]

Both rehabilitation and deviance have to be defined against the background of the norms of the society in question. The social scientific air of neutrality and objectivity has to be seen in the light of these assumptions and the support which social science gives to these values by defining in quasi-medical terminology the failure to meet them as pathological, and the subsequent ability to live in terms of them as rehabilitation. Of course, the critic will argue that the same is true of medicine – treatment and diagnosis take place against assumed standards of health and illness, and yet this does not seem to cast doubt on the role of medicine in our society. It is at least arguable, however, that there is a much higher degree of consensus in society about the types of physical conditions which constitute health and disease, and there is a much higher degree of agreement that physical health and the absence of physical injury are valuable than is true of what might be called 'social health' and 'adequate social functioning'. In a pluralistic society there are bound to be disagreements about standards of behaviour and the extent to which we can define a norm for social health. These can range from the view that the norms of society do articulate as an adequate standard of social health to the anguished outburst of R. D. Laing when faced with theories of rehabilitation and adjustment: 'Adaptation to what? To society? To a world gone mad?'[10]

Herbert Morris, in an influential article, has put the problem less dramatically but perhaps more rigorously when he argues that:

> The logic of cure will push us toward forms of therapy that inevitably involve changes in the person made against his will. The evil in this would be more apparent in those cases where the agent, whose action is determined to be a manifestation of some disease, does not regard his reaction in this way. He believes that what he has done is, in fact 'right' but his conception of normality is not the therapeutically accepted one. When we treat an illness we normally treat a condition, relieving the person of something preventing his normal functioning. When we begin treating the person for actions that have been chosen, we do not lift the person from something that is interfering with his normal functioning but we change the person so that he functions in a way regarded as normal by the current therapeutic community. We have to change him and his judgements of value.[11]

Granted the possibility of a good deal of intractable disagreement about the norms of society, a conception of rehabilitation, defined in terms of *certain* norms rather than others, loses its veneer of scientific neutrality. Obviously there is the possibility in the context of rehabilitation for mental health and illness to be new words for describing moral values as Szasz[12] has argued. It is not necessary for us to believe this to be the case – we may ourselves see the rules of society as embodying a healthy way of life, but the very fact that *some* may disagree with this and see these norms as repressive, or whatever, shows the necessity for the justification of these norms. And this justification which, as we have seen, defines the ends of rehabilitation, cannot be a scientific one – it has to be a *moral* justification.

This realization of the normative assumptions behind the rehabilitative process and the questionability of those assumptions has been a major cause of the loss of confidence in it at a theoretical level. The other major moral problem with the rehabilitative ideal, and this perhaps takes us much closer to the heart of the matter, is that it appears manipulative and not to respect persons as persons. It appears manipulative in the sense that 'punishment' or 'treatment' is given not on the basis of what the crime deserved, but rather on the basis of how the person can be changed so that he or she will be able to meet more adequately society's expectations. It also seems to involve manipulation in that when the length of punishment is linked to rehabilitation, then release will only come when the offender has satisfied a group of experts that he is rehabilitated – rehabilitation which, as we have seen, is likely to be seen in terms of the moral consensus of society. An interesting and dramatic illustration of this is to be found in the tragic story of George Jackson:

> In 1960 Jackson at the age of 18 was convicted of second degree robbery for driving a getaway car while a friend robbed a petrol station of seventy dollars. Under the Californian state law, which claims to have the most reformist penal code, Jackson and his accomplice were sentenced to a period of between one year and life imprisonment. After serving the first year the parole board determines when the prisoner should be released on parole. Under that system, parole is granted when the board thinks a prisoner has been sufficiently reformed to be let out. Jackson's accomplice was released in 1963. Jackson remained until 1970 and subsequently died in prison. He claimed that his political beliefs prevented him from being granted parole – he was a black revolutionary and as long as he expounded those beliefs he was not considered reformed.[13]

The critic of the rehabilitative ideal will argue that the reformist view shifts the centre of attention away from the *crime* to the *character* of the criminal and that as a consequence the length of time to be spent in an institution becomes dependent on a parole board comprised of experts who claim to know when reform or rehabilitation has been achieved. This is thought to be manipulative – an offender has to act in a way consistent with the norms which define rehabilitation and these norms represent the interests of society at large, and may or may not reflect the offender's own values.

The claim that the rehabilitative process is manipulative is also justified with reference to punishment which is based upon a predictive estimate of the chances of the offender acting in a similar manner again in such a way as to be a danger to society. Here a person may be deprived of his liberty not because of what he has done, but of what he is thought likely to do. The fact that the deprivation of liberty is called therapy instead of punishment does nothing to disguise the substantive issues of personal liberty and due process of law which are being bypassed in this kind of procedure, a procedure which is clearly maintained as being in the interests of society. The moral principle of respect for persons involves the idea that a person should never be used solely for the purposes of others, but as an end in himself. Clearly to talk about therapy in these circumstances gives the impression that it is being done in the interests of the offender, but it seems clear with the introduction of the concept of 'dangerousness' that the interests of society are obviously at stake and restraints on the offender are largely undertaken in response to a predicted danger to society.[14]

At the same time, there does seem to be something odd about the claim that the rehabilitative ideal is inhumane. Surely it might be argued that it is this reformist rehabilitative ideal which has led penology out of the dark ages of brutal and savage treatment inflicted upon offenders in the name of retribution. Clearly, if being humanitarian means being concerned with *physical pain* inflicted upon human beings, then the rehabilitative model has some claim to be humane – it is clearly the case that punishment conceived in rehabilitative terms is likely to involve far less physical pain than would be the case with some other model – but nevertheless it is certainly plausible to suggest that the rehabilitative model is at the best insensitive to certain other aspects of humanitarianism, particularly in the crucial importance of notions of agency, moral capacity and responsibility in our conception of ourselves. Strawson, in his important essay 'Freedom and Resentment',[15] has pointed out the extent to which our view of the humanity of another becomes attenuated when we see another person's behaviour as a result of antecedent causal factors. He points out that in normal human relations a whole range of attitudes, what he calls 'reactive' emotional attitudes between one person and another, are central to their relationship, whereas in the case of a person whose behaviour is seen as pathological only 'objective' or clinical attitudes may be appropriate:

To adopt the objective attitude to another human being is to see him perhaps as an object of social policy; as a subject for what in a wide range of sense might be called treatment; as something to be taken account, perhaps precautionary account of; to be managed or handled, cured or trained ... The objective attitude may be emotionally toned in many ways, but not in all ways ... it cannot include the range of reactive feelings and attitudes which belong to involvement or participation with others in interpersonal relationships.[16]

In addition, granted that the therapist is going to operate with *some* sociological and psychological model of human behaviour (if this is not so then the language of rehabilitation and therapy becomes redundant) this model is likely to determine in the end what are seen to be the needs, or better the 'real' needs or desires of the client or offender and perhaps even to be rather dismissive of the desires which the offender himself articulates. A good example of this which, because it operates with a strong although in my view unintelligible notion of the unconscious, is to be found in Clare Winnicott's article 'Casework and Agency Function' in which she talks about the role of the probation service in relation to crime:

When a child or an adult commits an offence of a certain degree and kind he brings into action the machinery of the law. The probation officer who is then asked to do casework with the client feels that he ought to apply techniques implying the casework principle of self determination, but he loses everything if he forgets his relationship to his agency and to the court, since symptoms of this kind of illness are unconsciously designed to bring authority into the picture.[17]

Here there is very little respect shown for the principle of individualization. In the first place the probation officer is being advised not to treat his client as being responsible, and then the client's committing the crime is supposed to be seen as an illness which has been unconsciously designed to bring an authoritarian personality into the life of the client. In addition, of course, it is difficult perhaps to see how such basic moral principles as respect for persons, self-direction, individualization etc., can in fact exist alongside a strong commitment to the view that human behaviour has the sufficient causal explanation, given this implies a presumption that the behaviour of the criminal has to be seen as falling within some general paradigm of explanation.

Utilitarianism and punishment

There are, however, alternative theories of punishment, most particularly the utilitarian and the retributive theory. I have aleady discussed the general structure of utilitarian theories of ethics and the application of this view to the practice of punishment should be fairly clear. As with everything else in utilitarian theory, punishment has to be guided by welfare-maximizing considerations. Crime lowers welfare in that it deprives individuals of life, property or physical integrity in the case of assault and rape. Equally, punishment, as the inflicting of pain and deprivation of various sorts, involves pain or diswelfare for the criminal. The justification of punishment for the utilitarian will lie in the trade-off to be made between the welfare which will accrue to society as the result of the assumed deterrent effect of punishment and the diswelfare experienced by the criminal. If punishment promotes social welfare as the result of its deterrent effect, through reforming criminals or by removing them from society, then it is justified if this degree of welfare outweighs the diswelfare of the punishment visited upon the criminal.

This kind of calculation can take two forms in utilitarianism which correspond to the distinction drawn in chapter 4 between *act* and *rule* utilitarianism. Under the act utilitarian model, the issue of justification would be individualized so that for any individual criminal a judgement would have to be made about whether punishing him and to what degree would maximize social welfare, counting that person's interests equally with those of all other members of the society. The obvious difficulty with an act utilitarian approach to punishment is that it could appear to sanction the punishment of the innocent in particular circumstances. If the aim of punishment in a particular case is to maximize welfare by means of deterrence, then it is conceivable that a further commission of a particular sort of crime could be deterred by punishing an innocent person. This could happen in a number of different ways. In wartime, for example, innocents could be killed in order to deter subsequent attempts to attack occupying forces after one such attack. This certainly happened in the Second World War in many cases, that of Lidice being perhaps the most harrowing. Alternatively, the innocence of the person involved might be disguised from people at large and subsequently punishing this person might deter other people from committing these sorts of crimes. Given that in each case the degree of welfare accruing to society will be increased by these forms of punishing the innocent, then it would appear that act utilitarianism can find no real way of ruling out in principle the potential legitimacy of punishing the innocent. Usually our ordinary moral intuitions would lead us to the view that the innocent ought not to be punished or, to put the point another way, that the innocent have a right not to be punished, but as we saw in the chapter on utilitarianism the act utilitarian can really find no place for any absolute moral standards or rights, when these are regarded as being independent of utilitarian calculations. Although the act utilitarian would claim that his point of view incorporated a conception of respect for persons in the sense that each person's interests are to be counted as being equal in the utilitarian calculation, or as Bentham put it, each is to count for one and not more than one, the fact is that for the act utilitarian the interests of the innocent in not being punished can be overridden in any particular case if somehow a judgement could be made and defended which envisaged an increase in social welfare accruing from punishing a particular innocent individual.

This kind of consideration has led many utilitarians in the direction of espousing rule utilitarianism. As we saw in chapter 4, the rule utilitarian does not accept the view that each individual action has to be assessed in terms of its utility-producing consequences but rather that rules of action have to be so assessed. In the case of punishment the question would not be whether in any individual case that individual should be punished for committing a crime, but rather the rule that punishing crimes in general maximizes welfare or utility. If this rule is justified on consequentialist grounds, then particular cases falling under the rule are justified not by the particular circumstances of *that* case, but by the general rule. From this, the rule utilitarian would go on to argue that a general rule which allowed the punishment of the innocent could not pass the utilitarian test. This might be so for two sorts of reasons, both of which are connected with the public scrutiny which would clearly follow from applying utilitarian tests to a *rule* as opposed to a particular action. First of all a rule allowing the punishment of the innocent would be likely considerably to increase public anxiety. After all, if any individual would be liable to punishment whether or not he or she had committed the crime in question anxiety and uncertainty produced by such a rule might lead to a general lack of acceptance in society and the rule of law. Secondly, on the act utilitarian model the theoretical efficacy of punishing the innocent will depend in many cases upon the population at large not knowing that an innocent person has been punished – an act calculated to deter other would-be criminals, which depends for its deterrent effect upon the widespread but false belief that a guilty person has in fact been punished. However, this degree of deception is impossible with rule utilitarianism, because as general rules which are to govern the society, rules have to be publicly discussed and evaluated in consequentialist terms on the utilitarian model. Once this has been done, it can be argued, a general rule of punishment which would permit punishing the innocent would not pass the utilitarian test because it would be difficult to see how it could then be effective as a deterrent which is the sole justification of punishment. Once again, however, as we saw earlier in the discussion of utilitarianism in chapter 4, every moral judgement is conditional and provisional and there is nothing absolutely wrong in punishing the innocent. In addition, we have to recall, in the context of a defence of punishment on a rule utilitarian basis, that there are strong arguments for believing that rule utilitarianism actually collapses back into act utilitarianism. If this is so, and the arguments appeared cogent when discussed earlier, then the attempt by utilitarians to avoid the problem of punishing the innocent, which as we saw was allowable under act utilitarianism, by a move towards rule utilitarianism would be undermined.

Rationality, agency and retribution

In one respect retributive theories of punisment do not regard rehabilitative or utilitarian theories of punishment as being definite enough or absolute enough. In the first place guilt becomes problematic in both cases. In the rehabilitative cases where rehabilitation is linked to a medical model, guilt becomes problematic just because of the view about the causation of criminal behaviour; in the case of act utilitarianism guilt is not a necessary condition of punishment. In addition, the retributivist believes that basic types of punishment exhibit only a very shallow commitment to humanitarian concerns because they are both inherently manipulative. In the case of the rehabilitative ideal we have seen how discretionary the process of punishment can become, and as the result of that how professionalized, so that the way a prisoner is dealt with is not determined by his past crimes, but also by his subsequent and future action. This is particularly true once ideas about dangerousness are brought into play as they are in some 'treatment' models. Utilitarian theories are also inherently manipulative on the retributive model because the explicit rationale for punishment is that it will involve doing something to a person which will have as its explicit aim the good or the welfare of others, in this case, the rest of society. Kant and Hegel on the other hand, took the view, as do some modern critics, that the humanitarianism of the utilitarian view is rather shallow and, in fact, in inflicting pain, or therapy, as a form of social control infringes the right of the person to be treated as an end in himself and not merely as a means to the ends of others. As Kant argues in a famous passage:

> Judicial punishment can never be used merely as a means to promote some other good for the criminal himself or civil society, but instead it must in all cases be imposed on him only on the ground that he has committed a crime; for a human being can never be manipulated merely as a means to the purposes of someone else ... He must first of all be found to be deserving of punishment before any consideration is given of the utility of this punishment for himself or his fellow citizens.[18]

Desert for Kant is therefore a central moral notion in thinking about punishment, and desert implies agency and responsibility. One can only make claims to deserve anything on the basis of things for which one can claim at least some degree of responsibility. Thus to entrench desert as a necessary condition of punishment, as Kant does in this passage, is to place at the very centre of this theory of punishment a very strong commitment to human responsibility. This is paralleled by Hegel who, in *The Philosophy of Right*, goes on to suggest that punishment is the *right* of the offender.[19] It is an affirmation of the person's status as a human being and not just something to be controlled or, as Strawson says in his essay 'Freedom and Resentment', to be taken precautionary account of. It is important, however, when considering Kant's statement of his position as found in the above quotation that his use of the word 'merely' admits that there can be justifiable aspects of the dealing of society with the offender which do take into account the interests of society, but these are not to be seen as overriding. And the question of the infliction of punishment and the particular character which it has in each case should be decided independently of these other interests. On this sort of basis punishment would be justified on the grounds of desert alone, and should be meted out in the light of the gravity of the offence, but equally during the sentence of an offender fixed by desert criteria there might well be offered the possibility of help: therapy, traning, education etc., which might help him to be rehabilitated or reformed. However, these opportunities should be offered and taken up quite independently of considerations about the length of sentences, the possibility of parole etc. The length of a sentence should be based upon what the crime deserves and not on the basis of whether the offender has reformed or not.

If this was all that Kant and Hegel were arguing then it might appear to be entirely unexceptionable for all but the most thoroughgoing utilitarians, but it is not all that they were committed to in their arguments. Kant is arguing that desert is not just a necessary condition for punishment but also a sufficient one. If a person has been found guilty of a crime then not only does his guilt make it possible to punish him, it makes it necessary to do so. Kant has a very powerful commitment to the anti-utilitarian consequences in this view. For example, in a famous passage he argues the most extreme cases possible against the utilitarians:

Even if civil society were to dissolve itself by common agreement of all its members ... the last murderer remaining in prison must first be executed so that everyone will duly receive what his actions are worth and so that the blood guilt thereof will not be fixed upon the people because they failed to insist on carrying out the punishment.[20]

Anti-consequentialist assumptions could hardly be taken further than this! There is no gap of justification between finding guilty as charged and therefore punishable, and actually punishing him. If he is guilty then he ought to be punished. Kant's reason for saying this is obvious – at least on first inspection – because if there was a gap between finding a person punishable and punishing him then the question, 'ought we to punish this guilty (punishable) person?', could only be answered by utilitarian arguments such as 'it is in the interest of society that we should do so', or 'it will deter him if we do'. But all answers of this sort for Kant can only be secondary if we take the principle of respect for persons seriously, because they all claim the right to inflict punishment in a manipulative way.

While this accounts for why Kant wishes to resist any suggestion of a gap between guilt and punishment, however, this does nothing to justify the principle, 'the guilty ought to be punished', unless of course we take the view that it is the only consequence in terms of punishment which is allowable under an acceptance of the principle of respect for persons. Some commentators have suggested that Kant's argument is an illusion; either the principle 'the guilty ought to be punished' has to be taken as a fundamental but disputable moral intuition, or else the reasons we give for accepting it must be broadly speaking of a utilitarian type – the balance of social advantage lies in punishing the guilty. However, there is perhaps a third type of justification which we might call analytical rather than either utilitarian or intuitive, although it is perhaps closer to the latter than the former. An analytical justification would be an attempt to see a particular theory of punishment, such as Kant's or Hegel's, as set within a broader framework of political and social analysis, and in particular an analysis of the nature of the state and social and political obligation. This is certainly the kind of argument which both Kant and Hegel sought to provide, and incidentally it is perhaps just what is lacking in the work of those who wish to resurrect, under the 'justice' model, some of the central features of Kant and Hegel's retributivism. Such an analysis would have to take us very deeply into each particular thinker's conception of the social and political order, the nature of the rules and laws which characterize that order and the obligations of individual citizens to that overall order. Perhaps only background theories of this sort are going to be able to provide the final basis for a desert-based theory of punishment which seeks to avoid either a utilitarian foundation which would be paradoxical, or lapse into an appeal to moral intuition which would be implausible to those who do not share the intuitions. However, the difficulty with such background theories is that they are never finally capable of completely compelling the intellect. They are more like contestable visions of the actuality and the possibility of man's social life rather than scientifically testable hypotheses about the nature of social experience – although, as we shall see, empirical evidence is relevant in a crucial way to determining the applicability of the Kantian model to existing societies.

In this chapter it is obviously impossible to try to discuss in other than the most superficial terms the visions of society which inform both Kant's and Hegel's views of punishment, and I shall discuss here only Kant's view: partly because it is much more manageable, and also because I have discussed Hegel's theory, which is rather different, elsewhere. Kant's theory of political obligation is contractual, one of the sort that Rawls has sought to update,[21] and he places a very great deal of weight on the notion of reciprocity. The laws of a just state are laws which would have been chosen by any rational person to govern social relationships in a position of initial choice. Kant is not, of course, saying that such a position of original constitutional choice ever existed, but rather than *if* we wish to determine the content of just and impartial laws we should try to work out hypothetically which legal rules *would* have been chosen by a group of rational persons forming a society for the first time. Such laws would, in Kant's view, embody both a degree of self-restraint and benefit. Without law a particular individual might well be able to derive more benefits than he or she would under a system with law, but this will not be true of persons generally, and since no person could know in advance whether he or she would be able to benefit under a system without law it would follow that it would be in his or her interest to accept a system of rules which would secure benefits to all men, though in certain contexts keeping such laws is going to require a certain amount of self-restraint. Any individual derives and accepts the benefits which the existence of law brings, so an individual owes obedience to the law as a *debt* to his fellow citizens who equally, by their self-restraint, keep the laws. If an individual chooses not to pay this debt to his fellow citizens by keeping the law then in Kant's view he or she has opted to pay the debt in another way – by punishment. If the law is to remain just and impartial it is centrally important to guarantee to those who obey the law that those who disobey will not gain an unfair advantage over those who obey voluntarily. Punishment is a debt to be paid to the law-abiding members of the community, and once it has been paid it allows re-entry into the community of citizens on an equal basis. Only within a theory about the nature of law and political obligation can we provide a basis for the retributive theory of punishment.

However, it is still arguable that even a theory of this sort does not sanction some of the sorts of remarks typically made by retributivists such as 'one wills one's own punishment', or 'punishment is the criminal's right'. It can be argued that while the language of rights in this kind of context is misleading, nevertheless the retributivists are touching on an important problem when they talk in their rather strange way of having willed one's own punishment and having a right to be punished, and once again the issue comes down to what we think is implied by respect for persons. On the view put forward by Kant and Hegel, when we claim to respect someone as a person we respect his autonomy as a rational moral agent. We may not respect his character, we may abominate what he does, but we respect him as a person having in some degree a moral capacity for rational and autonomous conduct. We respect not the person's episodic desires and whims, but rather the desires, goals and purposes which he has as a rational moral agent or *would* have *if* he were a rational moral agent. We do not necessarily respect persons when we treat them how they *actually want* to be treated, but rather in accordance with the ways in which they *would wish* to be treated if and when they have a rational view of their situation. Obviously such a view as this would lead us very quickly to being able to say that punishment is my right as a rational being. While I may, under the influence of fear, prefer to be dealt with in a way other than by punishment, to accede to this would not be to respect me as a rational moral agent. In punishing me and thus recognizing that I am a responsible agent and in sound mind the state respects me by doing to me what, if I were at that moment capable of rational appraisal, I would myself wish them to do.

Clearly there are many dangers with this argument and the most obvious one, interestingly enough, parallels one of the criticisms by retributivists of the rehabilitative ideal. The retributivist often claims that in the rehabilitative model the offender is usually thought not to be capable of a rational appraisal of his position and thus is in need of therapy; however, in the retributive model the individual's desire not to be punished is equally dismissed in terms of a view about what the offender would really want if he were more rational than he is capable of being at the present time. In the rehabilitative case the difficulties posed could only be solved if we had some objective account of the nature of mental illness, and some view about the ways in which the norms of our society embody a standard of social health to justify the inference that the offender's deviance from those norms is pathological; in the retributivist case the problem is analogous, although the language is less that of health or illness and more that of rationality and justice. If we could determine some objective standard of rationality and the laws which a rational person would choose then we might avoid some of the obvious dangers in saying that the offender, if he were rational, would will his own punishment. On this view I could be shown to have willed my own punishment as a rational moral agent *if* the laws of my society are the laws which would have been chosen by rational persons in an initial situation of choice, and if punishment would have been chosen in that situation as the means whereby adherence to such laws would have been secured. My willing my own punishment is thus shown by an argument about hypothetical rational choice. This issue here is a very central one in Western political philosophy – is it possible to see the coercive power of the state in such a way as it is the product of each person's rational, though not necessarily current operant, will.

This clearly leads on to the problem of social rather than narrowly criminal justice. This issue is squarely faced by Kant in his theory. The whole Kantian framework depends upon certain conditions being met before laws can be considered just – it would have to be capable of being defended in terms of an argument of the contractual form. The laws are just if they would have been chosen by rational persons in a situation of impartiality. If, however, the existing structure of law cannot be regarded as just in terms of criteria such as these, then clearly the Kantian theory of punishment will fail to apply. This is the great merit of seeing the theory in the wider context of Kant's political philosophy. The retributive theory only stands if it is in the context of laws which can themselves be defended as just. There are, however, a number of objections to Kant's enterprise, which has been taken over very largely by Rawls in his *Theory of Justice*, a book to which many current defenders of the justice model appeal. In the first place, of course, there is the view of legal positivists that it is a mistake to look for some external standard for the justification of law – in this case the social contract. On the positivist view, laws which are enacted according to the proper procedures within a constitutional system are *just* by definition. But more importantly, as we have seen, it is arguable that it is impossible to derive a substantive theory of just law from an a priori theory about rational choice in situations of impartiality. Before persons can make choices they have to have information, and choices about laws will have to be based upon information concerning the human condition, but are there any data about the nature of man and his relationship to his fellow beings which can be taken as objective and neutral and thus be able to play a role in a procedure which is seen as providing a firm foundation for external judgements about the just nature of particular laws? A Marxist would argue that if the information on which these hypothetical choices are made is based upon bourgeois social science and social theory, embodying assumptions, say, about the basic competitiveness and acquisitiveness of persons, then we shall end up with a bourgeois theory of justice. This is precisely what Marx accused both Hegel and Kant of doing and what latter-day Marxists have accused Rawls of doing. In his celebrated article on capital punishment Marx says the following:

> From the point of view of abstract right, there is only one theory of punishment which recognises human dignity in the abstract, and that is the theory of Kant, especially in the more rigid formula given to it by Hegel. Hegel says 'Punishment is the right of the criminal. It is an act of his own will. The violation of right has been proclaimed by the criminal as his own right. His crime is the negation of right. Punishment is the negation of this negation, and consequently an affirmation of right, solicited and forced upon the criminal himself.' There is no doubt something specious in this formula in as much as Hegel instead of looking at the criminal as a mere object, the slave of justice, elevates him to the position of a free and self-determining being. Looking however more closely into the matter we discover that German Idealism here, as in most other instances, has given but a transcendental sanction to the rules of existing society. Is it not a delusion to substitute for the

individual with his real motives, with multifarious circumstances pressing down upon him, the abstraction of 'free will'.[22]

What Marx is arguing here is that the theories of both Kant and Hegel presuppose a just society in which the law is seen as a system of rules which free, impartial, rational persons would have chosen as just laws. The rehabilitative ideal has to provide and has lamentably failed to provide a social theory which would allow us to say with objectivity that a particular system of law embodies pathological features; the retributivist, however, equally has failed to do this and that enables both parties to claim to respect persons while at the same time constructing elaborate theories which enable them to bypass what Marx calls the real person with his existing motives and pressed in by social circumstances.

The recognition, plausible as it is, that the retributive or justice model requires some broader framework of social and political philosophy and in particular a theory about the nature of a set of just laws, in order to back it up, leads to some difficulties for the model. If in fact all conceptions of justice are contestable, as some political theorists argue, and no single theory of justice can command the rational assent of all persons, then the form which retribution takes in a particular society is obviously going to be equally contested.

It is often argued that there is no real difference between retribution and vengeance and that it is surely wrong in the civilized world to base the criminal justice system on what is often seen as a crude and destructive emotion. However, this assimilation would be a mistake. Certainly revenge and retribution do have some things in common. Punishment is, as Nozick argues, 'inflicted for a reason (a wrong or injury) with the desire that the other person know why this is occurring and to know that it was intended'.[23] However, Nozick goes on to give some criteria which make it possible to draw a cogent distinction between revenge and retribution, and in what follows I take his criteria as the framework.

1   Retribution is inflicted for a wrong that has been done whereas revenge can be inflicted for a slight or an injury but not for a wrong. One way of putting this point is that retribution is inflicted for the infliction of a harm which society recognizes is a serious wrong done to an individual.

2   Retribution exhibits some idea of proportionality, that there is some

kind of internal limit to the degree to which retribution is justified and this is set by the nature of the wrong done. Whereas vengeance is not or may not be limited but if it is, it is for the reasons other than the internal proportionality of the crime committed.

3   Revenge is personalized whereas retribution is exacted in an impersonal way by an agent or agents who have no personal relationship with the crime or with the accused or victim.

4   Related to (3) vengeance has an inextricably irrational tone – taking pleasure in the suffering of the person on whom vengeance is taken. This is not true retribution, it is done impersonally and in a sense objectively and 'clinically'.

5   Retribution is general or universal in a way that revenge is not. If a wrong has been done to me I may seek vengeance of a degree and kind which is personal to me and to my emotional state at the time whereas in the case of retribution the retributive agent or agency is committed to the idea that all others in similar circumstances who are guilty of that crime should suffer the same degree of retribution.[24]

These seem to be good grounds for distinguishing between vengeance, which is personal and emotionally formed and not subject to proportionality, and retribution, which is impersonal, neutral and proportionate.

However, the emphasis upon proportionality raises a central issue for the retributive or the justice model of punishment and one which looks set to allow utilitarian or consequentialist considerations to gain a foothold again because the issue of moral pluralism comes into the picture in another respect too, namely that of the degree of punishment which will be a just retribution for a crime. This idea is central to retributive theories of punishment and it goes back to Aristotle's idea that the purpose of legal justice is to right wrongs and to share a kind of equality between the crime and the punishment:

When one party is struck and the other strikes, or one kills and the other is killed, that which is suffered and that which is done may be said to be unequally or unfairly divided; the judge then tries to restore equality by the penalty or loss which he inflicts upon the offender, subtracting it from his gain.[25]

This idea is also central to the Old Testament view of an eye for an eye and a tooth for a tooth which is frequently cited in discussions of the retributive theory of punishment. One might imagine that in a small homogeneous community, in which there were shared attitudes and understandings, there would be a high degree of agreement about what would count as an equal punishment. This would not depend upon some abstract or metaphysical principle but would be an accepted feature of the texture of that way of life. In *The Philosophy of Right* Hegel appeals to the idea of the equal value of the crime and punisment as a central feature of the retributive theory. We cannot accept, he argues, the idea that punishment should fit the crime in some literal sense.

> This identity rests on the concept, but it is not an equality between the specific character of the crime and that of its negation; on the contrary, the two injuries are equal only in respect of their implicit character, i.e. in respect of their value.[26]

In a more morally fragmented society, however, what would count as the just and proportionate punishment for an action which had to be determined independently of the calculation of consequences such as reform or deterrence, would be a difficult if not impossible task.

It is the recognition of this sort of fact together with the point about justice made earlier that might lead one again in a utilitarian direction. The utilitarian might well argue as follows: if a retributive theory of punishment requires a theory of just law to make it morally cogent and we lack such a consensual theory; and if retribution requires some idea of equality and proportionality about which again there may be little consensus in society, then a formula such as that proposed by the utilitarians in which punishment is seen in relation to the welfare of society as a whole might be thought to bypass these difficult issues. Utilitarianism, so it is argued, as we saw earlier, is concerned with fewer moral values, or seeks to transform other moral values into utilitarian ones. On this view, utilitarianism recognizes the facts of moral diversity, while securing to as many people as possible whatever they happen to want and punishment only comes into play when the actions of an individual conflict in a severe manner with the operation of the want-satisfying formula. It is not at all clear, however, that this is so, partly because of the internal difficulties in utilitarianism which were discussed in an earlier chapter, and partly because of the specific issues under consideration in the case of punishment. As we saw earlier, utilitarians experienced very great difficulty in trying to avoid questions about justice in favour of considerations about welfare and it seems likely that any theory of punishment if it is to be morally acceptable will have to be linked to a theory of justice. Secondly, while the utilitarian sees a problem in proportionality in the retributive theory which may be difficult to solve in a morally pluralist society, does not the utilitarian experience rather similar problems when seeking to determine the level of deterrence? Clearly the judgement to be made is not the crude one of what punishment will stop a particular crime, because then the most draconian punishments would be imposed, but rather which reasonable punishments will lead to a reasonable level of deterrence. In a sense there is a similar problem of proportionality between punishment and deterrence in the utilitarian view as there is between punishment and retribution in the retributive theory. In neither case can difficult judgements be avoided by operating a formula.[27] Again we see the problem of providing a philosophical foundation for the social function of an institution in the context of moral diversity.

Notes

1   K. Menninger, *The Crime of Punishment*, Viking, New York, 1968, p. 17.
2   Ibid., p. 95.
3   B. F. Skinner, *Science and Human Behaviour*, Macmillan, London, 1953, p. 115–16.
4   B. Karpman, 'Criminal Psychodynamics', *Journal of Criminal Law and Criminology*, 47, 1956, p. 47.
5   Menninger, *The Crime of Punishment*, p. 139.
6   F. Biesték, *The Casework Relationship*, Allen and Unwin, London, 1961, p. 46.
7   K. Menninger, 'Therapy Not Punishment', *Harper's Magazine*, August 1959, pp. 63–4.
8   See, for example, P. Winch, *The Idea of a Social Science*, Routledge, London, 1958, passim; C. Taylor, 'Interpretation and the Sciences of Man', in *Philosophy and the Human Sciences: Philosophical Papers*, vol. 2, Cambridge University Press, Cambridge, 1984; see also C. Taylor, *The Explanation of Behaviour*, Routledge, London, 1964.

9   H. Morris, 'Persons and Punishment', *The Monist*, 52, 1968, p. 480.

10 R. D. Laing, *The Politics of Experience and the Bird of Paradise*, Penguin, London, 1967.

11 Morris, 'Persons and Punishment', p. 487.

12 T. Szasz, 'The Mental Health Ethic', in *Ethics and Society*, ed. R. de George, Macmillan, London, 1968.

13 P. Bean, *Rehabilitation and Deviance*, Routledge, London, 1976, p. 10.

14 There is a good theoretical discussion of these themes in J. Murphy, *Kant: The Philosophy of Right*, Macmillan, London, 1970.

15 P. F. Strawson, *Freedom and Resentment and Other Essays*, Methuen, London, 1974.

16 Ibid., p. 9.

17 C. Winnicott 'Casework and Agency Function', in *Social Work and Social Values*, ed. E. Younghusband, Allen and Unwin, London, 1967, p. 108.

18 I. Kant, *The Metaphysical Elements of Justice*, ed. and trans. J. Ladd, Bobbs Merrill, Indianapolis, 1965, p. 331. See also the excellent discussion in Murphy, *Kant: The Philosophy of Right*.

19 G. W. F. Hegel, *The Philosophy of Right*, trans. R. M. Knox, The Clarendon Press, Oxford, 1952, paras 97ff.

20 I. Kant, *Metaphysical Elements of Justice*, op.cit., p. 102.

21 J. Rawls, *A Theory of Justice*, The Clarendon Press, Oxford, 1972.

22 K. Marx, 'On Capital Punishment', *New York Daily Tribune*, 28 February 1853.

23 R. Nozick, *Philosophical Explanations*, Harvard University Press, Cambridge, Mass., 1981, p. 368.

24 Ibid., pp. 366–8.

25 Aristotle, *Nicomachean Ethics*, trans. J. A. K. Thomson, Penguin, London, 1953, Book 5, p. 148.

26 G. W. F. Hegel, *The Philosophy of Right*, trans. T. M. Knox, The Clarendon Press, Oxford, 1952, para. 101.

27 Some of these themes have been developed very well by A. Sivaramakrishanan in his unpublished PhD thesis submitted to Southampton University in 1988 – 'Social Science, Professional Authority and Citizenship'.

9

Political Philosophy on Dover Beach? Reasoning, Context and Community

> ... the world, which seems
> To lie before us like a land of dreams,
> So various, so beautiful, so new,
> Hath really neither joy, nor love, nor light,
> Nor certitude, nor peace, nor help for pain;
> And we are here as on a darkling plain
> Swept with confused alarms of struggle and flight,
> Where ignorant armies clash by night.
>
> Matthew Arnold, 'Dover Beach'

> At the foundation of well-founded belief lies belief that is not founded.
>
> Wittgenstein, On Certainty

> So are you saying that human agreement decides what is true and what is false ? It is what human beings say that is true or false, and they agree in the language they use. This is not agreement in opinions but in a form of life. Wittgenstein, Philosophical Investigations

> To drop the idea of languages as representations, and to be thoroughly Wittgensteinian in our approach to language, would be to de-divinise the world ... since truth is a property of sentences, since sentences are dependent for their existence on vocabularies, and since vocabularies are made by human beings, so are truths.
>
> R. Rorty, Contingency, Irony and Solidarity

320

Throughout this book we have been exploring a number of related themes. The first and most general is the assumption that a society needs some kind of moral foundation, a set of beliefs which either do or might hold it together, the idea here being that practical reason is rootless and arbitrary if it is not based on a set of agreed values which are taken as authoritative for that society. In the past such values might have been based upon custom, tradition or pervasively shared religious beliefs. But now in a world in which, in the words of T. S. Eliot, we live 'dispersed on ribbon roads',[1] a world of individualism and moral subjectivism, it is argued we have moved into a new era of individualism, and the task of political philosophy is to provide a set of coherent principles on which practical reasoning about politics can rest in this new environment. Without this philosophically based agreement about values, then society will be potentially anarchical without any clear and agreed criteria for political judgement and practice. In earlier forms of human society we might have been able to accept Eliot's claim in *Choruses from 'The Rock'* that:

> What life have you if you have not life together?
> There is no life that is not in community,
> And no community not lived in praise of God.[2]

Many political theorists have held the view that some kind of transcendental sanction is necessary for morality and for moral and political ties. Locke, for example, argued in his *Letter on Toleration* that:

> Promises, covenants and oaths, which are the bond of human society, can have no hold or sanctity for the atheist, for the taking away of God, even if only in thought, dissolves all.[3]

Religious belief, or more generally metaphysical beliefs of one sort or another underpinned values. However, if morality is subjective then we need a set of principles which will provide a foundation for political accommodation between subjective standpoints. This idea has its roots in Plato in his critique of the Sophists who argued that man is the measure of all things, of what is true and what is false, of what is right and what is wrong. On this view politics was turned into a criterionless matter of persuasion and rhetoric rather than truth and rightness. With his assumption that there is a clear distinction to be drawn between knowledge and belief he argued that the claim to authority of the ruler must be based upon his claim to possess such knowledge. As we saw earlier, Bentham's argument for the principle of utility being the ultimate criterion of political judgement made a not dissimilar point when he challenged those who dismissed the principle of utility to say whether or not 'he would judge and act without principle' and if not whether any other principle is neither more nor less than an 'averment of his own unfounded sentiments; that is, what in another person he might be apt to call caprice'. This claim that practical reason must have a secure philosophical basis has been repeated more recently by the important German philosopher Jurgen Habermas when he argues that:

If philosophical ethics and political theory can know nothing more than what is anyhow contained in the everyday norm of consciousness of different populations, and if it cannot know this in a different way, it cannot distinguish legitimate from illegitimate domination ... If, on the other hand, philosophical ethics and political theory are supposed to disclose the moral core of the general consciousness and to reconstruct it as a normative concept of the moral, then they must specify criteria and provide reasons; they must that is produce theoretical knowledge.[4]

This is a significant passage in that it shows Habermas haunted by the spectre of relativism. Without a clear basis for moral judgement we can make no transculturally binding judgements and we are left very much with Protagorean relativism. Habermas rubs the point home with reference to National Socialism which embodied a shared form of moral consciousness. Without some external standard of right or wrong how could it have been challenged? One of the tasks of philosophy is the cognitive validation of such an external standpoint.

As we saw in chapter 1, however, there are major difficulties in trying to determine the cognitive basis on which such a philosophical ethics could in fact be founded. Given that such a theory is likely to include a conception of the good, or a conception of human flourishing which in turn would involve either normative or empirical assumptions about human nature, then as the positivists argued, such a view becomes enmeshed in deep philosophical difficulty. We have no clear idea how conceptions of the good can be rationally grounded and we have no clear view about how the empirical aspects of an account of human nature would support a theory of human flourishing, nor how the normative aspects of any account of human nature could be supported rationally. The fact/value distinction makes such arguments deeply problematic – a feature which has not really disappeared with the collapse of the overall positivist programme.

The problem of the subjectivity of value then poses deep issues for political theory and part of the liberal project in political theory once it has gone beyond seeing liberalism and political neutrality as merely a response to moral nihilism and fragmentation, has been to try to determine whether there are any rationally compelling rules which could underpin practical political reasoning in a world in which first order moral agreement has become fragmented. Liberal political thought has been engaged in what T. S. Eliot in the poem mentioned above called disparagingly 'working out a rational morality'. In his view this is a hopeless enterprise because morality can only be supported through some sense of the transcendent:

> Much is your reading but not the Word of God,
> Much is your building, but not the House of God.
> Will you build me a house of plaster, with corrugated
> roofing. . . .[5]

The attempt to produce a rational morality, however, has proceeded either by emphasizing procedural devices such as Rawls's veil of ignorance, or by trading on the idea of minimum ethical commitments, as in Rawls's idea of primary goods which any person is thought to want, or as in Gewirth's idea of the minimal conditions of agency. We have also looked at three other approaches characteristic of modern political theory: the utilitarian, which again seeks some principles of practical reason on the basis of some limited assumptions about human desires; the theory of needs; and accounts of human rights. Again, to be cogent, such theories seem to require some conception of the good. In the utilitarian case, we came to doubt the idea that there could be purely procedural ways of discounting some types of preference. In the case of needs, in order to specify needs in any detail it turned out to be necessary to appeal to rather specific cultural norms. In the case of rights, if a basis for rights is to be found and if priorities between rights claims are to be adjudicated, then again it seems as though some reference has to be made to substantive theories of human flourishing and some account of the ordering of human needs, but where are the resources to come from to support such a theory? This is the central dilemma of liberal political thought. It recognizes the fact of moral autonomy and moral individualism, while at the same time it cannot just take its stand on the subjectivity or the incommensurability of values because if it does then as Michael Sandel says in his characterization of Isaiah Berlin's position:

> If one's convictions are only relatively valid, why stand for them unflinchingly? ... if freedom has no morally privileged status, if it is just one value among many, then what becomes of liberalism?[6]

If, therefore, it is true that the project of a liberal political theory, neutral between competing, subjective conceptions of the good, fails, because such theories always involve substantive accounts of human flourishing, then we seem to be back with the fundamental problem, namely whether conceptions of the good, so central to practical reason, are capable of being rationally grounded or whether this is to pose the wrong question. Perhaps we can get away without finding philosophical foundations for ethics even in a society in which there seem to be no other overall foundations available. In this chapter I want to consider some alternative answers to this question. The first has come to be called communitarian and rather crudely, at this stage of the argument, may be taken as saying that political goods cannot be determined by abstract reasoning, nor are they freely chosen by atomized moral agents, but rather arise out of and are implicit in the ways of life of particular communities. The second answer is that the search for external rational foundations for practical reasoning is misconceived because even if, *per impossible*, they could be found, they would in fact be inert in relation to practical dilemmas. We do not need theoretical foundations for a way of life and to conceive the political philosopher's task in this way is misconceived. Practical reason is not about sophia (wisdom), justified claims to objective knowledge, but rather phronesis (judgement), the capacity of practical deliberative judgement in particular situations. These two views tend to coalesce in the communitarian/interpretive approach to the discipline.

The communitarian approach in political philosophy, which has come to be associated with Michael Sandel, Michael Walzer and Charles Taylor, arose to some extent as a reaction to the work of liberal theorists such as Rawls and Dworkin, as the title of Sandel's book *Liberalism and the Limits of Justice* suggests. However, it is important to recognize that the idea of community has frequently been invoked over the past 200 years as an attempt to correct what has been seen as the individualism, the subjectivism, the atomism, the alienation, the instrumentalism, the contract-based and market-oriented character of liberalism. Hegel, T. H. Green, Bosanquet, Tawney, Raymond Williams and Robert Paul Wolff have all in different ways invoked the ideal of community as a way of trying to combat these baneful features of liberal society, so modern communitarian thought is not really new. Indeed, in Britain the Idealist movement, influenced more by Hegel than by Kant's emphasis on universal rules, saw the community as the source of political values and conceded a large and central place for groups in a liberal society in which one learned to acquire an identity. However, these critics appealed to the idea of community as an inescapable ideal which individualistic liberalism found it impossible to accommodate, whereas the role of community in the work of modern critics of the liberal project is in fact multifaceted and it has at least both a normative and an epistemological role. This latter role is not so clearly present in the work of earlier critics, but in the works which I have mentioned it plays a part in underpinning the ideal role which community also plays in their theories. I shall now go on to try to outline these different roles and their importance for the liberal project because they are often run together in the work of communitarian political theorists. However, before going on to discuss these two issues in detail I will attempt a broad sketch of some of the central themes of communitarian political theory which will show its importance, the ways in which it challenges some of the assumptions of liberal political thought and the role which the normative and epistemological aspects of the theory play within it.

The epistemological role played by the idea of community relates to the points made earlier in the chapter about conceptions of the good.

Communitarians reject the idea that we can develop cogent views of the good by abstract philosophical reasoning, nor are they the product of individual preference or emotional attitude. Rather they are embodied in the ways of life of particular communities. The philosopher cannot give them any external rational foundation. They are given, however implicitly, in particular forms of life and the task of the philosopher is to bring them fully to consciousness and, as it were, reclaim them. He is not creating them, however; they are implicit in particular ways of life. In a sense the community is the basis of practical reason and political judgement, but these bases are not universal in scope nor indubitable as the foundational assumptions of many political theorists seem to imply. This does not mean, however, that they are arbitrary. They are only arbitrary in the sense that they could have been different, but given they are as they are they enter into and constitute the way of life of the particular society in question. They are restricted and local but this is to be expected. Practical reason has to speak to the situatedness of human life. There is a big difference here between the aims of communitarian thought and at least the programmatic aspirations of liberalism. Rawls, for example, argues on the final page of *A Theory of Justice*:

> Thus to see our place in society from the perspective of this position is to see it *sub specie aeternitatis*: it is to regard the human condition not only from all social but also from all temporal points of view. The perspective of eternity is not a perspective from a certain place beyond the world, nor the point of view of a transcendent being; rather it is a form of thought and feeling that rational persons can adopt within the world. And having done so, they can, whatever their generation, bring together in one scheme all individual perspectives and arrive together at regulative principles that can be affirmed by everyone as he lives by them, each from his own point of view.[7]

This passage makes strongly universalist and foundational claims which, as we shall see later, Rawls modifies, claims which are criticized not so much in detail, but as a project by the communitarians. The same point is made more exactly although more prosaically by Dworkin when he argues as follows:

In the end, political theory can make no contribution to how we govern ourselves except by struggling, against all the impulses that drag us back to our own culture, toward generality and some reflective basis for deciding which of our traditional distinctions and discriminations are genuine and which spurious, which contribute to the flourishing of the ideals we want, after reflection, to embrace.[8]

Is the project of political theory to provide some universal values as a foundation for practical reasoning in politics, or is it to bring to a fuller consciousness the values which are implicit in the communities of which we are a part? If part of the project of political philosophy is, as T. M. Scanlon argues, to justify one's actions to others on grounds they could not reasonably reject,[9] who are these 'others' and what are the sorts of reasons involved? Are the others part of the same moral community and if so what are its characteristics and its boundaries? Are the reasons universal, or part of a complex set of reasons which are implicit in a specific way of life? The answers given to these questions clearly determine the scope of political theory and the vocation of the political philosopher.

This brings me on to the second aspect of the communitarian case which might be termed ontological. Communitarians criticize the ontology and in particular the theory of the self put forward by liberal theorists and the conception of the human condition which follows from this. This involves making the case for arguing that the self at least in part is constituted by the values of the community within which the person finds him or her self and therefore that choosing values in some kind of abstract way as envisaged by liberal theory just embodies a false moral ontology.[10]

There is another strong theme in communitarian writing too, which is perhaps implicit in what has gone before, namely that the liberal project, or perhaps more comprehensively the Enlightenment project of providing universal principles of political morality, whether based upon rights or justice, is misconceived, not only because such theories cannot be given a rational foundation for the reasons I have suggested, but because they mistake the relationship between theory and practice. The flourishing of society cannot be secured by agreement on abstract principle, but rather has to trade on values which are implicit in the way of life in society as it exists. Plato reflected, through the figure of Socrates, on the confusions and contradictions of conventional morality in Athens and felt compelled by that confusion to seek a form of society in which humans could properly flourish on the basis of a set of values which transcended the everyday world, the Forms or Ideas. These could be known fully only by the philosopher. The task of political theory therefore was to redeem the everyday world by leaving it behind and identifying a set of values which could found society on a different and more secure basis. Certainly this idea that knowledge and understanding can only be gained by leaving the everyday world behind has a long history as an image in Western thought. The prophet in the desert, living on the margins of society; John the Baptist in the Wilderness, Jesus in the desert for forty days and forty nights, Plato's philosopher leaving the cave of everyday life for the sunlight of the Forms: all with the aim of redeeming the world by initially escaping from the constraints of existing values and principles. Or in much more prosaic ways, as in Rawls's Original Position, in which the rational contractors discount all the specific knowledge of themselves and their interests and thus of their specific identities; in Dworkin's insurance game; or most bizarrely by Ackerman who imagines a perfect technology of justice in which on a spacecraft (to separate us wholly from the world of interests) we reason about the distribution of manna (a resource without any specific qualities other than being capable of being transformed into 'any of the familiar material objects in our own world'. However, Walzer, perhaps the most self-conscious communitarian, argues in *Spheres of Justice* that this approach cannot provide the foundation for practical reasoning about values which those who have exemplified it have thought:

> One way to begin the philosophical enterprise – perhaps the orig-
> inal way – is to walk out of the cave, leave the city, climb the
> mountain, fashion for oneself (what can never be fashioned by
> ordinary men and women) an objective and universal standpoint.
> Then one describes the terrain of everyday life from far away, so
> that it loses its particular contours and takes on a general shape.
> But I mean to stand in the cave, in the city, on the ground. Another
> way of doing philosophy is to interpret to one's fellow citizens
> the world of meanings that we share. Justice and equality can
> conceivably be worked out as philosophical artifacts, but a just or

egalitarian society cannot be. If such a society isn't already here — hidden as it were, in our concepts and categories — we shall never know it concretely or realise it in fact.[11]

Do we need a universal ethics to sustain our society or do we need an ethos, a set of values implicit within society which the philosopher can play a role in bringing to the surface as a basis for further critical reflection on whether our society lives up to the values which are present in a deep way?

The issues at stake here have been well described by Rorty,[12] when he rejects what he calls, following Lyotard, meta-narratives[13] in which the philosopher seeks to describe or predict the activities of such entities as the noumenal self (Kant), Absolute Spirit (Hegel), or the proletariat (Marx), or Ideas or Forms (Plato). These meta-narratives are stories about metaphysical entities which, in Rorty's view, purport to justify loyalty to or in some cases breaks with contemporary communities. These meta-narratives purport to provide a rational basis for political action and judgement. Again this is an old argument about the whole enlightenment project of a set of universal principles compared with what Justus Moser, the eighteenth-century German thinker called Local Knowledge — an understanding of the values implicit in a specific and localized way of life.

So what is at stake here is political philosophy's current relationship with the rationalizing, cosmopolitan assumptions of the Enlightenment:

the truth of generality versus the truth of specificity, that is, truth at the level of abstract principles, versus truth embedded in immediate circumstances.[14]

The final aspect of the communitarian case in a sense builds upon these other points. If the community is the source of values and is constitutive of the self then the idea of community becomes of normative significance and community itself as something to be valued, as opposed to the typical political values expressed by liberal individualism. Given that the locus of the good and the sources of personal identity are to be found in community, then community should be sustained as the necessary environment for human flourishing. I shall now go on to discuss these arguments in turn.

Reasoning and community

The epistemological basis of communitarian thought can perhaps best be seen in relation to the later philosophy of Wittgenstein. This is not because Wittgenstein is much referred to by communitarians and interpretivists, except Rorty, but rather because his fundamental work on the philosophy of language provided a background in modern thought from which communitarians could draw. Here we need to revert back to some of the themes of the first chapter and in particular Wittgenstein's earlier argument in *Tractatus Logico-Philosophicus* that language depicts reality because ultimately it consist of names which stand in a direct denotative relation to objects in elementary propositions. In his later writings, such as *The Blue and Brown Books*, *Zettel*, *Philosophical Investigations*, *On Certainty*, and *Remarks on the Foundations of Mathematics*, he was very critical of these earlier doctrines. In these later writings he advanced a number of claims about language which, while they may not enter directly into the arguments in political theory as communitarians advance them, nevertheless play an important background role in relating their political theory to a deep philosophy of language.

First of all, Wittgenstein rejected the view of language which he had advanced in his early *Tractatus* writings. The criticisms made, particularly in *Philosophical Investigations*, are too complex and diverse to be gone into here, but the main theme is that instead of seeing language as a kind of calculus resting upon a set of basic elementary foundations, the elementary propositions of the *Tractatus*, Wittgenstein seems to have rejected foundations of this sort altogether. Instead of trying to determine whether a proposition was meaningful by tracing its relationship to a set of basic propositions, which on the positivist's view of the *Tractatus* were to be construed as reports of sense experience, thus depicting the world in an incorrigible way, we should look at the sense which the statement has in the linguistic context of which it is a part. As Peter Winch elegantly makes the point: 'Reality is not what gives language sense, but what is real and unreal shows itself in the sense which language has.'[15]

We should therefore try to locate a proposition in its appropriate context and not dismiss it as nonsense, or at the least as not possessing cognitive content because it fails to fit into some grid which is imposed on language by a priori epistemological considerations. So, for example, in the case of the religious language which was dismissed by *Tractatus* inspired positivism as devoid of cognitive meaning, we should look at a statement such as 'There will be a last judgement' and try to see what sense it has within the life of religious discipleship, within the linguistic practices of religion, within the religious language game. A word does not derive its meaning from its link to some unmediated external reality as opposed to its use within a stream of life. If this is true it follows then that philosophical reflection on religious and political language cannot take place in a vacuum; rather we have to be concerned with those traditions, practices, language games and contexts in which words have a home. Philosophical reflection on political language cannot take place in formal or abstract terms employing formal devices such as the appeal to logical consistency or the law on non-contradiction. We have rather to look at the meaning of moral and political concepts within specific moral traditions and contexts. In so far as they have such a place within a particular moral practice, they are going to have close relationships with other terms within that practice. So philosophical reflection cannot ultimately be pursued in a piecemeal way but has to involve trying to become clear about interrelationships between ideas in a rich social context:

> A main source of our failure to understand is that we do not command a clear view of our use of words ... A perspicuous representation [*Die ubersichtliche Darstellung*] produces just that understanding which consists in seeing connexions. The concept of perspicuous representation is of fundamental importance to us. It earmarks the form of account we give, the way we look at things (Is this a *Weltanschauung*?)[16]

The term *ubersichtliche Darstellung* in this passage could equally well have been rendered by 'overall view'. We need an overall view of our use of language and that means of the way of life in which it is embedded and forms a part. Philosophy is therefore inherently contextual, but struggling for a clear view of the context.

There is a second theme in Wittgenstein's philosophy which is central to an understanding of its impact upon modern political thought and that is the rejection of essentialism: the view that there must be either a common element to all uses of a term and the view that there is a strict set of necessary and sufficient conditions governing the use of a term. Here, the stalking horse is primarily Plato, but Wittgenstein's rejection of this model has important implications across the range of political theory, not just those of a Platonist sort. In many of his dialogues, for example the *Theatetus* (147), *Meno* (70–74), *Euthyphro* (6–7), *Republic* (507), Plato depicts Socrates as becoming exasperated with his discussants when in response to a question such as what is justice or what is knowledge, they go on to give examples. In the *Euthyphro*, for example, Plato argues that there is a need for a general account (logos) of a concept or a principle:

> Socrates: Remember that I said I did not ask you to give me two or three examples of piety, but to explain the general form which makes all pious things pious ... Tell me what is the nature of this form, and then I shall then have a standard to which I may look, and by which I may measure actions, whether yours or of anyone else, and then I shall be able to say that such and such an action is pious and such and such another impious.[17]

Secure moral judgement, and by extension, political judgement, depends upon a philosophical theory which will give an account of the terms used in the judgement. Without this, as Plato says in the *Republic*, 'the many are seen but not known'.

Therefore, giving examples misses the point. We need rather an account, a logos, of what makes these cases of justice or knowledge. Wittgenstein rejects this approach. In *The Blue Book*, for example, he argues that:

> The idea that in order to get clear about the meaning of a general term one had to find the common element in all its applications has shackled philosophical investigation; for it has not only led to no result, but it has also made the philosopher dismiss as irrelevant the concrete cases, which alone could have helped him to understand the usage of the general term. When Socrates asks the question 'What is knowledge?' he does not even regard it as a preliminary answer to enumerate cases of knowledge.[18]

This tendency to look for a common element Wittgenstein links to a craving for generality[19] which he sees as infecting philosophy. This craving for generality misrepresents language which is more open-textured and multifaceted than the search for necessary and sufficient conditions to govern the use of terms theory allows, and in fact frequently the search moves on to involve highly metaphysical theories which become very far removed from the confusions which led to the asking of philosophical questions in the first place. So, for example, in the case of the assumption that there is a common element to all uses of a general term, this leads in Plato to a very complex theory about what the common element is, namely the Form or Idea. It is participating in this metaphysical entity which makes something the kind of thing that it is. It also leads to a theory about how particulars are related to the Forms, a problem which Plato never really resolves and leads to some devastating critical passages in the *Parmenides*.[20] On the other hand the common element may be considered to be some kind of abstract idea of the thing in our minds from which all particularity has been removed. For example, in Locke's account of abstraction in an attempt to explain the common element in a triangle, a leaf and in snow he argues for a highly metaphysical theory of the common element as an abstract idea which loses all the particularity of the individual leaf or snowflake.[21]

Instead of recognizing the multifaceted nature of language and its relation to social practices which inevitably means a good deal of particularity, the craving for generality leads us to develop these complex metaphysical theories in which, as Wittgenstein says, 'language goes on holiday'. It becomes detached from the contexts in which it naturally functions and become part of a complex theory which just because it abstracts from particularity, then really fails to shed light on that particularity. Although Walzer's vision of people leaving the cave (see *Republic* 517c), moving out of the city and climbing the mountain are, as metaphors for objectivity, hardly examples of going on holiday, nevertheless the images play the same role of detachment from particularity as a condition of objectivity. Indeed Thomas Nagel has argued that the philosophical position is 'the view from nowhere'.[22] However, on the Wittgensteinian view the metaphysical basis of objectivity is really inert. Objectivity is internal to context and there is no context-free standpoint from which we can evaluate the world and social practices. We cannot look to metaphysical theories and certainty to provide us with a basis for a secure way of life.

Metaphysical theories cannot provide a foundation for language. The meaning of language and the ways of life in which languages are embedded do not rest upon some kind of antecedent metaphysical foundation. On the contrary, what is true and false, the real and the unreal, a standard of right and wrong are internal to a language and a practice and cannot be determined independently of it. The concept of a reason has a place within a practice, but there is no transcultural standpoint which can define the absolute standpoint of reason independently of social practices. Within a game, for example chess, a particular move can be right or wrong, a good or a bad move, a justified or unjustified one. The game of chess itself, however, is neither rational nor irrational, justified nor unjustified. These are internal questions, not external absolutist ones. If we are involved in a process of justification of action we can go so far within the context or the practice in which we operate, but that context bounds the range of justification. It is itself neither rational nor irrational:

> If I have exhausted the justifications I have reached bedrock and my spade is turned. Then I am inclined to say: 'This is simply what I do.'[23]

> What has to be accepted, the given, is forms of life.[24]

> What people accept as justification is shown by how they think and live.[25]

Forms of life, linguistic practices and contexts are what give meaning to phrases like 'having a reason for doing something'. There are no a priori reasons for action, no a priori principles of practical reasoning which can be identified independently of the particularities of context and practice. Basic propositions of a system of thought 'do not serve as foundations in the same way as hypotheses which if they turn out to be false are replaced by others',[26] and Wittgenstein goes on to quote Goethe 'Im Anfag war die Tat' (in the beginning was the deed). The principles by which we live do not depict the world or some kind of antecedent moral order, so much as embody the commitments by which we live.

Within the religious language game to live one's life as if it were under a final judgement is a reason for acting in one way rather than another. Outside this context, however, both the reason and the behaviour which it justifies might seem to be bizarre or unintelligible. This argument applies not just to practical reasoning but also to mathematical reasoning in Wittgenstein's view. For example, he argues in *Remarks on the Foundations of Mathematics*:

This follows inexorably from that ... This is a demonstration for whoever acknowledges it as a demonstration. If anyone doesn't acknowledge it, doesn't go by it as a demonstration, then he has parted company with us even before it comes to talk.[27]

He parts company before it comes to talk because the talk is predicated on a practice which the person does not share. The point is not an incidental one because it comes up again in the context of contradiction. He talks about the civil status of contradiction in the sense that it has a part only within a set of assumptions and practices:

the laws of inference can be said to compel us; in the same sense that is to say, as other laws in human society ... If you draw different conclusions you do indeed get into conflict, e.g. with society.'[28]

This is not just a matter of disagreement, but disagreeing in a way that ceases to give the expressions the meaning they have in the practice. As the earlier quotation makes clear, that kind of disagreement makes rational discourse impossible.

This thesis might seem to imply that the practices and language games in question are arbitrary. One must be careful here, however. They are certainly arbitrary in that they could have been different and there is no metaphysical argument to show that they have to be as they are. However, in Wittgenstein's view this is really to misuse the word arbitrary, because not to be arbitrary would imply fulfilling some kind of impossible metaphysical standard. Language games are not arbitrary, however, in the sense that whole ways of life embody them and that within these ways of life things have meaning and significance. They are not arbitrary in the sense that they cannot be changed at will because such a change would involve a massive change in our lives. This is a point which Wittgenstein makes clear in a number of places in *Remarks on the Foundations of Mathematics* because he wants to deny that conventionalism implies some kind of commitment to arbitrariness.

This point of view also implies that since practices are not given support by metaphysical theories, by what Rorty calls meta-narratives, they are not refuted either because of some failure to measure up to some standard of metaphysical exactness, such as the verification principle which was discussed in chapter 1. There is no absolute standard of reason which is situated outside language games and human practices in terms of which such practices can be graded, evaluated, dismissed or put into some hierarchy of ascending order of adequacy. In our culture it has been typical to take the standards of science as paradigmatic of rationality and to asses our activities in terms of whether they do or do not meet such standards, and clearly this view animated positivism. However, on this Wittgensteinian view we cannot give some contextless account of reason nor can we take reason out of one context such as the logical positivists did with science, and make it paradigmatic for all others because that would assume that there was a reality independently identifiable to which science in some way corresponded. As Winch says in discussing this view:

> criteria of logic are not a direct gift of God, but arise out of and are only intelligible in the context of, ways of living or modes of social life. It follows that one cannot apply criteria of logic to modes of social life as such. For instance, science is one such mode and religion is another; and each has criteria of intelligibility peculiar to itself. . . . We cannot sensibly say that either the practice of science itself or that of religion is either illogical or logical; both are non logical.[29]

If we are interested in ideas of justification, of right, of truth, then we shall have to understand them in this contextual way. There can be no a priori theory of right and justification. Language games do not get refuted by metaphysical argument, they get forgotten because they lose their point and purpose in a particular social context.

It would be a mistake to think, however, that the context of a particular social practice or community is itself a foundation for thinking and reasoning. Wittgenstein wants to move us away from the idea of foundations altogether. It is not that we are replacing metaphysical foundations with communitarian or contextual ones, rather that:

> Giving grounds, however, justifying the evidence, comes to an end; but the end is not certain propositions' striking us immediately as true, i.e. it is not a kind of seeing on our part, it is our acting which lies at the bottom of the language game.[30]

> If the true is what is grounded, then the ground is not true, nor yet false.[31]

Again the insistence is that it is commitment to a practice which is the basis for reasoning and for practical reasoning not some pure attempt to argue for the incorrigibility of a particular set of propositions as a universal foundation for practical judgement.

The idea that words do not have common elements or essential definitions leads to other implications too for political theory. If instead of common elements, what links the particulars falling under a common term[32] is in fact the family resemblances between them, the criss-crossing interrelationships rather than a list of necessary and sufficient conditions, then this clearly has implications for any attempt at a general political theory in which, abstracted from context, the terms in the theory must be used in an exact way. However, we may try to fix the meanings of words in everyday life for practical reasons. So, for example, while Wittgenstein may be correct that the word 'game' does not contain a common factor, nevertheless for the purposes of drawing up a byelaw to allow notices such as 'No Games to be Played in this Area', there will be some definition of a game which is unlikely, for example, to include noughts and crosses. We are aware that we have not given an exhaustive definition of 'game', but equally we can fix the boundary of the concept for this particular purpose. However, when we move to political theory the position is by no means as clear-cut, because, in the case of political concepts, where to fix the boundary may itself be a matter of political dispute in the sense that the meaning of a term may be disputed between different political traditions and standpoints. Instead of clear definitions being a prerequisite for progress in political theory, a particular definition may well itself embody a particular political standpoint. For example, whether justice can include social justice in the distribution of resources as social democrats believe, or whether it should be restricted as neo-liberals think; whether communities of interest are genuine communities as liberals argue they are, or not as communitarians of both the right and the left deny; whether rights are social and economic or only civil and political; in each case we have to accept that drawing the boundary in one place rather than another implicitly involves making a political decision, or at least a decision with political consequences.

These decisions do not reflect the way the world is or some necessary order which the mind has to follow, but rather reflect more generally our needs, interests and purposes. Take an example from outside political philosophy used by Renford Bambrough:

> Let us suppose that trees are of great importance in the life and work of the South Sea Islanders, and that they have a rich and developed language in which they speak of the trees with which their island is thickly clad. But they do not have names for the species and genera of trees as they are recognised by our botanists. As we walk round the island with some of its inhabitants, we can easily pick out orange trees, date palms and cedars. Our hosts are puzzled that we should call by the same name trees which appear to them to have nothing in common. They in turn surprise us by giving the same name to each of the trees in what is from our point of view a very mixed plantation. . . . Each party comes to recognise that its own classifications are as puzzling to the other as the other's are puzzling to itself.[33]

These classifications are not arbitrary. They are linked to needs and purposes in each group and each reflects objective similarities and differences. The islanders are concerned about building boats and houses with wood and they classify trees according to objective differences relating to these purposes. The botanist classifies according to objective features according to his purposes. However, the question of whether one classification is more true or more objective than the other cannot be divorced from the different needs and purposes at stake. Whether one is more objective than the other could only depend on whether we have some metaphysical view of the world to which the classifications of science more truly correspond. Or a metaphysical account of the ranking of human purposes such that, for example, the needs which science serves are somehow more important than the practical needs of the islanders. Some philosophers, such as Habermas in his book *Knowledge and Human Interests*,[34] have linked knowledge to a set of human interests and then tried to give a transcendental deduction of a particular set of basic human interests. This latter point relates particularly to the foundationalist approach in political theory in the sense that a good deal of such theorizing has had to do with devising frameworks for ranking the importance of human interests according to some metaphysical scale of value. The problem for the foundationalist now is where the metaphysical resources for such a deduction are to come from.

This brings us back to the traditional concern of political philosophers with theories of human nature which are supposed to fulfil this function. This depends, however, upon our being able to formulate some kind of universal theory of the self, its ends and its interests outside of any particular society and its practices. If we were able to do this, it would allow us to engage in a transcendental deduction of the necessity of some types of classification as opposed to others and ground their objectivity, not in the way it reflects some necessary features of the way the world is, but rather the fundamental interests which all persons have in common. However, Wittgenstein's arguments about the nature of the human mind to which we now turn have been thought to deal a death blow to the idea that we can in philosophy determine in an asocial way what the fundamental purposes and interests of human beings are. We shall now look at these arguments in general and go on to discuss their relevance to political philosophy and why these arguments push political philosophy into a contextualist or communitarian mode.

The point at issue here is what might be seen as Wittgenstein's commitment to the view that there is a non-contingent link between the self and the social context of which it is a part. This insistence on the link between self and society relates centrally to one theme which critics of the liberal project have frequently invoked, namely the extent to which the self in liberal theory is seen as atomized, asocial, solitary. It has led one critic of liberalism to argue that central to liberalism is the attempt to solve the problem which arises when 'essentially solitary individuals'[35] come together in civil society. If this is indeed a fair characterization of liberalism, then if Wittgenstein is correct that there can be no logical separation of self from context, then a central element of the liberal position is defective. The idea that self and context can be separated received its most paradigmatic statement in the work of Descartes, who argued in *The Meditations* that it was possible to doubt the existence of the external world, the existence of other human beings and the existence of one's own body; but not the existence and the contents of one's own mind since the very process of doubting is in fact a vindication of the process of thinking. This must imply that it is possible to have definite states of consciousness, covering the whole range of human thoughts, feelings and emotions independent of the existence of other human beings or relationships. It is this central Cartesian idea that Wittgenstein denies.

The argument for its denial is found in *Philosophical Investigations* and is concerned with what would have to be the case for us to possess the whole range of mental concepts in the absence of other people and relationships. It would mean that one would have to learn mental concepts from one's own case and Wittgenstein spent some time trying to explain why this is impossible. The argument is subject to some subtle disputes among philosophers,[36] but its main thrust seems to be clear enough and involves arguing that one could never learn the language to characterize one's experience purely by reflecting on the internal nature of that experience, an argument which, if cogent, would mean that there is a non-contingent relationship between one's being a subject of experiences and membership of a social word of shared meanings.

The argument is that if experience could be characterized independently of such shared meanings, then it must be possible to learn the language in terms of which we describe experience from one's own case. Indeed, one can only come to ascribe experience to others after one has learned to characterize one's own. However, what is involved in learning a language from one's own case or as Wittgenstein puts it 'how do I use words to stand for my sensations'? If one is to learn a language from one's own case this must also include the idea of following a rule. Language is inseparable from rule following in that if I designate a particular experience S with the word 'S' then I must be able to develop a rule for the use of 'S' so that I can be sure that I am using 'S' to describe the same experience at different times. Wittgenstein, however, wants to argue that it is impossible both to derive and follow a private rule. The meaning of the sign 'S' has to involve a rule for the use of 'S' and it might be argued that I derive this rule by concentrating my attention on the connection between the word 'S' and what it stands for namely the state of consciousness S:

> A definition surely serves to establish the meaning of a sign. – Well, that is done precisely by the concentration of my attention: for in this way I impress upon myself the connexion between the sign and the sensation. But 'I impress it on myself' can only mean: this process brings it about that I remember the connexion right in future. But in the present case I have no criterion of correctness. One would like to say: whatever is going to seem right to me is right. And that only means that we cannot talk about 'right'.[37]

Language is inseparable from rule following and one cannot follow a private rule because one cannot discriminate in a purely private way whether one is following the rule or not. Justification for the use of a term means, as Wittgenstein says, 'appealing to something independent', whereas a private check on rule following is like a person who buys 'several copies of the same morning paper to assure himself that what it said was true'. The language in terms of which we describe our states of consciousness, such as desires, wants, needs and so forth, are words in 'our common language' not just 'intelligible to me alone' and this follows from the nature of rule following.

This may seem rather remote from political philosophy, but in fact it has very great importance in the sense that it is not possible to derive a set of values about human flourishing, or the nature of human needs and desires, without looking at the social context which makes that account of flourishing or needs intelligible and provides a justification for it. Take a specific example which has been much discussed in philosophy during the past twenty years, namely the nature of wanting, a concept which is linked to political philosophy particularly through the utilitarian emphasis upon desire. If one were to reject the Wittgensteinian account of consciousness then it would seem that in principle anything could be wanted. The intelligibility of a claim to want something would not depend upon a common stock of values and assumptions about wanting, but rather on the sheer occurrence of an inner state called wanting. There is no logical link between the claim to want something and a common stock of values which makes the want intelligible. Take the following example from Elizabeth Anscombe's book *Intention*:

> But is not anything wantable, or at least any perhaps attainable thing ? It will be instructive to anyone who thinks this to approach someone and say: I want a saucer of mud or I want a twig of mountain ash. He is likely to be asked what for; to which let him reply that he does not want it for anything, he just wants it.... Now if the reply is: 'Philosophers have taught that anything can be an object of desire; so there can be no need for me to characterise these objects as somehow desirable; it merely so happens that I want them' then this is fair nonsense.[38]

The first point here is that to be intelligible the want has to be linked to some characterization of the desirability of the object which makes it a possible object of desire. The second point, following from Wittgenstein's point about the impossibility of a private language, is that one cannot have desirability characteristics which are private to an individual. The intelligibility, and thus the rationality, of a want depend upon two things: first that the object wanted has characteristics which make it desirable and secondly that these characteristics are drawn from a common stock of such terms in the common language within which the claim to want something is articulated. As Richard Norman says, commenting upon a similar point,

> One cannot drive a wedge between 'intelligible for us' and 'intelligible for him'. I want to argue that the intelligibility of a want is essentially a matter of its relation to public, supra individual standards and norms ... a want or an action cannot be said to have meaning at all unless its meaning can be formulated by reference to public standards.[39]

Given what has already been said about the way in which ideas such as rationality, justification and explanation are internal to particular language games and the social practices of which they are a part and the ways in which these differ in potentially incommensurable ways so that there can be no supra or a priori substantive standards of rationality, it follows that the intelligibility of action has a non-contingent link with a common language and its norms, and also that justification for action takes place within such a context too. There can therefore be no a priori or metaphysical theory of reasons for action just because such theories are not internal to specific practices, but equally there can be no account of reasons for action which derive them from some Cartesian psyche separate from the world of common language and common norms.

We can now see how this Wittgensteinian framework provides something of an intellectual background to communitarian and interpretative political philosophy. Although communitarians do not frequently discuss the issues in the philosophy of mind and language which relate to their theories, I believe that it is possible to see arguments of the sort we have been considering as forming a backcloth to these more directly political arguments. Indeed Richard Rorty acknowledges this as a central theme in his book *Contingency, Irony and Solidarity*.[40]

The appeal to community

Most of the themes of communitarian political theory are implicit in the Wittgensteinian perspective on language. First of all is the idea of the internal relation of reasons to particular practices and the way in which ideas such as a reason for action have to be linked to a common understanding and a common vocabulary. Most of these themes are found, for example, in the programmatic statements in Walzer's *Spheres of Justice*, perhaps the most fully developed example of the communitarian approach to political philosophy in the modern idiom. In chapter 1 of that work he identifies a number of ways in which his approach differs from what he takes to be the more universalistic and a priori road of other modern political theorists and he certainly seems to have Rawls particularly in mind.

The first element is that of particularity and the social context. As we saw in the case of Rawls's *A Theory of Justice*, Rawls seems[41] to develop an a priori and universalistic view of the moral reasoning of individuals in a situation which discounted everything specific about them when they are behind the veil of ignorance, or in the Original Position. Instead of asking the Rawlsian question 'What would rational individuals choose under universalizing conditions of such and such a sort?' we should rather concentrate on the more specific question 'What would individuals like us choose, who are situated as we are, who share a culture and are determined to go on sharing it? What choices have we already made in the course of our common life? What understandings do we already share?' Questions of political philosophy are questions about specific societies with particular values. Justification, argumentation has to take place within such contexts and not external to them.

Secondly, the kinds of goods which concern political theory such as office, economic goods, membership, desert, leisure, and so forth are social goods in the sense that they do not have a neutral meaning which is uncontaminated by specific cultural identities. There can be no thin theory of goods, no substantive theory of primary goods, no theorizing about Ackerman's 'manna', a good which has no specific characteristics. Even life's necessities have ineliminable social meanings:

> A single necessary good, and one that is always necessary – food, for example – carries different meanings in different places. Bread is the staff of life, the body of Christ, the symbol of the Sabbath, the means of hospitality and so on.[42]

We should also beware the idea that the primary use here is the nutritional and perhaps materialistic one.

> If the religious use of bread were to conflict with its nutritional uses – if the gods demanded that the bread be baked and burned rather than eaten – it is by no means clear which use would be primary.[43]

We can make a universal list of goods incorporated into a priori theories of practical reasoning only if 'they are abstracted from every particular meaning – hence for all practical purposes meaningless.'[44]

In this sense, there can be no a priori theory of reasons for acting or for political judgement. In the liberal tradition these reasons have been broadly of two sorts. In the *Critique of Practical Reason* Kant argues for a set of a priori reasons for actions which have no connection with specific social norms or with existing human preferences. It is what Wollheim calls a 'bleached'[45] theory. This was in order to secure the autonomy of human agency, an autonomy which would be compromised by the heteronomy, the empirical and variable nature of existing values, preferences, interests and desires. In the early nineteenth century Hegel, in arguments which bear some resemblance to the communitarians' recent arguments, subjects Kant's views to withering criticism.[46] The other alternative is the sort associated with Rawls, who argued that we can reason in an a priori manner about certain goods, primary goods which all people are presumed to want. However, modern communitarians such as Walzer reject this approach.[47] The idea of the self and its goods have to be linked to specific forms of human society, whether for the reasons which Hegel gave, or drawing upon Wittgenstein for the parallel reasons which modern communitarians give. In this sense modern political philosophy can be seen as a rerun of the debate between Kant and Hegel. The big difference between modern communitarians and Hegel is that the moderns reject Hegel's attempt to link specific forms of society and the different accounts of the nature of the self and its ends together into some metaphysical theory which saw them as progressing towards more and more adequate forms of human fufilment in world history.[48] This meta-narrative of legitimation has now to be rejected.[49] There can be no way of justifying ways of life in terms of some broad architectonic metaphysical framework.

Modern communitarian theorists, however, do agree with Hegel that social meanings are historical, they change over time and present meanings have to be understood in terms of their historical development. This means that as there cannot be a universal political philosophy, so there cannot be a transhistorical one. What count as the relevant reasons for action depend not upon some essentialist or transcultural or transhistorical theory but upon the contingent circumstances of particular cultures. It is in the rejection of a transhistorical meta-theory that they differ sharply from Hegel's own account of the link between self, good and society.[50]

Getting a clear view of a practice has to be an internal exercise and is much more like developing an adequate understanding of a literary text than it is producing a representation which is clearly true or false in the sense that it depicts an independent reality, as Charles Taylor says in discussing this problem:

We have to think of man as a self interpreting animal. He is necessarily so, for there is no such thing as the structure of meanings for him independently of his interpretation of them.[51]

If an interpretation is contested, as is likely, then all we can do, as Taylor argues, is:

> to show him through the reading of other expressions why [the contested expression] must be read in the way we suppose. But success here requires that he should follow us in these readings and so on, it would seem potentially for ever. We cannot escape an ultimate appeal to a common understanding of the expression, of the 'language' involved.[52]

There are several important issues at stake here. The first is that the appeal must be to shared understanding, it must be to some community of discourse, it cannot be to a private set of understandings. There cannot be interpretation without agreement and thus a shared community of some sort. Also the meaning of the interpretation is not secured on some metaphysical foundation lying outside the text or the practice, but is internal to the shared understandings which we bring to bear in interpretation. Finally, it makes the achievement of a common interpretation, whether of a text or of a community's values, an exercise more like literary criticism than science.

There are no ways of ranking social meanings and social goods into some kind of hierarchy of adequacy. Cultures are specific and there is no metaphysical background, no meta-narratives against which they can be considered as a whole as rational or irrational. In his discussion of the Indian caste system Walzer is very clear about this:

> We are (all of us) culture producing creatures; we make and inhabit meaningful worlds. Since there is no way to rank and order these worlds with regard to their understanding of social goods, we do justice to men and women by respecting their particular creations. And they claim justice, and resist tyranny, by insisting on the meaning of social goods among themselves. Justice is rooted in distinct understandings of places, honours, jobs, things of all sorts that constitute a shared way of life. To override those understandings is (always) to act unjustly.[53]

Any struggle against a hierarchical system must take from within and cannot be based upon some claim that the system fails to meet some standard of rationality or of human flourishing or justice which is determined outside, whether from an alternative way of life or from an a priori set of reasons for acting, such as would be given in an account of what a set of hypothetical rational persons under certain kinds of conditions might choose as distributive principles.

There are two final themes which emerge from this Wittgensteinian background. The first has to do with the nature of the self; the second with the role of philosophy. As we have seen Wittgenstein provides strong reasons for thinking that the self cannot be understood independently of society because of the non-contingent link between language, the characterization of inner experience and social standards. This provides the background for the communitarian claim that the self cannot be considered in an unencumbered way. It is argued by communitarians that the self has to have a non-contingent relationship with the standards and values of the society within which the individual lives. That is to say, in the view of communitarians it implies a clear rejection of Rawls's view that 'the self is prior to the ends which are affirmed by it'. If this were not so then we would be able to give some content to the nature of the self which is prior to an account of its embodiment in a particular society with its associated practices and norms. However, the thrust of Wittgenstein's argument seems to be against this position. Rawls argues that it is not our aims and values that primarily reveal our nature, but rather our capacity to choose our aims. Similarly with Gewirth what matters is our capacity for action and its necessary antecedents, not what we act for, what ends we seek in action.

It is not clear, however, that this is a coherent conception. If, for example, we turn back to Elizabeth Anscombe's example of wanting, it is not the case that here is a self that can decide to make anything the object of desire. Rather to claim intelligibly to have a want or desire is to make a claim with an implicit social and contextual dimension. The communitarians want to argue for situated selves in which the self is socially constituted and the reasons for action available to the self are those which are available as the common stock in the community. Lyotard draws the conclusion from this to which we shall return that: 'the social subject itself seems to dissolve in this dissemination of language games.' Liberal political theory in so far as it seeks to derive some universal reasons for action from the idea of the unencumbered self, agency, a thin theory of the good, all done in abstraction from any particular social practice, is sending language and thought on holiday.

The final implication of Wittgenstein's thought which might be held to support a communitarian approach in political philosophy is a claim that philosophy is inert in attempting to provide foundations for a way of life or set of beliefs. As we have seen, in some forms in Western thought the role of political philosophy has been seen in terms of drawing out the moral and political implications of a theory of human nature, or more broadly a cosmic theory within which human beings are thought to have a particular nature and significance. However, the Wittgensteinian view of the role of philosophy involves a rejection of this. Philosophy cannot give to society or to particular practices within society any particular foundation. What Lyotard has called meta-narratives, philosophical theories which hold practices together in some kind of total outlook, whether it is as with Plato participating in the Form of the Good, with Hobbes's mechanistic and geometrical understanding of human nature with a complete naturalistic framework, or Hegel's account of the role of particular aspects or moments of human nature in the movement of *Geist*, have collapsed and we should not be looking for alternative philosophical foundations of a totalizing sort. Such grand narratives have lost their credibility. We live in a radically pluralistic culture and the legitimacy of particular practices is misconceived if that legitimacy is seen as depending upon their place in some overarching philosophical position. Drawing upon Wittgenstein, Lyotard, who has been a great influence on Rorty, argues as follows:

> The social bond is linguistic, but it is not woven with a single thread. It is a fabric formed by the intersection of at least two (and in reality an indeterminate number of language games obeying different rules . . . Speculative or humanistic philosophy is forced to relinquish its legitimation duties, which explains why philosophy is facing a crisis whenever it persists in arrogating such functions.[54]

The grand narratives of the good, the noumenal self, the proletariat in history or *Geist* do not in fact hold societies together, they are dislocated from the societies whose beliefs they are thought to sustain and legitimize. Moral philosophy may be in crisis because of the lack of credibility of metaphysical meta-narratives but this does not mean that social morality is in crisis since it has never been sustained by metaphysical argument. As Rorty argues, 'These metaphors are stories which purport to justify loyalty to or breaks with certain contemporary communities, but they are neither historical narratives about what these or other communities have done in the past nor scenarios about what they might do in the future.'[55]

What gives a practice cohesion and legitimacy is internal to it. It is a matter of ethos[56] rather than grounds or foundations. Loyalty to institutions, belief in their value, is not grounded in anything other than the fact that, as Rorty argues, they overlap with lots of other members of the group with which we identify for purposes of moral or political deliberation and the fact that these beliefs, values and loyalties are distinctive of the group and it is through these that it builds up its self image and its sense of worth.

This approach refocuses the nature of political philosophy. Instead of trying to secure some metaphysical or epistemological foundations for general political judgement outside of particular ways of life and practices, political philosophy is interpretive, bringing to light the values, principles and the reasons which count in a particular context for action. Political philosophy and political judgement are linked much more to Aristotle's idea of phronesis rather than Plato's sophia; more to practical deliberation weighing the factors which count in a given context rather than some general theory about what would ground political judgement *sub specie aeternitatis*. On this kind of approach philosophical ethics 'does not propose any new ethics, but rather clarifies and concretises given normative contents'.[57] This also means that philosophy does not necessarily play any kind of privileged role in this clarification process. It can, as both Gadamer and Rorty argue, be achieved just as effectively by other means, such as art or literature, by narrative and story telling as much as by 'theory'. The arts in Rorty's view may well bring a community's self-consciousness to life because they 'serve to develop and modify a group's self image by, for example apotheosising its heroes, diabolising its enemies, mounting dialogue among its members and refocussing attention'.[58] This links also with Heidegger's claim in 'Letter on Humanism' that the 'tragedies of Sophocles preserve the ethos in their sagas more primorially than Aristotle's lectures on ethics'.[59] If philosophy is to play a role in bringing to self-consciousness the values and principles, the reasons for action in groups and societies, then it has to change the focus of its attention from rather universalistic terms such as good, right, obligation and so forth which form part of the liberal canon of political thought just because of their thin and universal nature, in favour of much more specific, thicker accounts of reasons for action in particular societies. This fits closely with Wittgenstein's argument that philosophy 'consists in assembling reminders for a particular purpose' and the importance of what he calls intermediate cases. If we are to gain an overall view of the use of language then we have to be concerned with thick concepts, those which are replete with meaning from those particular circumstances, and play a role in particular societies, such as cowardice, brutality, loyalty, honour, gratitude etc.,[60] not just with rather general concepts such as happiness or obligation as if one could generate a foundational theory of reasons for action from reflection on such concepts. Part of the reason for emphasizing thin concepts is just the desire for universality, or what more disparagingly Wittgenstein called the contempt for the particular case which goes along with the craving for generality.

It would follow from this argument that if the focus of ethical judgement is the ethos of a society or the set of values and norms which give reasons for action in that particular society, then if an ethos has become degenerate and no longer gives guidance, it cannot be restored by philosophy. It was not grounded in philosophy in the first place for the reasons which have been given and once it has begun to decompose it cannot be restored by philosophical argument. This point has been made quite frequently in recent years, particularly in relation to the idea of obligation which has played a major role in the development of deontological theories. It was argued by Elizabeth Anscombe, in her article 'Modern Moral Philosophy',[61] that much contemporary moral philosophy was an attempt to provide philosophical grounding for an idea of obligation which had as its original background a religious and indeed specifically Christian context from which it is in fact inseparable. We are still haunted by a ghost of obligation and deontology which can in fact only be made sense of and filled out in the context of a particular set of values. A new ethics can only emerge from the fragments of the old, it cannot be derived from some universal form of abstract reasoning, nor from some meta-narrative about the role of *Geist* or the Good.

Liberal thought and community

We need now to turn to the contrast between communitarian and liberal political thought to see how sharp the methodological disagreements in fact are. The alleged contrasts are between: universality and particularity; foundations and interpretation; the relationship of philosophy and praxis; and the understanding of the role of the Western tradition in political thought and particularly its contemporary deontological form. In some ways these polarities can be put in terms of Aristotle versus Kant. Many communitarians look to Aristotle for inspiration since his thought in both the *Ethics* and the *Politics* seems to be concerned not so much with universalistic claims but rather reflection on the aspirations, values and ethos of citizens in the Athenian polis of his day.[62] He was concerned with reflecting on the circumstances and the values of the polis and trying to put into some theoretically self-conscious way the links with and differences between values so that they could illuminate phronesis – practical judgement in particular circumstances. Aristotle's distinction between sophia and phronesis is taken as prefiguring the current concern with the inert nature of theoretical and universalistic reason in the context of practical judgement about ethics and politics within a particular society. Kant, on the other hand, seems to be the founder of modern deontological theories. He claims that his account of moral judgement is independent of any psychological theory about human nature, or any particular assumptions about human desires and interests drawn from a particular society. He claims to be able to produce a general theory about the requirements for moral action. Moral and political judgement is detached from particular ends and purposes in a particular community. It is formal, abstract and universal but for the very same reason, inert. So we need to consider how sharp these contrasts actually are and this is crucial because what is at stake is the nature and ambition of political theory and also the vocation of the political theorist.

Perhaps the first point to start with is the contrast between foundational claims and interpretive strategies. A good deal of the history of political thought and almost all of contemporary deontological liberal thought is considered by communitarian critics to be concerned with providing foundations for judgements, practices and institutions and to be neglectful of circumstance, particularity and locality. Certainly some figures in the history of political thought can be read in this foundationalist way and perhaps Plato is the best example. However, there are dangers in looking at the history of political thought as if it does embody this sharp distinction. It is easy to assume that political philosophers, most of whom after all wrote about other branches of philosophy, were trying to provide some kind of universal foundation for their political conceptions, starting either with some metaphysical theory about the cosmos, or an epistemological claim about the nature of knowledge, or some strong claims about the universal nature of human capacities and powers, and from these they have then tried to work out the implications for more peripheral areas of philosophical concern in ethics and politics. Two examples might serve to illustrate this tendency.

The first example is taken from Isaiah Berlin when he argues that:

The ideas of every philosopher concerned with human affairs in the end rest on his conception of what man is and can be. To understand such thinkers, it is more important to grasp this central notion or image (which may be implicit, but determines their picture of the world) than even the most forceful arguments with which they defend their views and refute actual and possible objections.[63]

The second example of how to read the history of political thought in this way is taken from Martin Hollis:

Take about 2000 hom. sap., dissect each into essence and accidents and discard the accidents. Place essences in a large casserole, add socialising syrup and stew until conflict disappears. Serve with a pinch of salt ... the exact ingredients vary with the chef. In particular the magic socialising syrup varies with the analysis of human nature.[64]

Despite the consciously caricaturing mode of Hollis's analysis, this is a common enough view. Theories of human nature determine ethical and political theories and those theories of human nature in their turn depend upon conclusions in metaphysics and epistemology. The assumption here is that metaphysics and epistemology are at the heart of philosophy and the foundationalist is concerned to draw out the ethical and political implications of his foundational metaphysical and epistemological assumptions. With the collapse of this model of epistemology and metaphysics, so the foundational model has to collapse too.

This, however, can involve a misreading of a good deal of political philosophy, although it was the model which we followed with reference to some central authors in chapter 2. The reason why this may be a misreading has been well stated by Alasdair MacIntyre:

> There is an important, although common misreading of the structures of ancient and medieval thought which projects back on to that thought an essentially modern view of the ordering of philosophical and scientific enquiries. On this modern view, ethics and politics are peripheral modes of enquiry, dependent in key part on what is established by epistemology and the natural sciences ... But in ancient and medieval thought, ethics and politics afford light onto other disciplines as much as vice versa. Hence from that standpoint, which I share, it is not the case that I first must decide whether some theory of human nature or cosmology is true and only secondly pass a verdict upon an account of the virtues which is based upon it.[65]

If this is a correct interpretation of at least some of the history of political thought, then the contrast between communitarian and interpretive models is overdrawn in that figures such as Aristotle and Hegel were not just deriving political conclusions as remote consequences from metaphysical first principles and conceptions of human nature. Rather as MacIntyre argues elsewhere:

> I cannot look to human nature as a neutral standard, asking what forms of social and moral life would give it the most adequate expression. For each form of life carries with it its own picture of human nature. The choice of a form of life and a choice of a view of human nature go together.[66]

Whether this is a plausible view of the history of political thought is an issue which we cannot really discuss in detail here, but if, for example, the work of Aristotle or Hegel[67] is considered, it is certainly not clear that how they think about politics fits into the foundationalist model as outlined by Berlin. Indeed in the case of Hegel it would be odd if this were so, in that his thought is all about the transformation of human nature and our understanding of ourselves in complex historical circumstances. As he argues in his work on human nature in *The Philosophy of Subjective Spirit*:

> The Ego is by itself only formal identity. Consciousness appears differently modified according to the difference of the given object and the gradual specification of consciousness appears as a variation in the characteristics of the objects.[68]

Certainly Hegel's argument that self-consciousness is not a given but an achievement which develops of necessity in relationships of mutual recognition provides as strong a link between self and others as Wittgenstein's argument about private languages and it could not be argued that he sees human nature in a static way to which correspond appropriate forms of social and political life.

It is not just that the contrast between foundational and communitarian approaches is a mistaken account of a good deal of the history of political philosophy, it also fails to do justice to recent developments in the subject, particularly relating to the work of John Rawls, who can be credited with the revival of liberal deontological political theory which seems to have the universalist overtones which communitarians reject. *A Theory of Justice* does appear to have such universalist tendencies – I portrayed it as such in chapter 3 above – and certainly the book has been read in that way and for good reason, particularly if one considers the whole argument in relation to the eloquent summary on the final page of the book. Even within the book, however, there are features which give pause for thought and more particularly in Rawls's subsequent interpretation of the scope and nature of his enterprise in his essay 'Justice as Fairness: Political Not Metaphysical'.[69]

In the book itself Rawls makes two points which are of the utmost importance in seeing how he thinks that his very abstract arguments apply to understanding political judgement in particular societies. The first is the early analogy which Rawls draws between theorizing about justice and grammatical theory, which leads him on to his account of what he calls reflective equilibrium. In Section 9 of the book he argues that it is possible to draw an analogy between moral theory, of which the theory of justice is a part, and the theory of grammar. In a grammatical theory we begin with the fact that people have the capacity to speak a language and to recognize well-formed sentences within that language. Clearly the ability to do this on the part of a native speaker requires some implicit knowledge of grammar which may reach various degrees of sophistication and articulation. However, the theory, if there is one, which will account for all of these capacities will be very complex if it is to be systematic and coherent and will 'require theoretical constructions that far outrun the *ad hoc* precepts of our explicit grammatical knowledge'. Similarly, moral theory does not operate in a vacuum. It is concerned with a coherent conceptual grasp of our everyday moral judgements, and he goes on to argue that this will 'certainly involve principles and theoretical constructions which go beyond the norms and standards cited in everyday life'. In particular in Rawls's view it will require the contract theory and the mathematics associated with the maximin theory. However, the important point for the moment is that the theory, however complex it becomes, is an attempt to set out in a coherent and systematic way the principles and values which inform first order moral judgements. In this sense it is not a priori or metaphysical. It is a theoretical attempt to understand the connections or lack of them between our deep-seated moral judgements. In this sense therefore part of the communitarian criticism of Rawls becomes muted because he is not trying as he sees it to produce a metaphysical theory (despite what he implies intermittently in the book with its talk of Archimedian points and a conception of justice *sub specie aeternitatis*) but a coherent theory of our first order moral judgement. In this sense he starts where the communitarian starts, with the moral judgements of a particular community, and as Rawls sees it in his later work, those judgements to do with liberty and equality which are characteristic of a liberal democratic society.

This point is further reinforced when he discusses the device of reflective equilibrium in the book. The attempt to produce a coherent account of moral judgement is a two-way process. Moral theory has to start with existing moral judgements but equally, as the process of theorizing gets under way, some of these judgements may have to be modified in the light of what their implications for other judgements are seen to be in the light of trying to achieve a coherent picture. In this theoretical attempt we are trying to do justice to those moral judgements which we accept in a considered way; those which we arrive at when we are not frightened or upset, those which we arrive at when we are not excessively concentrating on our own interests and when we do not expect to gain from making the judgement in one way rather than another. In trying to arrive at such a theory we shall move to higher levels of abstraction but these abstractions, such as the contract theory, the device of the Original Position and the like, which we discussed in chapter 3, are ways in which we try to shed light on some of the basic moral intuitions of a liberal society such as that all citizens are free and equal and that they have some capacity for autonomy in relation to their moral values. The important point, however, is that as in the theory of grammar our theories can be brought into some illuminating and explanatory relationship with our ordinary judgements.

We saw in Chapter 3 how Rawls's argument worked in relation to desert not just as a theory about desert, but his claim that the way he accounts for desert in his theory reflects one of the 'fixed points of our moral judgement', namely that no one deserves his native endowments nor his starting place in society; these, he argues at the level of ordinary moral judgement, are arbitrary from the moral point of view. The overall aim here has been described very well by Dworkin when he argues:

> the structure of principles must explain the convictions by showing the underlying assumptions they reflect ... it must provide guidance in those cases about which we have either no convictions or weak or contradictory convictions.[70]

I have said already that moral theory as Rawls sees it is a two-way process: the theory completes and renders coherent first ordered moral judgements while at the same time the theoretical construction is constrained by this first order moral data in the same way as the theory of grammar is constrained by the features of our being able to speak a language. At the same time, the demand for a coherent theory may well require some revision of first order judgements if that turns out to be so. It is essentially a two-way process. Given this, the problem clearly arises as to which judgements might be displaced by the demands of theoretical coherence. Are there any moral judgements which are so fundamental that they can never be displaced by theoretical considerations?

In his account of reflective equilibrium in *Taking Rights Seriously* Dworkin argues that in a crucial respect the device is relativistic because in his view 'the ground of intuition shifts' within groups and between groups. That is to say, there may not be just one set of moral judgements to theorize and there could be different theories of justice as part of the theorization of the stable moral judgements of different groups. If this is so, then Rawls is faced with a dilemma. On the one hand he could provide independent moral reasons for arguing that some sorts of moral judgements or intuitions are so basic that they cannot be discounted even though some groups within a society may not hold those judgements. These reasons will be of an external and perhaps foundational sort. On the other hand, he could accept the particularism of his own theory: that is, that it is a theory which tries to do coherent justice to one linked set of moral judgements while at the same time accepting that there might be other groups either within society or in other societies who do not hold those judgements and for whom an alternative theory would have to be provided. If Rawls wanted to maintain that *A Theory of Justice* is a foundational work as some of the language in that book suggests, then he has to give external reasons for arguing that the moral judgements which he is theorizing are the best ones and this he does not do. The other alternative would be to move away from any claims for the foundationalist or universalist aspects of the theory and argue that the theory provides a conceptual grasp of the judgements of one group while recognizing that there could be other theories to do justice to other groups. It is indeed this latter approach which Rawls has adopted in his most recent writings. In this sense he is closer to an interpretive account of the nature of political philosophy, trying to bring out in a coherent way the values of a particular group or type of society with a particular political culture. In his essay 'Kantian Constructivism in Moral Theory' he argues this sort of case, namely that he is not trying to find a conception of justice suitable to all societies regardless of their particular social or historical circumstances. Indeed, he goes on to argue that his argument is addressed basically to American political culture and to what he sees as the 'impasse in America's recent political history'. *A Theory of Justice* therefore is taking as its data the considered judgements of a particular political culture in which citizens are seen as equally free moral personalities. In this sense political philosophy as he sees it is political and not metaphysical; it does not provide a theory based upon some ahistorical metaphysical foundation:

> What justifies a conception of justice is not its being true to an order antecedent and given to us, but its compliance with our deeper understanding of ourselves and our aspirations, and our realisation that given our history and traditions embedded in public life, it is the most reasonable doctrine for us.[71]

Given that Rawls is now accepting explicitly that the moral judgements which philosophy has to theorize are specific to a particular way of life which cannot be given any metaphysical foundation, they are thrown up by history and tradition, Rawls sees two roles for political philosophy. In a society without much disagreement, the task of political philosophy would be that of reflecting 'upon and getting a clear view of the political life expressed in that culture'. Political philosophy would seek a kind of 'public self understanding'. This would be quite like what Wittgenstein called a perspicuous representation of a way of life. However, in a society in which there are cleavages between considered judgements, for example between liberty and equality,[72] the task of political philosophy would be to consider ways in which these values can be reconciled by drawing upon the underlying values of the culture particularly those of freedom and autonomy:

> Thus the real task is to discover and formulate the deeper basis of agreement which one hopes is embedded in common sense ... In addressing the public culture of a democratic society, Kantian constructivism hopes to invoke a conception of a person implicitly affirmed by that culture, or at least one that would prove acceptable to citizens if it was properly presented and explained.[73]

Indeed, this is the only way political philosophy could work in a society characterized by liberal democracy, which is the kind of society Rawls regards himself as theorizing. It has to work with the values implicit in the culture, not by attempting to draw upon some kind of metaphysical view of morality which Rawls, like Walzer, regards as inert in a democratic society marked by different conceptions of the good and of human flourishing:

> Thus the essential agreement in judgements arises not from the recognition of a prior and independent moral order, but from everyone's affirmation of the same social perspective.[74]

In this sense, therefore, Rawls assumes that a liberal democratic society does have a community of meaning and this has to be drawn out, rendered perspicuous and made coherent by political philosophy. As we shall see later in the argument, this links Rawls's view with that of Michael Walzer, a more avowedly communitarian thinker, the main point of disagreement now appearing to be the role of theory and the level of abstraction in theory in attempting to make sense of our shared values. But for the moment the point that needs to be made is that in the light or this more Hegelian stance which Rawls is taking, he himself could no longer be regarded as a foundationalist theorist. However, there are still forms of foundational theory both in the history of political thought and among contemporary theorists and a good recent example is to be found in T. M. Scanlon's reflections on Rawls's account of his philosophical method in his essay 'Contractualism and Utilitarianism'. In this essay he is clearly worried by the abandonment of some kind of external vantage point in political philosophy:

> An explanation of how we come to know the truth about morality must be based on such an external explanation of the kind of things moral truths are rather than on a list of moral truths, even a maximally coherent list ... Coherence among our first order moral beliefs – what Rawls has called narrow reflective equilibrium – seems unsatisfying as an account of moral truth or as an account of justification in ethics just because, taken by itself, a maximally coherent account of our moral beliefs need not provide us with what I have called a philosophical explanation of the subject matter of morality. However internally coherent our moral beliefs may be rendered, the nagging doubt may remain that there is nothing to them at all. They may be merely a set of socially inculcated reactions, mutually consistent perhaps but not judge-

ments of a kind which can properly be said to be correct or
incorrect.[75]

Scanlon's use of the word 'merely' here is instructive because this is the
only basis for philosophizing about morality and politics in Walzer's
view and in Rawls's modified position. Scanlon is closer to the classical
tradition, however, when he argues that 'a good philosophical theory
... [gives] us a clearer understanding of what the best forms of moral
argument amount to and what kind of truth it is that they can be a
way of arriving at.' In his view: 'Like first order moral judgement, a
philosophical characterisation of the subject matter of morality is a
substantive claim about morality.'

Taylor criticizes this view, however, from the standpoint of someone
who is sympathetic to the pluralist/communitarian position when he
argues that:

> the price of this formalism ... has been a severe distortion of our
> understanding of moral thinking. One of the big illusions which
> grows from either of these reductions (formalism or utilitarianism)
> is the belief that there is a single consistent domain of the 'moral',
> that there is one set of considerations, or mode of calculation,
> which determines what we ought 'morally' to do.[76]

Hence it is still important to consider the general theoretical differences
between foundationalists and communitarian/interpretive political
philosophers and to get as clear as we can about the precise issues at
stake between them.

We therefore turn to a more explicit examination of how communitarians operate with the concept of human nature and the idea of
basic interests and needs, powers and capacities of the human mind
which have been central to the foundationalist approach to political
theory. The basic question is whether communitarians can in fact get
along without universalistic values of their own. Some communitarians
are concerned by what appear to be the deeply relativistic consequences
of something like Wittgenstein's philosophy in the sense that if we have
no external standards of evaluation then it might be that not only can
we not give a way of life any foundation, but we may not in fact be able
to understand at the end the values, principles and concepts which are

part of a way of life which we do not share. In some cases this has led back to a concern with human nature in the sense that we have to appeal to some limiting features of human life as a standard in terms of which we make other societies comprehensible, leaving aside the question for the moment of an evaluation of such ways of life and practices. This point is made very well by Peter Winch in his famous essay 'Understanding a Primitive Society':

> I wish to point out that the very conception of human life involves certain fundamental notions – which I shall call limiting notions – which have an obvious ethical dimension, and which indeed in a sense determine the ethical space within which the possibilities of good and evil in human life can be exercised. The notions which I shall discuss very briefly here correspond closely to those which Vico made the foundation of his idea of natural law, on which he thought the possibility of understanding of human history rested: birth, death, sexual relations. Their significance here is that they are inescapably involved in the life of all human societies in a way which gives us a clue where to look, if we are puzzled about the point of an alien system of institutions. The specific forms which these concepts take, the particular institutions in which they are expressed, vary considerably from one society to another; but their central position within a society's institutions is and must be a constant factor ... I will say that it does not seem to me a merely conventional matter that T. S. Eliot's trinity of 'birth, copulation, death' happens to be such deep objects of human concern.[77]

While Winch himself makes it clear in another essay on human nature, to which we shall return, that he does not want to see this as providing a general criterion or a foundation for moral judgement based upon some account of human interests turning upon these fundamental concerns,[78] let us for the moment continue with the idea that such limiting conditions which are, as he says, of a universal nature, might link up with the foundationalist's argument that political values and moral principles could in fact be grounded in such limiting conditions of human nature. It is certainly arguable that communitarian political philosophers do in fact appeal to similar limiting features of human life within which their own communitarian thought is conducted. If they do operate with a notion of some universal features of human life and with evaluative principles which follow from these, then it might be held that the difference between communitarian and foundational political thought in the context of arguments about the role of ideas about human nature in political philosophy are in fact not so marked as protagonists on each side might want to contend. These issues come out most clearly again in Walzer's arguments in *Spheres of Justice*.

The first way in which Walzer invokes some idea of human nature, or at least certain fundamental concerns from which he draws evaluative conclusions, is in terms of his argument about the nature of human beings as culture-producing creatures. He says this in *Spheres of Justice*:

> We are all culture producing creatures; we make and inhabit meaningful worlds. Since there is no way to rank and order these worlds with their understanding of social goods, we do justice to actual men and women by respecting their particular creations.... Justice is rooted in distinct understandings of places, honours, jobs, things of all sorts that contribute to a shared way of life. To override these understandings is (always) to act unjustly.[79]

Here the moral principle that we should not invade self understandings and accepted cultural and political values is rooted in a universalistic claim that in fact human beings are culture-producing creatures and thus presumably have a fundamental concern with the status and integrity of what they have produced. This feature of human life provides both a limiting condition of political theory, namely that we should respect the cultural productions of people, and of political practice, namely that an invasive society which overrides the values which groups within a society have produced is a less just polity than one which grants autonomy to cultural groups and what they have produced. Whether this is a foundational claim or not (and given the ethical consequences which follow from it it is difficult to see why it is not), it is certainly a universalistic one.

There are other features too of Walzer's argument which point in the same direction. Take as another example his argument about rights in both *Spheres of Justice* and in *Just and Unjust Wars*. On the face of it a doctrine about basic moral rights would fit rather badly within a communitarian framework just because such rights are universal in scope and they aim to provide a transcultural set of moral limitations on how people should be treated. Rights are ascribed to human beings as such, not to people as Englishmen or Nigerians, men or women, Muslims or Christians. A communitarian should have some difficulty in accommodating such a conception. However, in *Just and Unjust Wars* Walzer trades on such arguments in a way which links them explicitly with some universal concept of what it is to be a human being. He argues that there are basic rights to life and liberty and these are entailed 'by our sense of what it is to be a human being'. This point is reiterated in the Preface to *Spheres of Justice* in which he argues that:

Justice in war can indeed be generated from the two most basic and recognised rights of human beings – and in their simplest (negative) form: not to be robbed of liberty. What is perhaps more important, these two rights seem to account for the moral judgements that we most commonly make in time of war. They do real work.[80]

He goes on to argue that he wants to forgo these arguments in relation to his theory of justice, just because they are of less help in that context. However, this is a difficult argument to interpret given that the negative right to liberty has often been used to block claims in favour of redistribution of resources. It might be held of course that these rights are most important in war because in that context we have a situation of a fundamental and irresolvable clash between two cultural forms, e.g. between National Socialism and Western liberalism or Soviet Communism and if war is to have any kind of moral limit we have to appeal to transcultural values such as basic moral rights are supposed to embody. However, again this seems to involve the idea that there are at least some moral values which can be derived from a transcultural understanding of what it is to be human and the basic interests of human beings which follow from that.

In a more recent work, *Interpretation and Social Criticism*, Walzer goes further and argues that we can, in fact, think in terms of there being some transcultural, minimal morality. All societies have prohibitions on 'murder, deception, betrayal, gross cruelty'. Again these are, to use his own words, 'a kind of minimal and universal moral code'.[81] In this case, however, he wants to see them not as discovered, or invented by philosophers so much as emerging out of 'many years of trial and error of failed, partial, and insecure understandings' and he goes on to argue 'that these universal prohibitions barely begin to determine the shape of a fully developed or livable morality. They provide the framework for any possible (moral) life, but only a framework ... One cannot simply deduce a moral culture or for that matter a legal system from the minimal code.'[82] These would on the contrary be filled in by the understandings implicit in different ways of life which cannot be put into any overall framework of adequacy or inadequacy. These 'variations are necessarily plural in character'. Walzer wants to preserve his pluralism within a universalistic framework, a framework which is not based upon some kind of philosophically discovered framework so much as a set of limits which emerge from the general circumstances of human life.

In *Spheres of Justice* this argument takes its richest form in relation to needs as we saw in chapter 5. Here Walzer argues that need is a fundamental idea in politics resting presumably on needs as basic interests of human beings, while at the same time arguing that what we take to be needs and the degree to which they met has to be decided within particular societies. There cannot be any universal, objective and foundational way in which we can specify human needs and what should then meet such needs. In this sense Walzer seems to make common cause with Winch, arguing that there are various limiting conditions of human life of which needs would be one, but equally that a theory of needs cannot specify concrete political institutions and arrangements. However, Winch goes much further in this than Walzer because in his 'Human Nature' essay in which he criticizes MacIntyre he argues that using needs in this way really empties the notion of content. If we try to have the best of both the universalist and foundationalist position and the pluralist one, we will end up with a theory which is empty of content. If we say that 'men's particular needs vary from society to society' (the pluralist position) while at the same time arguing that what is not variable is that 'an intelligible morality must provide for the satisfaction of its practitioner's needs', then this has drained the concept of needs of all content and this is no more than a 'juggling act' with the word need.[83] The limiting conditions of human nature cannot, on this view, provide a general criterion of political morality. Either it is a universal conception which will be rich enough to provide a basis for clear and grounded political judgement, or it will collapse into a complete pluralism. On the one hand we have no way of arriving at a universal account of human needs to guide political judgement across societies; on the other, the idea of needs collapses completely into pluralism and relativism. In this sense there seems to be no stable position between universalism and foundationalism on the one hand or pluralism and relativism on the other. Walzer's position seems to want to fix on such a stable position, allowing certain ideas such as needs, or the importance of life and liberty to be fundamental human concerns and to act as a universal framework for morality while at the same time arguing that all the content of these ideas has to be filled in a pluralist manner. For our purposes, however, we can see that even the most fully developed communitarian theory makes some ineliminable reference to universal features of human life and morality and therefore that the contrast between foundational and communitarian approaches is not so clearly demarcated as protagonists would like to think.

This point comes out in two other ways too. The first of these is the idea that the basis of political judgement has to be the social meanings internal to particular practices, communities and cultures. As I argued, the most obvious philosophical roots of this idea are to be found in Wittgenstein's later philosophy of language and I want first of all to look at some of the difficulties which arise in that context before going on to discuss the more obviously political ramifications of the issues involved. As we saw earlier, Wittgenstein's argument was that in order to understand a word or a concept we have to link it to the conceptual framework of which it is a part; we have to bring words back from their metaphysical to their everyday use and doing this will mean in fact putting the term back into the language game of which it is a part. The language game, the social practice, is the context in which we will get clear about the meaning of the terms which puzzle us. We shall not get illumination through some kind of universalistic approach in which we try to develop some general theory to account for the concept we use. Equally, we cannot give a concept a philosophical justification outside the language game of which it is a part. However, this assumes that we do have a clear idea of what is the appropriate context in terms of which the concept can both be rendered intelligible and some justification for its use found. Wittgenstein seems to regard this as relatively unproblematic, but we can question whether this is in fact so. Use, as much as ostensive definition, can be variously interpreted and this issue can arise in two ways.

First of all, we might have a genuine puzzle about the appropriate home for a term. What is the appropriate linguistic context to illuminate what we mean by it? To put the point in a way which might make its salience to political philosophy more obvious, what community of discourse is the appropriate one for our understanding the term? There is no clear-cut answer to this question in many cases. The boundaries of the context may be very obscure, as Wittgenstein's own reflections on essentialism make clear. In the *Philosophical Investigations* he uses very simplified examples, for example, people building a house in which words like 'slab' and 'building block' are used. In these cases the individuation of the language games is a comparatively easy matter. But for many terms and perhaps for those which most interest the phil-osopher this may not be the case. There may be acute boundary problems which may not be solved by closer inspection. This point is in fact made in passing by Winch when he argues that while the criteria of logic differ from language game to language game, for instance science and religion, he goes on to say, 'This is, of course, an over simplification, in that it does not allow for the overlapping character of different modes of social life.'[84] This is obviously the case, but then it is not clear how we determine the appropriate context for locating a concept and therefore the conditions which will make the concept intelligible and its use justified by the basic assumptions of that context or language game. We might therefore have to look for external reasons of a philosophical sort for placing the concept in one place rather than another. Again it may not be possible to avoid a need to consider external reasons of precisely the sort that the Wittgensteinian approach was determined to avoid. A particular example of this might be the use of the idea of obligation by moral and political philosophers. Alasdair MacIntyre has argued very forcibly that the notion of obligation has a sense only within the context of a society in which people have very clear roles and that deontological theories in which the idea of duty and obligation are central make sense only within that kind of context which has now effectively broken down. Whether this argument is plausible is not our main concern here; what matters is how such an argument about the appropriateness of context is to be resolved and it is at least arguable that resolving it will not be achieved by following the Wittgensteinian argument to look rather than to think. Again, what is the context of use, intelligibility and justification cannot be determined without considering external reasons.

This issue comes up in a more specific way in relation to communitarian political thought. The context of justification is the community with its shared social meanings. But following from the arguments above we have to ask the question what is the community in question? Here there are at least two difficulties. One of the deep paradoxes of communitarian approaches to political theory is that we are not really offered a theory of community, as Nancy Rosenblum has argued.[85] Communitarians will have to reply that we do not need a theory of community, just because this will look like a foundational or universalist theory of the sort they want to disavow. However, it is clear that they cannot do without such a theory. The first reason is that in Walzer at least the assumption seems to be that the moral community, with its shared understandings, is coextensive with the legal, juridical, national or political community; that, as Galston argues, 'the community of shared meaning is in fact the nation state.'[86] The communitarian project is to interpret and reclaim the sense of shared meanings in Rosenblum's words 'latent' in the nation state. However, it is not clear why community should be understood in this way. There may be nation states with a strong sense of community – Iran and Japan might be examples which spring to mind. Equally, however, the opposite seems to be the case with regard to other states in which there are substantial cleavages, Spain with the Basques, Sri Lanka with the Tamils, Britain with its problems of Northern Ireland and its Muslim community, Nigeria with its deep cleavages between Ibo, Yoruba and Hausa Fulani groups are just a few examples. There may be deep communitarian cleavages within a society which forms a juridical whole. Do these jurisdictions possess a latent community which the communitarian can reclaim as a basis for understanding and justifying political practices? Certainly the problem caused within British society by the publication of Salman Rushdie's *The Satanic Verses* leads one to think that there are in fact deep cleavages here which may not be resolvable by appealing to shared understandings. The publication of the book offended the religious sensibilities of Muslims; liberals however argued that in a secular society religious beliefs should not be made immune from criticism which involves irony and ridicule. This issue also relates to Rawls, who as we have seen has to trade upon the idea of an implicit community of values in a liberal society.

The second point is that other forms of community may well transcend nation states and again Islam might be a good example here. The sense of identity may well be linked to shared meanings which transcend national frontiers and may not in fact be found within national frontiers, as again the British example of the Salman Rushdie affair in relation to its own Islamic community may show, or the fact that people are killed in the Punjab as the result of a book published outside that society. In this sense the assumption that the appeal to community as the source of values as opposed to any kind of external reasons of a universal and foundational sort may appear to be optimistic. As Rosenblum argues, the communitarian appeal to the latent community which is supposed to be found at a deep level within the procedural republic of Western liberal societies may not respect the deep disagreements which such societies embody:

> What these shared meanings are, how widely they are shared, and what degree of conflict is permissible without the loss of latent community remains an open question.[87]

Without some general theory of community, which would transcend the appeal to particular communities, the communitarians' approach seems to be flawed. They cannot accept that the typical values of a liberal society – mutual toleration, some degree of distributive justice and the free market economy – are sufficient for an account of community just because the values involved here are of a procedural sort. For there to be a community there have to be shared meanings, shared goals and purposes for the society, but there is little account of how these things are latent within liberal societies. Let us take a specific example which is used by Dworkin to criticize Walzer,[88] namely the issue of the proper way to distribute health care in our society. There is the view that health is a basic need of all human beings and that it should therefore be distributed with reference to this shared meaning without other considerations such as the ability to pay becoming a criterion for access to health care. On this view the social meaning of health is that it is not a commodity to be traded in the market like other commodities. However, it is also clear that there are many in our society who disagree with this approach. Richard Titmuss argued in *The Gift Relationship*[89] that if human tissue is a commodity to be bought and sold, then anything can be a commodity. Over a long period, however, free market theorists, particularly those associated with the Institute of Economic Affairs in Britain, have argued for a market in human tissues such as blood. Is there any way that an appeal to shared social meanings can resolve this dispute? Do we have a shared meaning of health and a shared meaning about the boundaries of commodities which would allow us to resolve this kind of dispute without appeal to some kind of external reasons? Dworkin points to the place in which Walzer discusses this kind of disagreement when he argues that:

A given society is just if its substantive life is lived in a certain way – that is, faithful to the shared understandings of its members. (When people disagree about the meaning of social goods, when understandings are controversial, then justice requires that the society be faithful to the disagreements, providing institutional channels for their expression, adjudicative mechanisms, and alternative distributions.)[90]

Dworkin regards this as a feeble answer just because there is no account given about what being faithful to these disagreements might actually mean, for example, in the context of health care. To allow for alternative distributions reflecting the cleavages between those who see health as a commodity to be distributed by the market and those who do not may be too bland in that in many cases allowing the alternative social meanings to ground different forms of distribution may well undermine one form of social meaning and its concomitant form of distribution. Titmuss argued that to allow for a market in blood alongside a donor system might well undermine the donor system and devalue the 'gift' which the donor gives. Equally the idea of comprehensive education in Britain, which in its pure form would require all pupils to go to the same schools and undergo the same kinds of experiences, would not be possible and indeed would be undermined by the existence of other sorts of schools which embody different understandings of the nature of education. For strong believers in meritocracy selective education is required; for those who believe that education makes a crucial contribution to the formation of a common culture and social cohesion, then comprehensive education is essential. Neither can exist alongside the other. In order to resolve this issue we have to go beyond being faithful to shared meanings and appeal to some other notion such as justice. For Dworkin, the idea of justice is our critic, not our mirror as Walzer implies. He argues that:

We need to argue for any theory of justice of that kind, by finding and defending critical principles of the appropriate sort.[91]

This point is made even more forcefully by Gewirth when he argues in very similar circumstances:

Hence there still remains a need ... to adjudicate rationally among different competing moralities, for each of which supreme moral authoritativeness is claimed and each of which propounds different answers to the distributive and substantive questions about whose interests and which interests should be considered in the various possible ways of life and society.[92]

In doing this we shall be committed to a liberalism of the deontological sort which recognizes moral diversity and tries to formulate a set of general principles of right conduct which will be neutral between different conceptions of the good. However, Rorty comes back on precisely this point in 'Post Modernist Bourgeois Liberalism', in which he argues that it is precisely by reference to historical data and anecdote that we can deal with these cleavages, rather than by an appeal to general principle.

This leads to a further point at issue between the communitarian and Dworkin's approach, namely the role of the political philosopher in a democratic society. Walzer is rather worried about the general claims of political philosophy and the role of the political philosopher in a democratic society and this is a worry which has its roots in his response to Plato. Plato argued that the philosopher should rule because he has greater insight into the nature of the good, or more generally that the political philosopher can find, in Dworkin's words, a set of values which would show the right way of dealing with the value cleavages of the type we have been considering. If we thought for the moment that cleavages cannot be coped with by Walzer's strategy of remaining faithful to the disputed meanings which are manifested in the polity and took Dworkin's view that we could identify general critical principles, how would these relate to the democratic politics of a liberal society? After all, if we take Gewirth's line, it follows that the results of such deliberations are binding on each moral agent. On Walzer's view this approach leading to the formulation of general, critical principles would undermine democracy in the sense that when 'we have discovered them, or once they have been announced to us, we ought to incorporate them into our everyday moral life'.[93]

He rejects this approach, partly for all the reasons given; he does not believe that they can be found in the abstract way Dworkin insists upon. If we can hit upon the right principles they are 'only there because they are really here, features of ordinary life'. We can only come across such principles and regard them as morally binding because they are really linked with the social meanings of the community. However, his objection is not just to the epistemological problems involved in 'discovering' or 'finding' principles which do not already draw upon what is implicit in our way of life, but also to the conflict which would then exist between the role of the philosopher and the democratic attempt to negotiate a society in which there are deep cleavages between social meanings. Would this not mean that political authority would then rest with the experts who had determined the right principles? In *Interpretation and Social Criticism*, he argues that this is essentially a Leninist doctrine about the nature of political principles and sanctions a degree of coercion:

> The problem with disconnected criticism, and thus with criticism that derives from newly discovered or invented moral standards, is that it presses its practitioners toward manipulation and compulsion ... in so far as the critic wants to be effective, wants to drive his criticism home (though the home is, in a sense, no longer his own) he finds himself driven to one or another version of an unattractive politics. It is for this reason that I have tried to distinguish his enterprise from collective criticism, criticism from within, or as it is sometimes called, 'immanent critique.' His is a kind of asocial criticism, an external intervention, a coercive act intellectual in form, but pointing to its physical counterpart.[94]

Rights, entitlements, distributive justice, needs – their nature and what is required for their satisfaction – have to be negotiated democratically by 'temporary coalition of interests or a majority of voters'. However, Dworkin regards such democratic attempts to resolve such problems in a situation in which there are no shared meanings, unguided by general principles, 'only a selfish struggle'.[95] Galston[96] makes the interesting argument that a critic such as Andrei Sakharov in the Soviet Union appeals not to an internal critique of the Soviet system, but to the principles of Western liberalism which are not internal to his society, as a way of trying to change the system. This is done with an emancipatory interest and Walzer's strictures seem to be less appropriate in that sort of case even though the criticism is external and appeals to what he regards as a set of universal, but humane values. Hence, behind this debate about communitarian and foundational approaches lie different views about the nature of political philosophy's role in a democratic society.

Self and society

I now want to turn to the final aspect of disagreement between communitarians and liberal foundationalists, namely the theory of the self. It will be recalled that the communitarian critic regarded the liberal foundationalist as operating with a notion of an unencumbered self, a self which in Sandel's argument is prior to the ends which it espouses. This is necessary if we are to arrive at a general and foundational set of reasons for action. Of necessity this requires us to reason with an abstract theory of the self and with a very abstract set of goods such as primary goods. The communitarian rejects this assumption for two reasons. The first is that it is sociologically false for the reason that our identities are created out of our participating in shared ways of life and a politics that relies on theories which arise out of abstracts from these identities cannot move us. As Lyotard says in the passage quoted earlier, the social self becomes disseminated in a range of language games. Secondly, it is philosophically false for the reasons given by Wittgenstein about the necessarily social character of the self. The impossibility of a private language means that we cannot identify our experience except through concepts which are part of a common stock of experience. The idea of the unencumbered self is incoherent and cannot serve as the basis of shared political judgements and commitments.

When we look in detail at the communitarian political theorists, however, they are in fact very inexplicit about what in fact is the relationship between the self and its values and ends. While they believe in what Sandel calls the situatedness of the self, situated that is in a nexus of values and the social practices of which they are a part, they do not appear to want to say that the self is wholly constituted by such practices. This is partly no doubt for reasons which we have already seen in relation to Winch and Walzer, namely they do regard the self as having certain universal features which must be part of any recognizable form of human life even if what these mean in any society is going to be filled in with reference to the social meanings embodied in that way of life. However, this leaves the nature of these universal features of the self very inexplicit for the reasons which were given earlier. Either these universal features are going to be so filled in by the plural meanings in particular societies that we can say nothing of substance about the actual contents of these universal features, or alternatively, we can say something meaningful about these universal features in which case the contrast with the unencumbered selves of the liberal foundationalists is overdrawn. This is no doubt why, as Rosenblum argues, communitarians are very ambiguous when it comes to specifying the relationship between self and society, qualifying these formulations in crucial ways. Take the following examples:

Our experience is what it is, shaped in part by the way we interpret it; and this has a lot to do with the terms which are available in our culture . . .[97]

and Michael Sandel's argument in 'Morality and the Liberal Ideal' that we are partly defined by the communities which we inhabit. These are crucial although realistic qualifications to any theory which regards the nature of the self as wholly constituted by the community of which the individual is a part. As Rosenblum comments, this is a very modest thesis as it stands and thus not all the qualities of the person are in any sense intrinsically social and inalienable. We then need some account of what is not constituted by society because without it the liberal foundationalist can come back and say that it is precisely these unconstituted parts of the self on which he or she wishes to draw in working out some more universalistic theory of action. Again it would appear that the contrast at stake here is not all that clear cut. However, it is a crucial contrast for the communitarian to maintain, in the sense that many contrary thinkers have argued that it is precisely our ability to stand back, as it were, from the roles, the values, the practices of which we are a part that constitutes the basis of human freedom. This is certainly so with Kant, who has influenced the liberals so much. It is just because our actions are not determined by our heteronomous or situated nature, that we are ultimately autonomous agents able to act for universal reasons not determined by our situated nature. The same point is also made by Hegel, who is usually seen as being on the communitarian side of this argument, when he sees freedom as part of the 'infinite negativity of spirit, able to abstract from the particular situation of the self'. While no doubt our ability to act and choose always has to be based upon the weighing up of particular claims arising from our situation there is as Kymlicka argues 'nothing empty or self defeating in the idea that these communal values should be subject to individual evaluation and possible rejection'.[98] This evaluation may be with reference to standards which are independent of the particular situation of which we are a part, for example the criterion of universalizability which is crucial to Kant's notion of the categorical imperative. This would also fit with Rawls's idea that we always have the liberty to revise our ends however situated we are just because we are not wholly determined by them, a point which even communitarians adopt given the careful way they qualify the argument that the self is situated. Indeed, it is at least arguable that Lyotard accepts the same view, as in the passage quoted he talks only about the disseminated nature of the social self, while leaving it open as to whether there are other aspects of the self not susceptible to his analysis.

There is also little in Wittgenstein's argument about the social situatedness of the self to support the communitarian position here. The fact that we are not able to identify our experience except in ways that presuppose a common stock of terms to refer to inner experiences does not entail that once these terms have been learned from the common stock, they cannot be used in new and innovative ways, as A. J. Ayer pointed out in his essay 'The Concept of a Person'. This could only be true if we took the rather implausible view that words and concepts are totally tied to the sorts of conditions under which they were learned.

The argument does not entail that we cannot stand back from the common stock and evaluate that common stock of descriptions once we have learned that language.[99]

Overall therefore, the contrasts of a methodological sort at stake between communitarians and foundationalists are not clear cut. This argument still has a long way to go but I would imagine that we may move towards what might be called a left Hegelian position, in which we see a role for theorizing about universal features of human life and reasons for action based upon them while allowing as the communitarians have taught us that what fills in these universal features is going to depend a great deal upon context and social meanings. It is a left Hegelian position in that we do not think any longer that we can give a metaphysical basis of the sort that Hegel himself gave to the place of these universal features of human life, nor do we feel that we can put different social meanings of needs, justice and entitlement into some kind of architectonic framework of the sort that Hegel looked to a metaphysical philosophy of history to give. The pluralists are right in agreeing with Hegel that 'the shapes which the concept assumes in the course of its actualisation are indispensable to the knowledge of the concept itself',[100] but they go wrong in thinking that it is not possible to say anything of a transcommunitarian sort about what are the fundamental interests of persons and indeed their own practice belies this. Rawls's own development, which in *A Theory of Justice* was Kantian, has gradually moved in a Hegelian direction in his more recent writings, but he has not lost sight of the need for a general theory in which the disputes about the social meanings within a society and between societies have to be mediated. There is, therefore, scope for both the general and the particular in political theory, as Hegel saw very clearly in his account of concrete universals, and any full theory is going to have to do justice to both.

Notes

1 T. S. Eliot, *Choruses from 'The Rock'*, in *Collected Poems 1909–1962*, Faber and Faber, London, 1974, p. 168.

2 Ibid., p. 168.

3 J. Locke, *Epistola de Tolerantia*, ed. and trans. R. Kilbansky and J. Gough, The Clarendon Press, Oxford, 1968, p. 135.

4   J. Habermas, 'Legitimation Problems in the Modern State', in *Communication and the Evolution of Society*, trans. T. McCarthy, Beacon Press, Boston, 1979, p. 202–3.

5   Eliot, *Choruses from 'The Rock'*, p. 168.

6   M. Sandel, 'Introduction', *Liberalism and Its Critics*, New York University Press, New York, 1984, p. 8.

7   J. Rawls, *A Theory of Justice*, The Clarendon Press, Oxford, 1972, p. 587.

8   R. Dworkin, *A Matter of Principle*, Harvard University Press, Cambridge, Mass., 1985, p. 219.

9   T. M. Scanlon, 'Contractualism and Utilitarianism', in A. K. Sen and B. Williams, *Utilitarianism and Beyond*, Cambridge University Press, Cambridge, 1982, p. 116.

10 See C. Taylor, 'Atomism', in *Philosophy and the Human Sciences: Philosophical Papers*, vol. 2, Cambridge University Press, Cambridge, 1985.

11 M. Walzer, *Spheres of Justice*, Martin Robertson, Oxford, 1983, p. XV.

12 R. Rorty, 'Post Modernist Bourgeois Liberalism', *Journal of Philosophy*, 1983, p. 585.

13 J. F. Lyotard, *The Postmodern Condition*, trans. G. Bennington and B. Massumi, Manchester University Press, Manchester, 1984.

14 R. Beiner, 'Do We Need a Philosophical Ethics? Theory, Prudence and the Primacy of Ethos', *Philosophical Forum*, XX, no. 3, 1989. I am indebted to this paper for the formulation of some of the issues in what follows.

15 P. Winch, 'Understanding a Primitive Society', in *Ethics and Action*, Routledge, London, 1972, p. 12.

16 L. Wittgenstein, *Philosophical Investigations*, Blackwell, Oxford, 1963, para. 122.

17 Plato, *Euthyphro*, in *The Dialogues of Plato*, ed. and trans. B. Jowett, vol. 1, The Clarendon Press, Oxford, 1953, p. 314.

18 L. Wittgenstein, *The Blue and Brown Books*, Blackwell, Oxford, 1969, p. 19.

19 Ibid., passim.

20 Plato, *Parmenides* in *The Dialogues*, vol. 2, pp. 674ff.

21 J. Locke, *An Essay Concerning Human Understanding*, ed. W. D. Woozley, Collins, London, 1964, Book 4, Part 7.

22 T. Nagel, *The View from Nowhere*, Oxford University Press, Oxford, 1986.

23 Wittgenstein, *Philosophical Investigations*, para. 217.

24 Ibid., p. 226e.

25 Ibid., para. 325.

26 L. Wittgenstein, *On Certainty*, Blackwell, Oxford, 1979, para. 402.

27   L. Wittgenstein, *Remarks on the Foundations of Mathematics*, 2nd edn, Blackwell, Oxford, 1967, section 1, para. 61.

28   Ibid., section 1, para. 116.

29   P. Winch, *The Idea of a Social Science*, Routledge, London, 1958, p. 100.

30   Wittgenstein, *On Certainty*, para. 204.

31   Ibid., para. 205.

32   Wittgenstein, *Philosophical Investigations*, para. 66.

33   R. Bambrough, 'Universals and Family Resemblances', in *Wittgenstein*, ed. George Pitcher, Macmillan, London, 1968, p. 202; see also the essay by H. Khatchadourian in the same volume.

34   J. Habermas, *Knowledge and Human Interests*, trans. J. J. Shapiro, Heinemann, London, 1971, p. 313.

35   A. Jaggar, *Feminist Politics and Human Nature*, Rowman and Allenheld, Totowa, NJ, 1983, p. 40.

36   For example, see S. Kripke, *Wittgenstein on Rules and Private Language*, Blackwell, Oxford, 1986; C. McGinn, *Wittgenstein on Meaning*, Blackwell, Oxford, 1984.

37   Wittgenstein, *Philosophical Investigations*, para. 258.

38   G. E. M. Anscombe, *Intention*, 2nd edn, Blackwell, Oxford, 1963, p. 71.

39   R. Norman, *Reasons for Action*, Blackwell, Oxford, 1971, p. 55

40   R. Rorty, *Contingency, Irony and Solidarity*, Cambridge University Press, Cambridge, 1989.

41   I say 'seems' because of the subsequent discussion of Rawls later in the chapter.

42   Walzer, *Spheres of Justice*, p. 8.

43 and 44   Ibid.

45   R. Wollheim, *The Thread of Life*, Cambridge University Press, Cambridge, 1984, p. 202.

46   Hegel contrasts *Sittlichkeit*, the ethical life of the community, with *Moralität*, the self-assumed obligations of the autonomous self in *The Philosophy of Right* in the sections on Abstract Right and Ethical Life. G. W. F. Hegel, *The Philosophy of Right*, trans. T. M. Knox, The Clarendon Press, 1952. In Hegel's view the Greek city state was the prime exemplar of *Sittlichkeit*, and Kantian moral thought the prime exemplar of *Moralität*. The task of the modern world was to reconcile the two. See C. Taylor, *Hegel and Modern Society*, Cambridge University Press, Cambridge, 1979; R. Plant, *Hegel*, 2nd edn, Blackwell, Oxford, 1983.

47   For the most developed theory here see C. Taylor, *Sources of the Self*, Cambridge University Press, Cambridge, 1989.

48   See C. Taylor, *Hegel and Modern Society*, Cambridge University Press, Cambridge, 1979, p. 166ff.

49 See R. Rorty, 'Post Modernist Bourgeois Liberalism'.
50 See Taylor, *Hegel and Modern Society*, passim.
51 C. Taylor, 'Interpretation and the Sciences of Man', in *Philosophy and the Human Sciences*, p. 17.
52 Ibid.
53 Walzer, *Spheres of Justice*, p. 314.
54 Lyotard, *The Postmodern Condition*, p. 40–41.
55 Rorty, 'Post Modernist Bourgeois Liberalism', p. 585.
56 Beiner, 'Do We Need a Philosophical Ethics?'.
57 Ibid.
58 Rorty, 'Post Modernist Bourgeois Liberalism', p. 587.
59 M. Heidegger, *Basic Writings*, ed. D. Krell, Harper and Row, New York, 1977, pp. 232–3. Quoted in Beiner, 'Do We Need a Philosophical Ethics'.
60 For another defence of this view see B. Williams, *Ethics and the Limits of Philosophy*, Collins, London, 1985.
61 G. E. M. Anscombe, 'Modern Moral Philosophy', *Philosophy*, 33, 1958.
62 However, compare this account with chapter 3.
63 I. Berlin, *Against the Current*, The Clarendon Press, Oxford, 1981, p. 298.
64 M. Hollis, *Models of Man*, Cambridge University Press, Cambridge, 1977, p. 1.
65 A. MacIntyre, 'Bernstein's Distorting Mirrors', *Soundings*, 67, no. 1, 1984.
66 A. MacIntyre, *A Short History of Ethics*, Routledge, London, 1967, p. 268.
67 But again see the account given of Aristotle in chapter 2 of this book. Hegel does make some central assumptions about human nature, see Plant, *Hegel*, passim.
68 G. W. F. Hegel, in H. Glockner *Samtliche Werke Fromman Verlag Stuttgart*, 1927–30, vol. X, p. 259.
69 J. Rawls, 'Justice as Fairness: Political not Metaphysical', *Philosophy and Public Affairs*, 14, no. 3.
70 R. Dworkin, *Taking Rights Seriously*, Duckworth, London, 1977, p. 155.
71 J. Rawls, 'Kantian Constructivism and Moral Theory', *Journal of Philosophy*, 77, 1980.
72 Ibid., p. 519.
73 Ibid., particularly the second section.
74 Ibid., p. 518.
75 T. M. Scanlon, 'Contractualism and Utilitarianism', p. 106.
76 C. Taylor, 'The Diversity of Goods', in A. Sen and B. Williams, *Utilitarianism and Beyond*, p. 132.
77 Winch, 'Understanding a Primitive Society', p. 42.
78 See his essay 'Human Nature' in *Ethics and Action*.
79 Walzer, *Spheres of Justice*, p. 314.

80   Ibid., p. xv.
81   M. Walzer, *Interpretation and Social Criticism*, Harvard University Press, Cambridge, Mass., 1987, p. 24.
82   Ibid., pp. 24–5.
83   Winch, 'Human Nature', p. 87.
84   Winch, *The Idea of a Social Science*, p. 101.
85   N. Rosenblum, *Another Liberalism*, Harvard University Press, Cambridge, Mass., 1987, chapter 7.
86   W. A. Galston, 'Community, Democracy, Philosophy: The Political Thought of Michael Walzer', *Political Theory*, 17, no. 1, 1989, p. 121. My discussion here is indebted to Galston.
87   Rosenblum, *Another Liberalism*, p. 166.
88   Dworkin, *A Matter of Principle*, p. 216.
89   R. Titmuss, *The Gift Relationship*, Penguin, London, 1970.
90   Walzer, *Spheres of Justice*, p. 313.
91   Dworkin, *A Matter of Principle*, p. 219.
92   A. Gewirth, *Reason and Morality*, Chicago University Press, Chicago, 1978, p. 10.
93   Walzer, *Interpretation and Social Criticism*, p. 6.
94   Ibid., p. 64.
95   Dworkin, *A Matter of Principle*, p. 217.
96   Galston, 'Community, Democracy, Philosophy'.
97   Taylor, *Hegel and Modern Society*, p. 87. See M. Sandel, 'Morality and the Liberal Ideal', in *The New Republic*, 7 May 1984, p. 17, for similar qualifications.
98   W. Kymlicka, *Liberalism, Community and Culture*, The Clarendon Press, Oxford, 1989, p. 51.
99   A. J. Ayer, *The Concept of a Person and Other Essays*, Macmillan, London, 1963, p. 101.
100 Hegel, *Philosophy of Right*, p. 14.

Bibliography

Ackerman, B. *Social Justice in the Liberal State*, Yale University Press, New Haven, Conn., 1980.

Anscombe, G. E. M. 'Modern Moral Philosophy', *Philosophy*, 33, 1958.

Anscombe, G. E. M. *Intention*, 2nd edn, Blackwell, Oxford, 1963.

Aristotle, 'Physics', in *The Works of Aristotle*, ed. J. A. Smith and W. D. Ross, translated by R. P. Hardie and R. K. Gaye, The Clarendon Press, Oxford, 1910–52.

Aristotle, 'The Parts of Animals', in *The Works of Aristotle*, ed. J. A. Smith and W. D. Ross, The Clarendon Press, Oxford, 1910–52.

Aristotle, *Nicomachean Ethics*, trans. J. A .K. Thomson, Penguin, London, 1953.

Aristotle, *Politics*, trans. Sir E. Barker, The Clarendon Press, Oxford, 1946.

Ayer, A. J. *The Concept of a Person and Other Essays*, Macmillan, London, 1963.

Ayer, A. J. 'The Principle of Utility', in *Philosophical Essays*, Macmillan, London, 1963.

Ayer, A. J. 'On What There Must Be', in *Metaphysics and Common Sense*, Macmillan, London, 1967.

Ayer, A. J. *Language, Truth and Logic*, 2nd edn, Penguin, Harmondsworth, 1971.

Bambrough, R. 'Universals and Family Resemblances', in *Wittgenstein*, ed. G. Pitcher, Macmillan, London, 1968.

Barry, B. *Political Argument*, Routledge, London, 1965, p. 48.

Barry, B. *The Liberal Theory of Justice*, The Clarendon Press, Oxford, 1973.

Bay, C. 'Needs, Wants and Political Legitimacy', *Canadian Journal of Political Science*, 1, no. 1, 1968.

Bean, P. *Rehabilitation and Deviance*, Routledge, London, 1976.

Beiner, R. 'Do We Need A Philosophical Ethics? Theory, Prudence and the Primacy of Ethos', *Philosophical Forum*, XX, no. 3, 1989.

Bentham, J. *An Introduction to the Priciples of Morals and Legislation*, ed. W. Harrison, Blackwell, Oxford, 1967.

Berlin, I. *Four Essays on Liberty*, Oxford University Press, Oxford, 1969.

Berlin, I. *Against the Current*, The Clarendon Press, Oxford, 1981.

Biesték, F. *The Casework Relationship*, Allen and Unwin, London, 1961.

Bradshaw, J. 'The Concept of Social Need', *New Society*, 1972, p. 640.

Braybrooke, 'Let Needs Diminish That Preferences May Flourish', *American Philosophical Quarterly Monograph*, University of Pittsburgh, Pittsburgh, 1968.

Brittan, S. *The Role and Limits of Government*, Temple Smith, London, 1983.

Carnap, R. *The Logical Structure of the World*, Routledge, London, 1967.

Chisholm, R. *Perceiving: A Philosophical Study*, Cornell University Press, Ithaca, NY, 1957.

Connolly, W. E. *The Terms of Political Discourse*, D. C. Heath, Lexington, Mass., 1974.

Connolly, W. E. *Appearance and Reality in Politics*, Cambridge University Press, Cambridge, 1981.

Cranston, M. *What Are Human Rights?*, Bodley Head, London, 1973.

Dalton, H. *Some Aspects of Inequality of Incomes in Modern Communities*, Routledge, London, 1925.

Davidson, D. 'Agency', in *Agent, Action and Reason*, ed. R. Binkley, R. Branaugh and A. Marras, The Clarendon Press, Oxford, 1979.

Day, J. P. 'Threats, Offers, Law, Opinion and Liberty', *American Philosophical Quarterly*, 14, 1977.

Dworkin, R. *Taking Rights Seriously*, Duckworth, London, 1977.

Dworkin, R. 'What Liberalism Isn't', *New York Review of Books*, 20 January 1983.

Dworkin, R. *A Matter of Principle*, Harvard University Press, Cambridge, Mass., 1985.

Dworkin, R. 'In Defence of Equality' in *Social Philosophy and Policy*, 1983, Vol. 1, No. 1, p. 31.

Dworkin, R. *Laws Empire*, Collins, London, 1986.

Dyer, D. 'Freedom', *Canadian Journal of Economics and Political Science*, 30, 1964.

Easton, D. *The Political System*, Knopf, New York, 1953.

Eliot, T. S. *Choruses from 'The Rock'*, in *Collected Poems 1909–1962*, Faber and Faber, London, 1974.

Elster, J. *Sour Grapes*, Cambridge University Press, Cambridge, 1983.

Fitzgerald, R. 'The Ambiguity and Rhetoric of "Need"', in *Human Needs and Politics*, ed. R. Fitzgerald, Pergamon Press, Oxford, 1977.

Forbes, D. *Hume's Philosophical Politics*, Cambridge University Press, Cambridge, 1973.

Forder, A. *Concepts in Social Administration*, Routledge, London, 1974.

Freud, S. *Civilisation and Its Discontents*, Hogarth Press, London, 1963.

Frey, R. G. 'Act Utilitarianism', in *Utility and Rights*, ed. R. G. Frey, Blackwell, Oxford, 1985.

Fried, C. *Right and Wrong*, Harvard University Press, Cambridge, Mass., 1978.

Fromm, E. *The Sane Society*, Routledge, London, 1963.

Gadamer, H. G. *Kleine Schriften* 1, J. C. Mohr, Tübingen, 1967.

Galston, W. A. *Justice and the Human Good*, University of Chicago Press, Chicago, 1981.

Galston, W. A. 'Community, Democracy, Philosophy: The Political Thought of Michael Walzer', *Political Theory*, 17, no. 1, 1989.

Goldman, A. 'The Entitlement Theory Of Justice', *Journal of Philosophy*, 73, 1976.

George, V. and Wilding, P. *Ideology and Social Policy*, Routledge, London, 1976.

Gewirth, A. *Reason and Morality*, University of Chicago Press, Chicago, 1978.

Gewirth, A. *Human Rights*, University of Chicago Press, Chicago, 1982.

Gewirth, A. *Ethical Rationalism*, ed. E. Regis, University of Chicago Press, Chicago, 1984.

Glover, J. *Causing Death and Saving Lives*, Penguin, London, 1977.

Gray, J. 'On the Contestability of Social and Political Concepts', *Political Theory*, 15, 1977.

Gray, J. 'Classical Liberalism, Positional Goods and the Politicisation Of Poverty', in *Dilemmas Of Liberal Democracies: Readings in Fred Hirsch's Social Limits to Growth*, ed. A. Ellis and K. Kumar, Tavistock, London, 1983.

Gray, J. *Hayek on Liberty*, Blackwell, Oxford, 1984.

Gray, J. *Liberalism*, Open University Press, Milton Keynes, 1986.

Griffin, J. *Well Being*, The Clarendon Press, Oxford, 1986.

Habermas, J. 'Legitimation Problems in the Modern State', in *Communication and the Evolution of Society*, trans. T. McCarthy, Beacon Press, Boston, Heinemann, London, 1979.

Habermas, J. *Knowledge and Human Interests*, trans. J. Shapiro, Heinemann, London, 1971.

Harsanyi, J. C. 'Morality and the Theory of Rational Behaviour', in *Utilitarianism and Beyond*, ed. A. K. Sen and B. Williams, Cambridge University Press, Cambridge, 1982.

von Hayek, F. A. *The Constitution of Liberty*, Routledge, London, 1960.

von Hayek, F. A. *Law, Legislation and Liberty*, Routledge, London, vol. 1, 1973; vol. 2, 1976.

Hegel, G. W. F. *Samtliche Werke*, Fromman Verlag, Stuttgart, 1927–30.

Hegel, G. W. F. *The Philosophy of Right*, trans. T. M. Knox, The Clarendon Press, Oxford, 1952.

Heidegger, M. *Basic Writings*, ed. D. F. Krell, Harper and Row, New York, 1977.

Hirsch, F. *The Social Limits to Growth*, Routledge, London, 1977.

Hobbes, T. *Leviathan*, and C. B. Macpherson, Penguin, London, 1968.

Hollis, M. *Models of Man*, Cambridge University Press, Cambridge, 1977.

Hume, D. *Essays Moral, Political and Literary*, vol. 1, ed. T. H. Green and T. H. Grosse, Longman, London, 1875.

Hume, D. *An Inquiry Concerning Human Understanding and the Principles of Morals*, 3rd edn, ed. L. A. Selby-Bigge, rev. P. Nidditch, The Clarendon Press, Oxford, 1975.

Hume, D. *Treatise on Human Nature*, ed. L. A. Selby-Bigge, The Clarendon Press, Oxford, 1888.

Jaggar, A. *Feminist Politics and Human Nature*, Rowman and Allenheld, Totowa, NJ, 1983.

Jay, D. *The Socialist Case*, Faber and Faber, London, 1937.

Jencks, C., et al. *Inequality*, Allen Lane, London, 1974.

Kant, I. *The Metaphysical Elements of Justice*, ed. and trans. J. Ladd, Bobbs Merrill, Indianapolis, 1965.

Kant, I. *Groundwork for the Metaphysic of Morals*, Trans. H. J. Paton, Hutchinson, London, 1974.

Karpman, B. 'Criminal Psychodynamics', *Journal of Criminal Law and Criminology*, 47, 1956.

Kenny, A. J. P. *Action, Emotion and Will*, Routledge, London, 1963.

Kenny, A. J. P. 'Mental Health in Plato's Republic', *Proceedings of the British Academy*, London, 1969.

Kripke, S. *Wittgenstein on Rules and Private Language*, Blackwell, Oxford, 1986.

Kymlicka, W. *Liberalism, Community and Culture*, The Clarendon Press, Oxford, 1989.

Laslett, P. 'Introduction', *Philosophy, Politics and Society*, series 1, Blackwell, Oxford, 1956.

Laing, R. D. *The Politics of Experience and the Bird of Paradise*, Penguin, London, 1967.

Little, I. M. D. *A Critique of Welfare Economics*, Oxford University Press, Oxford, 1957.

Locke, J. *The Second Treatise of Government*, ed. J. Gough, Blackwell, Oxford, 1956.

Locke, J. *An Essay Concerning Human Understanding*, ed. W. D. Woozley, Collins, London, 1964.

Locke, J. *Epistola de Tolerantia*, ed. and trans. R. Kilbansky and J. Gough, The Clarendon Press, Oxford, 1968.

Lyotard, J. F. *The Postmodern Condition*, trans. G. Bennington and B. Massumi, Manchester University Press, Manchester, 1984.

MacCallum, G. 'Negative and Positive Freedom', *Philosophical Review*, 76, 1967.

McCloskey, H. J. 'Respect for Human Moral Rights', in *Utility And Rights*, ed. R. G. Frey, Blackwell, Oxford, 1985.

Macdonald, M. 'Natural Rights', in *Philosophy, Politics and Society*, Series 1, ed. P. Laslett, Blackwell, Oxford, 1956.

MacDowell, J. 'Virtue and Reason', *The Monist*, 63, no. 3, 1979.

McGinn, C. *Wittgenstein On Meaning*, Blackwell, Oxford, 1984.

MacIntyre, A. 'Against Utilitarianism', in *Aims in Education*, ed. T. B. Hollins, Manchester, University Press, Manchester, 1964.

MacIntyre, A. *A Short History of Ethics*, Routledge, London, 1967.

MacIntyre, A. 'Bernstein's Distorting Mirrors', *Soundings*, 67, 1984.

MacIntyre, A. *After Virtue*, 2nd edn, Duckworth, London, 1985.

Mackie, J. L. 'Can There Be a Rights Based Moral Theory?', *Midwest Studies in Philosophy*, 3, 1978.

Manning, D. *The Mind of Jeremy Bentham*, Longman, London, 1968.

Marcuse, H. *One Dimensional Man*, Routledge, London, 1964.

Marcuse, H. *Eros and Civilisation*, Sphere Books, London, 1969.

Marx, K. 'On Capital Punishment', *New York Daily Tribune*, 28 February 1853.

Maslow, A. *Motivation and Personality*, Harper and Row, New York, 1954.

Maslow, A. *Towards a Psychology of Being*, 2nd edn, Van Nostrand, Princeton, NJ, 2nd edn, 1968.

Menninger, K. 'Therapy Not Punishment', *Harper's Magazine*, August 1959, pp. 63–4.

Menninger, K. *The Crime Of Punishment*, Viking, New York, 1968.

Mill, J. S. 'Essay on Liberty', in *Utilitarianism*, ed. M. Warnock, Collins, London, 1910.

Mill, J. S. 'Utilitarianism', in *Utilitarianism*, ed. M. Warnock, Collins, London, 1962.

Miller, D. *Social Justice*, The Clarendon Press, Oxford, 1976.

Miller, D. *Philosophy and Ideology in Hume's Political Thought*, The Clarendon Press, Oxford, 1981.

Moore, G. E. *Principia Ethica*, Cambridge University Press, Cambridge, 1959.

Morris, H. 'Persons and Punishment', *The Monist*, 52, 1968.

Murphy, J. *Kant: The Philosophy of Right*, Macmillan, London, 1970.

Nagel, T. *The View from Nowhere*, Oxford University Press, Oxford, 1986.

Narveson, J. *Morality and Utility*, Johns Hopkins University Press, Baltimore, Md, 1973.

Narveson, J. 'Negative and Positive Rights in Gewirth's *Reason and Morality*', in *Gewirth's Ethical Rationalism*, ed. E. Regis, University of Chicago Press, Chicago, 1984.

Norman, R. *Reasons for Action*, Blackwell, Oxford, 1971.

Nozick, R. *Anarchy, State and Utopia*, Blackwell, Oxford, 1974.

Nozick, R. *Philosophical Explanations*, Harvard University Press, Cambridge, Mass., 1981.

O'Neil, O. 'Nozick's Entitlements', in *Reading Nozick*, ed. J. Paul, Blackwell, Oxford, 1981.

Oppenheim, F. *Political Concepts: a Reconstruction*, University of Chicago Press, Chicago, 1981.

Oppenheim, F. 'Facts and Values in Politics', *Political Theory*, 1, no. 1, 1973.

Partridge, P. H. 'Freedom' in *Encyclopedia of Philosophy*, vol. 3, ed. P. Edwards, Macmillan, New York, 1967.

Peters, R. S. *The Concept of Motivation*, Routledge, London, 1958.

Philips, D. Z. and Mounce, H. O. 'On Morality's Having a Point', *Philosophy*, 1965.

Plato, *Euthyphro*, in *The Dialogues of Plato*, ed. and trans. B. Jowett, The Clarendon Press, Oxford, 1953.

Plant, R. *Hegel*, 2nd edn, Blackwell, Oxford, 1983.

Plant, R., Lesser, H. and Taylor Gooby, P. *Political Philosophy and Social Welfare*, Routledge, London, 1981.

Quinton, A. *Utilitarian Ethics*, Macmillan, London, 1973.

Rawls, J. 'Justice as Fairness: Political Not Metaphysical', *Philosophy and Public Affairs*, 14, no. 3, 1972.

Rawls, J. *A Theory of Justice*, The Clarendon Press, Oxford, 1972.

Rawls J. 'Kantian Constructivism and Moral Theory', *Journal of Philosophy*, 77, 1980.

Raz, J. 'Liberalism, Autonomy and the Politics of Neutral Concern', *Midwest Studies in Philosophy*, 7.

Reeve, A. *Property*, Macmillan, London, 1986.

Robbins, L. *The Nature and Significance of Economic Science*, Routledge, London, 1932.

Rorty, R. 'Post Modernist Bourgeois Liberalism', *Journal of Philosophy*, 80, 1983.

Rorty, R. *Contingency, Irony and Solidarity*, Cambridge University Press, Cambridge, 1989.

Rosenblum, N. *Another Liberalism*, Harvard University Press, Cambridge, Mass., 1987.

Russell, B. and Whitehead, A.N. *Principia Mathematica*, 2nd edn, Cambridge University Press, Cambridge, 1925.

Sandel, M. 'Introduction', *Liberalism and Its Critics*, New York University Press, New York, 1984.

Sandel, M. 'Morality and the Liberal Ideal', *The New Republic*, 7 May 1984.

Sartre, J. P. *Existentialism and Humanism*, trans. P. Mairet, Methuen, London, 1948.

Scanlon, T. 'Contractualism and Utilitarianism', in *Utilitarianism and Beyond*, ed. A. K. Sen and B. Williams, Cambridge University Press, Cambridge, 1982.

Sen, A. K. and Williams, B., *Utilitarianism and Beyond*, Cambridge University Press, Cambridge, 1982.

Skinner, B. F. *Science and Human Behaviour*, Macmillan, London, 1953.

Skinner, B. F. *Walden 2*, Macmillan, New York, 1969.

Skinner, B. F. *Beyond Freedom and Dignity*, Knopf, New York, 1971.

Skinner, Q. 'Meaning and Understanding In the History of Ideas', in *History and Theory*, 8, 1969.

Smart, J. C. C. and Williams, B. *Utilitarianism*, Cambridge University Press, Cambridge, 1973.

Steiner, H. 'Individual Liberty', *Proceedings of the Aristotelian Society*, 1974.

Strawson, P. F. *Freedom and Resentment and Other Essays*, Methuen, London, 1974.

Szasz, T. 'The Mental Health Ethic', in *Ethics And Society*, ed. R. De George, Macmillan, London, 1968.

Taylor, C. *The Explanation of Behaviour*, Routledge, London, 1964.

Taylor, C. *Hegel and Modern Society*, Cambridge University Press, Cambridge, 1979.

Taylor, C. 'The Diversity of Goods', in A. K. Sen and B. Williams, *Utilitarianism and Beyond*, Cambridge University Press, Cambridge, 1982.

Taylor, C. *Philosophical Papers*, vols 1 and 2, Cambridge University Press, Cambridge, 1985.

Taylor, C. *Sources of the Self*, Cambridge University Press, Cambridge, 1989.

Thompson, D. 'The Welfare State', *The New Reasoner*, 1, no. 4, 1958.

Thomson, G. *Needs*, Routledge, London, 1987.

Thurow, L. 'Education and Economic Inequality', in *Power and Ideology in Education*, ed. J. Karable and A. H. Halsey, Oxford University Press, Oxford, 1977.

Titmuss, R. *The Gift Relationship*, Penguin, London, 1970.

Trammell, R. 'Saving Life and Taking Life', in *Killing and Letting Die*, ed. B. Steinbeck, Prentice Hall, New York, 1980.

Walzer, M. *Spheres of Justice*, Martin Robertson, Oxford, 1983.

Walzer, M. *Interpretation and Social Criticism*, Harvard University Press, Cambridge, Mass., 1987.

Weale, A. *Political Theory and Social Policy*, Macmillan, London, 1983.

Williams, A. 'Need as a Demand Concept', in *Economic Policies and Social Goals*, ed. A. J. Culyer, Martin Robertson, Oxford, 1974.

Williams, B. *Ethics and the Limits of Philosophy*, Collins, London, 1985.

White, A. R. *Modal Thinking*, Blackwell, Oxford, 1975.

Wiggins, D. 'The Claims of Need', in *Morality and Objectivity*, ed. T. Honderich, Routledge, London, 1985.

Winch, P. *The Idea of a Social Science*, Routledge, London, 1958.

Winch, P. *Ethics and Action*, Routledge, London, 1972.

Winnicott, C. 'Casework and Agency Function', in *Social Work and Social Values*, ed. E. Younghusband, Allen and Unwin, London, 1967.

Wittgenstein, L. *Philosophical Investigations*, Blackwell, Oxford, 1958.

Wittgenstein, L. *Tractatus Logico-Philosophicus*, Routledge, London, 1961.

Wittgenstein, L. *Remarks on the Foundations of Mathematics*, 2nd edn, Blackwell, Oxford, 1967.

Wittgenstein, L. *Zettel*, Blackwell, Oxford, 1967.

Wittgenstein, L. *The Blue and Brown Books*, Blackwell, Oxford, 1969.

Wittgenstein, L. *On Certainty*, Blackwell, Oxford, 1979.

Wolff, R. P. *The Autonomy of Reason*, Harper Torchbooks, New York, 1973.

Wollheim, R. 'Crime, Sin and Mr Justice Devlin', *Encounter*, 13, 1959.

Wollheim, R. *Need, Desire and Moral Turpitude*, Royal Institute of Philosophy/Macmillan, London, 1976.

Wollheim, R. *The Thread of Life*, Cambridge University Press, Cambridge, 1984.

Wood, E. *Mind and Politics*, University of California Press, Berkeley, Ca., 1972.

Index